GREEK ARCHITECTURE AND ITS SCULPTURE
IN THE BRITISH MUSEUM

GREEK ARCHITECTURE AND ITS SCULPTURE
IN THE BRITISH MUSEUM

Ian Jenkins

Line illustrations by Kate Morton

THE BRITISH MUSEUM PRESS

© 2006 The Trustees of the British Museum

Ian Jenkins has asserted the right to be identified as the author of this work

First published in 2006 by The British Museum Press
A division of The British Museum Company Ltd
38 Russell Square, London WC1B 3QQ

www.britishmuseum.co.uk

A catalogue record for this book is available from the British Library

ISBN-13: 978-0-7141-2240-3

ISBN-10: 0-7141-2240-8

Designed by Andrew Shoolbred
Printed in China by C&C Offset Printing Co., Ltd

Title page Centaur making off with a Lapith girl.
Parthenon South Metope 29. British Museum.

Contents

	Preface	8
	Introduction	10
	Map	12
CHAPTER ONE	Enlightenment and Renaissance	14
CHAPTER TWO	Greek Temples – Form and Meaning	26
CHAPTER THREE	The Temples of Artemis at Ephesos	47
CHAPTER FOUR	The Parthenon and Its Sculptures	71
CHAPTER FIVE	The Athenian Acropolis – Propylaea, Nike Temple and Erechtheum	108
CHAPTER SIX	The Temple of Apollo Epikourios at Bassai	130
CHAPTER SEVEN	Lycian Tombs	151
CHAPTER EIGHT	The Nereid Monument	186
CHAPTER NINE	The Mausoleum at Halikarnassos	203
CHAPTER TEN	The Temple of Athena Polias at Priene	236
	Notes	250
	Bibliography	258
	Index	266
	Illustration Acknowledgements	272

For Frances, Bonnie and Binky

Preface

To walk the galleries of the British Museum is to tour a world of antiquity. Nowhere is there a museum collection to compare with that of the British Museum in the range of places it covers, nor in the depth of history that it records. Passing from one room to the next, visitors can both discover the unique identity of ancient civilizations and explore the connections that once linked them. They can witness the strikingly individual culture of the Egyptians, Assyrians, Persians, Greeks, Lycians and Karians, to name but a few, and can see also how these peoples interacted with and influenced one another. This book is a journey through part of this ancient world visiting monumental tombs and temples on both sides of the Aegean Sea, from the Greek mainland and from western Turkey. These monuments are examined in detail and are set against a broad background of ancient history, landscape and people.

Frequently in this book, specific mention is made of modern scholars who have visited the monuments before us. Greek architecture and its sculpture usually comes down to us as a set of broken fragments, and our understanding of how these may be reconstructed inevitably depends upon the specialist knowledge of those who have, in some cases, dedicated an entire working life to a single monument. It is, for example, impossible to make even general remarks about the temple of Apollo Epikourios at Bassai without mentioning the work of Fred Cooper or the Mausoleum at Halikarnassos without the names of Kristian Jeppesen and Geoffrey Waywell. The notes and bibliography that accompany the text of this book have been compiled to guide the reader into the specialist publications that have informed my own account. With monuments so famous as those presented here, the bibliography is necessarily extensive. Some might argue that it should have been fuller still, but I have tried to restrict its scope to those studies I have myself found useful.

The customary apology must be made here about inconsistency in the spelling of names. All historians of the ancient Greek and Roman world have to decide whether to adopt Greek, Latin or anglicized spellings for Greek names. The tendency in recent years is towards Greek rather than Latin; so Halikarnassos is now usual, where before we wrote

Halicarnassus, and Perikles is preferred over Pericles. I have taken the same line here, but do not pretend to have achieved absolute consistency. Common English usage still inhibits total reversion to native forms. I have, for example, accepted Karia instead of Caria and can even cope with the 'Karians', but find myself unable to write Lykia for Lycia and feel especially uncomfortable with the 'Lykians'. I take courage from the fact that no one has yet insisted that we call the greatest adventurer of the ancient world Alexandros the Great, or call its greatest philosopher Platon. At best, I hope to have been consistently inconsistent.

Many people have assisted or been participants in the production of this book. Laura Lappin, its editor, has supported the project throughout. Kate Morton provided many of the illustrations that are a major part of this book. Dudley Hubbard and Ivor Kerslake took many of its photographs, while Beatriz Waters acquired others. A number of friends and colleagues have read and improved or otherwise informed all or parts of the text: they are John Banks, Jim Coulton, Peter Higgs, Kristian Jeppesen, Andrew Meadows, Olga Palagia, Nancy-Jane Rucker, Alexandra Villing, Susan Walker, Burkhardt Wesenberg, Dyfri Williams and Susan Woodford. All remaining errors are my own.

Ian Jenkins
Spring 2006

Introduction

From Athens and Arcadia on one side of the Aegean Sea and from Ionia, Lycia and Karia on the other side, this book brings together some of the great monuments of Classical antiquity. Among them are two of the Seven Wonders of the ancient world, the later temple of Artemis at Ephesos and the Mausoleum at Halikarnassos. Also featured are the Parthenon and other buildings on the Athenian Acropolis, the temple of Apollo at Bassai, the Nereid Monument and other sculptured tombs of Lycia, the Lion Tomb at Knidos, the Scylla Monument of Bargylia, and the temple of Athena Polias at Priene. These monuments are explained as archaeological artefacts and are considered in the context of the places where they were built and, not least, the people who funded, designed, built, used, destroyed and discovered them.

This book is primarily concerned with monuments in the British Museum, and is not therefore a history of Greek architecture and sculpture at large. Nor, however, is it a catalogue of one museum's collection. Individual chapters deal with the monuments in turn and these may be read as separate essays, but they may also be taken together as episodes in a continuous story. The overarching theme of this narrative is encapsulated in the title of the first chapter, *Enlightenment and Renaissance*, and the three hundred years of Graeco-Persian relations that it spans. The earliest Ionic architecture of East Greece or, if you prefer, of western Anatolia, was a product of that intellectual and artistic movement known as the Ionian enlightenment that flourished in the sixth century BC. Its great achievement was the archaic temple of Artemis at Ephesos which, until its destruction in 356 BC, was looked back on by successive Greek architects as the centrepiece of the grand tradition of Ionic architecture. The failure of the Ionian revolt against Persian imperial rule at the beginning of the fifth century, and Persia's destruction of Miletos, the principal Ionian city, brought to an end the great archaic age of Ionia and created a cultural and political vacuum in the Aegean world. This was to be filled amply by Athens, its empire and the amazing buildings that this city erected in the wake of its own stunning military successes against Persian attempts to conquer mainland Greece. Marrying together Doric and Ionic forms in the temples of its rebuilt Acropolis, Athens artfully assumed title to both mainland and East-Greek architectural traditions. Its own demise at the end of the fifth century BC, and the political stability that accompanied a formal reassertion of Persian control over the East-Greek cities, known as the King's Peace, gave rise in the fourth century BC to a renaissance of architecture in Ionia and Karia. This Ionian renaissance saw the creation of the Mausoleum at Halikarnassos and rebuilding of the colossal temple of Artemis at Ephesos. It culminated in the architecturally refined and sculpturally understated temple of Athena Polias at Priene.

Included in this story are the sculptured tombs of Lycian Xanthos. Recent scholarship greatly augments our understanding of Lycian history and reveals something of the political context in which Lycian tombs were built and of the personalities associated with them. Now, thanks to the efforts of experts in Lycian coins and inscriptions, with some confidence we can recite the names of the kings who built the great monuments of Xanthos. In what follows, Lycian tombs are taken together with Greek architecture, not with the intention of subsuming the identity of the Lycians into the grander legacy of the Greeks, as Hellenists have tended to do in the past, but rather to bring out the peculiar character of Lycian funerary monuments and to show how Lycian tomb builders participated in the wider story of the eastern Greeks and their neighbours in western Anatolia.

Among those neighbours were the Karians and the Ionians. As with the Lycians, so with the Karians, it is important to remind ourselves that, for all their imitation of Greek architecture and sculpture, they were none the less an indigenous Anatolian people who, under their Hekatomnid dynasty, inhabited a separate kingdom within the Persian empire. Even the Ionians who were traditionally seen as the Greeks of the East, immigrants from the Greek mainland to the shores of western Turkey, had nevertheless interbred with the indigenous peoples. Their brilliant culture had developed under the influence of these native peoples and the civilizations further east of Lydia, Assyria, Babylon and Phoenicia. In the sixth and fourth centuries BC the Ionians were directly ruled first by Lydia and then by Persia. Ironically, when governed by these non-Greek powers the Ionians were at their most creative, whereas during the fifth century BC, when imperial Athens dominated the Aegean, no major new buildings were erected in Ionia.

The rise of the Doric order around 650–600 BC is no less complex than that of the Ionic. Its origin in the Greek mainland may have been partly due to a renewal of native Mycenaean traditions in monumental architecture, but it may also have been influenced by the great buildings that stood on the banks of the Nile in Egypt. Whether we speak of the

Doric, Ionic or the later Corinthian order, Greek temple architecture exhibits a double character: on the one hand, there is its inventiveness and the independence of spirit that created the temple form in the first instance and ensured that architecture remained a dynamic art form, by which no two temples were ever made exactly alike. On the other hand, there is a conservatism and reverence for the past that preserved the orders and gave Greek architecture its timeless quality. This ability of Greek architecture to transcend its own time has been admired and exploited by generations of imitators in a Classical tradition that in the early nineteenth century saw the British Museum itself rebuilt as an Ionic Greek temple to provide a fitting home for the monuments that appear in the following chapters.

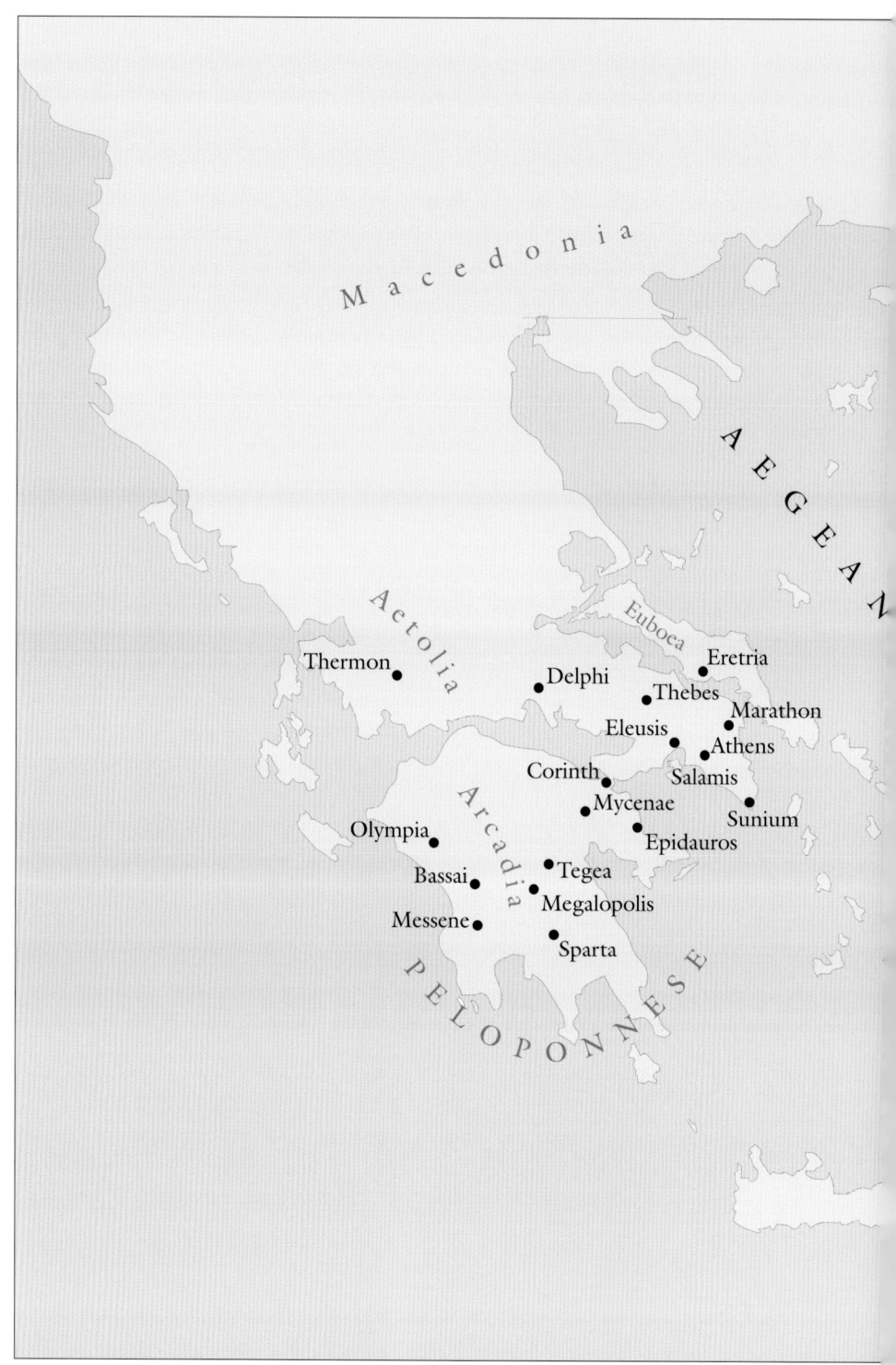

Map of Ancient Greece and Turkey.

Map 13

Chapter One

Enlightenment and Renaissance

EGYPT, MYCENAE, IONIA, THE NEAR EAST AND THE ORIGINS OF THE ORDERS

The Corinthian order was invented in the fifth century BC. The earliest evidence of its use is in Iktinos' temple of Apollo Epikourios at Bassai (see figs 123–4),[1] but it is said by the Roman architect Vitruvius to have been first thought up by Kallimachos, a sculptor from Athens. The idea came to him on a visit to Corinth, where he saw a tomb with an acanthus plant that had grown up around a basket of offerings, weighted by a tile. The three elements of the Corinthian capital were suggested by what he saw.

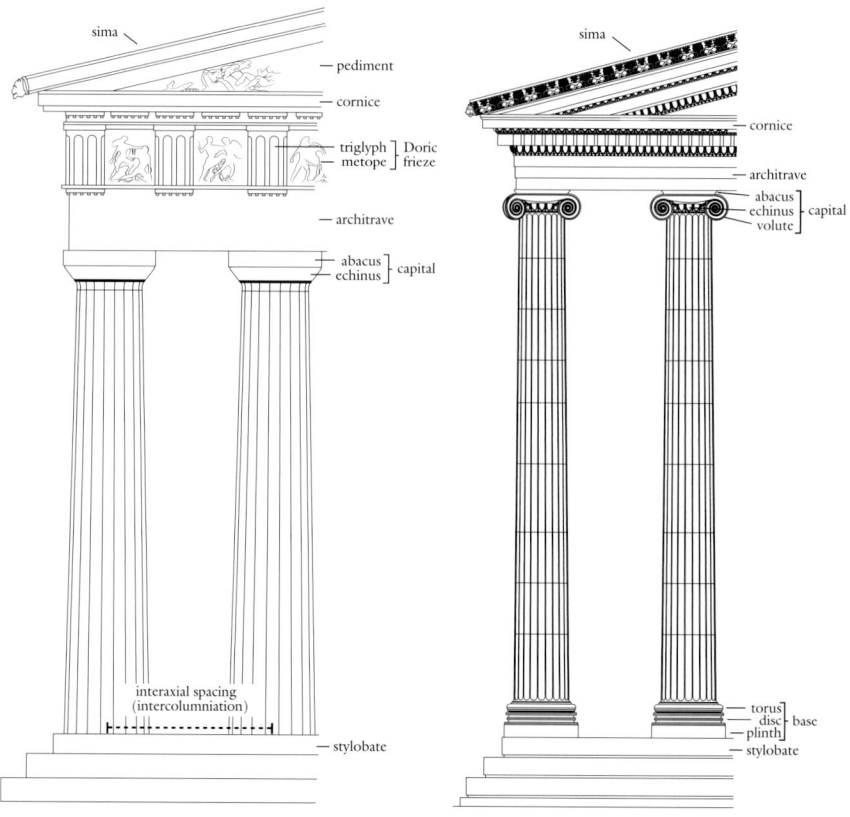

1 The Doric and Ionic architectural orders.

The basket became the inner, tapering body of the capital, while the living plant suggested its acanthus decoration. The rectangular profile of the tile became the flat moulding at the top, or abacus.[2] This picturesque anecdote may truthfully record the sudden appearance of the Corinthian capital in Classical Greece and points to how the forms of Greek stone architecture could have been developed from natural elements. The origins of the Doric and Ionic orders are often also assumed to lie in the inspiration of nature, but here the story is complicated by cross-fertilization from the architecture of Egypt, that of the Near East and, in the case of the Doric order, from a revival of the mainland Greek Mycenaean tradition of monumental building.

The Doric order takes its name from the Dorian tribes of Greek-speaking peoples who, according to Greek tradition, invaded mainland Greece following the collapse of the Mycenaean world around 1100 BC. Although they are said to have brought with them the use of iron, at first their world was impoverished in comparison with the palace culture of the

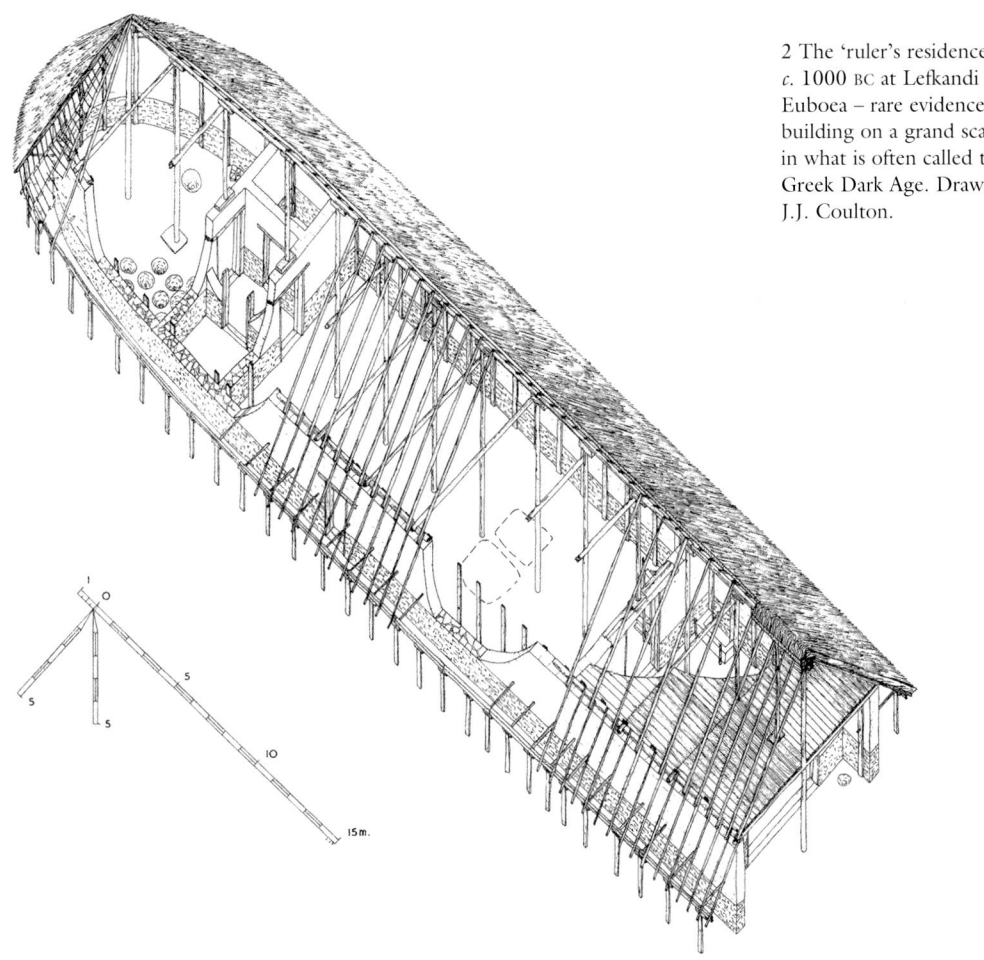

2 The 'ruler's residence', *c.* 1000 BC at Lefkandi on Euboea – rare evidence for building on a grand scale in what is often called the Greek Dark Age. Drawing J.J. Coulton.

Mycenaeans. Their homeland was to become the Peloponnese centred on the city of Sparta. The prototypes of Doric capitals and the characteristic metope and triglyph frieze are often presumed to have been made in wood and have not survived. We may search for glimpses of this proto-Doric architecture in terracotta models of lost building types and in excavated buildings, notably the so-called 'residence' (*c.* 1000 BC) at Lefkandi in eastern mainland Greece (fig. 2). Its pitched roof and overhanging eaves supported on external posts are evocative of the basic elements of temple architecture,[3] but nothing of what went before quite prepares us for the sudden appearance in the first half of the seventh century BC of a monumental architecture with stone masonry and terracotta roof tiles at Corinth and Isthmia, and around 630 BC at Thermon in north-west Greece (Aetolia).[4] Perhaps most striking are the painted terracotta panels from Thermon that may be the first tangible evidence for a metope frieze (fig. 3).

Egypt had a long history of monumental building in stone and it is possible to point to particular elements in Egyptian architecture that seem to anticipate the Doric order (fig. 4).[5] We may speculate on the extent to which the 'new' architecture was inspired by contact with Egypt, but the most immediate inspiration is likely to have been the visible remains of the great fortified palaces and tombs erected hundreds of years earlier by the Mycenaeans, and especially the monuments at Mycenae itself, Tiryns and

3 The beginnings of the Doric order? Painted terracotta architectural elements, *c.* 630 BC, found at Thermon in north-west Greece, tentatively explained as parts of a temple roof and a Doric triglyph and metope frieze.

other sites in the Argolid.[6] It is not too great a leap to imagine that the Mycenaean column and capital placed between the lions of the gateway of Mycenae or those flanking the entrance to the so-called 'Treasury of Atreus' were the inspiration for later Doric capitals (fig. 5). The Mycenaean monuments also carried architectural relief carvings, both patterned and figured, which represent the beginnings of the rich tradition of decorative sculpture for which Greek architecture is rightly famous.

The Ionic order is so-called after the Ionians, who fled the Dorian invasions and settled along the west coast of what is now Turkey. Athens came to be regarded as the mother city of the eastern Ionians, since Athenians claimed to have stood their ground during the upheavals at the end of the Mycenaean era and liked to see themselves as the indigenous people of mainland Greece. Ionic architecture developed first in the eastern Aegean, where early examples include the colossal temple of Hera on Samos and the Artemision at Ephesos (see fig. 11). The enormous size of these buildings was probably inspired by the great temples that stood on the banks of the Nile in Egypt.[7] Both temples mentioned had a double row of columns all round (dipteral), while forests of columns filled their

4 An Egyptian origin for the Doric column? Dair al-Bahri, portico of the shrine of Anubis, fifteenth century BC.

5 Mycenaean Greek inspiration for the Doric column? The doorway of the so-called 'Treasury of Atreus' restored.

6 Capital, floral necking, and distinctive base of a column of the Polykrates temple of Hera on Samos, c. 480 BC.

7 Painted floral ornament (c. 1555–1296 BC) may suggest Egypt as a possible source of inspiration for the development of the Ionic volute capital.

porches, calling to mind the copiously columned halls of Egyptian temples such as that of Amoun at Karnak. Eastern Greeks went to Egypt from at least as early as the middle of the seventh century BC, as the Mycenaean Greeks and Minoans had done before them.[8] Rhoikos, who partnered Theodoros as architect of the earlier colossal temple of Hera on the Aegean island of Samos (c. 570–560 BC), may be the same as the person of that name whose inscribed cup dedicated to Aphrodite was found at Naukratis, a Greek trading emporium in the Nile delta.[9] The remains of two temples of Apollo at Naukratis, one earlier and of limestone (c. 560–550 BC), the other later and of marble, have been found. The scale is much smaller than that of the Samian temple, but both had a decorated necking around the tops of the columns in the Samian manner, and, possibly, Samian bases as well (fig. 6).[10] Rhoikos was perhaps in Egypt to supervise the building of a Samian temple. Herodotos says that the Milesians built the Apollo temple, but also mentions a temple of Hera where the Samians worshipped.[11] The trading colony at Naukratis in the Nile delta was relatively close to the Mediterranean Sea, but the most dramatic evidence for the Greek presence in Egypt comes from a place far up the Nile to the south. At Abu Simbel are to be found the names of East-Greek and Karian mercenaries carved into the legs of the colossi of Ramesses II guarding his great rock-cut temple. The inscriptions date to the year 591 BC, when the Egyptian king Psammetichos II led a campaign against the kingdom of Nubia.[12] Knowledge of Egypt and its legacy certainly influenced the earliest Ionian builders, and the form of the Ionic capital may possibly be traced back to the lotus and lily columns of ancient Egypt (fig. 7).[13]

8 A relief carving from the North Palace of Ashurbanipal at Nineveh shows a pavilion in a park-like setting, *c.* 645 BC. The floral capitals of the columns call to mind the Aeolic order and probably reflect Phoenician influence from Syria going east to Assyria. British Museum.

If Egypt is one possible source for the origin of the Ionic order, then the Near East is another through the eclectic arts of Phoenician Syria (fig. 8) and from Cyprus.[14] It is difficult, however, to trace a direct line of descent from any one Near-Eastern or, indeed, Middle-Eastern source, and no longer can it be said with the confidence of the nineteenth century that 'all that is Ionic in the arts of Greece is derived from the valleys of the Tigris and the Euphrates'.[15] When they first appear, the various forms and systems of East-Greek monumental architecture are remarkably developed and individual. Around 600–550 BC two main types of volute capital were in use in the Greek world, only one of which would survive.[16] There was the so-called Aeolic type (fig. 9) which is associated with an ethnic group of Greeks, distinct from Dorians and Ionians. The Aeolians occupied the northern part of the west coast of Turkey. The Aeolic capital has volutes springing vertically from a common stem, usually with a palmette above and a necking of pendant leaves below. Such is the reconstructed capital from a row of columns that ran down the centre of a temple at Neandria. This Aeolic type was ultimately phased out in monumental architecture in favour of the Ionic capital, where, instead of springing up, the volutes hang down. Splayed low, they run parallel with a shallow abacus to present a broad flat upper surface, more suited to external colonnades where the capitals could help to spread the great weights of the entablature (see figs 1 and 11).

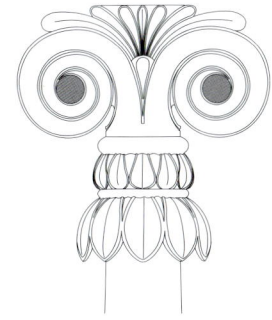

9 Aeolic capital from Neandria in north-west Turkey, *c.* 550 BC. The original is in Istanbul Archaeological Museum.

The Ionic order was early developed in East Greece along the coast of western Turkey, and perhaps even earlier still on the islands of the Cyclades, including Chios and Naxos. Notably, on the sacred island of Delos Ionic was chosen for the archaic temple of Apollo there.[17] In mainland Greece the treasuries built by East-Greek cities at the panhellenic sanctuary of Delphi were erected in Ionic styles that advertise the wealth and cultural identity of the cities that paid for them. Further west still, in southern Italy there are archaic instances of the Ionic order such as the colossal temple at Locri Epizephyri that was constructed with tall slender columns decorated at the neck in the Samian way.[18] Striking as this western Ionic architecture is, nevertheless Doric was the norm in southern Italy and Sicily, as the remains of great Doric temples at Syracuse, Paestum, Acragas and Selinus eloquently testify. Equally, in the archaic and Classical periods, Doric was rare in the east until the Hellenistic period, when it becomes popular for the façades of the long colonnaded halls that the Greeks called stoas. The archaic temple of Athena at Assos is the exception, combining its Doric columns and triglyph and metope frieze with an architrave carved pictorially, in the Ionian manner.[19]

GREEKS AND PERSIANS

In 612 BC the Assyrian empire was toppled by the Medes in an alliance with the Babylonians. The Medes had established themselves in western Iran and frequently clashed with their powerful neighbours, the Assyrians, to the west in what is now Iraq. The major centres of Assyrian power, including Nimrud and Nineveh, were sacked and left in ruins until their rediscovery in the nineteenth century of the modern era. The Median empire lasted from *c.* 600 to 550 BC. In the east, it stretched as far as the River Oxus, while its western limit on the River Halys bordered with the kingdom of Lydia. This was ruled by the fabulously rich Kroisos who, from his capital at Sardis, commanded the whole of western Turkey, including the Greek cities of the Aegean seaboard. The archaic temple of Artemis at Ephesos was partly funded by Kroisos, and his name may perhaps be made out in letters carved on fragments of the column bases.

The Persians were former subjects of the Assyrians who were incorporated into the Median empire. In 550 BC, however, Astyages, king of the Medes, was defeated by Cyrus the Great at the head of a Persian army, and a couple of years later Cyrus also took the kingdom of Lydia. Thus Cyrus founded the Persian empire that was to extend from the Balkans in the north to Egypt in the south, and from the Aegean Sea in the west to the River Indus in the east. It lasted for more than two hundred years until Alexander's conquest of 334–331 BC. The Lydian capital of Sardis was to become the centre of Persian power in the west and the seat of satraps governing both the Greek cities and the territories of the native Anatolian peoples, who included the Lydians, Karians and Lycians.[20]

The Persians had been a nomadic people with no tradition of city life or monumental building. When he came therefore to founding his new capital at Pasargadae (fig. 10), it was to the newly conquered peoples of western Anatolia that Cyrus looked for stone-working skills. Just so Darius, who ruled Persia from 522 to 486 BC, employed foreign craftsmen to build his great palace at Susa.[21] Ionians and Karians worked alongside craftsmen from all over the empire, and a sophisticated Persian court style was developed from the cosmopolitan mix of cultures that met at Susa. Darius began to build another palace complex at Persepolis some 640 kilometres to the south-east. The work continued under his successors, Xerxes (486–465 BC) and Artaxerxes (465–424 BC). Here again western craftsmen were employed and we see their influence in the masonry and in sculpture, such as the grand processions of the Apadana, or audience hall friezes.

10 The tomb of the Persian king Cyrus the Great (557–530 BC) at Pasargadae was probably built by Ionian or Karian masons.

Diodorus Siculus says that when Alexander reached the Persian heartlands he liberated some eight hundred elderly craftsmen.[22] They had been crippled by the Persians, who had spared only those limbs necessary for their especial craft. These men were likely to have been the descendants of slaves carried off in the Persian Wars that engulfed the Greek world towards the end of Darius' reign. In 499 BC the Ionians revolted and burned Sardis with the help of Athens and Eretria. The revolt was put down in 494 BC, and Miletos, centre of the Ionian enlightenment, was destroyed. The men of Miletos were executed, while the women and children were enslaved and sent down the royal road that connected Sardis with Susa, 2,500 kilometres to the east. The great archaic temple of Apollo at Didyma, linked by a sacred way to Miletos, was burnt and the cult statue carried off to Persia, where years later it was discovered and retrieved by Alexander the Great.

ATHENS AND ITS ACROPOLIS

In the sixth century BC, the Athenian tyrant Peisistratos had cultivated his city as a centre of international Greek culture to rival the Ionian cities of the east. He built at least one great temple on the Athenian Acropolis and augmented the Panathenaic festival as a celebration to rival the panhellenic festivals of Delphi and Olympia to the west and the great religious gatherings of Greeks in the east. The Athenian tyrant also initiated a colossal, dipteral temple, the Olympieion, that was designed to emulate the great temples of the east, at Ephesos and Samos. Like so many of the big temples begun in the sixth century BC, the Olympieion was to remain unfinished for centuries.[23]

The Peisistratid legacy was destroyed in 480 BC, when the Persians sacked the Athenian Acropolis and took their revenge upon Athens for the burning of Sardis during the Ionian revolt. Already in 490 BC, Darius had sent an army into mainland Greece, which was defeated at the Battle of Marathon. The second invasion force of 480/479 BC was finally repulsed through a naval victory at Salamis and a victory on land at Plataea. Athens emerged from the Persian invasions as the dominant Greek city. With Greece still officially at war with Persia, in the 470s Athens led the Greek defence by pursuing the enemy on the other side of the Aegean. A defence league was formed with its base on the island of Delos. The Ionian cities and islands of the eastern Aegean coast joined the league and paid their subscriptions into a central exchequer. The Athenian statesman Kimon became captain of the confederate fleet, and his campaign along the southern coasts of what is now Turkey drew the Lycian and Karian cities into the confederacy, which was fast resembling an Athenian maritime empire.

The Athenian Acropolis was not renewed immediately following the Persian sack. In 454 BC, however, the treasury of the Delian Confederacy was transferred to the Athenian Acropolis and in 449 BC a truce in the war with Persia was agreed. Controversially, Athens deployed confederate funds to finance the construction of remarkable buildings, both on the Acropolis itself, in the city and in the Athenian countryside. In new interpretations of the Doric and Ionic orders, sometimes combined in the same building, Athens usurped the grand tradition of monumental building. The great Ionic frieze of the Parthenon, with its carved procession of Athenians turned out in their festival best, was an expression of the city's self-image at the height of Athenian power, wealth and confidence and rivalled the great processional friezes carved around the columns of the archaic temple of Artemis at Ephesos. Athens, according to its own traditions, was the home of the original Ionian immigrants who founded Ephesos, Miletos and other Ionian cities of the eastern Aegean. In the vacuum left by the demise of Miletos, Athens naturally assumed the mantle of the Ionian enlightenment, cleverly marrying the Doric and Ionic orders to create hybrid forms that set new standards in architectural refinement and were to have enduring influence in both western and eastern Greece.

LYCIA, KARIA AND THE IONIAN RENAISSANCE

One of the striking features of the Athenian domination of the East-Greek cities is that 'liberation' brought no renewal of the great building projects of the previous century. We might have expected a limited period of economic and cultural decline following the catastrophic suppression of the Ionian revolt, but in Ionia the depression lasted for a hundred years. This protracted decline may be attributed to the compromised situation that the East-Greek cities found themselves in, caught as they were between Athens and Persia. On the one hand, they were part of a maritime empire paying tribute to the Delian Confederacy, while, on the other, they seem to have continued to pay land tax to the Persian satraps.[24] The Athenian allies were by no means always acquiescent, and among the least so were the Lycians. They had a tradition of national defiance, and evidence of a fire on the Acropolis at Xanthos around 470 BC suggests that Kimon violently suppressed them. With characteristic grit, the Xanthians under their King Kuprlli, who reigned from around 480 to 440 BC, set about rebuilding the sacred heart of their city in stone versions of wooden buildings lost in the fire. These are thought to have included the hero shrine of Sarpedon who, according to legend, had fought on the Asiatic side in the Trojan War.

The Athenian experiment in architectural self-aggrandisement was itself to falter with its military defeat at the end of the Peloponnesian War in 404 BC. Some of the stonemasons who had gathered in the service of the Athenian democracy appear to have left the city and sailed across the Aegean to seek employment with Athens' old enemy the Lycian city of Xanthos. In the Nereid Monument, constructed *c.* 390–380 BC as the monumental tomb of King Erbinna, we see in both its architecture and its decorative sculpture strong echoes of the Acropolis monuments. Further east in Lycia, other dynasts built monumental tombs that show, directly or indirectly, influence from Athens, including that of Perikles of Limyra. These Lycian monuments anticipated and influenced the eventual revival of the East-Greek tradition of monumental architecture, and the Mausoleum at Halikarnassos was directly inspired by the Nereid Monument.

Through all the upheavals of the Persian Wars and the rise and fall of the Athenian empire, the Ephesian Artemision continued to stand. It was spared the destruction that, following the failure of the Ionian revolt, had befallen the temple of Athena at Miletos and the temple of Apollo at nearby Didyma. It provided a seemingly permanent reminder of East-Greek achievements of the past, and the Greek world must have felt shock and outrage at its destruction by the arsonist Herostratos in 356 BC. The subsequent recreation of the temple modernized its archaic architecture and sculpture, while at the same time preserving the memory of the earlier temple. The rebuilding of it represents the centrepiece of a general renaissance of monumental architecture in East Greece that saw the Ephesian form of the Ionic order being used by the Karian descendants of Hekatomnos (Hekatomnids) in the temple of Zeus at Labraynda, the Mausoleum at Halikarnassos and the temple of Athena Polias at Priene. All three buildings are associated with the architect Pytheos, and it is entirely in keeping with the image we have of him as innovative traditionalist that he should take inspiration from the venerable Ephesian version of the Ionic order (fig. 11).[25]

It would be wrong to give the impression that the Karian court style of the Hekatomnid dynasty was all about Pytheos and his preference for the Ionic order. There are at the Hekatomnid sanctuary of Labraynda the remains of two ritual dining halls, one erected by Mausolus and the other by his brother Idreus.[26] The marble fronts of these buildings comprised a porch of two Ionic columns, which support a Doric entablature. The architraves carried the dedicatory inscription and above sat a metope and triglyph frieze. This mixing of orders was once dismissed as a Karian barbarism,[27] but no one would now assert the Hellenist's prejudice that the architecture of the Hekatomnids was the product of ignorant provincials. Rather, the mixed orders of Labraynda may be attributed to a sophisticated cosmopolitanism of the kind that in Athens had given rise to the experimental mixing of orders in the temples of the Acropolis.

Ephesos

11 The Ionic order of the archaic temple of Artemis at Ephesos had great influence on the temple of Zeus at Labraynda, the Mausoleum at Halikarnassos and the temple of Athena Polias at Priene. Drawing of Ephesos by F. Krischen.

Labraynda   Mausoleum   Priene

The Ionian renaissance happened in the wake of the political settlement in western Anatolia, known as the King's Peace.[28] In 386 BC the Persian king, Artaxerxes II (404–359) signed a treaty that largely put an end to uncertainty in the fortunes of the East-Greek cities brought about by protracted squabbling between Athens and Sparta, and placed them firmly back under Persian control, which was to last until Alexander's conquest of 334 BC. The satrapy held by the Hekatomnid rulers of Halikarnassos was the presiding power, less remote than the older satrapy that continued to have its seat at the former Lydian capital of Sardis. In its heyday Hekatomnid power extended as far west as Crete, south to Rhodes, east into Lycia and north into southern Ionia. The Athena temple at Priene, although eventually funded by Alexander the Great, was probably initiated under Hekatomnid patronage.

Pytheos' temple at Priene married the Ionian enlightenment of the past to the burgeoning Ionian renaissance of his day. Unlike his highly decorated Mausoleum at Halikarnassos, the Priene temple was more architecture than sculpture. Figured carving at Priene was restricted to the lids of the coffers, recessed into the ceiling of the colonnade and invisible to those standing outside the columns. Their subject matter was a battle between gods and giants, eloquent reminder perhaps of the age-old struggle between Greek west and Persian east. Inside the temple stood a reduced, yet still colossal replica of the Athena Parthenos of Pheidias, betokening Athens as mother-city to Priene and arch-protagonist in the struggle with Persia. When Alexander arrived at Priene in 334 BC, he found the temple partly built and evidently defrayed the cost of its completion from the spoils of his own victory over the Persians. His name was inscribed into the wall, and he became one of many powerful personalities who sought to legitimize their new status by associating themselves with a canonical symbol of Ionian culture. They include his adoptive mother, the Hekatomnid queen Ada I, whom he restored to the throne and whose sculptured portrait was found in the remains of the temple. The Romans were also to use the sanctuary for political propaganda. Portraits have been found there of Julius Caesar and the emperor Claudius, and Augustus had his name inscribed over the temple façade. With its rational Ionic order, restrained elegance and understated decoration, the temple of Athena Polias at Priene, which we shall explore in detail in the final chapter, was a paradigm of the Ionian renaissance in architecture.

Chapter Two

Greek Temples – Form and Meaning

THE LIVING PAST

Around 220–190 BC the architect Hermogenes deposited a temple plan, probably engraved on stone, in the shrine of Athena Polias at Priene, possibly a plan of the Athena temple itself (fig. 12).[1] Hermogenes was not the architect of the Priene temple which, as we saw in Chapter One, was designed by Pytheos 150 years earlier,[2] but it was exactly the kind of building that Hermogenes approved of and with which he would have wanted to be associated.[3] Pytheos' design had a simple harmony, exploiting the regular proportions and other rational properties of the mature Ionic order. Notable was its capacity to create equal spacing of the columns and to allow the alignment of the axis of select columns with the axis of the cella walls. Both Pytheos and Hermogenes are said to have complained of the inability of the Doric order to achieve such regular planning.[4] Pytheos wrote treatises on his works which, with Satyros, included the Mausoleum at Halikarnassos, and is said to have declared the Doric order to be the enemy of reason.

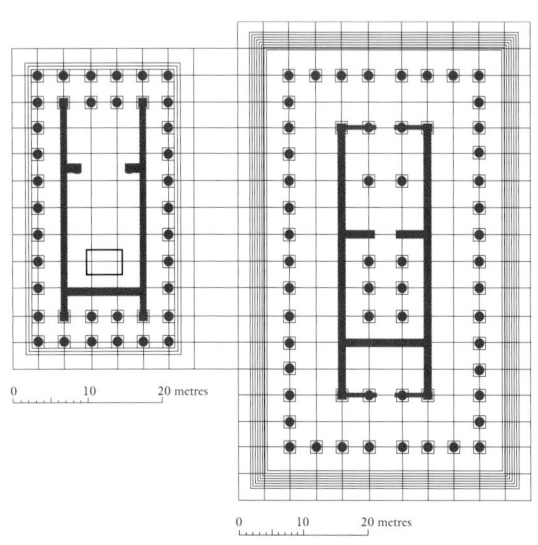

12 The plan of Pytheos' temple of Athena Polias at Priene (left), c. 350–330 BC, and that of Hermogenes' temple of Artemis at Magnesia, c. 130 BC, share the same grid-like regularity in design. After J.J. Coulton.

Hermogenes knew these texts of Pytheos and took the argument further with his own criticism of Doric architecture, codifying and championing the rules of the Ionic order, which he enshrined in written commentaries of his own works, principally the temple of Artemis Leukophryene at Magnesia on the River Maeander and a temple of Dionysos at Teos in Ionia.[5] Although the treatises are now lost, they were known to Vitruvius[6] and so, through his own treatise, which miraculously does survive, have come to influence modern revivals of Ionic style, such as Robert Smirke's exterior of the British Museum.[7] The modern Greek revival of the European enlightenment that brought the British Museum into being was a self-conscious attempt at resurrecting a lost ancient tradition of architecture. Hermogenes too had a strong sense of tradition and may therefore be called an *ancient* neoclassical architect. For him, however, the past was alive and he had none of the modern sense of a Classical tradition that had been lost and then found. Rather, in typically Greek agonistic fashion, he saw himself as competing with the ghosts of the great masters, intent upon establishing his own work as a model or paradigm – the kanon.

Vitruvius is apt to use the metaphor of beauty and strength in the human figure to explain the origin of correct proportions in architecture. This can express itself simply, as in his statement that plain and stocky Doric derives from the male body, while slender Ionic comes from the female form.[8] There is, however, a deeper awareness in Vitruvius of a persistent Greek tradition that conceived ideal beauty to be the sum of a set of calculated proportions that could be applied to the human body and temples alike.[9] That tradition is already evident in the later sixth century BC, in Pythagoras' application of mathematics to the understanding of the structure of music; in the fifth century BC we find it in the bronze figure, now lost, that was created by Polykleitos as the kanon of ideal male nude sculpture and the treatise that the sculptor is said to have written about it. It is, naturally, present in the truth-seeking dialogues of Socrates, in the cosmology of Plato and in the geometry of Euclid.

Euclid, who lived in the third century BC, is the first to mention a ratio that to the nineteenth century of our own era became known as 'the Golden Section'.[10] Applied to a temple plan, this rule of ideal proportion would determine that the ratio of the short to the long sides was equal to the ratio of the long side to the sum of the short and the long sides. Expressed arithmetically that would be 1 : 1.618.[11] The idea that a 'golden section' was the guiding principle of Greek builders is commonplace in an old-fashioned popular misunderstanding of Greek architecture. Nowadays there is widespread scepticism, first as to the practicality of trying to rediscover systems of ancient proportion, and second as to the extent to which theoretical rules of proportion were actually applied in any absolute terms.[12] Greek architecture, like Greek sculpture, was dynamic. No two ancient temples are alike, just as no two ancient sculptures, even when one obviously copies another, are ever exactly the same.

This tendency to nonconformity was intrinsic to the very tools and methods used. One obstacle to modern scholarly consensus about the design methods of Greek builders is the lack in antiquity of a standard system of measurement. The foot measure varied from region to region, and even in the same region two buildings may not have used the same unit.[13] Standard measures may in any case not have been very relevant in planning a temple where a *successive*, rather than a *modular* system of determining proportions seems to have been the norm. So, for example, in a

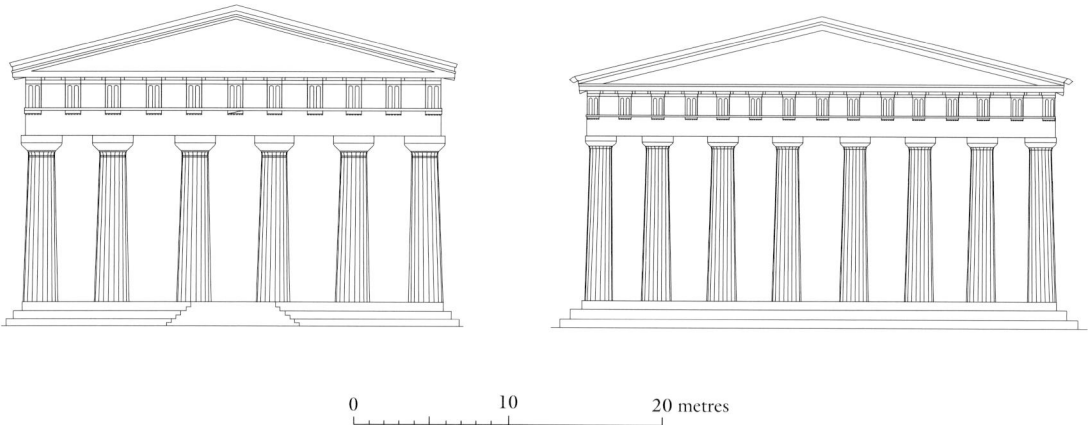

13 Elevation of the temple of Zeus at Olympia, *c.* 457 BC (left), compared with that of the Parthenon, *c.* 438 BC. Although roughly the same height as the Olympia temple, the Parthenon is broader, and its eight Doric columns are more slender than Olympia's six. Both buildings were designed according to a set of arithmetical proportions, not always easy to discover in other Doric temples (see also figs 64 and 66).

successive method the builders might take the width between the axes of adjacent columns and use this to determine the overall length and width of the temple platform. The diameter of the columns might in turn be multiplied by a given factor to arrive at their height. Following on from this, the height of the column capital could determine the height of the architrave immediately above, and so on. In a modular system, by contrast, one module or measurement, that say between the axes of adjacent columns, could be used to determine all other measurements.

Hermogenes' modular canon of proportions, as set out by Vitruvius, is much more the extreme exception of Greek temple building than the rule.[14] Nevertheless, some temples, even Doric ones, do exhibit conscientious efforts to develop a system of proportions for their order. For example, in the Doric temple of Zeus by Libon at Olympia (*c.* 470–457 BC) (fig. 13), the axes of the columns of the long sides are set 16 Doric feet apart, where one foot is presumed to equal 12⅞ inches or 32.6 centimetres;[15] the centres of the triglyphs were spaced 8 feet apart; the lion head spouts, 4 feet; and the tiles were 2 feet wide.[16] The height of the columns was 32 feet, double the column axial spacing, while the abacus was 8 feet wide, half the axial spacing. The Parthenon (447–438 BC), which in many ways sought to outdo the temple at Olympia, has a comparable set of different proportions which, together with its other refinements, contribute to what is sometimes seen as an almost mystical perfection. The Parthenon is certainly a remarkable building but, as many discrepancies in its architecture and sculpture show, it is far from perfect. Nor is it in any sense revolutionary; its achievement is best seen as a culmination of a long tradition.[17]

Greek architecture was traditional, but within that tradition there was change. This double dynamic of looking both forwards and backwards is encapsulated by Plutarch in his description of the works of Periklean

Athens as being at once eternally youthful and, from the outset, venerable (archaios). The nature of change was not in seeking new and innovative architectural forms, but in improving accepted ones and adapting them to changing circumstance. The principles of post and lintel construction and the design systems of the Ionic and Doric orders were unchanged from those of primitive wooden buildings and were to remain essentially constant. Visual refinement was achieved without the technical innovation and design virtuosity that commands today's architecture. Roman exploitation of cement made from Pozzolana sand for the construction of brick arches and domes was the nearest the world of Classical architecture came to a technological revolution.[18] Greek masonry, whether in marble or in cheaper limestone, was largely made without bonding cement. For stability it relied upon the precision of its cutting to achieve close jointing and on metal clamps that resisted seismic movement. There was besides an expertise in selecting, quarrying, shaping, lifting and placing stone that was practised as a craft tradition passed from generation to generation and even from civilization to civilization.[19] When Chersiphron, one of the architects of the colossal archaic temple of Artemis at Ephesos, was faced with the problem of how to raise the great architrave blocks into position he looked for the answer to Egypt, where for centuries blocks had been hauled on rollers up temporary ramps of earth or sand.[20] Such methods were especially suited to societies like those of Egypt and Assyria that could command large forces of cheap labour. The Greek city states, even when ruled by tyrants, will have found it difficult to assemble such labour without buying it in at great cost. By the time the Parthenon was constructed, therefore, ramps had been eliminated in favour of cranes and pulleys, which could be operated by a relatively small and specialist workforce.[21]

ARCHITECTS

The conservative nature of Greek temple construction and design meant that the men who cut and placed the stone were capable of putting up their buildings without an elaborate design process, which raises the question of the role of an architect. It is interesting, for example, to remark that, although the Parthenon and the temple of Apollo at Bassai are both by Iktinos, they are none the less very different buildings, arguably because they were constructed by different craftsmen. Conversely, the Parthenon and Propylaea gateway of the Athenian Acropolis are credited to different architects, Iktinos and Mnesikles, but have many features in common, because they shared a common workforce. Equally, the Nereid Monument from Xanthos is presumably by a different architect from those associated with the Erechtheum and the Nike temples, but bears resemblance to these Athenian monuments, in part because redundant workers from Athens migrated east to escape the collapse of the Athenian building industry at the end of the Peloponnesian War.

The capacity of expert craftsmen to control their own designs meant that even such a refined building as the Parthenon would have been erected without blueprint drawings. Its famous deviations from true horizontal and vertical lines, for example, were worked in at foundation level. The rest followed on, each course of masonry being individually tailored to match the previous and to anticipate the next course.[22] If such was the capability of the masons, what then was the role of the architect? Almost every shade of possible meaning has been given to the Greek word tecton.[23] At one extreme there is the model of the gentleman architect, a man of taste proficient in abstract geometry who was master of theory rather than practice; while at the other extreme is the clerk of works, responsible for letting and controlling contracts, what today we should call a manager, rather than a designer.[24] This, it has been argued, is closer to the norm, but such arch dismissal of the design genius of Greek architects almost certainly goes too far. The argument has its origins in the nineteenth-century moral aesthetic of William Morris, John Ruskin and the English Arts and Crafts Movement that they inspired with its insistence that labour should be united, that there should be no division of craft and design and no separation of construction and decoration. Design, it was argued, should arise from 'the simple putting together of material', in a practice where drawing is superfluous.[25] Certainly, Greek architecture, with its simple and often visible construction, appears to support the view that building in antiquity was done by the direct method. While, however, this may be true of some buildings, it is not necessarily so for all. By the late-Hellenistic period, Vitruvius takes architectural drawing for granted,[26] and there is in the third-century BC designs etched into the interior wall of the later temple of Apollo at Didyma tangible evidence of its actual practice.[27] Vitruvius certainly makes the case for architects to be more than mere builders or managers, when he writes: 'So architects who without culture aim at manual skill cannot gain a prestige corresponding to their labours, while those who trust in theory and literature obviously follow a shadow and not reality. But those who have mastered both, like men equipped in full armour, soon acquire influence and attain their purpose.'[28]

To Vitruvius, things should be constructed in a perfect harmony of parts, whether they be books, bodies or buildings. It is so with his very own book, and in occasional asides addressed to the emperor Augustus he expounds his approach to the writing of well-ordered treatises. Elsewhere, a good education is described as 'put together like one body from its members'. An architect should be what today we would call a 'renaissance man', educated in a range of interconnected disciplines. Besides mathematics, he should know optics so as to control perspective and lighting; he should be adept at arithmetic so as to manage costs; he should learn history so as to know the origins of architectural forms, and natural philosophy so as to understand the physical setting of buildings; he should understand the theory of music so as to comprehend acoustics, and medicine so that the siting and orientation of buildings will be healthy; he must have a command of property law so as to understand such matters as the rules governing boundaries.[29]

Vitruvius' perception of the image of an architect is likely to derive from the treatises of Pytheos who, to judge from Vitruvius' citation of him, appears to have expounded a similar argument for an architect as Jack of All Trades.[30] Pytheos no doubt saw his role as following on from that of the pioneer architects who c. 650–575 BC invented the Doric and Ionic orders. Their remarkable buildings were not the products of men locked into their craft tradition, but seem instead to be the work of independent minds.[31] Such personalities include Theodoros, credited by Pliny with the invention of the basic tools of architecture, straight-edge, compasses, rule, plumbline and square.[32] This tradition must be false, but he may have been among the first to encourage use of such tools, knowledge of which must have been borrowed from Egypt or the Near East. What is not in question is Theodoros' skill as a practical engineer with skills of calculation acquired perhaps in a Samian school of mathematics, which was also to educate Pythagoras in the later sixth century BC. Theodoros' great trick was to divert the River Imbrasos on his native island of Samos, thus making it possible to lay out a colossal temple platform measuring 105 by 52.5 metres. The temple, begun c. 570–560 BC, was never finished. No column capitals survive from this temple, and what remains of the rest of the building was incorporated into its successor. This latter was initiated by the tyrant Polykrates and intended to be the grandest temple that the Greek world had ever seen. The stylobate measures some 112.2 by 55.16 metres, but again it was never finished. The crucifixion of Polykrates in 525 BC probably marked the first major interruption, and thereafter construction was carried on intermittently into the Roman period. Remains of capitals and bases illustrate how distinctive was the Samian version of the Ionic order, and it was to have a powerful influence, both in the archaic period and in the fourth-century revival of the style.[33]

Having shown what he could do with the temple of Hera on Samos, Theodoros was engaged around 560 BC by the Ephesians to lay the foundations of the archaic Artemision on their notoriously marshy ground.

The cult of the architect was created by Theodoros and successive architects who like him wrote treatises, which are listed by Vitruvius.[34] The earliest treatises were among the first works of Greek prose literature and a considerable innovation in their own right. Subsequent generations could look back at them or, where they survived, refer to the buildings themselves. Most important was the archaic temple of Artemis at Ephesos that must have inspired similar wonder in would-be temple builders as our own Gothic cathedrals have inspired in the architects of western Europe and America. The archaic Artemision, until its destruction in 356 BC, stood sentinel over a grand tradition, and its particular form of the Ionic order was to be the one most commonly imitated. When finally the temple fell victim to the hand of a pyromaniac, it would rise bigger and more inspiring than ever on the same foundation, with new columns located over the very stumps of the predecessors.[35]

Contemplating the remains of the early monumental stone temples, it is difficult to avoid the conclusion that the principles of style and construction of the orders were first worked out in the early archaic period by exceptional men – we know of no women architects. 'The genius of subsequent architects', writes W.B. Dinsmoor, 'through centuries was mainly directed to a refining and modifying process, to a close study of every possible elegance and polish consistent with quiet and sound taste, to the obliteration of every crude line, harsh angle, or unseemly form. In such ways they reached the perfection of the temple of Athena Nike and the Erechtheum, which were not so much the works of their particular architects as the matured fruit of a succession of harvests.'[36]

WORKERS

If we have the names of too few of the architects of antiquity, then many are the anonymous but skilled craftsmen who, slave and free alike, laboured for a drachma a day – the standard wage for a working man at this time. They include those who quarried, carted, cut and carved the stone, besides those who fixed each member in position or gave it a final finish such as the fluting of columns. Glimpses of the organization of their work and payments made for it are given in inscriptions carved themselves into stone stelai and set up for public scrutiny. Tombs such as the Nereid Monument from Lycian Xanthos and the Mausoleum of Halikarnassos were erected with the private wealth of autocrats. The building of temples might be assisted by private funds, but they were usually commissioned by the state, and in litigious democracies, especially, it was in the interests of both the state and its officials charged with oversight of the works to keep records of expenditure. Where they survive such documents not only provide financial evidence but also assist our knowledge of how a temple looked and the sequence of its construction. They include records concerning the rebuilding of the Athenian Acropolis in the age of Perikles and, from the fourth century BC, the inscriptions found in the sanctuary of Asklepios at Epidauros in the Greek Peloponnese. A remarkable inscription from the Athenian Acropolis records the state of works on the Erechtheum in 409 BC, following several years of inactivity during an interruption caused by Athens' war with Sparta, and mentions the famous Caryatids (korai) as already in place.[37] Further records were kept for successive years with fascinating details of the work and its costs. Work on the temple and the great Athenian project as a whole came to an end in 404 BC with defeat in the Peloponnesian War. It took a quarter century for the building industry to recover, not only in Athens but all over mainland Greece, and one of the earliest of postwar enterprises was the construction around 375–370 BC of a new temple of Asklepios at Epidauros. Inscriptions chart the progress of the temple as it was put up, working from the outside in. As usual in temple construction, the outer columns were erected before the walls of the cella. The whole project comprised a series of contracts let to individuals, who were responsible for buying in materials and for finding and hiring skilled labour.[38]

Large-scale projects had considerable benefits in providing employment for craftsmen and the security within which to develop and refine their art. Plutarch's own account gives striking testimony to the social and economic prosperity that Perikles' building policy brought to Athens:

> For military expeditions brought good pay to the young and strong; and as he did not want the undisciplined artisan class to be without some share in the rewards, nor to take them while doing nothing and remaining idle, Perikles carried in the assembly great building projects and undertakings involving many crafts; so the people who stayed at home might take their share of the benefit from the public funds no less than the crews and the garrisons and the expeditionary forces. The raw materials were stone, bronze, ivory, gold, ebony, cypress-wood, and to fashion and work them were the crafts: carpenters, moulders, coppersmiths, stone-workers, goldsmiths, ivory-workers, painters, pattern-weavers, workers in relief. Then there were the men engaged in transport and carriage, merchants, sailors, helmsmen by sea, and by land cartwrights and men who kept yokes of beasts, and drovers; rope makers, flax-workers, shoemakers, road-makers, and miners. And each craft, like a general with his own army, had its own crowd of hired workers and individual craftsmen

organized like an instrument and body for the service to be performed; so, in a word, the various needs to be met distributed and spread prosperity through every age and condition.[39]

It is clear from this that building temples was more than a job merely for stonemasons. Greek architecture, like the sculpture that decorated it, was not about stone only, but was made up of various materials. Precious wood and ivory inlays have altogether disappeared. Metal attachments rarely survive in place, but their former existence can be detected in holes drilled for fixing them, such as those that pierce the eyes of the volutes of Ionic column capitals and those that pepper the Parthenon frieze, especially its cavalcade. A striking example of the composite, jewel-like nature of Greek architecture is the plait-motif moulding (torus) of the north porch column capitals of the Erechtheum. These were drilled and inlaid with coloured glass, which was remarked upon by nineteenth-century travellers, but has since disappeared (see fig. 117).[40]

POLYCHROMY

Besides inlays and attachments, Greek architecture and its sculpture was further embellished with applied colour.[41] It may seem strange that the ancients should choose beautiful and expensive white marble as the preferred material for tombs and temples and then, as the saying goes, proceed to gild the lily and paint the rose. The primary reason, however, for using marble was the sharp and durable edge it took in its carving, which allowed for a subtlety of plastic effect, especially in the creation of a play of light and shadow across the surface. Softer limestones were inevitably also used extensively, especially by the Greeks of southern Italy, where there were no marble quarries. Here, temple architecture was stuccoed and painted to resemble marble. In East Greece, as well as a plentiful supply of marble there was also a range of good-quality limestones, some as hard as marble, and these were sometimes selected for their intrinsic colour. In the Mausoleum at Halikarnassos, for example, an attractive blue-grey limestone was variously used to contrast with the white of the marble so that from a distance, and depending upon the light, the whole monument appeared to be banded with colour (fig. 14).[42] Nor was only one marble chosen, for scientific analysis has shown that this varies in origin according to each category of sculptured decoration.[43] The finest and most precious was imported from Athens' Mount Pentelikon and used for the colossal portrait figures. Where these different marbles and limestones were not painted, subtle variations in tone may have made their own contribution to the rich colouristic effects of Mausolus' tomb. Similar effects, as we

Greek Temples – Form and Meaning 35

14 The different stones of the Mausoleum at Halikarnassos, c. 350 BC, indicated on Waywell's proposed reconstruction, for which see Chapter Nine. Drawing S. Bird.

shall see in Chapter Six, may have been achieved by the different stones used in the temple of Apollo at Bassai.

Laying aside the intrinsic colour of stone itself, there is good reason to believe that the columns, walls and other non-painted surfaces of temples were washed with a varnish or tinted wax, akin to the so-called ganosis of the Roman period mentioned by Pliny and Vitruvius. Its purpose would have been to protect the surface against the weather and to take off the inevitable glare that comes with freshly cut marble or newly applied white stucco.[44] No one who has been blinded at noon on a summer's day

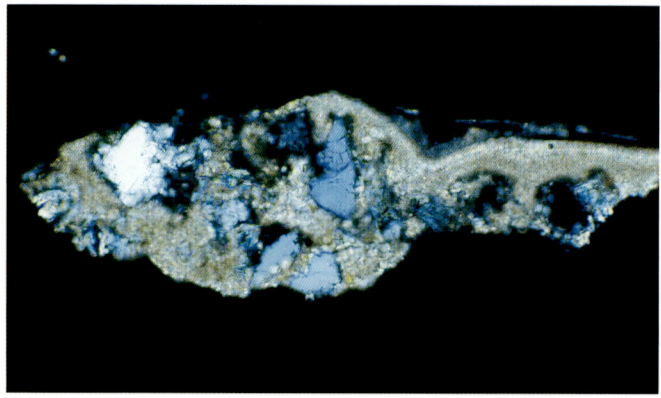

15 A cake of blue pigment found in a tomb at Camirus, Rhodes. British Museum.

16 A thin-section analysis of a sample of blue pigment from block 1019 of the Mausoleum's Amazon frieze. Fragments of colour appear suspended in a matrix, probably the adhesive by which the pigment was applied. British Museum. Analysis by Andrew Middleton.

by the whitewashed walls of Greek island houses will underestimate the unpleasant effect the Parthenon's blank masses of stark white marble must have had on the eye. Nor, contrary to popular belief, does Pentelic marble mellow quickly with time. The scars of the seventeenth-century Venetian bombardment that destroyed the Parthenon still show white against the west face of the Propylaea foundation wall. The patchwork of new marble that has been incorporated into the recent restoration of the Acropolis monuments will continue to jar the eye unless artificially coloured to match the original.

Many ancient monuments are today partially coated in an orange-brown patina that may be the remains of ancient varnish (see fig. 29). Besides mitigating the glare of newly cut marble, such a varnish would have served also to protect the polychromy and, as in the modern varnishing of pictures, to unify the tone. An alternative explanation of the patina, however, is that it is due to natural causes. If so, it does not seem to have formed as the result of a continuing, gradual process. Rather, it appears to have occurred relatively early in the life of ancient monuments and then to have been subject to an ongoing process of erosion. Thus, where such a patina is damaged by weathering or human hand, it does not regenerate itself, and the exposed white marble leaves a scar. The rusted appearance of ancient monuments could perhaps be explained by a sudden, global climactic catastrophe that with reduced light and increased humidity precipitated the growth of micro-organisms. These may have changed with time to become the mineralized deposits that we see today. The sixth century AD is remarkable in the texts of contemporary writers for its climactic disasters, including the notorious AD 536, a year without summer. A major volcanic eruption or meteor strike somewhere in the world may account for this.[45]

Varnishes and coatings apart, coloured paint and gilding were always a feature of ancient buildings, and those of the seventh and sixth centuries

BC were especially colourful. By the fifth century BC colour tended to be restricted to the upper reaches of a building. Here the visibility of decorative mouldings and sculpture, and the intelligibility of any story that the sculpture told, was enhanced with contrasting colour. Early Greek architectural polychromy probably experimented with a wider range of colours but, by the fifth century BC, the most popular seem to have been red, blue, and gold applied as leaf. These were combined with the reserved ground of the white marble, thus adding a fourth colour. Red will have been a naturally occurring or artificially produced pigment such as oxide of iron. Blue was usually a copper silicate, either naturally occurring, as in volcanic rocks, or manufactured (fig. 15). The colour was the deep, rich, inky blue of lapis lazuli and is sometimes called Egyptian blue. Gold was the warm yellow tone of pure unalloyed metal, possibly enhanced by an undercoat of red or blue (bole). The gold applied as leaf was attached to the marble by means of an adhesive but, since they were produced as fine particles of a mineral pigment, red and blue also had effectively to be stuck to the marble by means of a matrix solution in which the pigment

17 A red stripe painted on the drapery of an Amazon from the Amazon frieze of the Mausoleum at Halikarnassos. British Museum.

18 Detail of fig. 17.

particles were suspended (fig. 16). We hear in literary sources of the ancients using heated wax in a so-called 'encaustic' technique, but modern research argues for the use also of egg tempera in the painting of marble.[46]

In places colour traces still survive on architecture and sculpture in the British Museum. They include red and blue on the carved ceiling coffers of the Mausoleum and the temple of Athena Polias at Priene.[47] A painted face has been found on one of the coffers of the Nereid Monument with remains of a painted bead and reel and other ornament.[48] Red can be seen on the figures of the Amazon frieze of the Mausoleum, such as on the inside of a shield carried by a Greek warrior and again as stripes decorating the dress of an Amazon (figs 17–18). Blue can be seen on the background of the Amazon frieze and again on the background of the east side of Kybernis' tomb from Xanthos (see fig. 154), and there are other reports of red in the figures themselves. The freestanding sculptures of the Mausoleum also preserve traces of paint, including red in the mouths of the lions and blue and gold on what was once a painted saddle cloth of the colossal Persian rider (see fig. 211).[49] Traces of red and black occur on fragments of sculpture from the archaic Artemision.[50] The potential complexity of polychromatic technique is indicated by the use of gilded lead to fill the gap between two mouldings (astragal) of a colossal volute-capital from the same monument (fig. 19).[51] Lead has also been found on the horse fragments of the colossal chariot from the summit of the Mausoleum roof and this may have been laid over the marble as a thin base for gilding.

Not all paint traces on the sculpture can be taken at face value. A drip of red on the leg of one of the Greek warriors of the Mausoleum's Amazon frieze does not go back to antiquity but is probably an accident of the time when the sculpture was displayed on the walls of the Crusader Castle at Bodrum.[52] Some splashes of red on the Museum's architectural sculpture are yet more recent products of nineteenth-century colour schemes in the decoration of the gallery walls and ceilings, when the Victorians revived newly discovered ancient archaeological polychromy. That revival had been fostered by the eye-witness reports of European travelling architects who worked up their discoveries into dramatic reconstruction drawings.[53] Since much has been lost over the last two hundred years, their assertions cannot always now be checked against the evidence. Already in the nineteenth century there was scepticism about reported accounts of colour on architecture and sculpture. So frustrated was Charles Newton at the reluctance of his public to accept his observation of paint on the marbles he was digging up in Turkey, he bottled a sample of blue pigment scraped off a member of the Mausoleum as proof of its having been painted (figs 20–22).[54] One of Newton's difficulties was the fugitive nature of some colours. The colossal draped and seated male (see

19 Detail of a gap between two mouldings (astragal) on a column capital of the archaic temple of Artemis at Ephesos, where a fragment of gilding is preserved over a lead stopping. British Museum.

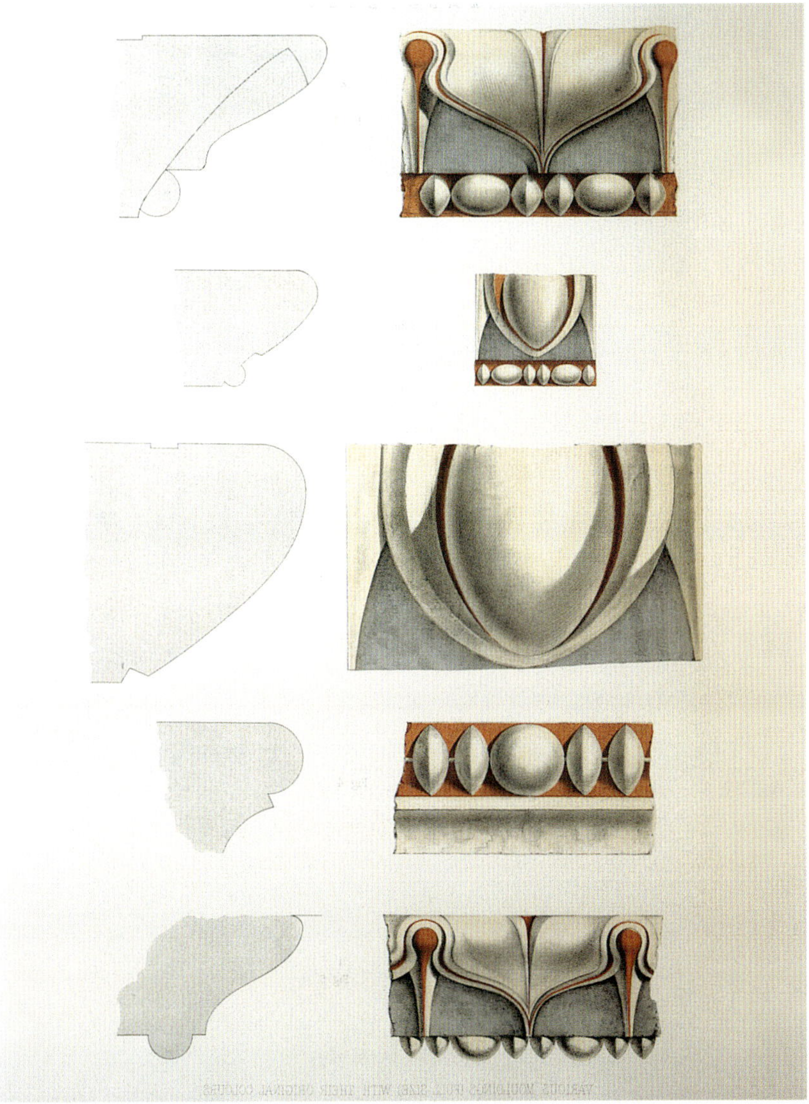

Greek Temples – Form and Meaning

20 C.T. Newton's lithograph showing coloured mouldings of the Mausoleum at Halikarnassos.

21 A miniature bottle containing blue pigment scraped by Charles Newton from one of the mouldings of the Mausoleum at Halikarnassos.

22 Detail of a bead and reel moulding on a coffer fragment of the Mausoleum at Halikarnassos, painted with red and blue pigment.

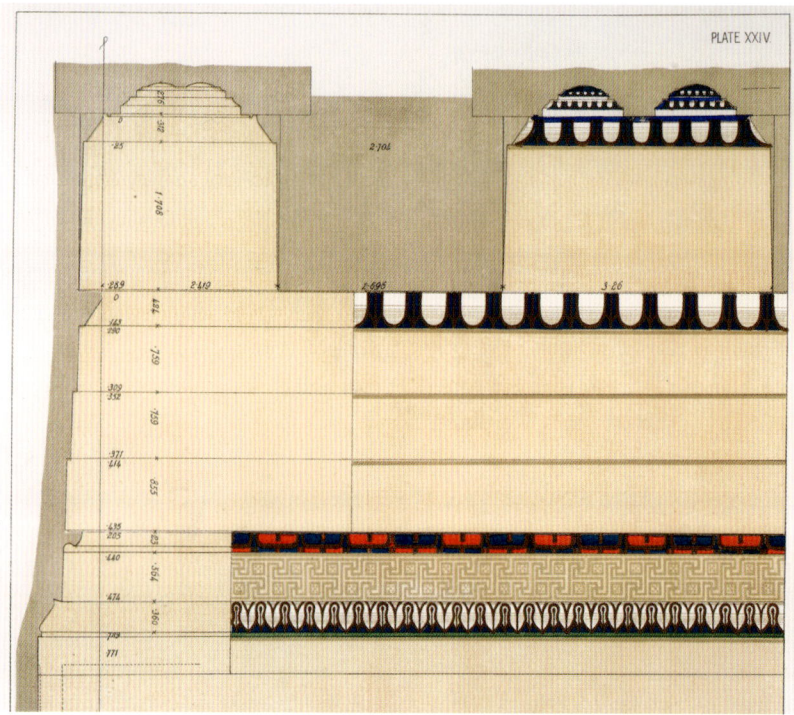

23 ABOVE RIGHT A wall-crown block from the interior of the Propylaea with incised and painted leaf and dart decoration, now discoloured to a dull brown. British Museum.

24 ABOVE Detail of fig. 23.

25 RIGHT Reconstruction by F. Penrose of the colouring of a wall crown of the Propylaea, surmounted by the architrave in the middle register and, above, the beam and coffers of the ceiling.

fig. 215) that may have been a cult figure of Mausolus himself was bright with purple paint when found, but upon exposure to the air this colour soon faded to the unpleasing brown that we see today.[55] The brown of many ancient sculptures in museums may in fact be the remains of an original colour. The painted decoration of a moulded wall block from the Ionic entablature of the Propylaea, for example, was carefully delineated with incised lines (figs 23–5). The lines remain but the paint itself has discoloured to a dull brown.[56]

Sometimes the paint has gone altogether and nothing survives but for a ghost of the decoration preserved through differential weathering.

26 Fragment of the crown moulding (thranos) over the Ionic frieze of the Parthenon preserving the ghost of a painted or gilded meander pattern. British Museum.

27 Reconstruction by F. Penrose of the colouring of the Parthenon frieze crown.

Imagine a sheet of marble that is partially painted with a pattern. Over time the painted surface weathers less quickly than the naked marble and, when finally every trace of the paint disappears, all that remains is the difference in the relative wear of the painted and unpainted surface. Such is the effect of the weather on the moulding (thranos) that crowned the Ionic frieze of the Parthenon[57] (figs 26–7) and less obviously on an anta-capital in the British Museum, thought to come from the south-east corner of the Nike temple on the Athenian Acropolis. It preserves the ghost of a painted floral decoration very similar to those carved on the Erechtheum.[58] Similar traces have been noticed on sculptures. We have

28 Reconstruction of the colouring of the Parthenon west frieze and ceiling.

already remarked upon the blue background and red detailing of the sculpture for Kybernis' tomb from Xanthos, and here is F.N. Pryce's summary of details where no paint remains, but a ghosted shadow survives:

> Considerable remains of this may be observed on the left angle of the north side, above the head, on the body between arms and talons and below the body of the 'Harpy'. A palmette scroll is clearly visible in silhouette between the bars of the throne on the east side. A.H. Smith saw palmettes on the right throne of the west side, which are now hard to trace; but cushion and interspace of the left throne of the same side show clear traces of patterns, probably similar palmettes, while the side shows remains of incised guide-lines for maeander. There was a maeander on the top border and an egg and dart on the bottom curved moulding.[59]

Greek Temples – Form and Meaning

It is often said that the sculptures of the Parthenon were brightly painted with contrasting colours (fig. 28). In reality, however, until very recently there has been little tangible evidence for the various claims that have been made. Certainly, the architecture does preserve traces of polychromy but, whether we speak of the sculptures in London, Athens or elsewhere, there is little by way of colour. In London this cannot be blamed on the notorious episode of the cleaning that took place in 1937–8, when much of the orange-brown coating or patina that hitherto had covered the sculptures was scraped away.[60] Already a century earlier during preparations for a casting of the sculptures to make plaster copies, the surface was inspected thoroughly by no less a scientist than Michael Faraday and found to retain no trace of colour.[61] Nor can colour be detected on sculptures that were not cleaned in the 1930s and still retain their patina. Now, however, important indications that the sculptures were in fact painted come from the west frieze. Most of this remained on the building in Athens until it was brought down for conservation reasons in 1993 and, as this work proceeds, there are unpublished reports of colour traces.

Verified observations have also been reported of colour on the east frieze of the temple of Hephaistos, a sister temple of the Parthenon built on the edge of the Athenian marketplace.[62] These were made in the 1950s when an orange-brown patina was scraped off in a cleaning process very like that earlier carried out on the Parthenon sculptures in the British Museum.[63] Red and blue were the predominant colours, but also green, which may be a consequence of the corrosion of the copper silicate in a pigment that was originally blue.[64] If the Parthenon frieze was also coloured, like that of the Hephaesteum, as now seems likely, then a blue background to the frieze and the colouring of individual elements of the figures will have aided the legibility of the subject. As for the pediments and the metopes, there is not yet firm evidence that they were coloured. Fragments of blue have been found on the triglyphs and on the plain moulding (taenia) above one of the metopes in Athens and another fragment of the same colour on the floor of the east pediment.[65] The only survival of actual paint on the sculptures in the British Museum is on the back of the box-like seat occupied by figure F of the east pediment (fig. 29). Here a brush loaded with a lead-rich paint was drawn across the marble in a place where it would not be seen and evidently before the sculpture was fixed into position on the pediment shelf.[66] It must have been a trial for a mixture intended to be used

29 A brush-stroke preserved on the rear of figure F of the Parthenon's east pediment. It is partially covered by an orange-brown patina, which may be attributable to artificial or natural causes.

elsewhere, exactly of the kind that we ourselves might make in home-decorating when choosing a colour or testing the density of a paint solution. What the actual colour of this paint was cannot now be determined.

CONTEXT AND MEANING IN ARCHITECTURE
AND SCULPTURE

Today, for conservation reasons much of the sculpture and architecture that survives from ancient buildings is seen in a museum. This naturally alters our perception of a subject, transforming it from being part of a larger whole into an object attracting the kind of curiosity that in antiquity would have been reserved for the cult statue inside a temple. Sculpture hung on the wall of a modern gallery like a picture naturally detaches itself in the viewer's mind from the architecture that once framed it. Moreover, because the sculpture is pictorial, the closer we are to it, the more we demand that it should yield the secret of its supposed meaning, that is to say over and above the obvious one of its immediate subject matter, which was normally an episode from Greek mythology.[67] Subsequent chapters of this book suggest ways in which, for example, the sculptures of the Parthenon or those of Lycian tombs can be viewed as 'programmatic', each image contributing to a corporate, overall message. In the case of democratic Athens the message is the civic image of a city, past and present, while in the case of the Nereid Monument, as in the Mausoleum at Halikarnassos, it is the self-image of royal autocrats and their pretensions to divinity.

In other cases the search for meanings is more problematic. The fragmentary nature of the remains of some buildings, such as those of the earlier and later Artemision at Ephesos, renders near impossible any attempt at extracting an overall programme. In the case of the archaic Artemision, for example, it is tempting to reconstruct the fragmentary figured scenes as processional and to conjecture that these scenes of a great pan-Ionian festival were an inspiration for the Panathenaic procession of the Parthenon frieze.[68] This, however, is to build one hypothesis upon another. Even where enough survives to make the subjects of the sculpture clear, other circumstances can render interpretation problematic. In the Parthenon metopes a battle between Greeks and Amazons or Greeks and Trojans, even strife between Greeks and Centaurs or between gods and giants, may be regarded as analogous to the real-life struggles between Greeks and Persians that disturbed the Greek world in the early years of the fifth century BC. The same, however, cannot be said of the appearance of such subjects on the funerary monuments of Lycians and Karians, who had been the allies of the Persians and had joined in the armies of invasion. Mausolus of Halikarnassos was a Persian satrap, and the battle between Greeks and Amazons on his tomb was hardly likely to be intended as a slap in the Persian face.[69]

Modern approaches to the understanding of ancient architectural sculpture must allow for the possibility that we expect too much by way of intended meanings. Subjects that appear time and again in the iconography of temples and tombs may simply have been the stock-in-trade images of masons, who did not anticipate the intense interest and quest for meaning that their work has provoked. Certainly, there is nothing in ancient building inscriptions to suggest that they did. Even Pausanias' descriptive guide to Greece, written in the second century AD, is disappointingly silent on the unusual subject of the Parthenon frieze, thus giving encouragement in the modern era to generations of would-be interpreters of its supposed hidden meaning.

The search for meanings is not restricted to figurative sculpture. Architecture too is sometimes discussed as having its own pictorial language.[70] Never has this idea been more current than among the architects of Revolutionary France with their *architecture parlante*, for which there are some ancient parallels. As we have already seen, Vitruvius speaks of the masculine qualities of the Doric order and contrasts it with the feminine forms of slender Ionic. There can be no doubt, moreover, that Doric was seen by mainland Greeks as a native style while, for the East-Greek cities of western Anatolia, Ionic had its own set of ethno-cultural associations. The mouldings of the rebuilt Artemision at Ephesos must be seen as a deliberate revival of archaic forms and a renaissance of past glories in what the previous chapter called the Ionian enlightenment.[71] Before the fourth-century renaissance of the Ionian golden age, Athens artfully created its own influential international style of architecture from a distinctive blend of Ionic and Doric forms that befitted the premier Greek city at the head of an empire made up of both Ionian and Dorian peoples.

To speak of the meaning of sculpture and architecture as separate entities is not to deny that sculpture on buildings is itself architecture.[72] Although the display of objects in museums may create a different impression, all sculpture fitted to buildings, whether carved in the round or in relief, was once architecture and can take many forms. Those that are carved in the round include: pediment figures; figures crowning the angles of pediments (acroteria); figures acting as columns – for example, Caryatids; figures set between columns, as in the Mausoleum and Nereid Monument. Reliefs include: continuous friezes, like the Ionic frieze of the Parthenon and that of the Bassai temple; friezes made up of individual panels like the metope and triglyph friezes of Doric temples; the neckings of columns or the lowest drums of columns, such as those of the

Artemisia at Ephesos; the stone guttering (sima) of roofs, most often with lion head spouts set amidst an ornamental frieze of palmettes or acanthus. Many of these elements were carved on the building, only after they were set as rough-faced, load-bearing members of the structure, and must, therefore, in all senses be considered parts of the architecture.

The original context in which architectural sculpture was conceived was the building that framed it, but that building was itself part of a larger context, namely the temple sanctuary or tomb precinct. Besides cult statues, temples housed oracles and treasuries and were a focus for festivals celebrating the divine personality with processional hymns, musical and athletic competitions and sacrifice. The building thus became the backdrop to a living drama and the space that surrounded it was a sacred enclosure, often planted with trees and with a source of fresh water, marked out by a boundary wall (temenos). Some temples, such as that of Apollo on the Aegean island of Delos or at Delphi, or the temple of Zeus at Olympia, or the Artemision at Ephesos, which we shall visit in the next chapter, might become the focus of international gatherings with an importance far beyond the local community that administered them.

When we contemplate the meanings of architectural sculpture, therefore, the matter of ancient context concerns more than just the building, more even than the temenos in which it stood, but has ultimately to do with the identity, values and experience of the living people who once gathered as festival celebrants and competitors.[73] These ancient witnesses cannot now be resurrected or interrogated as to what they saw and thought. Meanwhile, generations of modern viewers see architectural sculptures intended for the outside of a building displayed in museums on interior walls, where the gallery itself supplies a new architectural frame. It is sometimes said that museums are a false field in which to see ancient artefacts because the object is placed 'out of context'. It is incontrovertible that museums are not the original context, but they do represent a legitimate solution to the problem of preserving relics that can no longer be restored to the buildings from which they come. Moreover, displayed with other types of object and with the art of other civilizations, architectural sculpture can be used to construct narratives that transcend original function by becoming part of a bigger story.

Chapter Three

The Temples of Artemis at Ephesos

> My eyes have looked on the Wall of Babylon and on the Zeus by the Alpheus [Olympia], and on the Hanging Gardens, and the colossal Helios [Rhodes], and on the high Pyramids, and the gigantic monument of Mausolus, but when I saw the vast Temple of Artemis [Ephesos] soaring to the clouds, the others were all dimmed, for except in Heaven the Sun has never looked on like.
>
> Antipater of Sidon (*c.* 100 BC) on the Seven Wonders

On the night of 21 July 356 BC, Herostratos set fire to the great archaic temple of Artemis at Ephesos and, as this mention of him reluctantly demonstrates, fulfilled a prophecy that his name would live for ever.[1] Plutarch, writing in the second century AD, declares the event providential in occurring on the very night of the birth of Alexander the Great.[2] Already *c.* 395 BC, the building had suffered and survived a fire.[3] It had been immediately restored and probably enlarged by an unknown architect. This time the devastation was irreparable and the Ephesians decided to demolish the ruins and to rebuild. The so-called later or younger Artemision, bigger and more splendid than its predecessor, was to become listed as one of the Seven Wonders of the ancient world.[4] It survived until AD 263, when a surprise attack by the Ostrogoths laid the sanctuary waste.[5] The cult persisted until it was suppressed by the Christian emperors, and Justinian (AD 527–65) dismantled some of the columns for reuse in the imperial palace at Constantinople.

Ephesos was in the ancient Greek ethnic region of Ionia, which lay along the central part of the west coast of Turkey. According to tradition, it had been colonized by migrants from mainland Greece, fleeing the incursions of Dorian tribes at the end of the Greek Bronze Age. The Ionian Greeks flourished and, although never a nation, they nevertheless developed a strong sense of cultural identity, which centred upon their most important cult places. The wealth and prestige of the Ionian coastal cities made them inevitable targets for the expansionist ambitions of powers to the east, notably Lydia and Persia. Ephesos was originally founded on the sea, but suffered, like so many of the coastal cities of western Turkey, from the effects of river alluviation silting up the ancient harbour and pushing out the coastline. It prospered under the Romans to become one of the centres of Imperial rule in Asia, but, at the time of the building of the archaic Artemision in the sixth century BC, it was just one of several small Greek colony-townships that clung to the western edge of the Lydian and, later, Persian empires of Anatolia. Ephesos before the Romans was certainly less important than its sanctuary of Artemis and probably existed largely to service it.[6]

KING KROISOS OF LYDIA AND THE IONIAN ENLIGHTENMENT

The central personality in the creation of the archaic Artemision is King Kroisos of Lydia (fig. 30), the story of whose eventful life has happily been rescued from oblivion by that ever-helpful father of history, Herodotos.[7] Before their conquest by Cyrus the Great of Persia, the Lydian kings ruled western Anatolia from their capital at Sardis. Kroisos' mother was a Karian woman, and his father Alyattes had carried on the hereditary struggle of his Mermnad dynasty to subdue the coastal Greek cities. Around 570 BC, Alyattes commanded Kroisos to conduct a war against Priene, and Kroisos approached a rich Lydian by the name of Sadyattes for a loan. This request was refused, and so Kroisos went to Ephesos, where he vowed in the sanctuary of Artemis that, were he to become king of Lydia, he would there dedicate the entire fortune of Sadyattes.[8] Kroisos did indeed become king and fulfilled his pledge, having the very foundations of Sadyattes' house grubbed out and dedicated in the sanctuary. The unfortunate Sadyattes was put to death, drawn over the spikes of metal carding combs. Kroisos went on to fund the construction of the columns of a new Artemision, perhaps from the wealth of Sadyattes, and Kroisos' name is probably to be read on fragments of the inscribed bases.

Lydian interest in Ephesos was already a part of Alyattes' foreign policy. According to Herodotos, Lydia had tried for fifty-seven years to suppress Miletos, which was effectively the capital city of Ionia, deliberately ruining each year's new harvest. Alyattes brought this hostility to an end and founded two temples to Athena in Milesian territory. Miletos, however, whether in war or in peace, was never very pro-Lydian, and there was little prospect of Alyattes being able to control Miletos' great sanctuary of Apollo at nearby Didyma, with its influential oracle. Lydian interest concentrated, therefore, on building up Ephesos as a friendly centre of Ionian culture. Such was the independent Ionian spirit, however, that even Ephesian compliance to Lydian domination was not won without force. Kroisos attacked the city and, when its defences collapsed, the wily Ephesians sought sacred immunity from destruction by claiming the protection of their goddess. Lest there be any doubt, they stretched a rope from the city walls to the columns of the temple, a distance of some seven stades or about 1.5 kilometres. Amused by this ingenuity, Kroisos granted them immunity, but insisted on the expulsion of their tyrant Pindaros.[9]

Eventually Kroisos would himself succumb to the rising power of Persia. When at Pasargadae Cyrus the Persian defeated Astyages, leader of the Medes, Kroisos consulted oracles in mainland Greece as to what he should do. If he were to engage with the Persians, his agents were ambiguously told at Delphi and at Thebes, a great empire would fall. Indeed it did, Sardis was besieged and Kroisos captured in 547 BC. Records of oracles given to famous persons are now regarded as ancient forgeries, invented by

30 Kroisos on the pyre. Amphora painted by Myson, *c.* 500 BC. Paris, Louvre.

the priests to augment the reputation of the oracular cult. The story, however, entered the corpus of legend that grew up around Kroisos, including conflicting tales of his fate. It was said that his life was spared and he was made a guest and adviser at Cyrus' court. Another account had him placed alive on a pyre, only to be saved by the intervention of Apollo.

With the fall of Sardis, the Greek cities came to regret their refusal of an earlier invitation from the Persians to revolt against Lydia. They now offered themselves as Persian subjects under the same terms as those they had accepted from Kroisos. Cyrus refused and his general, Harpagos the Mede, set about capturing them one by one. Cyrus was to prove no less adept than Kroisos had been at controlling the Ionian Greeks' political independence, while permitting their cultural autonomy. There was healthy cultural exchange and cross-fertilization of ideas. At Pasargadae, Cyrus constructed his tomb employing Greek masons, as architectural motifs and masonry techniques testify;[10] while, on the island of Samos, Pythagoras nurtured the origins of the modern, western system of mathematics with knowledge acquired from Babylon.[11]

Samos in the sixth century BC, like Miletos and Kolophon, was a centre of Ionian learning and fashion.[12] Samos too had its great Ionic temple, dedicated to Hera and built by Rhoikos and Theodoros, the latter also being involved with the archaic Artemision.[13] As we saw in the previous chapter, the earlier temple of Hera on Samos, boasting a double row of Ionic columns standing on distinctive Samian bases, was begun around 570 BC. Poor foundations probably account for the fact that it was dismantled a generation later, and its successor was commissioned by the tyrant Polykrates, but was never completed.[14] Its forest of colossal columns, designed to overwhelm the senses, was almost certainly inspired by Samian contacts with Egypt and knowledge of monumental buildings there. Samians had their own trading post in the Nile delta, which was probably eclipsed by the trading colony founded around 620 BC at Naukratis. There was a tradition that the Samian architect Rhoikos had visited Naukratis in the Nile delta, and he was perhaps involved in the building of temples there, albeit on a much smaller scale than his work on Samos.[15] Douris of Samos quotes some verses of the Samian poet Asios, who flourished around 700 BC, that describe the striking appearance of the Samian people attending their temple in his day:

> He wrote of the joyous panache of the Samians as they made their way to the sanctuary of Hera by the stream of Imbrasos, west of the Samian city. Their hair was combed, they were closely wrapped in fine clothes, and they covered the floor of the wide earth with their snowy cloaks. On them were golden brooches, like cicadas, and their hair in golden bands tossed in the wind, while about their arms were delicately wrought bracelets.[16]

So may we imagine the Ephesians in their processions in honour of Artemis which, to judge from their fragmentary remains, was the subject represented on the carved columns of the archaic Artemision. Miletos too had its processions, not least along the Sacred Way that ran south from the city to the archaic temple of Apollo at Didyma. That temple, like the Artemision, had columns standing in the front porch carved with scenes of worshippers (figs 31–2).[17] Miletos was at the heart of the Ionian enlightenment, and its philosophers were to preside over the birth of western natural philosophy and its rational view of the world.[18] There, in the first half of the sixth century, lived Thales, one of the legendary Seven Wise Men of the ancient world, and his slightly younger contemporary the natural philosopher Anaximander, the first Greek map-maker. In the next generation was Anaximander's pupil, Anaximenes, and Hekataios, who shared an interest in maps and compiled a *Description of the Inhabited World* which has survived only in fragments, but which clearly had a great influence upon Herodotos. Ephesos had its own star-thinker in the

The Temples of Artemis at Ephesos

31 Reconstruction of the order and architectural sculpture of the archaic temple of Apollo at Didyma. After G. Gruben.

32 Fragment of a female figure carved onto one of the columns of the archaic temple at Didyma. Berlin Staatlichen Museen.

enigmatic Herakleitos, who was born around 540 BC and lived all his life in his native city. His thought has come down to us as a series of aphorisms, such as that commonly translated, 'You can't step into the same river twice'.[19]

The great archaic age of Ionian creativity was brought to a bloody end, when in 499 BC Aristagoras the ruling tyrant of Miletos, with encouragement and help from Athens, led a general revolt of the Ionian cities against Persia. It failed, and in 494 BC Miletos was captured, most of its males put to death, and women and children sold into slavery. The great temple of Apollo at Didyma was destroyed[20] and would not rise again until the time of Alexander the Great 150 years later. The Artemision, however, was left unscathed, perhaps because of Persian patronage following on that of Kroisos.

J.T. WOOD AND THE SEARCH FOR THE ARTEMISION

John Turtle Wood (1805–94) was an engineer and architect who, through the 1860s, was engaged in the construction of a new railway from Izmir to Denizli (fig. 33).[21] As an amateur diversion, but at the cost

33 John Turtle Wood (1805–94) by L.S. Canziani. British Museum.

of considerable personal hardship, he began excavations in the ruins of ancient Ephesos. In February 1866 he began to excavate the great theatre (fig. 34), estimated to seat 24,500 people, and in the course of these excavations found an important inscription that had been mounted upon the eastern wall of the entrance. It recorded a series of decrees, chiefly relating to a number of gold and silver images, each weighing from 3 to 7 pounds (1.36 to 3.17 kilos), which were dedicated in the temple of Artemis by a wealthy Roman citizen, C. Vibius Salutarius.[22] On 25 May, on the birthday of the goddess, these images were to be carried by the priests in procession from the temple, which lay outside the city, to the theatre. They made their way to the Magnesian gate, which was the principal southern entrance of the city and took its name from the nearest town, Magnesia-on-the-Maeander. There they were met by ephebes, young men of military age, who joined the procession and helped carry the images to the theatre. After an assembly, the statues were returned in procession to the temple, escorted by the ephebes as far as the so-called Coressian gate. Mentions of the emperor Trajan, and of the specific Consuls for AD 104, date the decree.[23]

Wood saw that, if he were able to locate the Magnesian and Coressian gates, he could follow the roads that would lead him to the temple. Before the end of 1867 he had located the Magnesian gate, and eventually found the Coressian near the stadium on the north side of the city. From the Magnesian gate he traced the road, which passed through an ancient cemetery, identifying the tomb of the Ionian hero Androklos, reported by Pausanias as being 'on the road that leads from the sanctuary past the Olympieion towards the Magnesian gate'.[24] He came across the stone piers of a portico, which he identified as that given by Damianus, and was described by Philostratus as providing a covered walkway from the city to the temple. North-east of the town, Wood came across a wall,

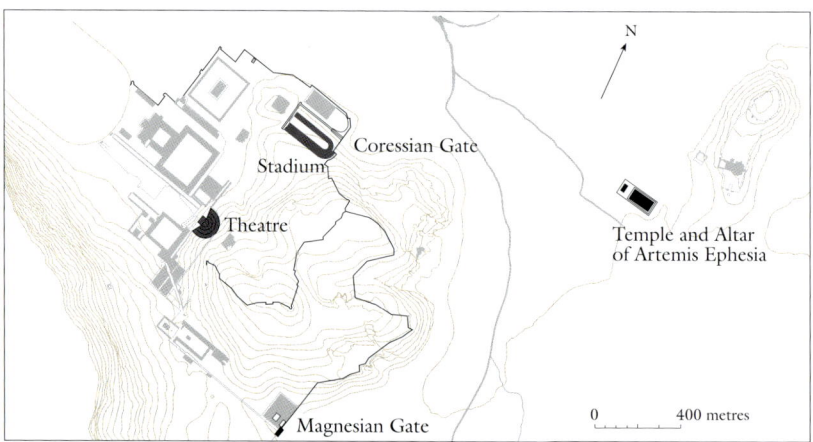

34 Plan of Ephesos.

35 The Artemision under excavation in December 1871.

which bore inscriptions in Latin and Greek that showed it to have been built by the emperor Augustus in 6 BC. This was the temenos or sanctuary wall constructed by the Romans to restrict the area in which renegade suppliants could claim the protection of the goddess. Finally, on the last day of 1869 the temple was found, 'so long lost, so long sought for, and so long almost despaired of'.[25] Its marble pavement was located at a depth of 6 metres below the surface, such was the extent of the silting up of the area around Ephesos. By pumping water out of the remains, Wood excavated into the foundations of the later temple and found them to incorporate the demolished remnants of the archaic temple (fig. 35). Wood published an anecdotal account of his discoveries in 1877, with his own reconstruction of how the later Artemision might have looked. The topic has been much debated ever since, not least because much of the evidence for the plan of the principal, western front of the building is missing.

In 1904–5 D.G. Hogarth and A.E. Henderson returned to the site and researched the older buildings that had stood there before the archaic and late-classical temples. They identified three earlier building phases, the earliest being an apsidal shrine dating back to the late eighth or early seventh century and situated to the west of the later temples. These earlier buildings were given letters 'A–C', and the archaic Artemision was designated 'D'.[26] Since 1965, the Austrian Institute of Archaeology in Vienna has been active at the site. The initial investigation was an attempt to locate the altar, which was said to have been embellished with sculpture by Praxiteles. The altar was found and the sculpture finds are largely held in the depot of the museum at nearby Selçuk.[27]

36 Roman replica of the Artemis of Ephesos. Naples Archaeological Museum.

THE TEMPLES

The primary purpose of both the earlier and later Artemision was to house the cult statue of the goddess (fig. 36). The cult seems to have been a fusion of Anatolian mother goddesses and the Greek Olympian deity Artemis. The statue, like the temple, was renewed more than once, but retained an archaic stiffness enlivened by much decoration and the extraordinary multi-breast-like appendages that make Ephesian Artemis unique.[28] Neither the earlier nor the later Artemision is thought to have been roofed entirely, and the statue must have stood in a kiosk (naiskos) within the open courtyard at the heart of the architectural complex. Both the archaic and the late-classical temple were designed to be among the grandest and most impressive buildings of the Hellenic world. They belong to a rare group of colossal temples, which include the Rhoikos and Polykrates temples of Hera on Samos, that of Apollo at Didyma, Artemis at Sardis, the Olympieion in Athens, so-called Temple G at Selinous and the temple of Zeus at Akragas on Sicily. The column heights were around 12.08 metres for the archaic Artemision and a massive 17.65 metres for the younger. The Parthenon with 10.43-metre-high columns was substantially smaller and in plan occupied barely a third of the area of the later Artemision. Moreover, the two Artemisia both had a double surrounding colonnade (fig. 37). The front of the later temple, and possibly of the earlier temple in its last phase, also had a third row of columns, behind which stood an avenue of columns filling the deep porch.

Some of our knowledge of the Artemision comes from the ancient authors, but this is not always reliable.[29] The literary sources, for example, do not always make a distinction between the earlier and later temples. The information supplied by these authors derives ultimately from

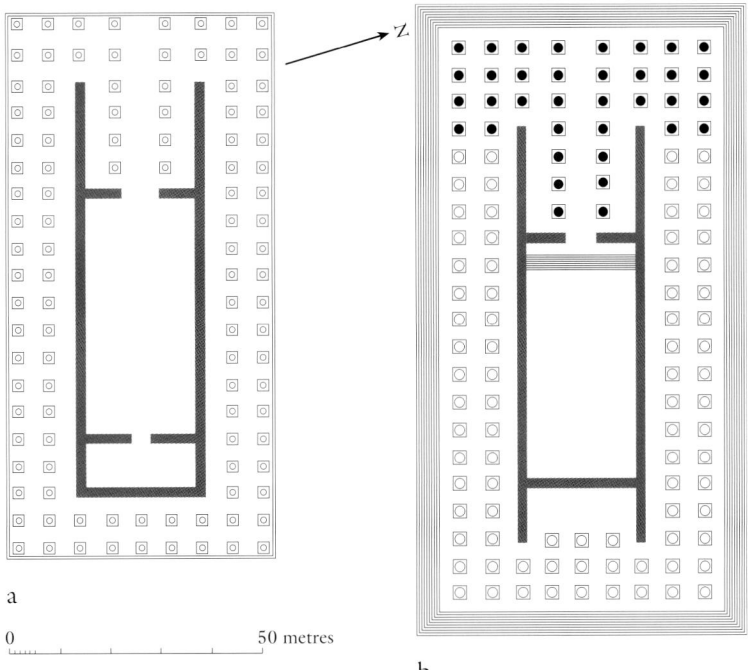

37 Plans of (a) the archaic and (b) later Artemisia.

the architects' own treatises. It was common practice for Greek architects to compile an account of their completed work, but sadly none of these texts survives, and we feel the loss of the treatise on the archaic Artemision by the Cretan architects Chersiphron and Metagenes[30] and on the later temple by Demokritos of Ephesos.[31] The foundations of the archaic Artemision, as we saw in Chapter Two, were prepared by Theodoros, who appears to have been succeeded, as architect of the temple itself, by Chersiphron, who was perhaps replaced in turn by his son Metagenes. The architect of the later Artemision was perhaps Cheirokrates, as Strabo has it, or Deinokrates according to Vitruvius. The Ionian architects Paionios and Demetrios took up the task from him.[32]

The primary literary source for the Artemision is Pliny.[33] Without distinguishing which temple he has in mind, he says that it measured 225 by 425 feet and had 127 columns, each 60 feet high, which height would imply the later temple. Thirty-six of these were described as columnae caelatae, or carved with sculptures, one by the famous fourth-century sculptor Skopas. Vitruvius describes the temple as a dipteros (i.e. a double row of exterior columns on all four sides) with a run of eight columns front and back, and says that the middle part was open to the sky.[34] Philo of Byzantium tells us that it had a podium of ten steps.[35] Helpful as these sources appear, they leave many questions unanswered. It is not known, for example, which measurement for the ancient foot length Pliny had in mind, a problem we shall encounter again in attempting to reconstruct the Mausoleum at Halikarnassos (Chapter Nine).[36] Then there is the question of how the odd number of 127 columns is to be accommodated. If both the long sides of the temple and its short ends had an equal number of columns, then the total would be even. To get an odd total, one of the sides must differ from that opposite. The Polykrates temple of Hera on Samos had eight columns along the front, but nine at the back.[37] The lesser number at the front allowed for a processional avenue through the central column spacing leading up to the great entrance doorway, and this was probably also the case at Ephesos. Then we must ask which temple at Ephesos had thirty-six carved columns and how exactly these were deployed. Which temple had the stepped podium? Answers can be found only in the material remains.

THE ARCHAIC TEMPLE AND ITS SCULPTURE

Wood found two sorts of archaic relief sculpture. There were fragments of round, drum-like reliefs and flat, rectangular-shaped ones.[38] The round reliefs must have been from carved column drums, while the flat reliefs are of two kinds. There are those carved with figures that are less than life size, which formed a decorative sima or parapet masking the stone guttering around the bottom edge of the roof. Then there are the reliefs with life size figures, which may have belonged to a decorative frame for the doorway. A second possibility is that these last may have been part of a frieze running along the bottom of the cella wall (an orthostate frieze) or, third, they may have belonged to carved cubic pedestals forming the supports of columns, such as those that, as we shall see, were certainly used in the later temple.[39]

Carved column drums there certainly were and these were a striking feature of both the early and later temples. Not all the columns were carved and Pliny's figure of thirty-six columnae caelatae may have applied equally to both temples. It is unlikely that any column had more than one carved drum. The total number of columns, carved or not, is disputed and few scholars accept the figure of 127 for the archaic temple.[40] The Austrian architect Anton Bammer, for example, chooses the option of placing two rows of eight columns along the front with nine at the rear and arrives at a total of 106 (fig. 37a).[41] The German scholar Axel Rügler arrives at 109: like Bammer, he has a double row of eight along the front and nine at the back, but his arrangement of columns in the rear porch is different from Bammer's, and he also believes that after 395 BC a further eight columns were added to the front to make three rows there and a total of 117.[42]

Disputed too is the deployment of the relatively few carved members among the many columns. It is not known whether the carved columns appeared at both the front and rear of the temple, or at the front only; there is also the question of how high up the column the carved drum was placed.[43] It has been suggested for the later Artemision (see fig. 46) that the carved drums were placed at the neck of the column (hypotrachelion),[44] and a case has been made also for the relief drums of the archaic Artemision being displayed at the top of the columns.[45] Such carved elements are known from buildings elsewhere in the Greek world, following the lead of the temple of Hera on Samos. A decorative necking of lotus flowers, for example, ran around the top of the columns of the sixth-century temple of Apollo at Naukratis in the Egyptian Nile delta.[46] The Hellenistic temple of Apollo Smintheus at Chryse in the Troad in northwest Asia Minor had drums carved with figured reliefs under the capitals.[47]

According to Herodotos, Kroisos funded most of the columns[48] and this would seem to suggest that they were set up, but not all carved, in his

38 and 39 Fragments from sculptured columns of the archaic Artemision: the lower part of a male figure draped in a cloak; the head and torso of a beardless male figure with long flowing hair and draped in a panther skin. British Museum.

40 and 41 Fragments of female heads from sculptured columns of the archaic Artemision. British Museum.

lifetime. The earliest sculpture, judging by style, has been dated to around 560 BC, but some of the column reliefs appear more advanced. A date of around 525 BC has been suggested for some column reliefs on the basis of a comparison with the frieze of the Siphnian Treasury building, which once stood in the sanctuary of Apollo at Delphi.[49] This stylistic discrepancy in the sculpture shows that the temple took many years to complete, as indeed we might expect with so great a project.

The subject of the column reliefs (figs 38–41) appears to have been a procession, and among the fragments that survive we glimpse tantalizing snatches of figures standing or walking, some with arms bent as if to hold an offering.[50] Occasionally, the offering itself occurs, as in a ritual vessel decorated with bull heads. As well as human figures, cattle and horses are seen. Their appearance on the columns could never have been as a continuous frieze, but together the carved columns presented the elements of a procession, perhaps reflecting the real-life events that carried the Ephesians dressed in their festival-best to and from the temple. Alternatively, George Hanfmann speculates: 'It may well be that the thirty-six sculptured drums of the Croesan Artemision presented a processional vision of the court of King Croesus which was as much a projection of his ideology as the frieze of the Parthenon is of the Periclean democracy.'[51] The comparison with the Parthenon frieze is strikingly apposite, and while some have sought the inspiration for that great work in the processional friezes of the Apadana at Persian Persepolis,[52] it is worth remembering that in the archaic Artemision the Athenians had a more accessible, Hellenic source.

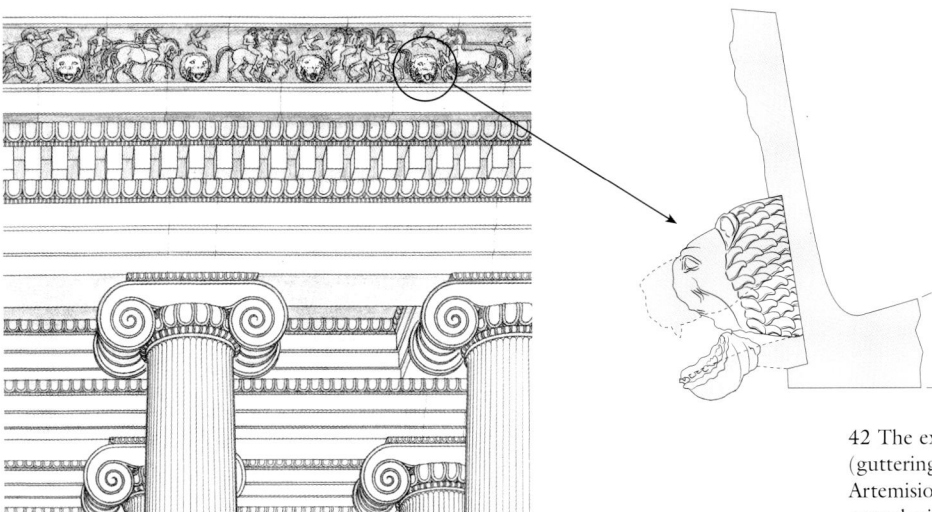

THE ARCHAIC DECORATED SIMA

The greater number of fragments of surviving sculpture from the archaic temple come from the sima or parapet that concealed the stone rain-guttering along the edge of the roof (fig. 42).[53] Such simas, pierced with spouts in the form of open-mouthed lion heads, were usually decorated with floral ornament. Those of the Artemision were especially elaborate and perhaps took their inspiration from the terracotta sima of the palace of Kroisos at Sardis, which was decorated with figures of Pegasos.[54] Again there are doubts as to how exactly the sculpture was arranged. Temples of the scale of the Artemision are often thought to have had roofs that were partially open to the sky. It is supposed that the exterior parts – the walks around the columns, the porch and doorway – were covered, but the space within was only partially so, creating an interior courtyard. In such an arrangement, the roof might slope both out, towards the columns, and in, towards the courtyard (fig. 43). Thus rainwater running both ways necessitated two sets of guttering, one outer and the other inner, and two simas. Two scales represented among the fragments of sculptured sima would seem to suggest such a double arrangement of guttering, the larger scale of sculpture assigned to the outer and the lesser to the inner sima.[55]

As in the column reliefs, the parapet fragments present no coherent design. Various subject

42 The external sima (guttering) of the archaic Artemision was elaborately carved with sculpture in relief and with spouts in the form of lion heads with open mouths, which allowed rainwater to drain away.

43 Schematic diagram of a suggested roof arrangement of the archaic Artemision showing the location of the exterior and interior sima.

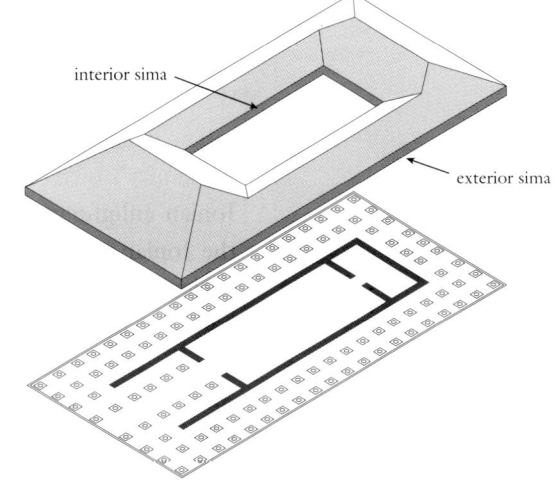

60 Greek Architecture and Its Sculpture

44 and 45 Sculptured sima fragments from the archaic Artemision: the head and neck of a horse with the torso and arm of a youth holding the reins; part of the head of a female wearing a conical cap with a protruding pony tail. British Museum.

categories, however, can be identified. They include processional chariots and horses (fig. 44), armed men in battle, a fight between human males and Centaurs, men and women in procession, Amazons, mythical beasts, a seated assembly and animals such as lion and ox. The date of the sima reliefs is later than that of the columns. On a comparison with the oldest reliefs in the Siphnian Treasury frieze in the museum at Delphi, the sima reliefs may be judged to begin around 530–525 and appear to continue down to around 470 BC.[56]

THE LATER TEMPLE AND ITS SCULPTURE

Following his defeat of a Persian army at the Battle of Granikos in 334 BC, Alexander the Great travelled south through the Greek coastal cities offering them their freedom and inviting them to expel their Persian garrisons. When he reached Ephesos, the great temple was in the process of being rebuilt, following the fire that was said to have destroyed it on the night of Alexander's own birth in 356 BC. The old temple was a rare survival of the Ionian enlightenment that had been suppressed by Persia's crushing of the Ionian revolt in 494 BC. It must have been famous throughout the ancient world and will have been a vital symbol of the cultural unity of the Ionian Greek cities. The archaic temple had been financed by King Kroisos of Lydia, a now legendary enemy of the Persians, and various sources say that the reconstruction was funded by several cities,[57] for whom the Artemision had acted as a bank.[58] Always mindful of his own legend, Alexander offered himself to pay for the completion of the new temple.[59] The Ephesians no doubt feared that their 'liberation' would be short-lived, and that the Persians would return and destroy so blatant a record of a pact with the Macedonian upstart. Once before, when Alexander's father Philip II had sent his general Parmenio to free the coastal cities of western Anatolia, an image of Philip had been set up in the temple of Ephesian Artemis, only to be toppled when the Persian faction in the city regained control. This time the Ephesians came up with a diplomatic refusal: it would, they suggested, be improper for one god to make a dedication to another.

Such was the power of attachment to the old temple that many of its features, albeit modernized, were incorporated in the design of the new building. Its plan was repeated in the new temple with column resting on column and wall on wall. The columns were, however, higher and thicker; their bases were enlarged, and their arrangement at the front and back of the temple may not have been quite the same. The stylobate or floor was enlarged and raised on a stepped platform 5 metres high, which must be that mentioned by Philo of Byzantium as having ten steps. This was designed to augment the grandeur of the building and to lift it further above the marshy ground, which even then threatened to submerge it. Stumps of columns left over from the old temple were thus incorporated into the foundations of the new structure.

THE LATER COLUMNS

As remarked earlier, Pliny mentions 127 columns, a figure which is usually assumed to apply to the larger, later temple. Even here, however, so great a number is hard to accommodate and it may be a mistaken report for 117.[60] As in the older, so in the younger temple, the front porch columns lined an avenue leading up to the door. The location in the ground plan of Pliny's thirty-six columnae caelatae is as problematic in the later temple as it is in the earlier. It could be argued that carved drums were placed at both front and back, but equally it is possible to assign all thirty-six to the front columns only.[61]

As with the earlier, so with the later temple the placement of the carved drums in the elevation of the column is disputed (fig. 46). Besides carved drums in the later temple, we also find carved pedestals.[62] These pedestals were each made up of four separate corner quadrants clamped together (fig. 47). The question arises as to whether these were placed at the foot of plain fluted columns or whether they were in some way combined with the carved drums.[63] When placed side by side the relief drums and carved pedestals are both exactly 184 centimetres high.[64] It has been

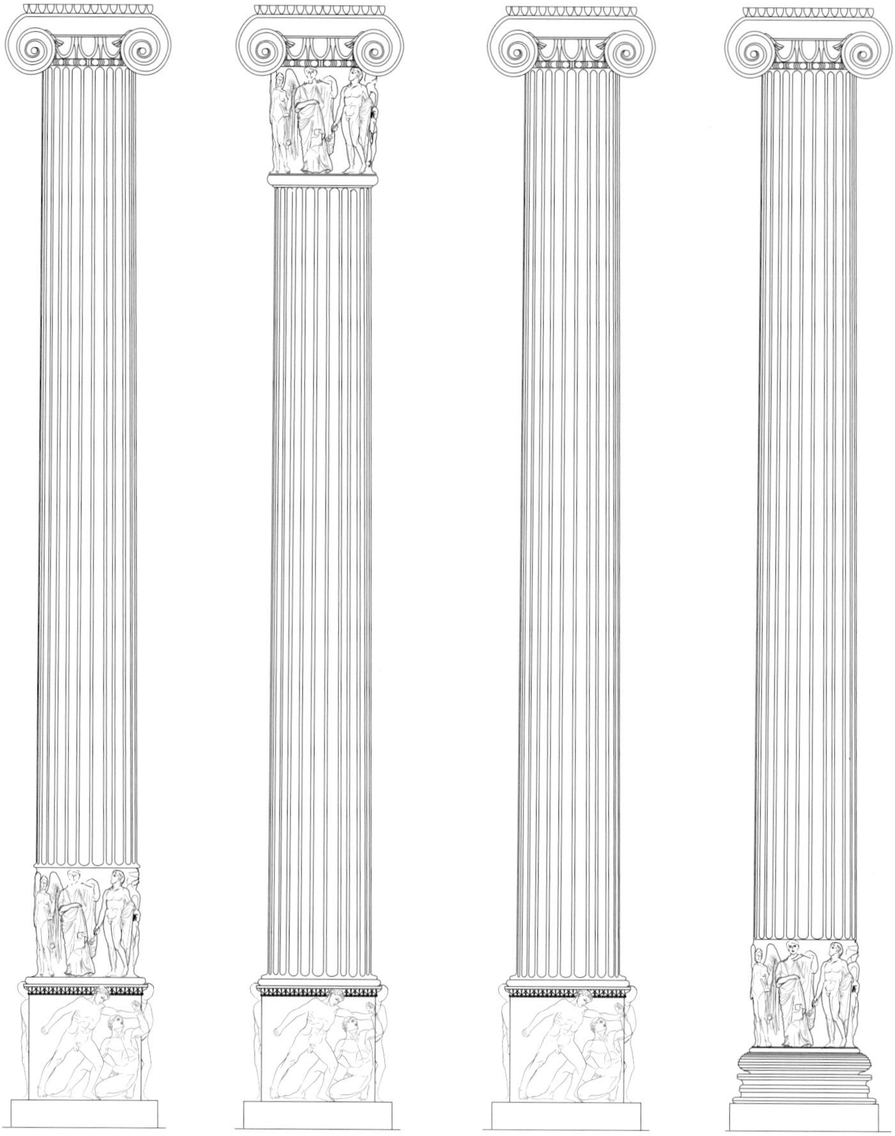

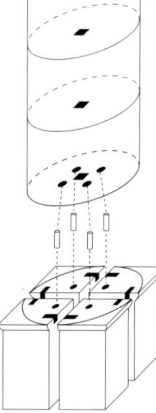

46 ABOVE Four options for locating the carved column drums and pedestals of the later Artemision. After B. Wesenberg and A. Rügler.

47 LEFT Diagram to show the fixing of the carved drums to the quadrants of the squared pedestals. After A. Rügler.

48 Carved drum of the later Artemision mounted on a reconstructed pedestal in the British Museum's former Ephesos Room (now dismantled), *c.* 1920.

49 West front of the later temple of Artemis at Ephesos showing the 'forest' of columns with carved drums mounted on squared pedestals. Drawing F. Krischen adapted by K. Morton.

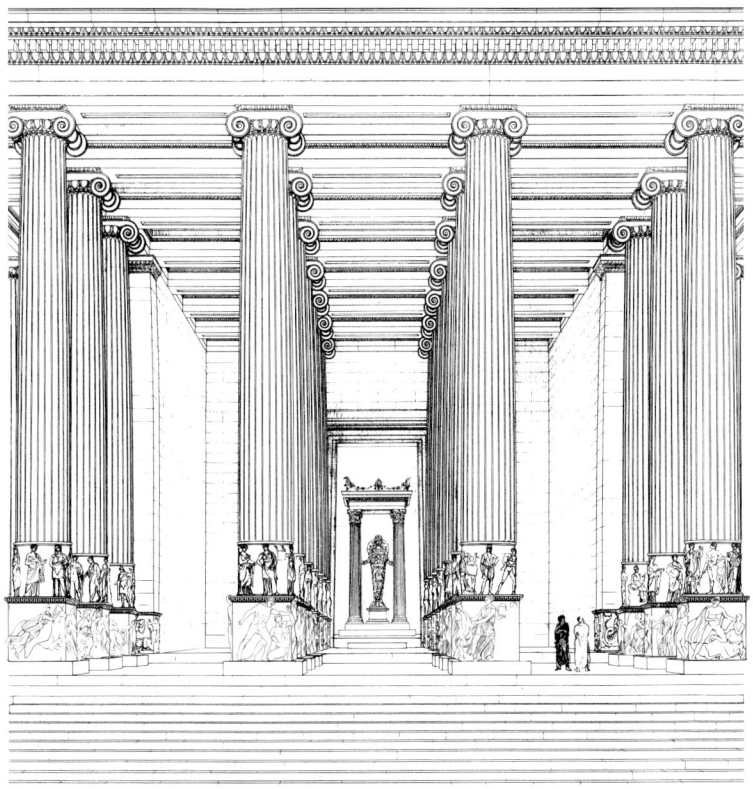

suggested, therefore, that the drums stood at the foot of some columns, the pedestals at the foot of others. It may, however, be objected that although the two are the same height, their respective relief fields are not consistent and the heads of the figures on the pedestals are higher than those on the drums. The top beds of the cubic pedestals, moreover, were drilled four times, one in each corner of each quadrant, with a circular dowel hole, while the bottom beds of the carved drums were also cut with four holes corresponding to those in the pedestals (figs 48–9).[65] These holes must be for fixing carved drum to carved pedestal and would seem to provide proof of the one having stood upon the other.

50 Cistophor of the emperor Augustus showing the Artemision. British Museum.

A possible source of pictorial reference, which could have helped resolve this issue, is coins (fig. 50). Even those who prefer one theory over another, however, must admit that the coin evidence can afford no clear conclusion. Roman imperial coins often show on their reverse an artwork or building for which the city in which the coin was struck was famous. The coins of Ephesos, therefore, sometimes feature the west front of the Artemision. A special study of the coins concluded that they did not support the theory that the carved drums were placed under the capitals.[66] Evidence was found only for the carved drums being featured at the foot of the columns and it was concluded that the cubic pedestals must have been employed elsewhere than on the front of the temple. It has, however, been argued that coins of the emperor Hadrian show relief elements at both the lower and upper parts of the columns, and this would seem to support the theory that the carved drums were in fact column neckings.[67] Finally, the coin evidence allows for a third possibility: a Hadrianic silver cistophor and a bronze coin of Antoninus Pius appear to show that the cubic pedestals supported the columns on the front, and that the carved drums sat immediately on them.[68] In such contradictory circumstances, the coin evidence is best left to one side.

THE SUBJECTS OF THE SCULPTURE

Let us assume that there were thirty-six carved column drums and thirty-six cubic pedestals, each with four sides. Let us also imagine the carvings of the circular drums rolled out straight, and those of the four-sided pedestals, as it were, folded out. Then, placed end to end, the figured carvings of the later Artemision, it has been calculated, would stretch for half a kilometre. The colossal undertaking of manufacturing them may be compared with the by no means insubstantial Parthenon frieze, which was only half as high and some 160 metres long. While the latter, moreover, as a continuous ribbon of stone arguably represented a single, unified

The Temples of Artemis at Ephesos

51 and 52 Two sides of a fragmentary pedestal quadrant showing the hero Herakles and a female figure tugging him. British Museum.

53 Reconstruction of figs 51 and 52. After W.R. Lethaby.

narrative, the pedestals and drums of the Artemision could have shown up to 180 individual 'pictures', counting thirty-six drums together with the four separate sides of thirty-six pedestals.

This number of 180 separate images need not imply that there were the same number of subjects, and some carvings are likely to have worked together to illustrate episodes of a smaller number of themes. So, for example, a single pedestal may have represented four of the labours of Herakles, and three columns together could have accommodated all twelve labours. Indeed, Herakles was one of the mythical heroes featured in the pedestal scenes (figs 51–3), and in other pedestal fragments it is suggested that we find the exploits of the hero Theseus.[69] Unfortunately, the few fragments that survive do not permit a clear judgement. The most substantial piece is the greater part of one quadrant of one pedestal. On one side we find Herakles, unmistakably draped in his lion skin, apparently attempting to escape the clutches of a predatory female shown round the corner on the other side.[70] It is difficult, however, to parallel this composition within the range of known formulae for representing the deeds of Herakles. On another quadrant a fight is shown between a muscular male figure standing over a nude male crouching on the ground (see fig. 46).[71] Neither figure has an attribute to identify him. Nor does this subject recognizably relate to a female with a hind shown on another side of the same quadrant, which may indicate the goddess Artemis. The solution to both problems is perhaps to see here a battle between the Olympian gods and the giants, by which the Olympians established their new order in the universe. In such a gigantomachy, familiar figures such as Artemis and Herakles can appear along with unidentifiable giants. On other pedestal fragments are shown: a Centaur crouching, while a human male stands over him; sea-nymphs riding sea-monsters; Victories, one leading an ox and another a sheep.

Of the carved drums only one survives in anything approaching a good state of preservation, and this great treasure serves sadly to remind us of what we have lost (figs 54–6).[72] Even here, where most of the figures of the subject are present, there is scope for differing interpretations. The likeliest is that first suggested by Carl Robert, who saw the myth of Alcestis, best known from its dramatization in a play by the fifth-century Athenian tragedian Euripides.[73] According to the story, Alcestis offered to die in place of her husband, but was rescued by Herakles. She is perhaps here shown on the point of departure. The winged youth looking over his shoulder and naked, but for a sword on a strap across his chest, may be identified as Thanatos (Death) leading Alcestis, who follows arranging the elaborate folds of her mantle. To her proper left is Hermes, the only figure to be identified for certain. In his right hand he holds his herald's wand or

The Temples of Artemis at Ephesos 67

54 and 55 Thanatos (Death) and Hermes, leader of souls, accompany Alcestis in the underworld on a sculptured column drum from the later Artemision. British Museum.

56 The scene on the sculptured column drum shown in figs 54 and 55.

caduceus. Hermes here seems to serve in his capacity of psychopompos, or leader of souls to the underworld. To his proper left is another female figure whose dress and demeanour and the wedding wreath she holds suggest Persephone. She was the daughter of the fertility goddess Demeter whose death was her marriage to Hades, god of the underworld. Like Alcestis, Persephone was destined to return from the dead but only for a limited period each year. Her advent coincided with the return of spring to the world of mortals and her departure with the onset of winter. Hades is probably to be identified with the damaged figure seated by her. The sculpture is remarkable for its vivid handling of the shallow relief and for the breathing vitality and pathos of the figures. It is remarkable too for the seemingly self-conscious variety of styles exhibited in the individual figures. Thus Thanatos has soft, rounded forms, suggestive of the works of the fourth-century sculptor Praxiteles, while Hermes has the proportions and marked musculature of a study by Polykleitos, who flourished some two generations earlier. It is almost as if a sculptor were making a deliberate play of his academic knowledge of the styles of great masters.[74]

Other tantalizingly fragmentary drums appear to show: unidentified standing and seated women, perhaps goddesses;[75] men in Persian dress walking in procession;[76] and a youth with a bearded man who appears to be pulling on a rope or branch. While these fragments and others are not sufficient to reconstruct an iconographic programme, they do allow comparison between the handling of the relief in the carved drums and that of the pedestals. In the latter, the figures stand out in high relief, while that of the drums is more shallow. In the pedestals figures are usually moving rapidly, while those of the drums are still or moving slowly. In the drums there is less tendency to overlap figures and create an illusion of depth than in the pedestals. Several figures encircle a drum, while the pedestals usually show only two figures per side, as in a metope.[77]

As with the older Artemision, so with the younger temple, the duration of the building process can only be guessed at from the earliest and latest style of sculpture. There is nothing exact in this method, especially when we consider that both pedestals and drums are likely to have been set as rough-faced blocks, which were then given their carved finish *in situ*, perhaps some time after construction was completed. The Alcestis drum is usually dated as early as 340 BC, but its academic eclecticism might warrant a date of a generation later. On the basis of a comparison with other datable fourth-century works, the carving of the Ephesos reliefs, or at least those that survive, was completed by around 300 BC. Since carving sculpture may be regarded as one of the finishing processes of making a temple, it is tempting to argue that the building work is likely to have been completed at some time previous to that date. Fifty years,

57 Lion-headed water spout from the later Artemision. British Museum.

however, seems a very short time for so large an undertaking, and we must keep an open mind as to the possibility that construction itself continued into the Hellenistic period.

The later temple of Artemis at Ephesos was as remarkable for its architectural detail as it was for its sculpture. Although not as elaborate as that of the earlier Artemision it boasted a fine gable sima, carved with a creeping acanthus. This motif later became popular in East Greece and was used, for example, on the temple of Athena Polias at Priene. Although it was already found in mainland Greece, its appearance on the late-classical Artemision was a first in East Greece. Impressive were the lion heads that also decorated the sima along the roof line of the long sides of the temple (fig. 57). They are very close in form and style to those of the Mausoleum at Halikarnassos, which building slightly predates the Artemision. Also similar to that used on the Mausoleum is the carved moulding which ornaments the top edge of the sculptured pedestals. Such correspondence between near contemporary buildings should not be surprising. It is evidence of specialist carvers moving from one centre of employment to another and of the common language of architectural ornament that they and their patrons developed for expressing shared cultural values.

CONCLUSION

The earlier and later Artemisia may be seen as icons, respectively, of the Ionian enlightenment and its eventual renaissance. The rebirth of the Artemision, grander and more splendid than before, is emblematic of a general revival in monumental building projects in East Greece in the middle of the fourth century BC. Sometimes referred to as the Ionian renaissance, it featured among other buildings the Mausoleum at Halikarnassos, the temple of Zeus at Labraynda and the temple of Athena Polias at Priene, in all of which buildings the Ephesian version of the Ionic order was used. The interlude between construction of the archaic temple in the sixth century BC and the later temple of the fourth century saw great changes in the political and economic fortunes of East Greece. The collapse of the Ionian revolt and the destruction of Miletos by the Persians had brought the Ionian enlightenment to an end and tipped the region into an architectural depression. Meanwhile, on the other side of the Aegean, Athens, mother of Miletos and other cities of Ionia and now leader of the free Greek states in their defence against Persia, was well placed to take over the Ionian tradition in architecture. As we shall see in the next two chapters, she did so in spectacular fashion.

Chapter Four

The Parthenon and Its Sculptures

PERIKLES AND HIS BUILDING PROGRAMME

Around 450 BC the Athenians embarked upon the architectural renewal of their city with works that ostensibly were the creation of the people but which arguably were the products of the vision of Perikles, the leading statesman of the day (fig. 58). 'In theory' wrote the historian Thucydides, 'there was democracy, but in fact political power was exercised by one man.'[1] Athens was then the pre-eminent city of the Greek world. At the beginning of the fifth century, its new democracy had valiantly played its part in the struggle against two Persian invasions and gained the respect and admiration of all the Greeks. In succeeding decades, Athens capitalized on this success and soon overtook its arch-rival Sparta to assume leadership of a naval defence league of Greek states designed to keep the Persians at bay. As Athenian confidence and ambition grew, so the nature of the relationship changed. Voluntary contribution of funds by its allies for the maintenance of a naval home guard developed into the enforced payment of protection money for the exchequer of what was in all but name an Athenian empire. At first the central bank of the confederates had been kept on the sacred Aegean island of Delos, but in 454, it was transferred to the Athenian Acropolis, and soon after the first work was carried out on the Acropolis.

58 The portrait of Perikles represents a model soldier-citizen, one who was 'kalos kai agathos', fair of face and sound of heart. Second-century AD marble copy of a lost original in bronze. British Museum.

Although a sanctuary, the Acropolis was also a castle. In the Bronze Age, a thousand years before the Parthenon was built, it had been the fortified palace of the Mycenaean rulers of Athens, and in places the characteristic, so-called Cyclopean masonry of the Mycenaean defence walls survives to this day. In the Classical age the Acropolis fortifications proved ineffectual against the Persian army of invasion, and the temples and other monuments were destroyed in 480 BC. It was said that following the battle of Plataea in 479 BC, at which the Persians were finally routed from mainland Greece, the Greek cities which had suffered at Persian hands made a pact never to rebuild their temples, but to let the ruins stand as a memorial of barbarian sacrilege. Already in the fourth century BC, the Oath of Plataea, as it came to be called, was being dismissed as a patriotic invention of the Athenians, and we cannot now say whether or not it was sworn.[2] Opinion recently has swung in its favour, and it would help to explain how a rich and powerful city like Athens came not to rebuild its temples until long after their destruction. The rescinding of that oath through the inauguration of a peace treaty with the Persians,[3] perhaps the so-called Peace of Kallias, would also account for the change of Athenian heart around 450 BC, when a new phase of public building activity began on the Acropolis and elsewhere in and around the city.

The person who had directed events that led to the new peace was Kimon, the Athenian general and statesman who was the son of the Persian War hero Miltiades. Kimon had taken the war with Persia into enemy territory. Harrying the Persians in the eastern Aegean, he scored a great victory in the autumn of 468 BC in two battles fought on the same day on land and at the mouth of the River Eurymedon in Pamphylia, east of Lycia on Turkey's southern shore. With the proceeds of the sale of booty from around two hundred enemy ships, Kimon funded civic works in Athens, including reinforcement of the south wall of the Acropolis, the planting of plane trees in the marketplace and the transformation of the open-air gymnasium, known as the Academy, from arid dust bowl to well-watered grove.[4] Seeing what popularity could be gained from the provision of such civic amenities probably inspired Perikles to deliver an even greater prize, the renewal of the Acropolis at the very heart of the city.

We know of both men through the collected biographies of Plutarch. Writing around AD 100 and at the height of the Roman empire, his was an age of burgeoning philhellenism. Plutarch's are not critical biographies, but rather they are records of an anecdotal tradition of stories gathered from various sources, generated at various times. Veracity, therefore, may not be their greatest virtue and, to some extent, they are best seen as monuments of the impression left on contemporary Rome of great figures of the past.[5] Perikles emerges from Plutarch's account as the very model of a soldier-citizen, brave and steely on the inside, and yet always courteous and moderate in his outward demeanour. Perikles' character is encapsulated in the surviving marble portraits of him. These are Roman copies of a lost Greek bronze original, the copies dating to around the time of Plutarch's writing.[6] The helmet betokens Perikles' office as strategos (general), which was a civic as well as a military post. Here it is pushed to the back of the head to reveal the idealized face of a man who is *kalos kai agathos*, fair and good. It is not asked of this image of a leader that he be an individual, nor that he exhibit any peculiarities of personality. The image simply presents a type, an abstract embodiment of community values, easy on the eye and reassuring of the mind.[7]

Perikles himself is said to have cultivated this public persona:

> He not only had a spirit that was solemn and a discourse that was lofty and free from plebeian and reckless effrontery, but also a composure of countenance that never relaxed into laughter, a gentleness of carriage and cast of attire that suffered no emotion to disturb it while he was speaking.[8]

He never accepted invitations to dinner. It was not that he did not enjoy good food or company, but he feared compromising his own studied self-image, not to hold forth and lose control of his celebrated reserve. Only once while head of state did he go out to dine at the wedding feast of a relative, but, as soon as the wine was brought in, he made his excuses and left.[9]

Plutarch's portrait, like the marble head, shows us only one side of the man. It stands as a record not of what Perikles was actually like but of what people came to believe he was like. The same *megalophrosyne* or high-mindedness is found in the impression we gain of him from Thucydides, an Athenian author of Perikles' own era. His great *History of the Peloponnesian War* chronicles the hostilities between Sparta and Athens that would lead in 404 BC to the collapse of Athens' empire, and to enemy occupation of the city. Thucydides portrays Perikles in his prime in 431 BC addressing the people at the grave of the war-dead, who had fallen in the first year's fighting. Perikles does not deliver a lament, but praises the dead by praising their city. He lists numerous points of comparison in which the Athenian is superior to the inhabitants of other Greek states: 'We throw our city open to all the world and we never debar anyone from learning or seeing anything which an enemy might profit by observing. We place our trust not in deception but in our courage.'[10] Thus Perikles puts the case in favour of the open society over the totalitarian system of Sparta. He goes on, 'We are lovers of beauty yet without extravagance; and lovers of wisdom without weakness' – Sparta's refusal to cultivate the arts was notorious throughout the Greek world. 'In a word then', Perikles concludes, 'I say that our City is the School of Hellas.'

Thucydides' text by no means represents a transcript of an actual speech. Indeed, the historian himself says as much. The fact that it cannot

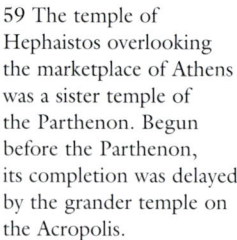

59 The temple of Hephaistos overlooking the marketplace of Athens was a sister temple of the Parthenon. Begun before the Parthenon, its completion was delayed by the grander temple on the Acropolis.

be taken literally, however, does not detract from its documentary value for revealing how Thucydides saw Perikles and the city over which he presided. Nowhere is the self-image of the city expressed more eloquently than in the great programme of new building works initiated *c.* 450 BC for the purpose of beautifying Athens at the height of its fame, wealth and power. The wave of new building was centred upon the Acropolis, but also featured other shrines, both within and outside the walls of the city.[11] Collectively, these buildings can be seen as an ornament of the city's prestige and also as a commemoration of its valour during the Persian Wars. Thus, a temple of Poseidon at Sunium was dedicated to the god of the sea, in whose waters Athenian ships had gambled and won against the Persian fleet at the Battle of Salamis in 480 BC. The temple of Nemesis, personification of divine retribution, was erected at Rhamnous a short distance away from the plain of Marathon, where in 490 BC the Athenians almost alone had defeated the Persians. A temple of Hephaistos, god of smiths and other crafts, was built on the edge of the marketplace to boast of the city's powers in the arts (fig. 59). These four temples, built in the Doric order, have many features in common and have all been attributed to a single unknown architect, working around 450–430 BC.[12]

Plutarch presents Perikles and his impresario Pheidias as heroes in a drama guaranteed to appeal to modern sentiment, in which artistic vision is realized in the face of small-minded opposition from politicians.[13] Plutarch relates the story of how Pheidias is said to have worked portraits of himself and his patron into the figured scenes on the shield of the great statue of Athena Parthenos, which he constructed to go inside the Parthenon (fig. 60).[14] In Roman copies of the shield we do in fact see two figures, whom some have identified as Perikles and Pheidias fighting back to back, defending the Acropolis from an invasion of Amazons.[15]

The fiercest critic of the project was another Thucydides, who always

60 The 'Strangford Shield', a smaller and simplified Roman copy of the shield held by Pheidias' Athena Parthenos. The two figures fighting back-to-back below the central mask of Gorgon are sometimes identified as portraits of Pheidias and Perikles. British Museum.

carries the patronym 'son of Milesias' to distinguish him from the historian of that name. When Kimon died on Cyprus, Thucydides took over the leadership of Athens' democratic conservatives. He competed through the 440s with Perikles for control of the assembly until he was voted into political exile (ostracism) in 443 BC. His line of attack, according to Plutarch, was a bid for the high ground of a moral parsimony:

> And Greece seems to be the victim of monstrous and manifest tyranny, when she sees us using what she is forced to contribute for the war to gild and deck out our city like a wanton woman, decorating her with costly stones and statues, and thousand-talent temples.[16]

Perikles is reported artfully to have replied to this criticism that if the people found the burden too heavy on the public exchequer, then he would himself pay the cost from his own purse and inscribe his own name on the buildings. Such patronage had been the *noblesse oblige* of tyrants, and Perikles will have known that his 'undemocratic' offer would have been unacceptable to the electorate. Unable, however, to afford by any other means the grand buildings they desired, the Athenians were themselves obliged to pilfer the treasury of the Delian League.

61 The west front of the Parthenon compared at the same scale with the south front of the British Museum.

62 OPPOSITE TOP The ever-changing Parthenon viewed from the north-west. The ruin seen here represents the product of nearly 2,500 years of construction, demolition, adaptation and restoration, which is continuing.

63 OPPOSITE BOTTOM The Parthenon in 1804 painted by Lancelot Theodore Turpin de Crissé (1782–1859). The artist has filled the west pediment with more sculpture than was there at this date. A small mosque occupies the floor of the ruined temple.

THE TEMPLE

The centrepiece of the Acropolis renewal was the Parthenon (figs 62–3).[17] Made entirely of fine white marble quarried from Mount Pentelikon, some 16 kilometres outside the city, the building rose between 447 and 438 BC. The quarry works and preparations of the site are likely to have begun perhaps as early as 450/449 BC.[18] It was erected on the site of a previous temple, which was under construction on the south side of the Parthenon when the Persians destroyed the Acropolis in 480 BC. The pre-Parthenon was intended to commemorate Athens' victory at the Battle of Marathon in 490 BC over a Persian army of invasion, and it is natural therefore to see the Parthenon itself in a similar commemorative role. The later temple was to be both wider and longer than its predecessor. Unusual for a temple built in the Doric order, it had eight columns on the short sides and seventeen on the long, counting the corner columns twice. The plan (fig. 64) shows a principal chamber for the temple statue, entered from the east, and a smaller rear chamber, which served as a treasury, entered from the west.

Including the floral ornament crowning the centre of the pediment, the Parthenon measured 24 metres high. This was to be the largest and richest temple on the Greek mainland, outdoing even the great temple of Olympian Zeus at the panhellenic sanctuary of Olympia, and challenging if not actually rivalling in size the great archaic temples of Asia Minor, notably the greater by far archaic Artemision at Ephesos. The increase in

The Parthenon and Its Sculptures 77

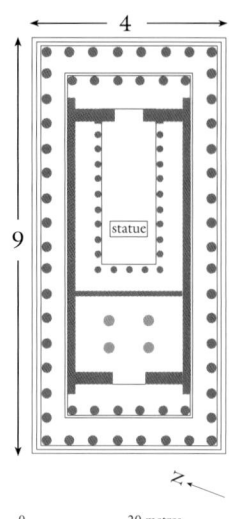
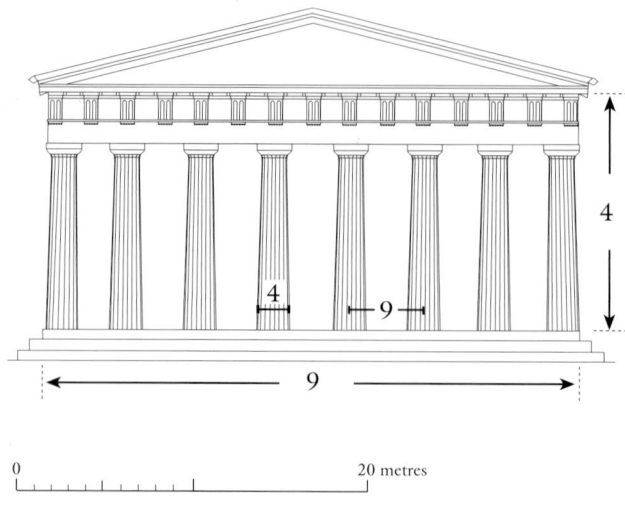

64 Plan and elevation of the Parthenon indicating the 9:4 ratio of its design.

width was determined specifically by the function of the Parthenon as a space in which to display the statue of Athena Parthenos. The platform of the temple (stylobate) measures some 69.51 by 30.86 metres, about 5 metres longer and 3 metres wider than Olympia's Zeus temple. These dimensions represent a proportion of 9 to 4, which governs other metrical relationships. There is, for example, the diameter of the underside of the lowest column drum in relationship to the distance between the central axis of one column and the next. Another instance is the width of the stylobate in relation to the height of the building from the floor to the cornice forming the base of the pediment.[19]

As remarked in Chapter Two, these features are sometimes pointed to as evidence of the Parthenon's supposed geometrical perfection, which was set out, so the argument goes, in the architects' lost blueprint. Already in the nineteenth century, however, Francis Penrose was the first to publish accurate measurements that revealed a number of discrepancies and apparent changes of plan in the construction.[20] From these it could be argued that the builders of the Parthenon worked without a master plan, but constructed it according to an empirical tradition of building practice, applying a more than usually high degree of craftsmanship. Even the famous frieze, it now emerges, was the product of a change of plan and an afterthought.[21] Although not the perfect building it is sometimes said to be, it has none the less been called the most remarkable in the world by one who was fully aware of its imperfections.[22] Among many remarkable features are its construction refinements, which occur in other temples but not to the same degree.[23] These include deliberate avoidance of true horizontal and vertical lines, such as by curving the stylobate upwards towards the centre, in both its length and its width. The upward lift of the stylobate (fig. 65) was built into the foundations of the previous temple ruined by the Persians, raising the centre of the length of the stylobate by some 11 centimetres and that of the short sides by some 6 centimetres. Naturally this helped to shed rain water from the floor of the temple but also, when carried into the upper reaches of the building, countered the tendency for long horizontal lines to appear to sag. The columns taper in a curve, more above and less below. This refinement is called entasis (tension). Corner columns, moreover, are thickened, so as not to seem thinner when seen against the sky. Like the walls, the columns lean inwards, and it has been calculated that if the columns of the long sides were extended they would meet at a height of some 2 kilometres above the temple floor, while those of the façade would meet at nearly 5 kilometres. Such refinements were highly labour-intensive. They determined that virtually no two blocks were the same and that each element had to be cut on site, its form dictated by that of the previous member. When we consider this and the fact that the jointing of blocks is finer than a human hair, and so fine that in places horizontal joints of the stepped podium (crepidoma) have fused together,[24] it seems incredible that the Parthenon took only nine years to build and a further seven to finish.

The architects are said to have been Iktinos and Kallikrates. The former is also said to have designed the temple of Apollo at Bassai, which is explored in Chapter Six. Vitruvius says that, together with a certain Karpion, he wrote a book about the Parthenon.[25] What exactly the nature of the architects' co-operation was, or their relationship with Pheidias, we cannot say. Iktinos is sometimes credited with the subtleties of the design, Kallikrates with production and engineering and Pheidias with the sculpture, that is to say both the statue within and the external sculpture.[26] There is, however, reason to think

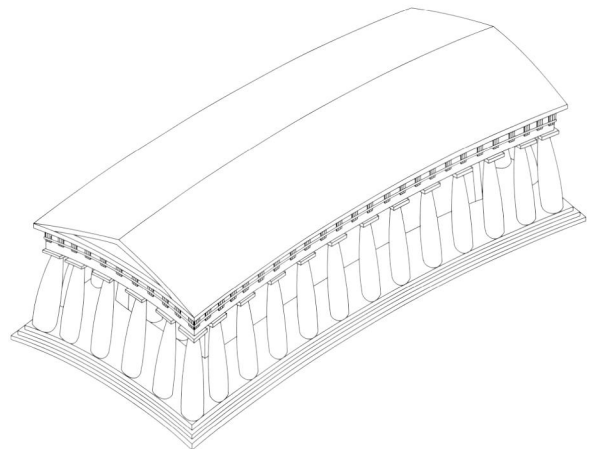

65 ABOVE The architectural refinements of a Doric temple greatly exaggerated.

66 BELOW Section of Zeus' temple at Olympia compared at the same scale with that of the Parthenon. While at Olympia Pheidias had to squeeze his colossal statue of Zeus into an existing space, with the Parthenon he was able to influence the design to accommodate better the Athena Parthenos statue (see also fig. 13).

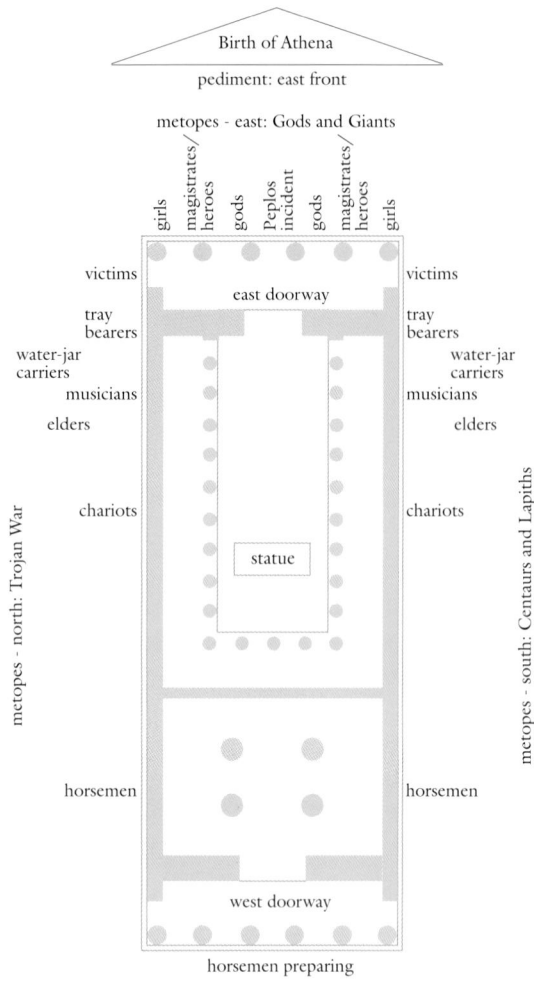

67 Plan of the Parthenon indicating the subjects of its sculpture.

that Pheidias substantially influenced the architects in creating a setting for his colossal Athena. A comparison of the Parthenon with the temple of Zeus at Olympia (fig. 66), for which he created a colossal statue of Zeus, only goes to show how different is the result when the sculptor had no opportunity to intervene in the architecture. The Zeus temple has a front of just six columns, and the outside width of the cella is about three-fifths of the overall width of the temple. Two rows of columns divide the interior of the temple into three. Pheidias squeezed his colossal Zeus somewhat awkwardly into the central corridor just 6.35 metres wide. The Parthenon, by contrast, has a front of eight columns allowing for a ratio of cella to temple width of five-sevenths and a central space framed by the interior columns that measured 9.82 metres, thus allowing the colossal Athena to appear fully accommodated.[27]

THE SCULPTURE

The Parthenon both contained and was decorated with some of the most beautiful sculpture the world has seen[28] and, in spite of centuries of vandalism and neglect, we are fortunate that so much of it survives (fig. 67).[29] Although certainly responsible for the statue that stood within, it is doubtful that Pheidias ever raised a chisel to any of the marble figures that decorated the outside of the temple, but he may have designed them. There is especially in the pediments and Ionic frieze much evidence of careful planning by one individual so as to obtain the best marriage of sculpture and architecture, and both pediments and frieze exhibit the genius of a single imagination in the manner in which each narrative unfolds as a series of episodes. One of the hallmarks of the Parthenon sculptures is the way they lead the eye from one to another, each figure or group of figures drawing energy from the previous and passing it on to the next. If this

68 Full-scale replica of the Athena Parthenos in gilded plaster by Alan LeQuire, 1982–2002. Nashville Parthenon, Tennessee.

is not Pheidias's handiwork, the design at least can certainly be attributed to one intelligence, perhaps to one of his pupils.

THE COLOSSUS OF ATHENA

The Parthenon was designed to hold the statue of Athena Parthenos that with its base stood nearly 12 metres high in the temple, framed on three sides by a two-tier set of interior Doric columns (fig. 68).[30] It was constructed of sheets of gold and ivory around a plastered wooden armature.[31] The statue itself was destroyed in antiquity, but we regain something of its appearance from miniature marble replicas of the Roman period. These and a brief description by Pausanias are the principal inspiration for several modern reconstructions, notably the full-scale plaster version by Alan LeQuire for the impressive full-scale replica of the Parthenon in Nashville, Tennessee, in the United States.[32] Visitors to Nashville can understand how the spectator of Pheidias' masterpiece must have been overpowered by the awesome presence of the goddess looming up in front of them. Although not strictly architectural sculpture, as we have seen, the design of the colossus of Athena was intimately connected to the design of the temple, and its great size accounted for the unusual width of the building. The statue was probably dedicated at the Great Panathenaic festival of 438 BC, by which date the roof must have been on the temple. Pheidias is thought to have quit Athens for Olympia soon after the Athena was completed and there to have made the comparable chryselephantine statue of Zeus.[33]

Athena was portrayed as a warrior resting after successful combat. A figure of winged victory alighted on the palm of her outstretched right hand, while her left hand supported a round shield. A spear rested against her left shoulder. The goddess was draped in the simplest form of tunic, the peplos, her shoulders and chest hung with the aegis, the snake-fringed, fish-scaled poncho that had been the gift of her father Zeus and had protective powers. Worked into the design of this garment was the mask of the gorgon Medusa. Athena's head was covered by an elaborate helmet, the cheek pieces hinged up on the sides. A sphinx supported the crest, and the forepart of a winged horse sprang up on either side. Herself a sculpture, Athena was also decorated with other sculptures, the mythological themes of which were echoed in some of the sculptures on the outside of the building. The exterior of the shield was carved with a battle between Athenians defending the Acropolis against Amazon attack, the subject being that of the western metopes. The interior was painted or inlaid with a battle between gods and giants, the theme of the eastern metopes. Around the edges of Athena's sandals were battles between Greeks and the part-man, part-horse Centaurs who appear again in the southern metopes. Athena stood on a high base, the position of which can still be determined on the floor of the Parthenon. It too was decorated, this time with the Olympian gods present at the birth of Pandora, the Eve of Greek myth. Athena and Hephaistos, the gods of craftsmanship, were shown on either side, dressing the doll-like Pandora.

THE METOPES

The temple itself was a vehicle for a rich assemblage of marble sculptures (fig. 69). Above the architrave, resting on the columns, ran the Doric frieze comprising on all four sides of the building a series of alternating metopes and triglyphs. The former were panels of sculpture measuring 1.2 metres high and between 1.22 and 1.33 metres wide. They numbered ninety-two in all, fourteen on the short sides and thirty-two on the long.[34] Metopes slotted into place behind the lip of the triglyphs, an architectural device said by Vitruvius to be a relic of a time when temples had been of wood, and the wooden beam ends had been a decorative feature.[35] The metopes were built into the roof-supporting entablature and had therefore to be in place when the roof was constructed. It is thought that this happened in time for the Great Panathenaic festival of 438 BC, at which it is likely that Pheidias' Athena Parthenos was dedicated. All of this provides a date by which the metopes would have been carved, and the pressure on the sculptors to complete the job in time may account for some of the unevenness in style and quality found in them, especially in the better preserved south metopes.[36]

Each side of the building relates to a different theme: on the west Amazons fighting Greeks, on the north scenes from the sack of Troy, on the east the Olympian gods fight for their supremacy in the universe over the old order of giants. On the south side the majority of metopes showed the Centaurs fighting Greeks. Apart from the Centauromachy of the south, the metopes of all other sides have been badly mutilated and are now virtually illegible. One only of the north side and from the western corner has survived, although even here the two figures have lost their heads. Two goddesses are shown in lively conversation, one seated and the other facing her standing. It is thought that this scene was spared destruction by Christian fanatics because it was taken to show the Virgin Mary and the Angel Gabriel in a New Testament scene of Annunciation.

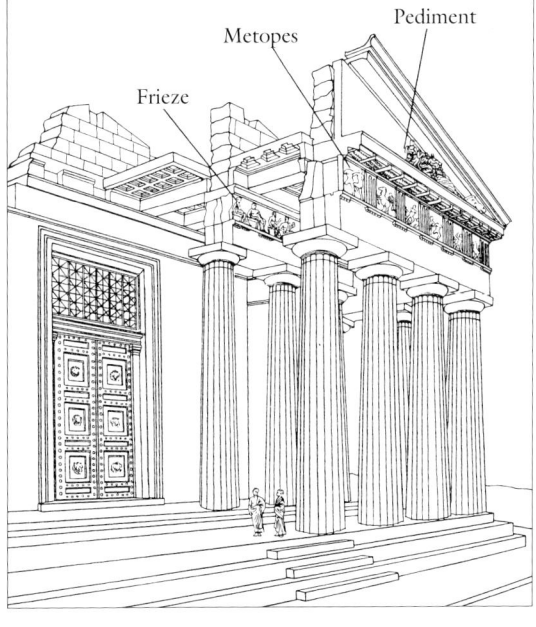

69 Cut-away to show the location of the Parthenon's three kinds of external sculpture.

All fifteen metopes in the British Museum come from the south side of the building and relate to the Centauromachy. The battle rages at the wedding between Hippodameia and Perithoos, king of the Lapiths, a mythical Greek people living in northern Greece. In myth, the outlying regions of civilization were often thought to be inhabited by fabulous beasts, and the Lapiths shared their homeland with Centaurs. They could be cultured and wise, like Cheiron who educated the hero Achilles, but, as their dual form implies, there was another side to their nature, and this was likely to come out when inflamed by wine. At the wedding feast,

70 A Lapith youth draws himself up to deliver a fatal blow as he prevents the escape of a wounded Centaur. South Metope 27. British Museum.

the Centaurs abused Lapith hospitality and tried to make off with the women. The men resisted and a battle broke out. One of the combatants, linking the theme to Athens, was probably Theseus, legendary king of the city, but he cannot now be identified for certain.

Each metope tells its own tale of rape or mortal combat. Two figures only are ever represented, usually Centaur and male Lapith, with the contest more convincingly rendered and, indeed, the carving better executed in some instances than in others. There is variety too in the manner of conceiving the Centaurs. In one, his face may be that of a mild old gentleman gleefully making off with his Lapith 'filly' (see title page), while in another it is a fierce mask of tragedy. In the battle scenes the contest is usually undecided, although the outcome may be guessed. In one especially successful composition a powerful Centaur presses a hidden right hand to a wound in his back and attempts to escape (fig. 70). The head is broken away, but we can see that it was pulled back by the outstretched left arm of the Lapith, who raises his other arm, the lost hand equipped with some weapon, which will soon descend to deliver a fatal blow. The sculptor poses the action at the moment just before the drama concludes. The pivotal point of the composition is located in the gulf between the two bodies, which is filled by the backdrop of the Lapith's cloak. Around

71 Life ebbs away from the body of a fallen Lapith, as the Centaur rears in triumph over him. South Metope 28. British Museum.

this central point the energy revolves in a circle made up of the arching bodies of the combatants, one pulling in one direction and the other in another. Such formal compositions are the product of a calculating and confident designer, successfully making best use of the square format of the marble block. The carving is done in very deep relief, so deep that the Lapith appears to hang off the picture, his limbs carved free and attached only by little bridges of marble left in during the carving. All too often, these proved insubstantial, and vulnerable parts have become detached and gone missing.

No less accomplished, but different in that it reveals the outcome of the drama, is the metope that on the building was placed immediately to the right (fig. 71). Here, exceptionally, we are informed of the fate of the Lapith. His youthful body has fallen and he lies supine along the ground line of the image. His head lolls to one side and he is not expected to rise again. Death and our mortal pity are all that remain for this young warrior felled before his time. In direct contrast and provoking very different feelings is the Centaur rearing in triumph. One arm brandishes the skin of a panther, trophy of a previous contest. The tail and paw of this flayed beast fly behind, decorating the open spaces of the picture, while the Centaur's own flame-like tail rises to meet them. The left arm of the Centaur is

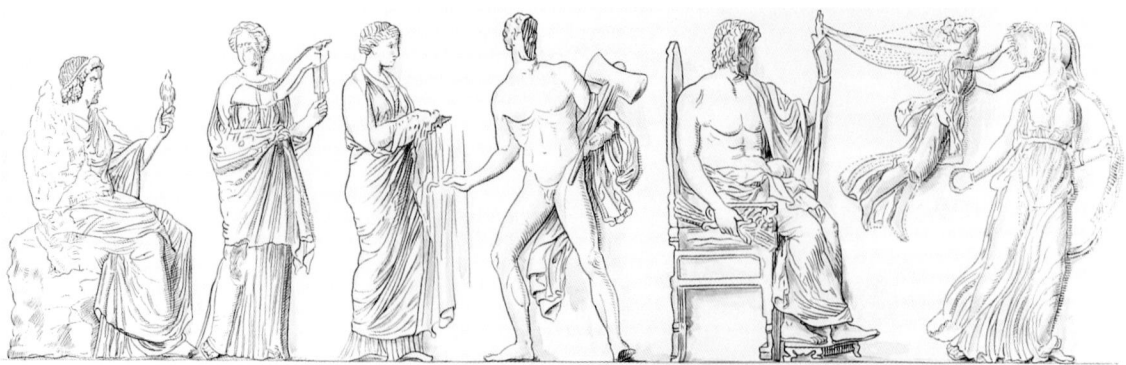

72 The birth of Athena shown on a Roman wellhead now in Madrid perhaps holds the key to reconstructing the lost figures that once filled the centre of the east pediment of the Parthenon.

broken away, as is the weapon. We can just make out, however, the curve of a vessel. This is one of those intended for the feast, probably a wine-mixing bowl. An instrument of conviviality is here corrupted in the hands of this most perverse of guests to become a club with which to bludgeon a host. The power of the image for an ancient Greek lay in the horror it provoked, not only at the premature death of a fellow human being but also at the transgression against the laws of hospitality.

THE PEDIMENTS

The most impressive parts of the Parthenon sculpture must have been the two pediments, the triangular gables, one at each end of the temple.[37] On this sculpture-rich building, the apex of each triangle was itself crowned by a central, 'floral' ornament (acroterion), marble fragments of which survive. The side angles also supported acroteria but, because of the type of plinth and cuttings for their metal anchors, these are now thought to have been forward-leaning figures of Victory.[38] The base of each triangle comprises a narrow shelf where, against a blank wall, were set two great

73 Left to right: the sun god Helios and his horse-drawn chariot emerging from the sea at dawn; Dionysos reclining naked; probably Persephone seated with her mother Demeter; perhaps Hebe (youth), cup-bearer of Zeus. Parthenon east pediment figures A to G. British Museum.

A   B   C   D   E   F   G

compositions, comprising sculpture carved all round. The elongated triangle was not the most promising of templates into which to set a narrative subject. At the centre there was sufficient height for figures to stand more than twice life size, while the sharp angles of the corners implied a much smaller scale. As we shall see, the designer of the Parthenon pediments cleverly arranged his figures, both in relation to the frame and in the relationship of one figure to another, so as to minimize the potential for extreme variation in scale. The style of the carving seems, like that of the frieze, more advanced and consistent than some of the metopes, and the evidence of the Parthenon building inscriptions indicate that the pediment sculptures were carved between 438 and 432 BC.[39]

Both the east and west pediments have suffered much vandalism. The east was almost emptied when in late antiquity the temple was converted into a church, and almost all of what survives comes from the two corners and is in the British Museum. The larger figures that filled the heart of the composition are lost, and with them would have gone all knowledge of their subject, if not for the testimony of Pausanias writing in the second century AD. This compiler of the ancient tourist guide to Greece briefly mentions the sculpture of the Parthenon and says that the pediment over the entrance, that is to say the east pediment, showed the miraculous birth of Athena. According to the story, Athena was conceived by the union of Zeus and Metis, the female personification of intelligence. Fearing that any child of such parentage would come to threaten his authority, Zeus attempted to put an end to the pregnancy by swallowing Metis whole. The child, however, grew in the head of the father until released by a blow from the axe of her half-brother Hephaistos, god of smiths. Vase-paintings show the brain-child of Zeus, fully grown and armed, popping out of his head. So tall a composition, with one figure rising above another, could not be accommodated, even at the apex of the

74 Perhaps Hestia, goddess of the hearth (seated left) with possibly Aphrodite reclining luxuriously in the lap of Dione, her mother. Parthenon east pediment figures K, L and M. For figure O see fig. 77. Figure N, the torso of Selene, is in Athens. British Museum.

K   L   M

75 A girl recoils from witnessing the birth of Athena. Her draperies brilliantly express excitement. Parthenon east pediment figure G. British Museum.

pediment triangle, without awkwardly reducing the figure of Zeus. It is therefore likely instead that Zeus was shown seated or standing at the centre, with Hephaistos on one side and Athena moving away on the other. None of these figures survives, although a few doubtful fragments in Athens have been assigned to them. That Zeus was seated is suggested by a round marble altar of the Roman period, later converted into a well-head and now in Madrid (fig. 72). It is carved with scenes thought to have been inspired by the east pediment.[40] The altar shows Olympian Zeus enthroned, while on one side of him Athena moves away at speed, looking back and crowned by a flying Victory; on the other side of Zeus, Hephaistos, having delivered the miraculous birth, retreats but also looks back. This motif of moving one way and looking another is typical of the dynamics of representing human action elsewhere in the pediments and in the frieze, and the scene may well hold the key to reconstructing the lost design for the birth scene of Athena on the Parthenon.[41]

A dynamic arrangement of the lost central

76 Dionysos relaxed and resting on a rock draped with the skin of a panther watches Helios rise, giving dawn to a new day. Parthenon east pediment figure D. British Museum.

figures of the east pediment is to be preferred over the suggestion that there were static standing figures since, to judge from those that do survive, the central drama was sufficiently animated to send an electrified charge through the groups on either side.[42] In the British Museum are displayed five figures from the left-hand side of the pediment and four from the right (figs 73–4 and 77). The innermost figures of these groups exhibit the impact of the shock transmitted by events at the centre. Their identity is uncertain and for convenience they are referred to by letters. The figure of a young girl, G, lurches sideways, as if blasted, and, as she moves one way, her drapery swings in the opposite direction or flies behind her head (fig. 75). She has been called Hebe, cup-bearer of Zeus. Her sudden movement disturbs figure F seated to her right. The head is missing but, from the turn of the torso, it can be reconstructed glancing towards the advancing girl. The matronly presence of this figure absorbs the energy of figure G, and the second seated figure, E, is seemingly unaware of the commotion. While figure F sits at an angle, figure E sits full on to the viewer, and the next, D, carries the turn through space a stage further (fig. 76). He reclines on a rock, cushioned by the skin of a feline animal, and his head looks out and away to the left.

The diminishing height of these four figures, the running girl, the two seated women (perhaps Demeter and her daughter Persephone) and the brilliantly studied reclining male nude (probably Dionysos god of wine) are artfully adapted to the downward slope of the pediment frame. The line of their composition descends with grace and ease, each figure relating naturally to the next. In order to fill the corner itself, and to trap the right-to-left flow of energy precipitated by the running girl, the designer marked the time of Athena's birth by showing the chariot of the sun god Helios (A). There was no space for a naturalistic rendering of the complete vehicle and its four horses, and so we are asked to imagine the greater part sunk beneath the horizon. Only the arms and now lost head of Helios were shown along with the heads of his team, two of which are displayed in the British Museum (B and C). In a curious attention to realism, the sculptor carved the waves of the sea covering Helios' breast, a feature that would never be seen when the sculpture was set in place on the pediment. The daring concealment of the greater part of Helios' chariot implies great confidence on the part of the designer in his own ability to suggest the whole of a subject by indicating only a part of it.

Another group of figures survives from the right side of the same pediment, four in the British Museum and one in Athens (K, L, M, N and O) (fig. 74). A female is seated front on to the viewer and, disturbed by the commotion to her right, she seems on the point of rising. Her right foot is tucked under her thigh, and she appears to be pressing down on it.

77 The head of one of the team of four horses that drew the chariot of the moon goddess, Selene, across the night sky eloquently portrays the strain of the task. Parthenon east pediment figure O. British Museum.

78 In 1674, before the explosion that wrecked the temple in 1687, the artist Jacques Carrey drew the west pediment sculptures. Athena and Poseidon dominate the centre, while their respective chariots fill the spaces between these two gods and those figures in the two corners, who witnessed and perhaps judged the competition.

As she does so, the drapery over her knee becomes smooth and taut. The missing head glanced in the direction of Athena's birth. To her left another seated female, equally richly draped, sits at three-quarters to the spectator, and in her lap an even more luxurious figure reclines to be seen side-on. These two have been identified as Aphrodite resting in the lap of her mother Dione. The reclining figure is the female equivalent of the male nude in the opposite corner and completes a trio of figures, which artfully balance those on the left. Like them, these figures descend with the sloping cornice and, at the same time, turn through space. The reclining female, M, carries our attention away from the central drama, to the very

corner itself, where to balance the chariot of the rising sun was shown Selene, the moon goddess, sinking beneath the horizon. The torso of Selene, N, survives in Athens, along with fragments of three heads of her team of horses. A fourth, O, is in London and is perhaps the most famous and best loved of all the sculptures of the Parthenon. It presents the essence of the stress felt by a beast that has spent the night drawing the chariot of the Moon across the night sky. As the Moon sinks low, her horse lays back its ears, the jaw gapes, the nostrils flare, the eyes bulge, veins stand out and the flesh seems spare and taut over the flat plate of the cheek bone.

Both sets of figures respond in diminishing degrees to the surge of energy discharged by the now missing central tableau. On the left, figures G and F feel it most, while figure D does not seem to have been at all affected. Just so, on the right, figure K takes the brunt of the shock of Athena's birth, while the languor of figure M goes undisturbed. The scenario is a credible one of energy rippling out from the centre, strongest at points closest to the source and weakening the further it travels. There are those who would discount the Madrid well-head as evidence for reconstructing the lost central scene and would restore a static group of standing figures. This may, however, be rejected as failing to connect adequately with what we see to left and right. A static central composition does not provide the necessary 'dynamo' for the motion that runs through the surviving figures that exhibit it.

79 The once colossal figure of Athena was reduced in the seventeenth century to fragments: the draped torso in the British Museum joins the plaster cast of a fragment of the helmeted head in Athens. Parthenon west pediment figure L.

80 The battered torso of Poseidon in the British Museum joins a fragment of his well-built chest in Athens. Parthenon west pediment figure M.

81 A languid youth artfully designed to fill a corner of the west pediment probably portrays a river god. Parthenon west pediment figure A. British Museum.

82 From the back, the body and drapery of the reclining youth seems especially water-like.

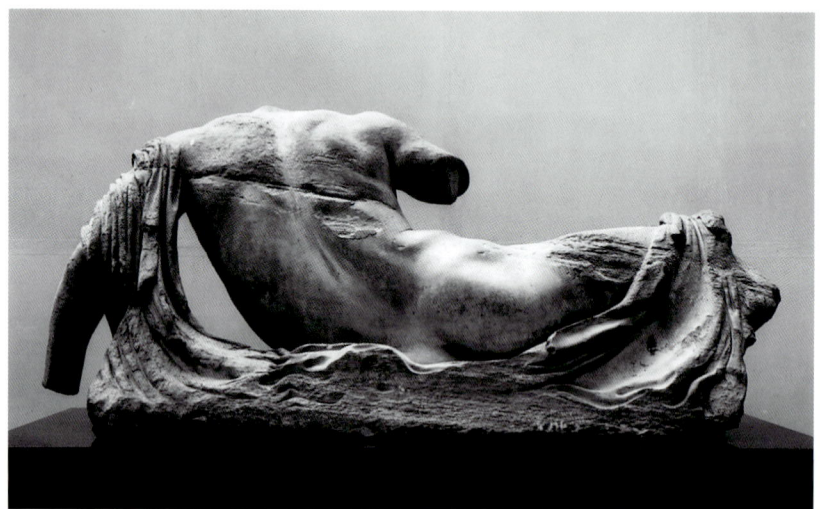

As the drama of Athena's birth was being played out in the east pediment, another momentous episode in her life was taking place in the west pediment at the opposite end of the building. The west pediment sculpture had survived well until the explosion that wrecked the Parthenon in 1687. Up until then, it would have been possible, even without the account of Pausanias, to identify Athena and Poseidon and their struggle to command the land of Attica (by which is meant Athens and its countryside). Drawings attributed to Jacques Carrey, thought to have been done in 1674, show how the pediment looked then (fig. 78). At the centre, the colossal figures of the contestants were shown moving suddenly away from each other (figs 79–80). According to one interpretation, they have just delivered the miracles by which their performance was to be judged. Poseidon had struck the rock to cause a salt spring to gush forth, while Athena caused the first olive tree to grow. Athena's was judged the greater gift, and Attica was given to her. On either side were ranged the chariots that had delivered the gods to the Acropolis. According to a different interpretation, it was the race to the Acropolis and the timing of the delivery of the miracle that won the prize, rather than the miracle itself.[43] The vehicles with their rearing teams of horses provided ideal compositions with which to respond to the sloping frame. To left and right were ranged descending groups of figures thought to represent legendary heroes of Athens, by whom the judgement was made. They include on the left one of the first kings of the city, Kekrops, and with him a daughter. In the very corners, the problem of the angle was solved by causing the figures to lie down.

Divided largely between Athens and London, the sculpture that survives affords us tantalizing snatch-views of the west pediment's once rich and impressive composition. Two relatively well-preserved figures are displayed in the British Museum. One comes from the left-hand angle and portrays a youth, whose lissom form is thought to personify one of the streams that flow through the city of Athens, perhaps the River Ilissos or possibly the Eridanos (figs 81–2). He appears to be drawing himself out of the water on to a bank. A fall of drapery, wet and clinging, flows over his left arm. It pours behind the back and buttocks of the figure, where it is indistinguishable from water. The other figure that has survived better than most is Iris the herald of Poseidon's chariot, a messenger goddess and spirit of the rainbow (fig. 83). She was portrayed as if alighting on the rock of the Acropolis after flight. Her wings, probably of bronze and now lost, rose behind her and were attached at fixings in her shoulders. Iris is a girl in a short tunic, the cloth of which is pressed against her body by the rush of the wind. The clinging fabric shapes her youthful form, or breaks free to flutter out at the sides.

Together, Iris and the river god exhibit the Pygmalion-like power of the sculptors of the Parthenon to turn stone into life. These figures, broken as they are, still live and breathe with the vitality carved into them by some unknown mason of the fifth century BC. More than merely lifelike,

83 The figure of Iris heralded the chariot of Poseidon. This once winged goddess of the rainbow and of the upper atmosphere, breathed only by the gods, seems to personify the spirit of the air. Parthenon west pediment N. British Museum.

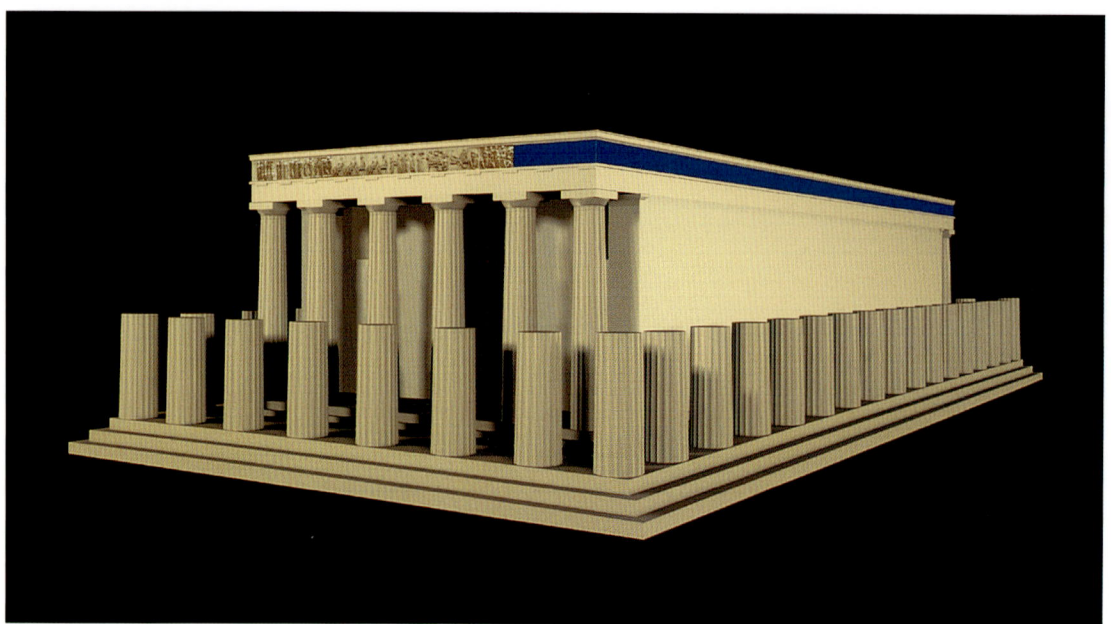

84 The Ionic frieze of the Parthenon ran within the outer colonnades, around all four sides of the building. Computer-generated photograph. British Museum.

they transcend the human form and become universal representations of elements in nature, water in the case of a languid river god, air in that of the wind-blown Iris. This abstraction has nothing to do with the cold idealism that is sometimes attributed to Greek sculpture, especially when seen through anodyne Roman copies of lost Greek statues. It is, rather, the product of the Greek conception of gods as living, breathing men and women, who are yet immortal, better than ourselves and possessed of unfading beauty.

THE IONIC FRIEZE

Such undying gods as those of the pediment sculptures are also to be found in the continuous band of sculpture that comprised a carved Ionic frieze.[44] Not only gods were shown in the frieze, but also godlike men and women. The norm in choosing subjects for temple sculpture was to portray some event from the tales of mythical gods and heroes. In the Ionic frieze of the Parthenon, exceptionally, the Athenians chose to represent themselves as an idealized, living community.

While the pediments were filled with figures carved in the round and the metopes are in very high relief, the frieze is a band of low relief, a metre high and 160 metres long, which was carved over four sides of the building. On the long sides, it ran within the colonnade along the top of the masonry wall of the cella, some 12 metres above the temple floor (fig. 84). On the short sides, it was located at the same level above the porch

85 The central scene of the east frieze in position above the approach to the main doorway of the temple. Computer-generated photograph. British Museum.

columns, again within the columns of the outer colonnade. Thus on all four sides of the building, the frieze could be viewed only in snatches through the peristyle, and this position for so great a work must be called inconspicuous, if not obscure.

The frieze was carved into blocks of marble some 60 centimetres deep. Their length varies, but those of the long sides measure generally 1.22 metres. It is sometimes argued that the blocks were carved in a workshop at ground level and afterwards hoisted into place. The likeliest procedure, however, is that blocks were first set as a continuous course of masonry, the face left proud and rough for the frieze to be carved into it.[45] On the west and east sides the carving observes the vertical frames of the block divisions, but on the north and south sides the figures are carved across the divisions, as if into one continuous ribbon of stone. The carving is likely to have happened after 438 BC, that is to say after the roof was on the temple and the major construction work was completed. The carving of the frieze and of the pediment sculptures may be seen as finishing processes, along with final dressing of masonry surfaces, fluting of columns and application of painted decoration.[46]

The frieze took as its subject a procession that divides into two branches, each starting out from the south-west corner. This is thought by many to be the procession of the Panathenaea, a festival in honour of Athena held annually in Athens during the summer month of Hekatombaion, and every four years celebrated with especial splendour, when it was known as the Great Panathenaea. One branch of the procession was

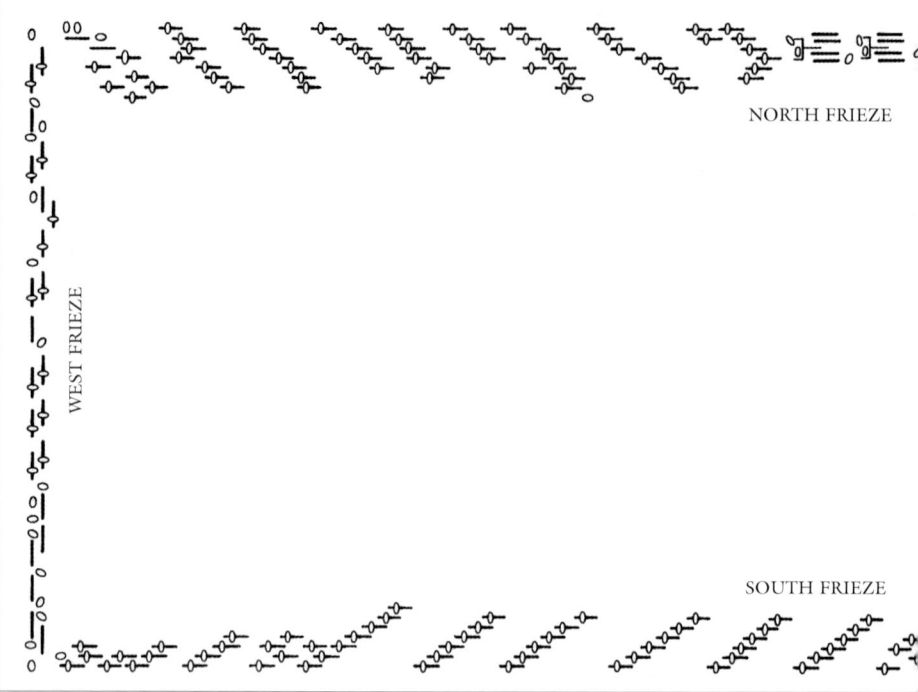

carved along the south side of the building, turning on to the east, where it ran to face a group of gods seated to look south. The other branch ran along the west side and then on to the north, until it too turned the corner on to the east and there faced a group of gods seated and looking north. Between the two banks of gods is seen a group of cult officials engaged in some rite involving children with stools and a blanket of cloth (fig. 85). This is thought to be the peplos, a robe newly woven each year by Athenian girls and women and dedicated at the Panathenaea to the statue of Athena Polias on the Acropolis.

The composition and carving of so long and complex a work required much forethought. This is especially so on the long sides, where the illusion of depth created in the picture through overlapping figures is particularly ambitious. It has been possible to reconstruct some of this planning process by plotting the figures in the procession as if they were seen from above (fig. 86).[47] This bird's-eye view enables us to understand at a glance how the procession was laid out, and the designer of the frieze can be imagined drawing up just such a diagram in order to show the teams of carvers how to execute his vision. That the Parthenon frieze is the product of a single and superior intellect, there should be no doubt. It has a coherent unity of design and episodic narrative structure that render its internal logic comparable with that of the pediment compositions. Just as there, so in the frieze, a distinguishing characteristic is the way figures

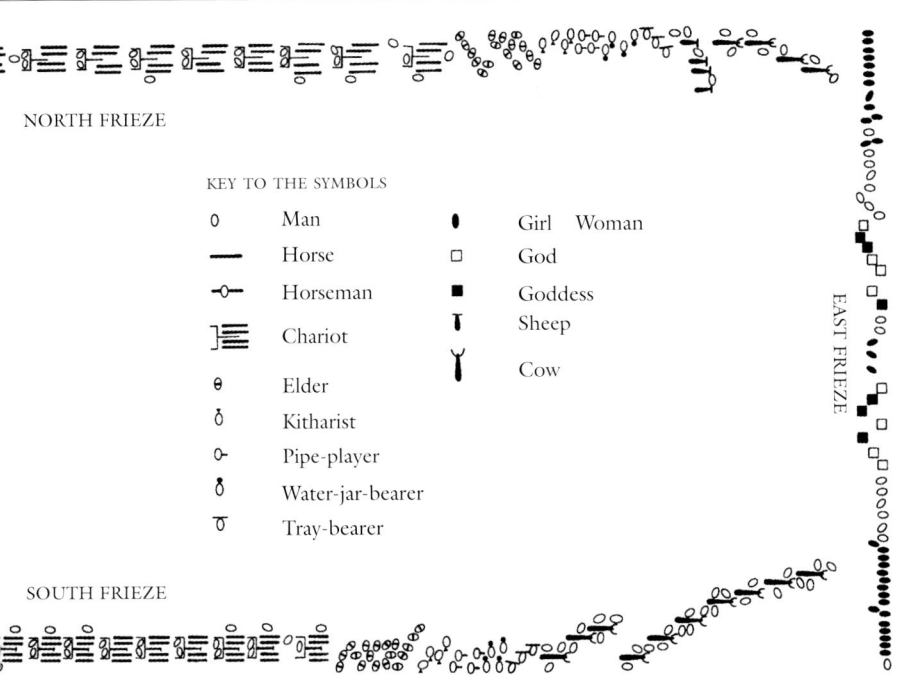

86 The procession shown in the Ionic frieze symbolically mapped as it would appear from above. The designer of the frieze must have made such a plan. Drawing S. Bird.

or groups of figures give energy to or take it from those that go before or come after.

The northern branch of the procession actually begins on the west frieze with a troop of horsemen, some mounted some not, some facing one way and others another, to provide an introductory episode of preparation for the cavalcade that lies ahead. This cavalcade makes up the second episode of the narrative and is to be found around the corner on the north side, where sixty horsemen occupy about half of the entire long flank (figs 87–8). The north-side cavalcade is one of the most complex and visually demanding passages of the entire frieze. Horsemen are divided into ten ranks of unequal number, each rank divided by a rider who is placed nearest the viewer, and not overlapped by any other figure in his rank (fig. 89). The rank of overlapping riders may contain as many as eight, before the capacity of the shallow relief to extend the illusion of receding depth is stretched to the limit. The next rank in the sequence begins with a rider, again placed nearest us in the relative depth of field, and not overlapped by any other. The image of a ride-past is thus constructed by layering one horseman on another and one rank on the next. It is an ideal solution to the problem of accommodating so many figures in so narrow a band of such shallow relief. As was the case in Egyptian, Assyrian and in earlier Greek art, where a procession was to be represented, so in the Parthenon frieze figures placed nearest to the viewer and

87 The start of the north-frieze cavalcade shows figures yet to mount their horses and thus echoes the preparation scenes of the west frieze. A boy helps a rider to belt his tunic, while a companion looks on impatiently. Parthenon north frieze block 47. British Museum.

88 Viewing the cavalcade at an angle reveals the rhythmic lines of composition that run through the heads of the horsemen, the heads of the horses, the hands of the horsemen, their hanging feet and the rearing forelegs of the horses. British Museum.

89 The cavalcade is made up of a series of ranks of riders, each divided by a figure who is placed nearest the viewer and not over-lapped by any other rider in his rank. Drawing S. Bird.

those furthest away fill the same distance between the top and bottom frame of the picture. The process makes no use of perspective, and nor was there a need for it. Once the rules of this game of make-believe are known and seen to work, they can be readily accepted by the viewer, ancient and modern.

Ahead of the horsemen were chariots, ten on the south frieze and eleven on the north. The first one or two are stationary and then the teams appear to fly headlong in a race, before being reined in to anticipate the figures of pedestrians who walk ahead. Two figures ride side-by-side in the car, a driver in flowing tunic and an armed foot soldier. The latter seems to leap out of the cars to complete the race on foot, which was in fact the task of the so-called apobates (the one who leaps out) in a race of that name at the Panathenaic festival. Occasionally a marshal on foot directs the traffic. Much damaged by the explosion that wrecked the Parthenon in 1687, the chariot race is one of the less well-preserved episodes of the frieze. It can in parts, however, be reconstructed by Jacques Carrey's drawings, and some marvellous carving survives from it. Most dramatic in the south frieze is the team of four horses with flickering flame-like manes, miraculously conveyed in the shallow relief never more than 6 or 7 centimetres deep (fig. 90). Their manes are echoed in the flying horse-hair crest of the helmeted foot soldier and his billowing cloak.

The lead chariots are reined back to acknowledge the groups of figures that walk ahead of them. The first of these are bearded elders, perhaps officials of the Athenian democracy, or possibly the winners of a male

The Parthenon and Its Sculptures

HORSEMEN

90 A chariot runs at speed, drawn by four horses, their fiery manes echoing the flaming crest and flying cloak of the soldier behind. Parthenon south frieze block 31. British Museum.

beauty contest that was one of the festival events. The winners carried branches in the procession, and some hands do look as if they are holding something. None of these objects survives and they were perhaps painted on to the relief.

Ahead of the elders walked musicians. Little survives, but with the help of Carrey's drawings it is known that there were both string and wind players. The strings were provided by the kithara, a kind of harp equipped with a large, resonating sound-box. In the festival there were competitions both for 'kitharists', solo instrumentalists, and for 'kitharodes', accompanied singers. The wind instrument featured in the frieze was the aulos, a wind-blown pipe, played in pairs. There is room in the reconstructed frieze for four of each type of musician on both the north and south sides. Their presence is a token representation of the real-life musical accompaniment to the procession and, no doubt, a deliberate reference to Perikles' own augmentation of the part played by music in the festival competitions.[48]

The musicians were led by youths carrying water-jars (hydriai) and, ahead of them, trays (fig. 91). The contents of these vessels probably have

91 Three young men carry water jars on their shoulder, while a fourth bends down to lift his jar. Parthenon north frieze block 6. Athens, Acropolis Museum.

to do with the sacrifice of animal victims, which event, with its roasting and sharing of meat among the onlookers, was the culmination of the festival. The animals were slaughtered in honour of Athena, and their inedible parts were consumed by fire on the great altar that stood at the east end of the Acropolis. Anybody who has followed the path of a recent drove of cattle will understand why it seems very unlikely that the full quota of one hundred were included in the Panathenaic procession, but there may have been token representatives. Certainly, the frieze shows some only of the many: on the north side were carved a tight bunch of four sheep and ahead of them a longer file of four cattle, accompanied by their handlers. On the south side were ten cattle.

The poetic properties of the frieze are revealed fully in the victim scenes, where the designer was challenged to render the broad, flat flanks of the animals interesting to the spectator. In the south frieze in particular, the line of ten beasts could have become tedious in the hands of a lesser artist. Monotony was avoided by weaving together the blank hides of the cattle with the contrasting, complex drapery of the youths. A drama unfolds, moreover, as the line of animals proceeds. The three hindmost go quietly, but the fourth in sequence bolts and sends a shock-wave through those immediately ahead. The leaders are again tranquil, and order is restored to convey the propitious sign that victims go willingly to the altar. The line made by the backs of the beasts describes the narrative, running straight and then rising and falling to run straight again. The crest of this wave is marked by the tip of the nose of a beast, the head raised up

92 Three draped youths strive to control a bucking cow. The complex folds of their cloaks contrast pleasingly with the broad, flat flank of the beast. Parthenon south frieze block 44. British Museum.

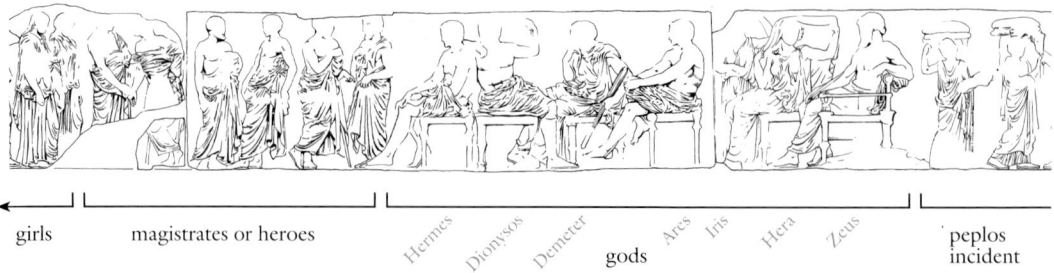

93 On the east frieze the two branches of the procession converge but do not meet, divided by standing draped male magistrates or perhaps heroes and, innermost, seated gods. Between the gods can be seen the peplos incident. Drawing S. Bird.

and pulled back by the tension of a restraining halter (fig. 92). This is the animal that the poet John Keats so memorably described as 'the heifer lowing to the skies'.

The victims lead the procession to the north-east and south-east corners of the frieze. The north-east corner is lost, but the south-east survives, and there a marshal leads the procession from the long south flank of the temple to its short east side (fig. 93). Here young women appear for the first time in the frieze, their tunics and cloaks concealing their bodies. This modesty contrasts with the nudity of many of the male figures seen hitherto. A number of the women carry jugs and bowls for the pouring of liquid libations, and at least one carries a stand for burning incense (thymiaterion). Girls and women of well-to-do Athenian families were involved in the manufacture of the tapestry-woven peplos for the goddess, and this may account for their prominence at the head of the procession.

The women bring the procession and its offerings nearly to the gods, fulfilling the role of women in Greek religion as intermediaries between the world of mortals and that of the divine. The two groups of seated gods are flanked, however, by two corresponding groups of men, who stand or lean on staves, as if in casual conversation. These have been seen as either magistrates, possibly waiting to preside over the sacrifices, or heroes of Athens' legendary past. They are perhaps the eponymous heroes, who gave their names to the ten tribes of the city. Some of these same heroes, for example Theseus, Kekrops and Erechtheus, may be represented again in the metopes and pediments.

The gods are shown as the dignitaries of a grandstand audience, seated and thereby on a larger scale than the human figures of the frieze. The two outer aisles, as it were, are occupied by personalities who may be said to have most to do with the world of mortals: on the south side is Hermes, messenger of the gods and leader of human souls into the Underworld; on the north side is Aphrodite, goddess of amorous affairs. These two appear deliberately placed to represent the most profound of human passions, respectively death and love. The inner aisles are reserved, on the south side,

| peplos incident | Athena Hephaistos Poseidon | gods | Apollo Artemis Aphrodite Eros | magistrates or heroes | marshals | girls |

for Zeus as father of the gods and the supreme Olympian and, on the north side, for Athena whose temple is the Parthenon.

The gods sit on stools, with the exception of Zeus who occupies a throne with back support, and arm-rest poised on a diminutive sphinx. The human characterization of Zeus and his family of gods in the frieze is very much of the same kind as that of the divine family portrayed on Olympos in the epic poems of the early Greek poet Homer. An ancient Athenian would have had no difficulty in recognizing each individual. There are clues in the form of attributes, some carved or attached in metal, now lost, and others painted. The southern group from left to right is made up as follows: Hermes alert and attentive to the approaching procession sits with the hat (petasos) of a traveller. His short boots were perhaps carved with wings, and a drill-hole in the right hand probably indicates the attachment of a metal wand or caduceus. To the right is Dionysos, god of wine. He cuts a very different figure slouching on the shoulder of his companion with one arm raised. It was supported by a staff, now lost, but this must have been the thyrsos or pine-cone-capped emblem of the god of ecstasy, often carried by his female followers, the maenads. Dionysos' feet are interlocked with the left foot of the female deity next to him. She carries in one hand a torch of tightly bound wheat or barley stems, while the other hand supported her chin, before this was broken away. Her mournful expression becomes Demeter, goddess of the Earth's fertility, who lost her daughter Persephone to Hades, god of the Underworld. Next comes Ares, god of war, with both feet off the ground. One rests on a spear that was carved in part only, the remainder having been indicated in paint now worn away. The right knee is cradled in clasped hands to raise the other foot as part of a remarkably naturalistic pose, closely observed from life. To the right again stands Iris, another messenger god, who is caught in the action of arranging her hair with her raised left hand. She is close to Hera, Zeus's queen and goddess of marriage, who turns a glance towards her husband and, as she does so, holds out her veil in the manner of a new bride. Zeus himself gazes in the direction of the procession approaching from the south, and carved along his right arm is a sceptre.

94 Three gods: left to right, Poseidon, Apollo and Artemis. Parthenon east frieze block 6. British Museum. Athens, Acropolis Museum.

The gods facing the northern branch of the procession are, from right to left, Eros, the boy god of love, leaning into the knee of his mother and holding the long handle of a parasol. Aphrodite extends her right arm over the boy's left shoulder to point out the approaching procession. Her other arm rests on the thigh of Artemis, goddess of the hunt. Artemis looks in the same direction as her sister and links arms with her. Her right hand was probably supported by a bow, attached in metal. Next to Artemis, Apollo's right arm was also supported by a missing object, perhaps a bow, as he turned to the older figure of bearded Poseidon, god of the sea (fig. 94). Poseidon taps Apollo on the shoulder to alert him that the procession has been sighted. The arm movements of these gods, culminating in the pointing gesture of Aphrodite, create a balletic and expressive sequence that carries the eye pleasingly from one to another. Next comes Hephaistos, lame god of smiths, whose right side is supported by a crutch just visible under his armpit. He turns to his half-sister Athena, goddess of the temple and chief honorand of the festival, who sits with the snake-fringed aegis in her lap, while a metal spear was attached along her right side.

Iris, Hera, Zeus, Athena and Hephaistos are all carved on one block of stone, located above the approach to the east door of the Parthenon. They form part of a tableau that was visible through the gap between the fourth and fifth columns of the peristyle (see fig. 85). The columns framed the gods, and the gods themselves framed the centre-most image, where two adults were shown with three children engaged in a drama involving a piece of cloth and two cushioned stools. These figures stand and do not share the enlarged scale of the seated gods. The uncertainty of their identity has provoked much controversy, but they are usually taken as mortal players of a real-life drama, rather than heroic figures of some mythological event. The most enduring suggestion is that they are all cult officials of the Panathenaic festival, and that the cloth is the peplos of Athena. The man is perhaps the archon basileus, the chief magistrate and overseer of Athenian state religion. The woman may be the priestess of Athena Polias, while the two girls are perhaps arrephoroi who, between the ages of seven and eleven, spent part of the year on the Acropolis in Athena's service. The sex of the semi-naked child with the cloth is disputed, but we may see a boy here, at least to judge from the profile of other naked boys in the cavalcade. In handling the peplos, his role in the cult seems especially important, but no ancient literary source survives that will help specifically to identify him, nor the nature of the ritual act in which he and the others are involved. There is, therefore, plenty of scope for scholars to exercise their learning in finding ever new and ingenious interpretations of the scene.[49]

The presence of the peplos at the centre of the east frieze, flanked by the gods, seems to indicate that the procession is that of the Panathenaic festival. Outside this central image, however, it could be argued that the procession is a generic one with no specific reference to any one festival. The horsemen, chariots and various pedestrian figures could be seen as collectively emblematic of all Athenian festivals, and the presence of all the major gods suggests that such a general, abstract idea of celebration was intended. Attempts to see it otherwise and to make the frieze a pictorial record of the Panathenaic procession will always show up the mismatch between the procession of the frieze and that of the collected literary sources that document the festival. Horsemen, for example, so prominent in the frieze, are not mentioned by any ancient author as having participated in the Panathenaic procession. Instead we hear of foot soldiers, hoplites, who represented the real strength of the Athenian fighting force. The horsemen of the frieze probably have more to do with ideal representation, that is to say with the idea of festival itself rather than with any particular reality. They are also there to flatter contemporary Athenians and Perikles especially, one of whose innovations was to expand the Athenian cavalry from some three hundred to a force of a thousand.[50] The new Periklean cavalry of a thousand was divided into ten units of a hundred riders in each, the ten units individually representing the ten tribes of Athens. Parading in the marketplace of the city, they must have been a thrilling new experience and one that no doubt captured the imagination of the designer of the frieze. This anonymous artist, perhaps

Pheidias himself, brilliantly captured their essence in the ten ranks of the north frieze and, indeed, the ten ranks of the south frieze. In the south frieze, by contrast with those of the north frieze, the ranks are made up of a regular six riders in each. Every rank, moreover, was distinguished by a different form of dress. This sartorial difference renders the emphasis on ten divisions even more explicit in the south frieze cavalcade than it does in the north.

In the horsemen, but also in the other groups representative of the Athenian community, the frieze seems to transcend specific festival celebration to present a larger idea, that of festival as the embodiment of the polis or city itself. It epitomizes the physical city in the movement of the procession between the outskirts and its sacred heart. It defines the social makeup of the city in comprising participants who are both young and old, male and female, citizen and non-citizen. It creates a hierarchy of Athenian life, of beast serving man and of men and women serving god. Capturing the essential elements of festival, it presents a paradigm of a religion in which mortal communicates with the divine, through contest in the horse parades and the chariot race, through pomp in the pedestrian figures, and through sacrifice in the victims being led to the unseen altar. It moves between real life and legend in a pageant evocative of Athens' heroic past: chariots and their flowing-robed drivers had long been anachronisms, figures of romantic imagination rooted in the legendary age of heroes.

At the heart of the frieze was the peplos, woven with scenes of the gigantomachy, in which the Olympian gods had struggled to evict the old order of giants from the cosmos. Gods and men alike now enjoyed the rational order that had been achieved by victory over the giants. The peplos was for the people of Athens therefore an image full of meaning and one that was renewed every year in the weaving of it for the Panathenaic festival. The very art of weaving was itself a celebration of the goddess Athena, whose gift to humanity it had been. On the frieze, the gods frame the ritual handling of the sacred robe, but they do not observe it, and their location in the drama of the frieze is seemingly deliberately questionable: are they on Olympos, surveying the coming sacrifice from afar, or are they on the Acropolis as honoured guests of the Athenians? Whereas in the west and east pediments we are left in no doubt that the drama unfolds on the Acropolis and Olympos respectively, in the frieze the distinction between the Acropolis and Olympos is confused. This ambiguity was no doubt intended, so that the Athenians who ascend in procession to pay homage to their gods may seem themselves to achieve a glamorous apotheosis.

CONCLUSION

The sculptures of the Parthenon are exceptional both for their quality and for their apparent significance as a collective and coherent embodiment of Athenian identity, expressed through mythical and civic imagery. The metopes with their scenes of fantastic battle evoke Athens' legendary past in the Centaur and Amazonomachy of the south and west side of the temple. On the north side Athens embraced a panhellenic struggle in the scenes of the Greek sack of Troy and, in a different dimension again, the east side showed the cosmic battle of Olympian gods fighting the giants. In these images of strife between culture and nature, Greek and barbarian, rational and irrational forces, it is difficult not to see a thinly veiled reference to the real-life war between Greeks and Persians that had destroyed the building that preceded the Parthenon on the Acropolis. This paralleling of myth and history seems intended both to commemorate Athenian valour and to elevate the Graeco-Persian struggle to the level of an archetypal triumph of the Greek virtues of moderation and self-restraint (sophrosyne) over Persian arrogance (hybris). Athenian propaganda presented the city as one constrained by principles of divinely sanctioned 'good order' while Athens' enemies were portrayed as the epitome of wanton excess.[51]

This idea of Athens' legendary and historical past mirrored in the myths of the gods and heroes recurs in the pediments where, in the west pediment, the focus is upon the Acropolis on which are gathered participants in or witnesses to the contest of Poseidon and Athena. In the east pediment, Athena is again at the centre of the action, but here it is her birth on Olympos. This juxtaposition of Olympos and the Athenian Acropolis implies that the gods have their home on both the holy mountain and the sacred citadel. The comparison of one with the other is found again in the frieze in a most unexpected and even shocking way.

The Ionic frieze is the most ambitious of all the sculptures of the Parthenon and the most expressive of a national ideology. It presents a story narrated episodically as a festival procession spanning the outer limits of the city and its sacred heart, connecting the legendary past with an idealized present and uniting the mortal inhabitants with their divine patrons. In this fusion of godlike men and manlike gods the spectator is unclear as to whether the gods are on the Acropolis or the Athenians are on Olympos. This beautiful and eternal paradox is the ultimate Athenian conceit and, even now, when all the ancient political, civic and religious meanings of the frieze bear no relevance for the modern viewer, except in academic terms, none the less we are touched by its ability to transcend period and place and to present a timeless and incorruptible humanity in which we can find and refresh our own best selves.

Chapter Five

The Athenian Acropolis – Propylaea, Nike Temple and Erechtheum

THE PERIKLEAN BUILDING PROGRAMME

The newly built Parthenon was the architectural centrepiece of Athens' identity as the premier city state of Greece and it was conceived as part of a general renewal of the city in the second half of the fifth century BC (fig. 95). Our principal literary source for the Periklean building programme is Plutarch,[1] who mentions six projects, and the names of some of their architects: Iktinos and Kallikrates built the Parthenon; Koroibos, Metagenes and Xenokles built the 'Hall of Initiation' in the great Demeter sanctuary at Eleusis; Kallikrates built the southern of the two parallel, so-called long walls, connecting the fortifications of Athens with those of its harbour at Piraeus. The Odeion, a music hall, was constructed at the

95 A festival procession passing through the Propylaea enters the Acropolis. In the foreground is the temple of Athena Nike, in the distance is the Parthenon and to the left the Erechtheum. Drawing P. Connolly.

south-east foot of the Acropolis and next to the theatre. It was designed by an unknown architect to echo, or so it was said, the captured tent of Xerxes, the Persian king forced to abandon his camp following defeat in his failed assault on Greece of 480/479 BC. The Propylaea or 'gateways' were erected by Mnesikles as a monumental entrance to the Acropolis. The last work mentioned by Plutarch is Pheidias' gold and ivory colossus of Athena Parthenos displayed in the Parthenon.

96 The ruins of the Ilissos temple incorporated into a Byzantine church.

This list has some of the highlights, but by no means completes the full catalogue of works that might be deemed Periklean. It could be argued that the extent of the building programme has been exaggerated and Perikles' involvement in it overstated.[2] There is no absolute authority for assigning every fifth-century work even on the Acropolis of Athens to a unified Periklean vision, and certainly not all the buildings that have been associated with him were erected during his lifetime. And yet the case might still be made for attributing to Perikles' initiative the little Ionic temple of Athena Nike (Victory) perched prettily on a rocky spur (the Nike Bastion) overlooking the western approach to the Propylaea.[3] There is also the so-called Erechtheum, which housed, among others, the principal cult of Athena, that of the city goddess Athena Polias. Her earlier temple had been destroyed by the Persians and it is unthinkable that during his lifetime Perikles made no plans for its renewal. Mention should also be made of a building situated to the southeast of the Acropolis that strongly resembled the Nike temple (fig. 96). Constructed on a bank of the River Ilissos, it was later converted into a church, and subsequently fell into ruin. In the middle of the eighteenth century it was recorded by the travelling architects James Stuart and Nicholas Revett. Around 1780, it altogether disappeared, presumably reused as building material elsewhere.[4] Its design, architectural detailing and a few surviving fragments of its sculptured frieze all compare closely with those of the Nike temple. The distinctively Athenian column bases and capitals of these two Ionic temples form part of a group with those of the Propylaea (438–432 BC) and the Erechtheum (420–413?; 409–405 BC).[5] The date of the Ilissos temple is much disputed and has been put earlier than or, because of the similarities between the two, contemporary with the construction of the Nike temple.[6]

The Nike temple was subject to interruption caused by war with Sparta, which affected not only this but also other major works of the Periklean era, including the building of the Hephaesteum. The temple of

Hephaistos stands overlooking the Athenian marketplace and is the best preserved of all the Periklean monuments (see fig. 59). It is thought to have been begun at about the same time as, or a little before, the Parthenon, but it competed for resources with the building of the Parthenon and was not therefore finished until after it. The construction of the Erechtheum was also interrupted by the Peloponnesian War, while other buildings, notably the Propylaea and the temple of Nemesis at Rhamnous, were never finished because of it.[7] This chapter will focus on the Propylaea, Nike temple and Erechtheum, the three principal Acropolis monuments that provide insight into some of the best preserved of Perikles' works and the best that Greece ever produced.

PROPYLAEA

In 438 BC the team of masons that had been employed on the construction of the Parthenon handed that building over to the finishers to complete such details as the final dressing of surfaces, fluting of columns, external sculpture and decorative paintwork and, soon after, they began work on a new monumental gateway or Propylaea, designed by the architect Mnesikles (figs 97–8).[8] Propylaea or 'gateways' is a plural word used in acknowledgement of the five access points the building gave to the Acropolis. The principal of these entrances was the central opening. Processions would leave the broad,

97 Plan of the Propylaea showing the central passage and four other doorways. The pinakotheke or picture gallery is on the left, with its dining couches arranged around the walls; on the right is the truncated southern wing linking to the Nike temple.

98 Section through the Propylaea with its different levels and contrasting Doric and Ionic orders. The pinakotheke (picture galley) can be seen projecting on the left with the stepped processional ramp in front.

sloping ramp in front of the gateway and were fed up and into a narrower, central passage running west to east. This inner passage was flanked by three pairs of Ionic columns. Tall and slender on their moulded bases, they contrast with the shorter, fatter Doric columns of the east and west façades (figs 98–9),[9] which echoed those of the Parthenon. Although very different in plan, and forced to ascend the ground rising steeply from west to east, the Propylaea nevertheless shares many features of the Parthenon in architectural form, structural composition and decorative detail. These similarities are attributable partly to Mnesikles' apparent intention to complement the Parthenon with a building that harmonized with it and partly to the working practices of the masons who had been transferred from the Parthenon to work on the Propylaea.

99 The Doric order of the east front of the Propylaea deliberately complements the Parthenon. Unfinished at the outbreak of war with Sparta, the Propylaea was never completed. 'Lifting bosses' and other unresolved features remain visible in the south wall.

The Propylaea replaced a previous gateway, damaged in the Persian sack and afterwards patched up. The previous one stood on a rather different alignment and, in altering the siting of his building, Mnesikles straightened the approach from the Panathenaic ramp, continuing the processional way right through his gateway and into the sanctuary of the Acropolis. As well as demolishing the old Propylon, he knocked down a limestone apsidal building to its west and north. Its dismantled blocks were reused in the foundations of Mnesikles' replacement. His Propylaea is composed of three separate units, the central hall itself and the north and south wings. These two wings are far from symmetrical. The one on the north side is a proper room, with a cross-wall pierced by a door and two windows behind its columned façade. The southern building has no such features, and its columns screen a simple hall linking the Propylaea to the pavement of the sanctuary of Athena Nike.

The purpose of the northern room was to serve as a ceremonial dining place. Dining couches were arranged around its interior walls and the placement of these is the reason for the seemingly awkward off-centre location of the door and peculiar position of the windows in the south wall. The space came to be known as the pinakotheke or 'picture gallery' and is recorded as having large paintings on its walls.[10] This artwork apart, the Propylaea was given no figured sculpture. Its fine coffered ceiling and upper entablature were, however, richly painted, while the white marble walls and steps were detailed in five different places in dark-grey Eleusinian limestone.[11]

It is curious that for all its grandeur and the fineness of its architecture, the Propylaea was never finished. It is thought that the L-shaped spaces on the north and south sides were each to have been in-filled with halls. Redundant features such as cuttings for roof beams and door jambs bear witness to Mnesikles' intention. In addition, many of the lumps of stone used for attaching ropes for handling the blocks of ashlar masonry (lifting bosses) remain and were not cut away as they should have been. On walls, floors and steps the final dressing has not been given to the surface of the masonry. Clearly, when hostilities with Sparta broke out in 432/431 BC, work on the Propylaea was discontinued. Although the workforces reconvened later to construct the Nike temple and the temple known as the Erechtheum, the secular Propylaea would remain unfinished.

TEMPLE OF ATHENA NIKE

The western façade of the Propylaea overlooked a broad, sloping ramp, designed as a gathering point where participants in the Panathenaic procession would pause and await their turn to file through the central passage of the gate. Like modern tourists, from this high point the ancients could admire the view over the city and the sea beyond or they could scan the majestic façades of the Propylaea that rose before them while, to the right, they could look up at the little Ionic temple of Athena Nike, which stood on a rocky spur flanking the processional ramp (fig. 100).[12] This building and many of its ornamental sculptures have miraculously survived a complex history. In the seventeenth century it was dismantled and incorporated into a Turkish fortification. Four blocks of its carved frieze were left visible and were engraved in James Stuart and Nicholas Revett's *Antiquities of Athens*.[13] Vulnerable to abuse, in 1802 they were removed by Lord Elgin's men, who had them sent to England along with a few architectural elements from the same building, and they are now in the British Museum.[14] Meanwhile other blocks of frieze remained concealed in the fortifications and were discovered, along with the rest of the building's architecture when, after Greek Independence from Ottoman rule, the Acropolis was purged of its post-antique buildings and transformed into the surviving set of Classical works that we see today. In 1835–6, the temple was reconstructed from its remains, on the original base.[15] There it stood, the subject of many photographs and

100 The Nike temple viewed from the north-east.

travellers' drawings, until between 1935 and 1940 it was again dismantled and restored by Nicholas Balanos.[16] Unfortunately, iron used to join together fragments of marble afterwards expanded as it rusted and this did much damage that might have been avoided had a lesson been learned from the ancient masons and the iron contained in a sleeve of lead. Atmospheric pollution in Athens has also caused much erosion of surface in both sculpture and architecture. The frieze blocks were removed to the shelter of the Acropolis Museum in 1999, and in 2002 the entire temple was dismantled preparatory to its third reconstruction.[17]

The rock on which the Nike temple later stood had served as a bastion of the old Mycenaean fortification. It is thought that, around 580–560 BC, the Nike bastion was refaced and terraced with dressed masonry, and that a shrine and altar were dedicated to the cult of Athena Nike. This work coincided with a general development of the Acropolis and the creation of ceremonial space for the gathering of celebrants of the Panathenaea, which festival gained in importance at this time.[18] This phase of the sanctuary was almost certainly destroyed by the Persian sack of the Acropolis in 480 BC, which brought down the other temples along with the monumental gateway, predecessor to the Periklean Propylaea. A stone inscription discovered on the Acropolis in 1897 decrees a new temple on the bastion, to be designed by Kallikrates, one of the architects of the Parthenon. The date of the Nike temple decree is much disputed but it was perhaps passed in the 430s. Stylistically, the sculptured frieze seems to date around 425–415 BC, so the construction may have been interrupted, as other Athenian building projects were, by the outbreak in 432/431 BC of the Peloponnesian War.[19]

101 The Nike temple seen from the north-west. A sculptured parapet ran around the top of the bastion.

102 A winged victory bending over to fix her sandal, from the Nike temple parapet. Athens, Acropolis Museum.

The dressed limestone facing of the bastion that we see today (fig. 101) bonds with the stonework below the southern wing of the Propylaea, which suggests that it was done around 437 BC during the commencement of work on the Propylaea itself.[20] The walls of the Nike temple bastion were raised by more than a metre and the enlarged floor area was re-surfaced. The level of this floor and the perimeter lines of the sanctuary were now orientated to correspond with those of the newly erected Propylaea. Access to the space thus created was either through the southern wing of the Propylaea or via a narrow, steep stair, which climbed the north face of the podium. Around the north, west and south perimeter of the sanctuary ran a marble parapet, about a metre high and measuring about 30 metres in total length.[21] The parapet frieze blocks sat upon the overhanging marble crown of the podium and were themselves capped by a crowning member. The style of the sculpture carved in the outer face of this parapet seems to represent the full flowering of the school that first gathered to work on the Parthenon and it has been judged later than the frieze that ran around the entablature of the Nike temple itself (fig. 102). The subject matter of the parapet frieze represents a similar scene on each of the three sides, showing Athena Nike seated on a rock, approached by winged Victories. Some of these lead cattle to sacrifice, while others are seen decorating military trophies hung with hoplite armour, naval equipment and Persian spoils. These are thought to symbolize a run of successful campaigns fought in the eastern Aegean and Hellespont between 411 and 407 BC by the Athenians mostly under the leadership of Alcibiades, the colourful Athenian general and statesman. A good proportion of the original frieze survives, albeit in fragments. It was also much copied in the later Hellenistic and Roman periods in the genre of so-called neo-Attic reliefs, and these copies assist in filling in some of the compositional gaps.[22]

The Nike temple was constructed out of Pentelic marble. The order is Ionic with four columns making porches at both the east and west ends. It is small, its stepped base measuring just 8.17 by 5.4 metres.[23] Simple in plan, there is no separate room at the back of the cella (opisthodomos), and the entrance into the cella was between two rectangular pillars standing between the ends of the long flank walls. The rich detailing of the architecture has strong affinity to the Ionic order of the Propylaea and that of the Erechtheum. The bases of the columns are of the Attic-Ionic type, a distinctive variant of the Ionic order that had been established on the eastern seaboard of the Aegean. The Nike temple bases comprise a reeded torus on a scotia, on a plain torus of unusually shallow depth. The profile of the column bases is repeated around the foot of the walls and in the bases of the door pillars. The column capitals are again distinctively Athenian and, although much smaller, are nearly identical in design with those of the Propylaea. Apart from their overall proportions, shared features include: the egg-profile moulding of the echinus; the double fillet along the edges of the bolster, the egg and dart moulding below and the bulbous eyes to the volutes.

The exquisite architectural detailing nicely frames the sculptured ornament. Little survives of the pediment sculpture.[24] The apex of the triangle being just over half a metre high, the scale was small with each piece dowelled individually to the base of the pediment. It is thought that a scene of battle between gods and giants filled the east pediment, while an Amazonomachy was represented in the west. The corners and apex of the pediments were crowned with acroteria, thought to have been of bronze. Remains of complex dowelling and the evidence of inscriptions suggest

103 Battle between Greeks and Orientals. Nike temple south frieze. British Museum.

104 Battle between Greeks. Nike temple west frieze. British Museum.

105 Assembly of gods. Nike temple east frieze (a block is missing on the right).

that at least one of the central acroteria was a Bellerophon and Chimaera, while the side ornaments were Victories.²⁵

A continuous frieze ran above the architrave on all four exterior sides (figs 103–5). Measuring some 0.45 metres high, it shows scenes of battle on the north, south and west sides, and a gathering of gods on the east.²⁶ The frieze is far from complete: the east side is best preserved with a loss of only some figures, especially towards the north end; all four blocks of the west frieze survive, divided between London and Athens; all the south frieze blocks also survive, although the order is disputed, and again they are divided between London and Athens; the fragmentary north frieze is the least well preserved with only one block surviving whole. The relief of the frieze is deep with much undercutting. The illusion of depth is assisted by an extraordinary amount of so-called piecing, where individual elements are made separately and attached with metal dowels. The composition of the east frieze allows the largely static forms of the gods to stand or sit in their own space with little overlapping of one on another. It is an arrangement of gods familiar from the statue base of the Athena Parthenos of the Parthenon, at least to judge from surviving fragmentary copies. Whereas there, however, the motive for the gathering is explicit, to preside over the birth of Pandora, here the purpose of the divine assembly is unclear. The centre is dominated by Zeus seated on a throne and facing his daughter Athena. A gap between these two may have been filled with the figure of Hephaistos. This possibility has prompted the suggestion that we see here the moment of the birth of Athena, who was released when Hephaistos with his axe cleft open the head of their father.²⁷

Other interpretations of the subject of the east frieze favour the idea that the appearance of the gods is more closely related to the battles raging on the other three sides. Here the compositional arrangement of figures is very different; the battle scenes are a series of tableaux arranged around a fallen or falling warrior. The use of overlapping elements is greater than in the east frieze, but again restrained, and the sculptors rely upon the twisting and turning of individual figures and their flying draperies to intensify the illusion of a drama in real space. The battle subjects appear not to be all one. While the north and west friezes show Greeks fighting Greeks, the south frieze shows Greeks pitched against figures in oriental costume. Some prefer a mythological explanation, where subjects might include the legendary Trojan War or the story of the

Seven against Thebes; others prefer to see the battles taking place in an historical context, where the figures in oriental dress would be the Persians at the Battle of Marathon, and the scenes of Greeks fighting Greeks would refer to the contemporary contest of the Peloponnesian War between Athens and Sparta.[28] The history of that war by Thucydides has been filleted to find individual battles or skirmishes that would fit both the iconography of the frieze and the date of the supposed carving of it in the late 420s. It might be argued in favour of the historical and contemporary scenario over the mythological that this would fit the pattern apparently provided by the Parthenon frieze, where an assembly of gods is likewise shown on the east frieze to preside over an event seemingly drawn from real life on the other three sides. The major difference is that, while the arts of peace are shown in the frieze of the Parthenon, on the Nike temple the subject was war.

ERECHTHEUM

On the north side of the Acropolis terrace, balancing the Parthenon to the south but smaller and very different in style, was built the temple we know today as the Erechtheum (fig. 106).[29] It stood on especially sacred ground, the latest of a series of shrines to mark the oldest and most important cult places of the city. Even as new, the Erechtheum took on the identity of the archaios neos, 'the venerable temple'. The foundations of the major predecessor can still be seen, where archaeologists have exposed them, just to the south and so close that in parts the south wall of the Erechtheum, including the Caryatid porch, rests on the foundations of its predecessor. This earlier temple is thought to have been destroyed by the Persians in 480 BC. After the defeat of the invaders, a smaller, makeshift successor appears to have been constructed on the site and for a while may have coexisted with the Erechtheum.

The most important cult object in the Erechtheum was the ancient statue of Athena Polias, goddess of the city. Unlike the colossal gold and ivory invention of Pheidias, this was a primitive, standing or very possibly seated image, carved from olive wood and so old that its origin was explained by its having fallen from the sky.[30] It was this statue, and not the goddess of the Parthenon, that was honoured by the Panathenaic festival and, in all other respects, represented the heart of Athenian religious life. Unlike the Parthenon, however, the Erechtheum was not the temple of a single honorand since, from possibly Mycenaean times, there had gathered around Athena a number of gods and heroes of the city. Notable among them was Erechtheus, protégé of the goddess and legendary early king of the city.[31] Their cult places were included in the temple precinct,

106 The Erechtheum viewed from the Parthenon. In the bottom left foreground are the remains of an archaic predecessor.

where they were described by Pausanias, but in such confusion that it is difficult to place them. As one scholar has remarked, 'it is often quite as necessary to explain Pausanias from the Erechtheum as the Erechtheum from Pausanias'.[32] Erechtheum is not the name the Athenians themselves used for the building we know. For them it was 'the temple in which the ancient statue is'.[33] The term Erechtheum appears only twice in ancient sources of the Roman period.[34] Because of this confusion and doubt, some believe that Erechtheus did not share this shrine with Athena at all, but occupied a separate building.[35] That would make it wrong to call the Ionic temple of the Acropolis by the name we know it. All things considered, however, the majority view remains that Erechtheus' shrine and that of Athena Polias were one and the same.

When exactly the building was begun is not known. It seems inconceivable that Perikles' administration, before his death in 429 BC, did not have a plan to provide a permanent replacement for the late-archaic predecessor destroyed by the Persians in 480 BC. There is no document, however, to show that the Erechtheum is a Periklean building. The evidence is the building itself, but we do not know enough of the work and signature style of Periklean architects such as Kallikrates and Mnesikles to justify their designation as the likely authors of the Erechtheum.[36] Nevertheless, for links between the temple and Mnesikles, one might point out that in both the Erechtheum and the Propylaea there is the same conception of a building in asymmetrical parts, compartmentalizing its various functions and assisting in the transmission of worshippers from one level of steeply rising ground to another. There are comparisons to be made also between the Erechtheum and the Nike temple. Both have building techniques in common, such as an unusual form of metal T-dowel used in the clamping of stone blocks together. In building refinements too there are comparisons to be made. Both shun the extensive curvature of 'straight' lines, such as we find in the Parthenon, but equally both exhibit a barely discernible inward lean of columns. This coupled with similarities in the intricate mouldings of the two suggests that, if not the same architect, then at least the same labour force was responsible for both temples.[37]

If the Erechtheum was not begun earlier, then a likely moment of opportunity and optimism is the brief period of Athenian prosperity that followed the so-called Peace of Nikias in 421 BC. Allowing time for sufficient moneys to accumulate in the exchequer, the year 419/418 BC may have seen the breaking of new ground.[38] The presiding Athenian general and statesman of the time was Nikias, a religious conservative, and the renewal of time-honoured cult places, including the home of the ancient goddess, must have appealed to him. The progress of the building did not run smooth. The war with Sparta interrupted the works and for a period the site appears to have been abandoned, and the temple left unfinished. The evidence for this has survived in a remarkable report compiled in the summer of 409 BC and carved into a marble stele, the greater part of which is now in the British Museum.[39] As with the Nike temple, so with the Erechtheum, the various stages of the building work are usually dated according to the ups and downs of Athenian fortunes in the Peloponnesian War. The major interruption was probably caused by the disastrous naval expedition that Athens sent against Sparta's ally Syracuse on Sicily in 415–412 BC. This low ebb in Athenian fortunes did not improve until its general Alcibiades' successes across the Aegean at Cyzicus and the Hellespont in 410/409 BC.

The report was drawn up by five commissioners, one of whom was an architect and another was secretary to the board. They were responsible for work to be carried out in the year 409/408 BC, and their report was an assessment of the situation they found following the delay. The first part describes the condition of the building with a summary of the height reached by the walls and an indication of what remained to be done, such as the fine-dressing of wall surfaces, the carving of mouldings and the fluting of columns. All of these operations we learn were done when the rough-cut members were already in place. The second part of the report provides an inventory of blocks lying around the site waiting to be placed, those prepared and those in the roughest state direct from the quarry.[40] In addition to the commissioners' report, fragments have survived of three sets of accounts of work actually carried out in the years 409–404 BC. The first account for 409/408 BC details work on the frieze,

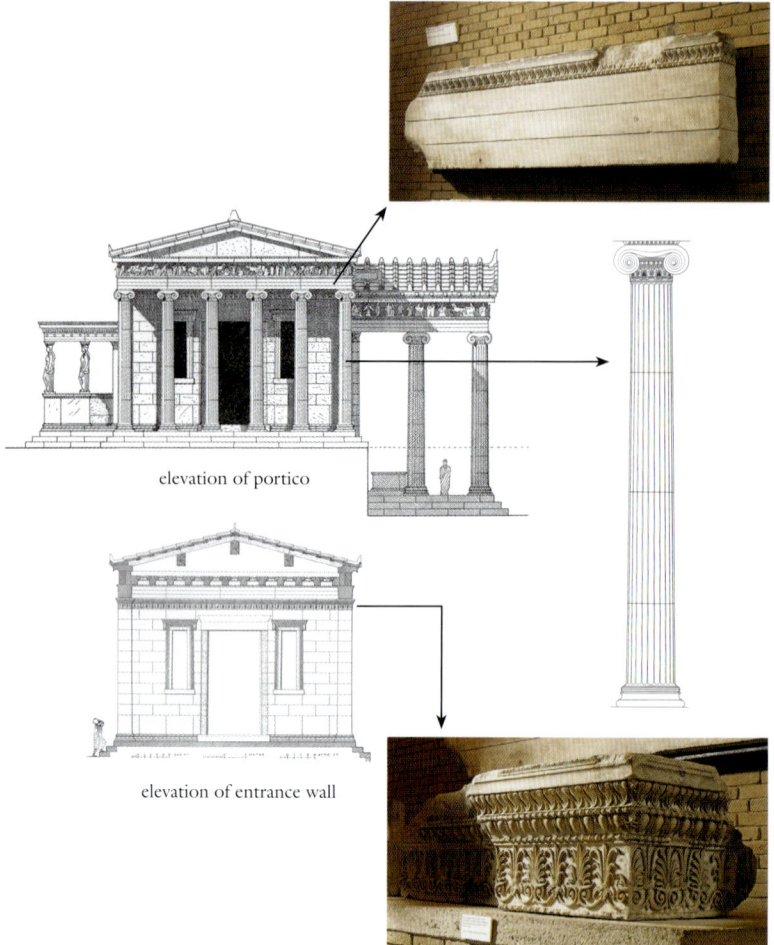

107 East elevation of the Erechtheum showing the locations of an Ionic column, a section of wall crown and a block of architrave in the British Museum. British Museum.

cornice and pediments and the manufacture of a wooden coffered ceiling.[41] The second for 408/407 BC includes records of payments for fluting the columns of the east porch and carving figures for the frieze.[42] The third set of accounts is less securely dated to 406/405 and 405/404.[43]

All of these inscriptions provide insight into the working practices of the skilled labour force. Let us, for example, take the reports of payments for the fluting of the columns of the east porch in the year 408/407 BC.[44] There are six columns in all and each was subjected to four processes carried out by a gang of up to five or seven men. As the work proceeded, each process became progressively more expensive than the last, adding up to a total expenditure of 350 drachmas per column or the equivalent of one working man's wage for a year. A column in the British Museum comes from the extreme north end of the row of six (fig. 107).[45] Either at this end of the row or at the south end – we do not know which – there stood an altar of the goddess Dione. The accounts number the columns in relation to this altar: 'The column by the altar; the second from the altar . . .'. The names of the workers responsible are given, and so we can say that the column in the British Museum was fluted by one of two gangs, led by either Laossos of the district of Alopeke or Theugenes of Piraeus. Their names are rare survivals of the identity of the usually anonymous masons of antiquity.

The Erechtheum has a unique design and prompted Vitruvius to remark that features normally found on the short end of a temple are transferred to the flanks, by which he meant the positioning of the two side porches, north and south.[46] The irregularity of the design can be partly explained by the slope of the ground it occupies, which drops by some 3 metres east to west. More to the point was the imperative to incorporate a number of traditional cult places.

108 Plan of the Erechtheum with its four doorways giving access to a variety of cult places.

THE EAST PORCH

The temple comprises a cella measuring 24 by 13 metres, with no fewer than four doorways, one on each side (fig. 108). Perhaps a helpful way to tour this potentially confusing building is to visit each of these doorways in turn. On the east a pedimented porch of six columns led to a door, through which the eastern chamber could be entered. Here almost certainly was placed the Polias statue facing the great sacrificial altar, which lay some distance to the east of the Erechtheum. Elgin removed the northernmost column of the east porch, which is now replaced by a cast. With it he took the corner block of architrave above.[47] A second fragment of architrave is also in the British Museum,[48] along with a pilaster capital and part of the wall crown (epicranitis) from the north corner of the east porch wall.[49]

THE NORTH PORCH

On the north side of the temple, at the western end, an even grander porch gave access to a smaller western chamber with a floor level much lower than that of the larger eastern chamber (fig. 109). There is material evidence to suggest that this western chamber may have been subdivided to form a complex of rooms, but the exact arrangement is difficult to reconstruct, owing to the destruction of the interior walls at the time of

109 The Erechtheum viewed from the north-west. The high walls of the garden of Pandrosos screen the basement of the west façade from view. Drawing P. Connolly.

the conversion of the Erechtheum into a church.[50] Certainly, the floor plan of the archaic temple to the south, which the Erechtheum is thought to have replaced, had such an arrangement of interior partitions. In the Erechtheum these spaces may have been designed to accommodate some of the many cult places that Pausanias saw.[51] According to him, there was a wooden statue of Hermes said to have been dedicated by Kekrops, the first king of Athens. Pausanias fails to mention that Kekrops' tomb was also housed in the temple. We know of it from the commissioners' report, where it is said to be located close to the porch of the maidens.[52] Four altars are mentioned by Pausanias, one to Zeus Hypsistos (Highest), one shared by Poseidon and Erechtheus, an altar to Hephaistos, and one to Boutes who, like Erechtheus, was a hero and founder of the Eteoboutadai family of priests. In addition there was a salt-water spring said to evoke the sound of the sea. Probably located in the westernmost chamber, it was later destroyed when the Christians enlarged the opening in the floor to create a water cistern.[53] In the south-east corner of the north porch was another opening in the paving, once framed by a small altar. Still visible in the rock below are three groups of fissures, enclosed in a small crypt incorporated into the masonry foundations.[54] In the marble coffered ceiling immediately above this spot, there was a curious opening through both ceiling and pedimented roof (figs 109–10).[55] It may plausibly be suggested that this aperture betokened the trajectory of the trident of Poseidon when that god struck the Acropolis rock in the struggle with his rival Athena for the land of Attica. As we saw in the last chapter, the story was represented in the west pediment of the Parthenon. Alternatively, it was perhaps thought to mark the spot where Zeus hurled his thunderbolt earthwards to bring to a close the contest that had already taken place

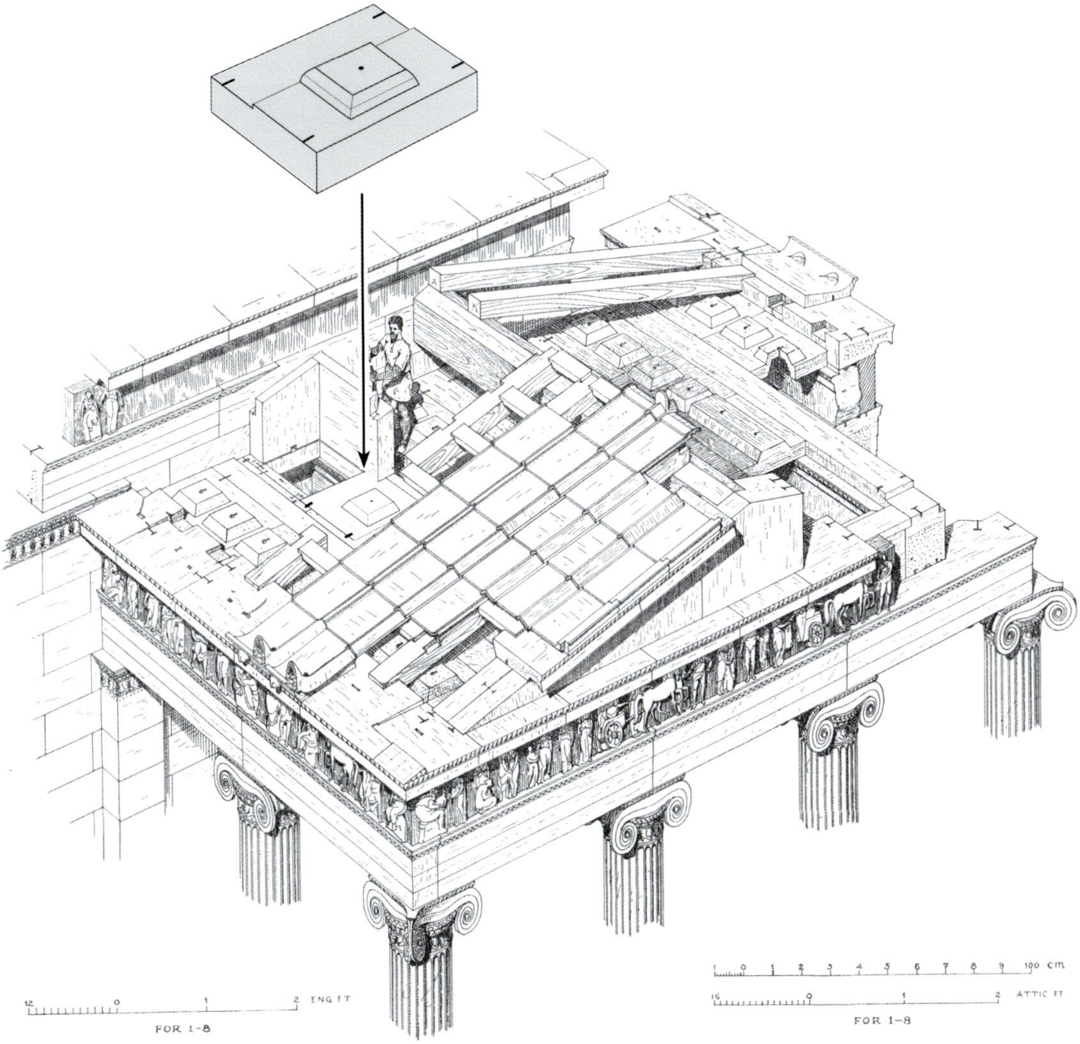

110 and 111 The roof arrangement of the Erechtheum's north porch included a rectangular aperture that symbolically marked the trajectory of Zeus' thunderbolt (or Poseidon's trident). One of the coffers placed next to one side of this opening is in the British Museum. The greater than usual width of one side of this coffer accommodated the end of one of the upright slabs of stone that framed the opening and connected with the raking roof beams above. British Museum. Drawing G.P. Stevens adapted by K. Morton.

between Athena and Poseidon. A coffer now in the British Museum comes from the ceiling of the north porch and was one of those that bordered the mysterious opening.[56] It was replaced by N. Balanos at the beginning of the twentieth century as part of his reconstruction of the north portico.

THE WEST DOOR

Our third doorway pierced the west wall of the western chamber. Exiting through it, one entered the walled garden-shrine of Pandrosos (figs 108–9), a daughter of the legendary king Kekrops and sister of Erechtheus.[57] Here was to be found the sacred olive tree of Athena, which was her gift to the Athenians in the contest with Poseidon. It was said to have been burned by the Persians, only to sprout green shoots upon their defeat. The western wall of the temple itself was divided into two levels. Below was a wall of plain ashlar masonry while, above this basement, there rose a grand façade of four engaged Ionic columns between pilasters (antae), and above these again ran an architrave and frieze, topped by a pediment to balance that of the east porch. Between the columns and pilasters of the west wall we now see five windows. These are a modern reconstruction of the windows let into the west wall as part of a renovation of the temple in the last quarter of the first century BC.[58] This renovation was part of a major overhaul of the temple carried out in the reign of the emperor Augustus following a catastrophic fire that gutted the interior, badly affecting the surfaces of the walls and damaging especially the west side, necessitating extensive repairs. The workmanship of these repairs closely resembles that of the round temple of Roma and Augustus that was erected around 20/19 BC, immediately to the east of the Parthenon. A piece of cornice from the Erechtheum was found during excavation of the foundations of this Roman building.[59] The decorated necking of a column in the British Museum comes from the Roma and Augustus temple and eloquently demonstrates the debt its unknown architect owed to the earlier temple in a deliberate attempt to link one to the other (fig. 112).[60] The Roman temple commemorated Augustus' victory over the Parthians, echoing the Athenians' own victory over their eastern enemies, the Persians. This thematic link nicely illustrates the many connections to be found between the monuments of the Acropolis, in both form and meaning.[61]

112 Necking of a column from the temple of Roma and Augustus. Its ornament was copied from that of the Erechtheum. British Museum.

Returning to the western façade of the Erechtheum and viewing it as it stands today, we may think that it has a very peculiar and unbalanced appearance, inharmoniously resembling three separate buildings, jammed close up against each other. There is the great northern porch on the left flank and, on the right flank, the diminutive Caryatid porch; while, in between and at yet another level, there stands the central, columned part, raised awkwardly on the plain ashlar of the basement. It must be remembered, however, that this lower level was not meant to be seen, at least from a distance, but was once masked by the western wall and shrine building of the sanctuary of Pandrosos. Further west still, there was the terrace wall, against which Pheidias' colossal bronze Athena Promachos (fighter) stood and drew the eye of those entering the Acropolis through the Propylaea. Altogether, it is clear that the west front of the Erechtheum was not intended, as now, to be fully exposed to view. Much of it was screened off, and its mouse-hole of a doorway is not to be compared with the grand porches of the north and east sides. It was without architectural pretension and served as a back entrance linking the Erechtheum with the adjoining garden of Pandrosos.

113 The Caryatid porch. Drawing G.P. Stevens.

THE CARYATID PORCH

Even less conspicuous was a fourth external entrance, this time in the south wall of the temple and accessed through the short east side of the Caryatid porch (fig. 113).[62] So inconspicuous is it and so uncomfortable of access that it could never have been in general use. The porch itself is the most distinctive feature of this unusual temple.[63] It comprises six girls, supporting an entablature and a coffered ceiling, and standing on a marble podium. It was almost complete in 409 BC: 'On the Porch adjoining the precinct of Kekrops the upper surfaces of three of the ceiling blocks over the maidens, thirteen feet long, five feet wide, needed to be dressed. The rosettes on the epistyle needed to be carved . . .'[64] Those rosettes never were carved and they remain today as the plain disks that the commissioners saw in 409. Their report, which refers to them simply as korai,

114 Caryatid from the south porch of the Erechtheum. Her stately pose seems inspired by the girls of the Parthenon's east frieze. British Museum.

'girls', demonstrate that the Caryatids were already carved and in place by 409 BC. How many years they were made before that depends upon when we place the start of the building project. It has often been said that the Caryatids echo in appearance the girls processing in the east frieze of the Parthenon, who are likely to have been carved between 438 and 432 BC. Because they are apparently in the Pheidian tradition, the Caryatids have been associated with the workshops of his pupils Alkamenes and Agorakritos. Certainly they bear a striking resemblance to Alkamenes' statue of Prokne and Itys in the Acropolis Museum, dated c. 430–420 BC.[65] Four of the girls stood in a line, with one more behind each end figure, echoing the number and arrangement of columns in the north porch. As in earlier uses of Caryatids, such as in the late-archaic Knidian and Siphnian treasuries at Delphi, the human figures stand in place of columns. This purpose determines their pose: the two outer figures support their body weight on the outer leg, so as to present a straighter, more architectural line than the relaxed inner leg. The figure immediately adjacent and that standing behind both do the same, with the result that three are posed one way, and three another, in mirror image.[66]

The Caryatid in the British Museum stood second from the west (fig. 114).[67] Like her sisters, one of her hands clutched her drapery, while the other, now lost, may have held some offering vessel. She wears the peplos form of tunic with a shoulder mantle hanging behind. Her face is rounded with full cheeks. The long, thick hair is braided around the head with a fall down her back. Early Caryatids connect with the entablature they support by means of the kalathos or basket they carry on their heads. Those of the Erechtheum bear a cushion supporting a moulding, carved with bead and reel and an egg and dart motif, and crowned by a further square moulding.

Elgin no doubt took the best preserved Caryatid and so saved her from the fate that befell the others. They deteriorated on the building and there suffered, especially in the later decades of the twentieth century, from the deleterious effects of weathering and city pollution. At last in the 1970s, they too were removed to the Acropolis Museum. Casts now occupy their places on the building itself.⁶⁸

In addition to its Caryatids, the Erechtheum bore other figured sculpture in the form of a frieze that ran around the outside (fig. 115).⁶⁹ This, unusually, comprised a band of dark blue-grey limestone from the region of nearby Eleusis. The blocks measure 0.617 metres high, except around the north porch, where they measure 0.683 metres. The frieze was sculptured, not in the usual way with figures carved out of the same block, but by cutting them separately in white marble and then attaching them individually with metal dowels. This was the method used for decorating statue bases in temples, as in the case of that of the Hephaesteum, made probably between 421 and 415 BC.⁷⁰ The blocks of the Hephaesteum's statue base were the same Eleusinian limestone and one of them has holes for fixing figures in relief. Embellished with touches of colour and gilding, the figures will have contrasted pleasingly against their dark ground. Interestingly, the mythological subject of the base in the Hepahaesteum was the birth of Erechtheus. No doubt the use of Eleusinian limestone both on the Erechtheum frieze and on statue bases was intended to simulate the painted blue ground of architectural friezes.

115 A girl in a belted peplos attributed to the sculptured frieze of the Erechtheum. Sir John Soane's Museum, London.

Fragments of over a hundred figures survive from the Erechtheum frieze. Some are single figures, standing or seated, while others are coupled with an object – armour or an altar – or with a horse or horses. No figure can be securely assigned to any one position in the frieze, and therefore no sequence can be reconstructed. What is more, although the subject (or subjects) of the frieze is assumed to be mythological, and more than half the fragments can be identified as being from female figures, no single figure can be identified for certain with a known mythical person. It is assumed by many that episodes from the life of Erechtheus are featured, but these cannot be confirmed. Nor, tantalizingly, do the descriptions of the inscribed accounts of 408/407 help for, as the following extract demonstrates, the figures are referred to only in the most general of terms:

> Phyromachos of Kephisia
> the youth beside the breast-plate, 60 drachmas
>
> Praxias, living in Melite,
> the horse and the man appearing behind it and striking its flank,
> 120 drachmas
>
> Antiphanes of Kerameis, the chariot and the youth and the two
> horses being harnessed, 240 drachmas.[71]

Although they may not help with the decipherment of the subject matter, these accounts do tell us exactly when the frieze was carved, the names of those who carved it and the amounts that they were paid. As in the case of other skilled labour, the going rate seems to have been a drachma a day. That applied both to citizens, such as Phyromachos, and to foreign workers or metics who were resident in the city, such as Praxias, and also to slaves. Single figures cost 60 drachmas, while pairs of figures (man and horse) took twice as long and so doubled the cost.

The Erechtheum was not so dramatic as the Parthenon in its sculptured ornament but it was richer in its non-figured decoration. The floral ornament of the Erechtheum has been much admired for its elegance and imitated in numerous neoclassical buildings. It displays great variety, notably in the form of the flowers and tendrils. Altogether nine different versions have been identified in different positions on the building.

116 Wall crown (epicranitis) carved with an alternating lotus and palmette decoration. Probably from the east end of the south wall. British Museum.

The simplest is that of the epicranitis, the band running around the top of the north, south and east cella walls (fig. 116). Three blocks of this moulding preserved in the British Museum,[72] together with one from the collection of the traveller-architect Haller von Hallerstein in Munich, are all thought to come from the east end of the south wall. They seem to have been in place at the time of the commissioners' report of 409 BC.[73]

CONCLUSION

When painted and, at least in the case of the columns, inlaid with glass, the decoration of the Erechtheum contributed to the exquisiteness of its Ionic order, making an elegant contrast with the Doric simplicity of the Parthenon.[74] The

Parthenon had its own Ionic and perhaps even pioneering Corinthian features,[75] but these were concealed within the peristyle or cella walls and did not show on the exterior. The Erechtheum made no such secret of its eccentricities. Multi-faceted in design, it was no less complex in its cults. Its recesses abounded in signs of gods and heroes, protective deities and legendary kings of the city. The Parthenon and the colossus it housed were showpieces of Perikles' new Athens. Less awesome, but holier by far, was the Erechtheum and its primitive wooden idols, mysterious spring of salt water, marks in the rock, hole in the ceiling and other tokens of divine presence.

117 Drawing by T.L. Donaldson (1795–1885) showing coloured glass beads set into the plait moulding of one of the Erechtheum column capitals. British Museum.

From around 450 BC, the Acropolis of Athens was developed as a showpiece of Athenian culture at the height of the city's political economic and military power. The Parthenon, Propylaea, Nike temple and Erechtheum are tangible and eloquent reminders of a golden age, in which Athens not only became the principal Greek city but also commanded a maritime empire that bonded together, albeit in a fragile and intermittent union, its allies among the Greek cities of southern Italy and those of East Greece. Athenian architects devised new distinctive forms of the Ionic order, which in the case of the Parthenon and Propylaea were married with Doric into highly refined hybrid structures crafted with an extraordinary degree of skill. In the Nike temple and Erechtheum, the Ionic order reached an acme of jewel-like perfection that was to have lasting influence and, in the Hellenistic and Roman periods, it was the Attic form of the Ionic order that was to prevail (fig. 117). The Greek mainland was at first slow to respond to the new architecture, and the temple of Apollo at Bassai, designed by one of the architects of the Parthenon, was a rare instance of a major temple being erected outside Athens during the Peloponnesian War.

Chapter Six

The Temple of Apollo Epikourios at Bassai

It was perhaps a welcome escape from war-stricken Athens and the plague that killed Perikles in 429 BC when Iktinos, one of the architects of the Parthenon, accepted a commission that took him out of the city. Pausanias says that Iktinos designed the temple of Apollo Epikourios (the Helper) at Bassai, a sanctuary situated in the mountains of south-west Arcadia in the Greek Peloponnese.[1] The temple was highly unusual: externally it was conventional Doric with six sculptured metopes in each of its two porches, but inside it had Ionic colonnades, crowned by an architrave and continuous frieze. More bizarre still, a rear chamber was screened from the main room by one or more Corinthian columns. The originality of this design is typical of the daring and sophistication of the architect, one of the stars of Athens' own building programme, whose artful fusion of Doric and Ionic orders was one of the peculiar features of the Parthenon. Much of what appears original, however, may have been determined by the design of the Bassai temple's archaic predecessor.

Bassai means 'wooded glens', and the name reflects the rural nature of the sanctuary site, which was owned by the nearby town of Phigaleia. The remoteness and beauty of Bassai reflects the Greek idea that gods were present in nature (figs 118 and 120). A temple in the mountains of Arcadia both complemented and concentrated the sense given by the landscape of a divine presence. The commission to adorn an exposed ridge on the slopes of Mount Kotilion in this remote region of Greece was very different from that of the Parthenon in the heart of the metropolis of Athens. And yet, its foundation and progress seem directly linked to events in Athens. Pausanias explains that Apollo's epithet 'Epikourios' was given to the god for the help he gave, not only to Athenians in delivering them from the plague, but also to the Arcadians who were similarly affected. Thucydides, however, the historian of the Peloponnesian War that brought the plague about, says explicitly that it never reached the Peloponnese.[2] Against Pausanias, therefore, it may be argued that the divine epithet originates in the name 'Epikouroi', which Arcadian mercenaries assigned to themselves.[3] As 'helpers' they had not only served Athens but nearer home had traditionally supported their neighbours the Messenians.

They frequently revolted against their oppressors, the Spartans, and periodically sought refuge in Arcadian territory. The Messenians may have been major participants in the Bassai cult of Apollo.[4]

In 421 BC, Athens negotiated a peace in its own war with Sparta and, as we saw in Chapter Five, the building of the Erechtheum on the Athenian Acropolis is thought to have begun shortly afterwards. The break in hostilities with Athens released Spartan fighting power, which was newly directed against Arcadia. Phigaleia was sacked in 421 BC, and the building of the Apollo temple was probably interrupted until around 415.[5] It was in that year that war between Athens and Sparta was resumed and, as a consequence, the construction of the Erechtheum was itself halted. Thus the great city temple on the Athenian Acropolis and the country shrine in the mountains of Arcadia were differently affected by the volatile fortunes of war with a common enemy, Sparta.

The temple of Apollo did not stand alone at Bassai. Pausanias' testimony and surviving remains attest to the fact that the site was part of a sacred landscape extending to the peak of Mount Kotilion, where in a shallow depression was a sanctuary of Artemis and other deities, including Aphrodite. The original cult of Apollo was that of so-called Apollo Bassitas, about which little is known. The association with the mercenaries of Arcadia introduced the epithet 'Epikourios' at a later date, but the god appears to have had a military importance from the beginning, and some of the earliest finds from the area are miniature shields and other arms and armour

118 The temple seen from the north-east. Watercolour drawing by John Foster, architect (1787–1846). British Museum.

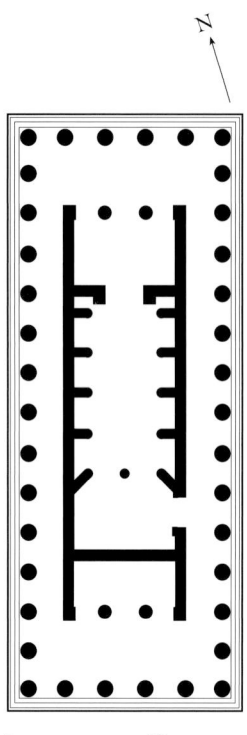

119 Plan of the Bassai temple with its unusual north–south axis dictated by the lie of the land along a rocky spur of Mount Kotilion. The rather narrow platform with fifteen columns along the flanks and six at the front and back gave the Bassai temple an archaic look.

dating from the early seventh century BC. Such objects are associated with, in all, four temples of Apollo, which have been dated to around 625 BC (Apollo I), around 575 (II), around 500 (III) and 429–400 BC (IV).[6]

The archaic cult was long known through the small votive objects discovered at the site dating from the seventh and sixth centuries BC, principally those excavated in 1908 by Nikolaos Kourouniotes.[7] Confirmation of the earliest temple itself, however, was established only in 1970 by the excavation of Nikolaos Yalouris.[8] Apollo I was situated immediately to the south of the Classical temple. Like the Classical temple, it had two chambers. The principal one was at the front and the lesser one at the rear. It had mud-brick walls, supported on stone socles, and a great roof of terracotta tiles. Antefixes in the same material were decorated with moulded sphinxes, each with a fish in its mouth. Interestingly, the same moulds were used to produce antefixes for the temple of Artemis, constructed at about the same time as the first Apollo temple.[9] Around 575 BC, the Apollo temple received a new roof and the side walls were lengthened to create a rear chamber. This phase is identified as Apollo II.[10] The identity of Apollo III is established only through the dressed masonry blocks that were reused in the foundations of Apollo IV, and it is not known where this temple once stood.[11]

There seems to have been no exterior colonnade in the pre-Classical temple, but the long thin plan of the building constructed immediately to the south of the Classical one determined the elongated plan of the temple that we know (fig. 119). This allowed there to be six columns along the short sides, but fifteen along the long, giving the temple an archaic appearance that is out of keeping with its Classical date. Also predetermined by its archaic predecessor was the rear room with its side entrance. Even the seemingly original interior colonnade of the Classical temple seems to have been anticipated in the internal arrangement of columns.[12]

DISCOVERY, STUDY AND CONSERVATION

'The temple of Apollo at Bassae stands in lonely isolation against the slopes of Mount Kotilion within the wild uplands of southwest Arcadia. It overlooks Messenia and surveys a panorama of nearby mountain peaks, coastal plains, and in the middle, the sea and full mountain ranges spreading into the far distance . . .'[13] Thus the archaeologist and architectural historian Fred Cooper, who has made a life's work of studying the Apollo temple, evokes its setting. As so often in this book, it is impossible to understand the history of the monument, without mention of those responsible for compiling that history. Cooper's poetic description is the product of familiar acquaintance, acquired over many seasons of work at the site. He stands in a long line of scholars who have studied the temple since its discovery in 1765 by Joachim Bocher who, after his first visit to the region, returned only to disappear in the untamed wilderness of the Arcadian mountains.[14] In 1812, a group of European architects and other travellers and adventurers assembled at the temple in a campaign to extract twenty-three sculpted blocks of frieze from its ruins. Some of them had already been involved in the discovery, excavation in 1811 and subsequent sale to Munich of the pediment sculpture from the temple of Aphaia on Aegina. The team at Bassai included the Estonian Baron Otto Magnus von Stackelberg and the Dane Peter Oluf Brønsted. Some of the group became owners of the frieze and other sculptures and architectural pieces, sold to the British Museum in 1814.[15] The chief scholars among them were Haller von Hallerstein and Charles Cockerell, youthful architects of the kind that pioneered the modern understanding of Classical buildings. The German died early, and it was left to Cockerell to publish the results of their labours, belatedly in a folio volume that coupled the Bassai temple with Aegina in the discovery of which Cockerell was also

120 The temple seen from the north-west. The table top of Mount Ithome rears out of the plains of Messenia in the distance. Watercolour drawing by John Foster, architect (1787–1846). British Museum.

intimately involved.[16] For his study, Cockerell had access to a copy of a manuscript by Haller, now in the British Museum.[17] After Cockerell, the next to use the Haller manuscript was the American scholar W.B. Dinsmoor, who made a full but largely unpublished study of the temple.[18] Others whose work on the building would remain incomplete include Peter and G.U.S. Corbett. The former was especially interested in the sculptures and, in particular, in the frieze. His proposed arrangement of the blocks, which is now the one exhibited in the British Museum, contradicted that of Dinsmoor and is at odds with that of Cooper and his co-worker Brian Madigan.[19]

Besides study of the remains that survive above ground, new light was shed on the temple and its history by a series of excavations from 1902 to 1908.[20] At this time the temple underwent substantial reconstruction. It had been pulled apart in the Christian era and left as a ruined heap of masonry on the temple floor by men looking for metal clamps that held the blocks together. The walls were rebuilt and column drums reassembled. There remained, however, many other pieces scattered around the building that had not been incorporated in the reconstruction. From 1970, Cooper and his assistants therefore set about drawing every stone, whether in place on the building or lying on the ground, or preserved in museums.[21] Concern was growing meanwhile for the long-term safety of the monument, vulnerable as it is to all kinds of weather in a mountain climate. Particularly worrying is the stability of the foundations, which rest ultimately on bedrock, but are cushioned with a layer of clay and sand, some 5 to 20 centimetres deep, serving as an anti-seismic shock-absorber.[22] Rain seeping into the foundations and washing this layer away

121 The tent protecting the temple from weather.

contributes to their instability. Other dangers include attack by the extreme frosts of the high altitude, causing the limestone to shale. In order to combat these effects, the temple has been enclosed in a white tent, and the stones scattered around it are protected by polythene sheets (fig. 121). The columns and walls have been trussed with wooden ties to combat especially the outward inclination of the columns. There is a difference of opinion about the cause of the tendency of the columns to lean. It has been argued that their shift is historical and non-progressive, while others attribute it to the current volatility of the foundations.[23] The future of the temple remains uncertain.[24]

ARCHITECTURE

The solid geometry of the Classical temple of Apollo Epikourios, with its regular artificial shapes and shining marble roof, perfectly complemented the rugged natural landscape of the surrounding mountains. Visible from a great distance, the temple and its setting epitomize the poetic contrast of art and nature that is so often a feature of the design and location of Greek temples. The temple itself had its own set of contrasts in the bands of different stones and their painted decoration. The principal contrast was between the glistening white of the imported marble and the grey-blue of the local limestone.[25] These stones took on their own contrasting colours according to the time of the day. So, as one commentator observes, 'The limestone is gray, very light in full sun, tending to lavender in the half shadow and to purple-blue in the deep shadows . . .'[26] The use of marble was restricted to the roof, the sculptured decoration, the capitals of the interior and the ceiling coffers of the front porch.

Unlike the Parthenon, there were no sculptures in the pediments[27] and none of the architectural refinements, such as upward curvature of the platform or stylobate, inward inclination of columns and thickened corner columns.[28] The discovery of a base for a floral ornament (acroterion) to adorn a corner of one of the pediments shows that attempts to reconstruct human, female figures at the apex and corners of the pediments are wrong.[29] The sloping frame or sima (fig. 122b) of the pediment was, however, richly carved (and probably painted) with thirteen-petal palmettes that alternated with five-leaf lotuses, as seen in the decorated face of two sima blocks in the British Museum.[30] A similar palmette was featured in the antefixes, an ornamental device that marked the ends of the lowest cover tiles of the roof (fig. 122c). The antefixes were carved in low relief and almost certainly painted. They were carved of a piece with the cover tile, which extended behind, together with the flat pan tile.[31] The roof ridge was decorated with a series of antefix-like mouldings

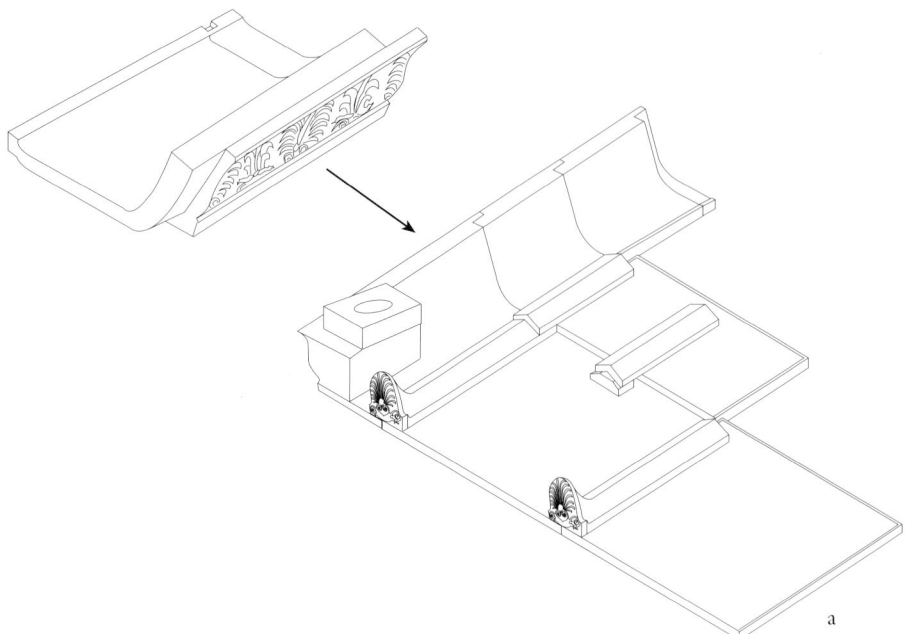

122 Elements of the marble roof: (a) the roof tiles and their antefixes with a back view of the raking sima; (b) two segments of the raking sima, British Museum; (c) marble antefix. Now broken away, it was carved of a piece with a tile. British Museum.

carved of a piece with some of the ridge tiles. The best preserved fragment is that in the British Museum. It is plain and carved rough but was perhaps intended to be finished with a carved or painted palmette.[32] Many reconstructions of the temple roof show it with a large opening to the sky (hypaethron), following the reconstruction of Cockerell, which was done at a time when historians of Greek architecture were more inclined to reconstruct Greek temples without continuous roofs.[33]

The distinctive features of the interior are the engaged colonnade and the continuous frieze. At Bassai the colonnade employed a variety of Ionic forms,[34] but most singular was the inclusion of a feature that here perhaps made its first appearance in Greek architecture. At the back of the principal chamber and marking the central point in the opening between it and the smaller room behind there was a freestanding column crowned with a Corinthian capital.[35] This was seen and recorded by the travellers who first excavated the temple. Unfortunately, they did not bring the capital with them, and it was smashed shortly after their departure (fig. 123). Fragments of it have surfaced in subsequent excavations. Its importance lies in its being one of the very earliest examples of the Corinthian order, and it may have been an Iktinian invention. There is, for example, a

123 Engraving of the temple when first cleared, looking south. The Corinthian capital is shown resting on a column stump with a rifle leaning against it on the left.

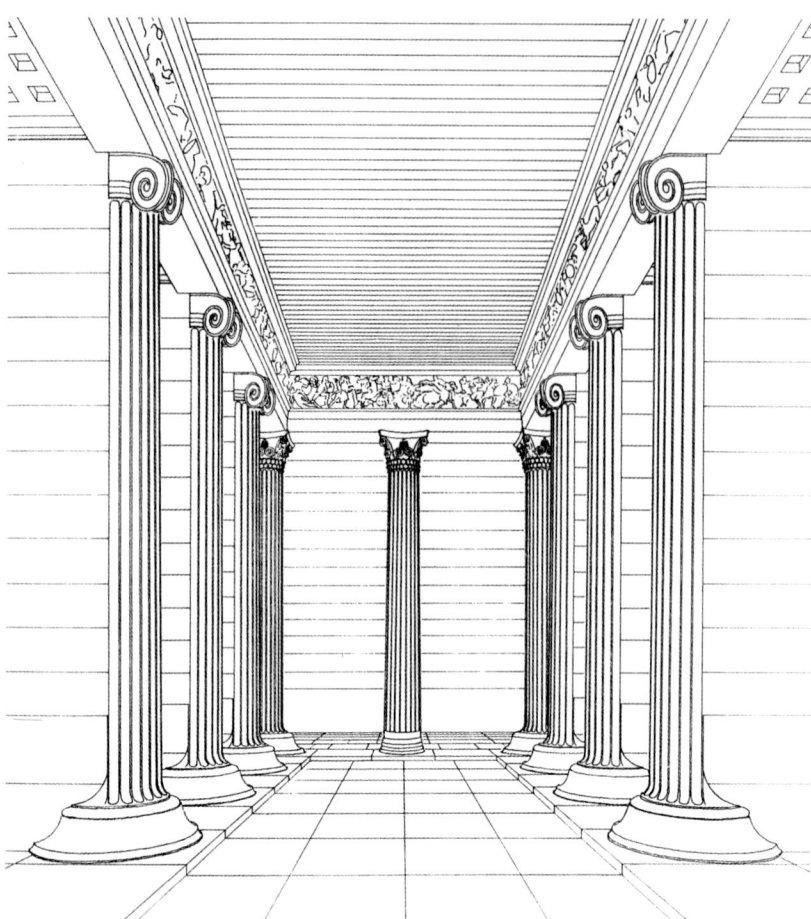

124 Temple interior reconstructed. Some restore three Corinthian capitals, as here, while others prefer to flank a central Corinthian column with two Ionic capitals. Drawing A. Mallwitz.

suggestion that the four columns that once supported the ceiling of the lesser room of the Parthenon were crowned with Corinthian capitals.[36] As we saw in Chapter One, however, there is also Vitruvius' explanation of the invention of the Corinthian order by the Athenian sculptor Kallimachos, inspired during a visit to Corinth.[37]

The Corinthian column was flanked by two other half-columns (fig. 124). These were engaged with spur walls set at an angle to the axis of the building.[38] The order of the capitals here is unknown and, while Cooper suggests Ionic, others would restore two further Corinthian capitals. The side walls were each lined with a further four half-columns, each one capped by a marble Ionic capital of a unique, hump-back design, and standing on Attic-Ionic bases.[39] The column shafts were again attached to spur walls. Such engaged columns were unusual in Classical Greek temples. Rare examples include the west front of the late-fifth-century Erechtheum in Athens and the temple of Athena Alea at Tegea in the Peloponnese (*c.* 360 BC), a building that shows the influence of Bassai.[40]

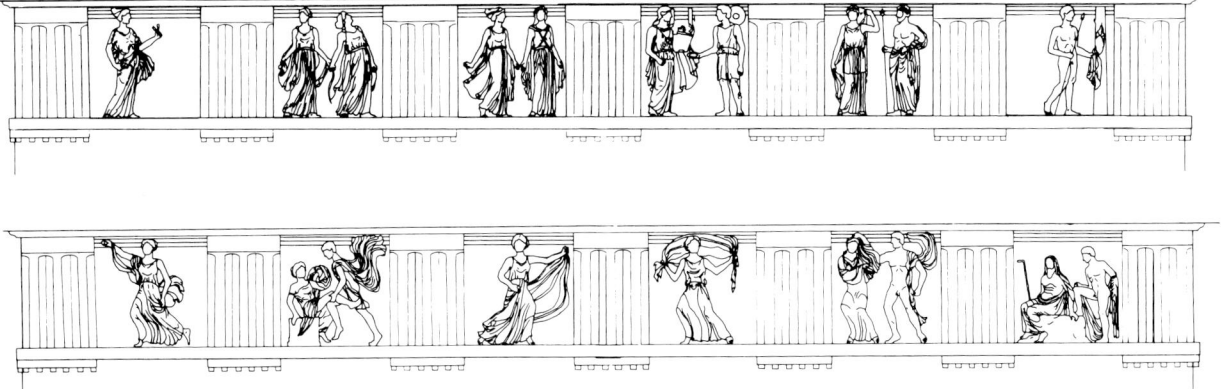

125 and 126 The north and south porch metopes restored by Brian Madigan.

METOPES

The temple had three sculptured friezes: the Ionic continuous frieze inside and two outside Doric friezes, one over the north porch columns, the other over the south porch (figs 125–6), and each comprising six metopes with alternating triglyphs. The metopes survive in fragments only and have been studied by the American scholar Brian Madigan.[41] Working from 1978 as part of Fred Cooper's team, he identified in the British Museum, in the National Museum in Copenhagen and in the National Museum in Athens a total of 127 fragments. Building upon the work of previous scholars, he reconstructed twelve impressive pictures on paper, each comprising one or two figures in a frame, which measures around 80 centimetres high.[42] The little evidence there is has been scrutinized to determine the likelihood of a metope belonging to the south or the north porch.[43] Work in the British Museum has since continued on the sculptures and, inevitably in such a painstaking task, some fragments that are assigned to separate metopes by Madigan have been found to join together and must therefore belong to the same metope and not to two different ones. Moreover, a number of previously unidentified fragments have been located both in the British Museum's own reserves and in the depot at the site of Bassai itself.[44] In addition, it has been suggested that a relief fragment in New York, carved with a figure of Victory, is part of a previously unrecognized metope from Bassai.[45]

The assignment of fragments to the north or south side of the temple, the attempt at their reconstruction and the identification of the mythical figures represented in the fragments are all part of the same endeavour to retrieve a pictorial story from broken and disjointed parts. It has been suggested that some of the many fragments showing females in flying draperies, including that of the girl with a hand gripping her neck (fig. 127), come from a composition in the south porch that showed the rape

127 Metope fragment showing a girl in wind-blown drapery. The fingers of a disembodied hand seem to clutch her neck and may suggest violence. British Museum.

128 Rape of the daughters of Leukippos by Castor and Pollux depicted on a red-figured water-jar by the Meidias Painter, c. 410 BC. British Museum.

of the daughters of Leukippos.⁴⁶ The subject was certainly current in contemporary art, as found on the red-figured water-jar (hydria) by the Meidias Painter in the British Museum (fig. 128).⁴⁷ It had, moreover, a particular resonance for the local Arcadians, since the incident took place in the nearby territory of Messenia. The victims of the rape by Castor and Pollux, twin sons of Zeus, were Hilaira and Phoibe, daughters of the Messenian king. The twins were important figures in Spartan cult, and to Arcadians the rape may have been seen as an allegory of Spartan violence against the Messenian struggle for political independence. A specific link between Apollo and the Leukippidai is to be found in the tradition that the god was their divine father, and Apollo is seen with them in other representations of the rape.⁴⁸ Their mortal father is perhaps to be found in the fragment of a torso of an older man (fig. 129).

If the assignment of a kithara-player to the north porch is right (fig. 130), then the subject of the north metopes may revolve around this musician.⁴⁹ Apollo was the god of the temple and of music, and he has been identified with this figure, who wears a fox-fur cap (alopekis) and the head of a gorgon on his breast and who plays the harp-like instrument known as

129 Torso of a bearded and veiled old man. British Museum.

130 Apollo? wears an animal-skin hat and holds a kithara, a stringed musical instrument. British Museum.

131 A girl dancer holds krotala (castanets). British Museum.

a kithara.[50] The alopekis hat, which is associated in Athens at this time with the inhabitants of Thrace, north of Greece, was not the standard headgear of the god. On the north side of the Bassai temple, the hat is thought to betoken Apollo's sojourn and, here, his return from the northern lands of the Hyperboreans, peoples whose territory was so remote that they were said to live beyond even the origin of the north wind. According to myth, immediately after his birth on the sacred island of Delos, Apollo was carried by swans to spend a year on the northern margins of the world. On a vase in the British Museum, he is shown riding a griffin home to Delphi, where he is greeted by his sister Artemis.[51] This is a very different rendering of the myth from that of the Bassai metopes, and there is much room for doubting the identification of the figure we see there.

If the person with the kithara in the Bassai metope fragment is not Apollo, then the mythical musician Orpheus is the obvious alternative. His death at the hands of the frenzied women of Thrace was a popular myth and one that inspired a number of vase-paintings.[52] However, the females of the Bassai metopes, to judge at least from the hand of one of them holding castanets (fig. 131), were not so much in the mood for murder as for dancing. Apollo is commonly accompanied in art and myth by a retinue of nymphs. Who better, then, to attend the god in the wooded glens of Arcadia than tree-nymphs or Dryads?[53] Building one hypothesis upon another, the trunk of a tree in one metope fragment may refer to them, or their sisters, the Hamadryads, nymphs who were coeval with the trees they occupied. Arkas, the eponymous hero of Arcadia, himself the son of the nymph Kallisto, married a tree-nymph. We may seek Arkas among the surviving fragments of males, but who is to say in which one?

There is little certainty in any of this, but we could perhaps argue that one of the two sets of metopes represented the nymphs, who abound in Arcadian lore. We may see them as the dancing retinue of Apollo, or the hand at the throat may indicate the ravishing of fantasy-females in the Arcadian shepherd imagination. It seems almost pointless to speculate, but out of the same fragments that have been used to conjure the rape of Leukippos' daughters, one could as easily invent the unrequited lust of Pan – an Arcadian figure if ever there was one – for the Arcadian nymph Syrinx. Arcadian Pitys fled Pan and was turned into a pine tree, singing out her tragic story when the wind sighed through its branches. Her fate brings to mind that of another more famous Arcadian nymph, Daphne, victim of Apollo's lust. Letting the imagination run wild, it could be argued that a fragment apparently showing drapery hanging on a tree is in fact part of a scene showing the metamorphosis of girl into tree.[54]

The date of the metopes is, of course, contested. The outer limits would seem to be 429–400 BC. Comparison can be made with the figures of the Erechtheum frieze, and the carving of the Bassai metopes can plausibly be placed in the last decade of the fifth century.[55]

THE IONIC FRIEZE

All twenty-three blocks of the interior frieze survive more or less intact: ten show a battle between human Lapiths and the part-man, part-horse race of Centaurs, calling to mind the south metopes of the Parthenon; twelve show a battle between Amazons and Greeks, the same subject as the west metopes of the Parthenon; and a single block shows Apollo and his sister Artemis in a stag-drawn chariot (fig. 132).[56] The frieze measures 64 centimetres high and comprises a series of rectangular slabs of varying lengths. Each one presents a picture which is largely contained within its own limits, and with very little of the image carried over from one block to another, such as we find in the north and south sides of the Parthenon frieze.

The relief is high, and the design and execution of the lunging, twisting, falling and fallen figures exhibits many virtuoso flourishes. Especially memorable is the drapery, now swirling in the turbulent air, now falling liquid-like, now vaporous and transparent revealing the human form beneath, now stretched tight in a stack of parallel folds. For all their apparent spontaneity and inventiveness, many of these compositions can

132 Apollo, the archer and god of the temple, and his sister Artemis ride in a chariot drawn by deer. The inconspicuous and awkward location of this block in the north-west corner of the temple suggests that the frieze blocks were not installed as intended. British Museum.

133 The imposing figures of Herakles and the Amazon queen, Hippolyte, dominated the south frieze facing the north entrance. Their composition in crossing diagonals is reminiscent of Athena and Poseidon in the west pediment of the Parthenon. Compare fig. 78. British Museum.

134 Kaineus forced into the ground by Centaurs. Once a Lapith girl loved by Poseidon, Kaineus asked the god to change her into an invulnerable youth. Here Centaurs pile rocks onto the hero's shield. British Museum.

135 The composition of Kaineus in fig. 134 is reused to represent a Greek warrior fallen at the mercy of an Amazon. Compare also the fallen warrior of the larger podium frieze in Chapter Eight, fig. 183. British Museum.

be shown, on comparison with contemporary Athenian art, to be formulaic and suggestive of a pictorial craft tradition that persisted through the centuries into the Roman period. In the near-contemporary battle friezes of the temple of Athena Nike on the Athenian Acropolis (figs 103–4), there are understated and seemingly more sophisticated versions of the same figure types. Some figures in the Bassai frieze can seem over-dramatized and almost cartoon-like in comparison with the refinement of such work, and indeed with that of the Bassai temple's own metopes. The word 'provincial' comes to mind for the frieze, distinguishing it from the sculpture of metropolitan Athens. That is not to say that the treatment of the human or animal form is the same throughout the Bassai frieze. Estimates of the number of different sculptors involved vary from three to nine, according to how subtle are the distinctions made between them.[57] Even a cursory glance, however, reveals that some humans are stocky with large, round faces, while others are of slighter, one might almost say quieter build; some Centaurs are similarly shown as powerful bulwarks, while others – and especially their horse parts – are barely sketched in.

The mythical subjects of the frieze are the standard ones for Greek temple decoration. Most protagonists are anonymous, but in the Amazonomachy Herakles can be identified by his lion-skin cloak (fig. 133).[58] He was placed on a long and particularly splendid block at the centre of the south frieze and facing the great north door of the temple. Here the hero battles with Hippolyte, the taking of whose girdle was one of his twelve labours. The bodies of the two opponents overlap at the legs in a composition that was formulaic in Greek art for representing strife. It was used most famously in the similarly posed figures of Athena and Poseidon at the centre of the west pediment of the Parthenon. In the Centauromachy, the single certainly identifiable figure is the hero Kaineus (fig. 134),[59] who was invulnerable and was vanquished only by his being beaten, literally, into the ground. It is interesting to remark in passing how the sculptor has adapted Kaineus' form in the Centauromachy to render a Greek in the Amazonomachy in similar pose, kneeling under the umbrella of his shield (fig. 135).[60]

When they are shown without specific attribute, naming the figures in either mythical battle is problematic. An attempt has been made to argue that two different Amazonomachies are

136 The death of the Amazon queen Penthesilea at the hands of Achilles depicted on a black-figured amphora signed by Exekias, c. 520 BC. British Museum.

137 A stricken Amazon pleads for her life in a scene reminiscent of Achilles and Penthesilea in fig. 136. British Museum.

139 Two powerful and near naked Greek warriors fight back to back. They are perhaps Perithoos, king of the Lapiths, and his friend, the hero Theseus. British Museum.

141 A mother protecting her baby fends off the assault of a Centaur. Drapery swirls around them and the woman's breast is uncovered in the struggle. British Museum.

The Temple of Apollo Epikourios at Bassai   147

138 A bearded warrior wearing helmet and body armour, perhaps the hero Ajax, terrorizes a fallen Amazon. The stacked folds of the male warrior's tunic, stretched taut between his knees, are a particular feature of the stone-carver's virtuosity, seen elsewhere in the Bassai frieze. British Museum.

140 The composition of Parthenon South Metope 2 is close to that of the Greek and Centaur shown on the right of fig. 139. Such comparisons indicate the formulaic nature of pictorial composition in Greek architectural sculpture, with one generation of stonecarvers passing on ideas to the next. British Museum.

142 Distressed Lapith women seek sanctuary at a shrine marked by the statue of a female deity. The Centaur, disregarding the religious laws protecting suppliants, attacks the women, but is himself attacked by a Lapith youth coming to their rescue. British Museum.

shown and that, while Herakles is the chief hero of one, Achilles is present in another.[61] In myth Achilles' battle with the Amazons is set in the Trojan War, when the female warriors fought as allies of the Trojans. Achilles slew the Amazon queen Penthesilea, and the death is shown dramatically on a black-figured amphora in the British Museum, where Achilles' spear pierces the throat of the Amazon and draws her blood, just as his eyes meet hers and he falls tragically in love (fig. 136).[62] In the frieze, the pair have been identified with a lunging Greek and a fallen Amazon raising her hand in supplication (fig. 137). It is tempting to extend this guesswork and give names to other figures. Is, for example, an imposing bearded warrior, terrorizing another fallen victim, mighty Ajax, who will one day carry the lifeless body of Achilles himself from the field (fig. 138)?

The likely setting for the Centauromachy is, as in the Parthenon's south metopes, the wedding feast of the Lapith king, when the Centaurs inflamed by wine attempted to carry off the bride and other Lapith women.[63] In Greek sculpture, Perithoos, king of the Lapiths, was occasionally shown fighting back-to-back with his friend the hero Theseus. Such a pair might be found in the imposing male warriors in fig. 139. The figure on the right is combined with the Centaur in a composition strongly echoing that of the Lapith and Centaur in the Parthenon's South Metope 2 (fig. 140).

The females feature in the Centauromachy as helpless victims, and thus provide a contrast to the representation of their sex in the warrior women of the Amazonomachy (fig. 141). They are shown trying to escape or fend off the Centaurs or, in one instance, they seek sanctuary at the shrine and standing image of a goddess (fig. 142). The tree pictured in this same block and the uneven ground line of the frieze indicate the rugged rural landscape of northern Greece, echoing that of Bassai itself.

One of the main impediments to understanding the frieze is uncertainty about the arrangement of the original sequence of the blocks.[64] It is ironic that, although for once virtually an entire set of architectural sculpture has survived intact, we are still left in doubt as to what went where. This is in part due to the fact that the sculptured scenes are largely contained within the frame of each block and so, unlike the Parthenon frieze, there is next to no continuity of carving from one block to another. Further, although great efforts have been made to discover the setting of the frieze in relation to the architrave blocks that went below and the so-called backers that went immediately behind, such evidence as has been assembled is incomplete or self-contradictory.[65]

There are those who have abandoned altogether the attempt to retrieve the arrangement as installed and instead attempt to argue the case for a hypothetical, intended arrangement, which, so the argument goes, was abandoned at the installation stage of work.[66] The uneven distribution of

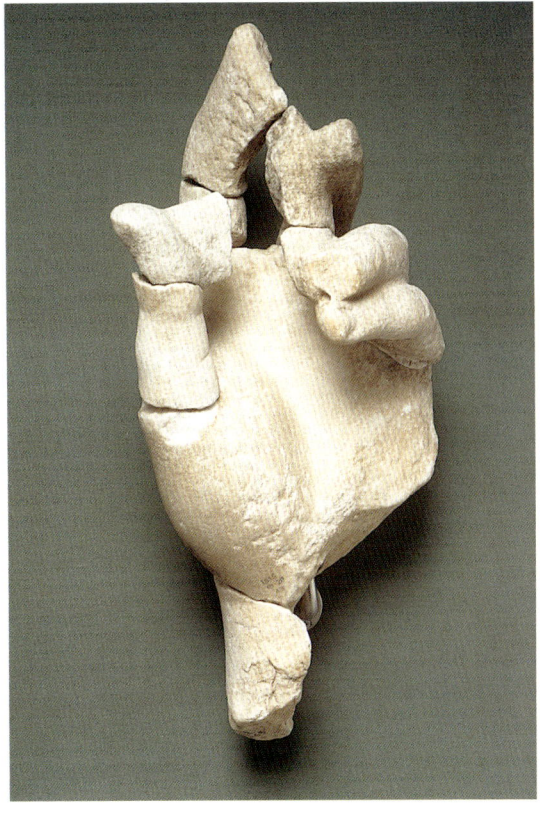

blocks between the Centauromachy and the Amazonomachy friezes and the crude reduction of the length of some blocks is seen as evidence that the frieze was shortened to accommodate a change of plan in the design of the interior of the temple.[67] By such reasoning, the frieze can be ordered to suit notions of what it should be like, without great regard for what it might actually have been like. Against this view, it is possible to insist that there was no change of plan and that the reduction of blocks is no more than one might expect in the installation of any frieze that was not carved *in situ*.[68] While the Parthenon frieze was carved into a pre-built wall, the Bassai frieze blocks were shallow panels that were set into place after the sculpture was executed. A pair of holes drilled into the face of each block may have served for ropes used in the lifting.[69]

143 Part of a colossal foot wearing a sandal and thought to belong to the cult statue of Apollo. British Museum.

144 A colossal hand from the temple statue. British Museum.

FREESTANDING SCULPTURE

Two colossal freestanding sculptures of Apollo that once stood in the sanctuary have all but disappeared. One was made of bronze and was said to have stood 12 feet high. Pausanias saw it in the marketplace at Megalopolis, situated in Arcadia to the south of Phigaleia.[70] It had been taken there as a gift of the Phigaleians towards the founding of the city in 370/369 BC. Pausanias thought the statue was fifth-century and contemporary with the Apollo temple at Bassai, but it is unclear whether it was the original cult statue and stood inside the temple or a votive that perhaps stood, as it was to do at Megalopolis, in the open air. If it was the cult statue, then the question arises as to what replaced it at Bassai. In conflicting reports, fragments in marble of two hands and two sandalled feet (figs 143–4) are said by the travellers to have been found either on the floor of the cella, just in front of the Corinthian column, or in the room at the back of the temple.[71] One of these hands is better preserved than the other and has been reconstructed by the present author through the identification of a previously unrecognized join of a finger fragment. Cockerell assumed that the marble colossus was a fourth-century replacement for the bronze, and he may well be right. Modern scholarship, however, has favoured a view that the figure was late-Hellenistic or Roman. This assumption is based largely upon the sandal type, and especially the indent of the sole between the big and first toes, which, it has been argued, is indicative of a later date.[72]

The fragments of feet and hands preserve traces of dowel holes for fixing them to the rest of the now missing statue. These have given rise to a persistent misunderstanding that the statue must therefore be acrolithic, that is to say a figure composed of marble extremities mounted on a wooden armature, concealed by actual drapery.[73] It was, however, commonplace in Classical and later sculpture to construct figures from pieces worked separately, and extremities especially tended to be treated in this way.

CONCLUSION

The temple of Apollo Epikourios at Bassai brought the new architecture of metropolitan Athens to rural Arcadia. Outwardly Doric, the interior was boldly designed in a novel use of the Ionic order, combined with the first documented appearance of the newly invented Corinthian capital. The Peloponnesian War and no doubt the remote setting of the temple restricted any influence, at least in the short term, that Iktinos' genius may have had in the Peloponnese. Later, however, we see echoes of Bassai's engaged Ionic colonnade in the fourth-century temple of Athena Alea at Tegea, while the Corinthian order, so tentatively introduced at Bassai, was to grow in popularity to become the preferred order of Roman architectural grandeur.

Construction of the Apollo temple at Bassai and the later Erechtheum and Nike temple on the Athenian Acropolis may be seen as tokens of defiance in the face of adversity dealt by Sparta to Arcadians and Athenians alike. There were those, however, who had cause to resent the hardship brought about by Athens' own imperial ambition. Among the reluctant and perfunctory contributors of tribute to the Athenian exchequer on the east side of the Aegean Sea were the Lycians.

Chapter Seven

Lycian Tombs

LYCIA – ITS PEOPLE, LANGUAGE AND HISTORY

Lycia in south-west Turkey is a beautiful land of dramatic mountains, pine forests and green valleys, fed by rivers flowing into a lapis-blue sea.[1] In mythology it is the home of the fire-breathing monster Chimaera, slain by Bellerophon on his winged horse Pegasos. In Classical times it was the home of the Lykioi, the name the Greeks gave to an indigenous people of south-west Anatolia, who called themselves Trm̃mili (Termilai to the Greeks).[2] The Greeks had various explanations for the name Lykioi. They derived it from Lykos the fugitive son of the legendary king Pandion. Alternatively, it was thought that it came from the wolves, lykoi, who led the goddess Leto to her refuge by the River Xanthos, after she had given birth to the divine twins Apollo and Artemis. The Lycians were in fact an ancient race whose ancestors were probably the indigenous Luwian-speaking people, the Lukka, mentioned in the Hittite records of the late Bronze Age. There was also an incompatible tradition that they had migrated from Crete.[3] They appear in Homer's *Iliad* as allies of the Trojans, led by the heroes Sarpedon and his cousin Glaukos (fig. 145).[4]

145 Death and Sleep carry the fallen Lycian hero, Sarpedon. Red-figured krater (wine-mixing bowl) signed by Euphronios, *c.* 510 BC. Formerly The Metropolitan Museum of Art, New York.

The Lycians were probably once semi-nomadic people moving between the mountains and the coastal plains and river valleys.[5] While they continued to practise this age-old pattern of transhumance, by the Classical period Lycia was divided into a series of independent city states. The principal and most powerful of them was Xanthos, her towering acropolis overlooking the river of the same name. Powerful dynasts ruled the city, competing with other chieftans for Lycian supremacy, while at the same time subject to the political ambitions of Persia to the east, Athens to the west and neighbouring Karia. Xanthos is the Greek name for the city, which the Lycians themselves called Arñna.

152 Greek Architecture and Its Sculpture

The Lycian language is imperfectly understood. It is probable that the Lycians took to writing their tongue only *c.* 500 BC, and the practice of doing so died out during the period when Lycia was fully hellenized in the wake of Alexander the Great's invasion of western Anatolia in 334 BC, when even in its spoken form the language may have been obsolete. It has its roots in the Indo-European group, of which Hittite and Luwian are also members. Unlike cuneiform Hittite, however, Lycian in its written form is alphabetic, adapted from the archaic Greek script of the island of Rhodes.[6]

Apart from a few graffiti on ceramic and metal vessels, the majority of texts comprise around two hundred stone inscriptions.[7] To these may be added the personal and place names that often appear abbreviated on coins (fig. 146).[8] This coin evidence has been especially important for reconstructing the lineage of Xanthian dynasts.[9] The earliest coins, probably struck *c.* 520 BC, bear the Greek inscription KYB, which is an abbreviation for the Xanthian dynast Kybernis. His successor Kuprlli came to power around 480 BC and struck the first coins with Lycian legends. The stone inscriptions tend to be short and formulaic. Although most can be read, their vocabulary does not assist much in the decipherment of the few, longer texts that survive, such as the Trilingual Stele.

The Trilingual Stele was found in 1973 by French excavators at the Xanthian sanctuary of Leto.[10] This Rosetta Stone of the Lycian language records a religious decree written on one side in Greek and on the other in Lycian. There is also a summary in Aramaic, a court language

146 Coins of the principal dynasts ruling Xanthos from the sixth to the fourth century BC. From top to bottom: Kybernis, *c.* 520–480 BC; Kuprlli, *c.* 480–440 BC; Kheriga *c.* 440–410 BC; Kherẽi, *c.* 410–390 BC; Erbinna *c.* 390–370 BC. British Museum.

of the Persians, which is inscribed on one of the two ends.[11] Probably passed in 337 BC,[12] the decree authorizes the establishment of a cult of Basileus Kaunios or 'King of Kaunos', the centre of which was at Kaunos in neighbouring Karia, close to the border with Lycia. Kaunos was one of the towns like Halikarnassos founded by the Hekatomnid rulers of Karia, of whom we shall hear more in Chapter Nine. The importation of this Karian cult into Lycia reflects the political influence of Pixodaros, the ruler of Karia, over the Lycians at this time. The inscription also mentions his appointment of an epimelete or garrison-commander at nearby Xanthos, which Lycian city must then have been under Karian control.

THE RULERS OF XANTHOS AND THEIR TOMBS

The sculptured tombs of Lycia are its most impressive remains (fig. 147). The majority of them can be enjoyed today as architectural adjuncts to the spectacular and romantic Lycian landscape, while a few have entered museum collections, principally in Istanbul, Vienna and London. The

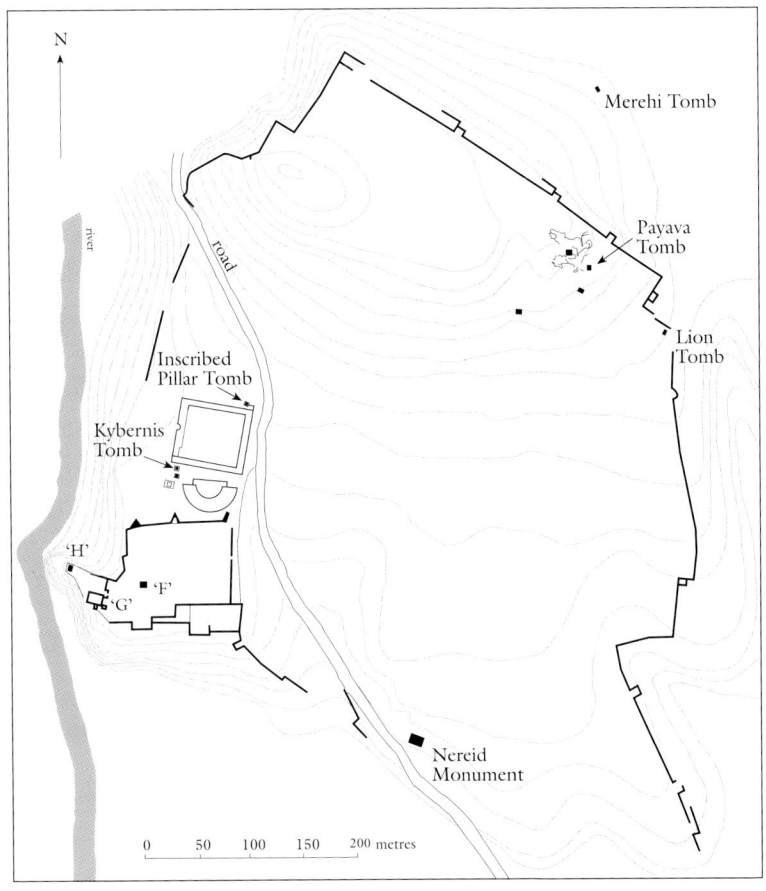

147 Map of Xanthos showing the location of monuments in the British Museum.

British Museum has the largest assemblage of Lycian monuments outside Turkey, acquired as the produce of two expeditions in 1842 and 1844, led by Charles Fellows, the pioneering discoverer and champion of ancient Lycia.[13] The most important of them is the Nereid Monument (Chapter Eight). Temple-like in its architectural grandeur, it was more hero shrine than ordinary tomb, erected around 390–380 BC for the Xanthian dynast, whose name was Erbinna in Lycian, Arbinas in Greek.

Besides such hero shrines as the Nereid Monument, there were more regular types of Lycian tomb. These may be divided into four main categories. Perhaps most distinctive are the tall pillar tombs, like the Inscribed Pillar, Lion and Harpy (Kybernis) tombs, each with a sculptured burial chamber supported on a high monolith, standing on a stepped base. Then there are the so-called house tombs, which are clearly a translation into stone of constructions in wood. The earliest of these are the buildings archaeologists call F, G and H, erected on the acropolis of Xanthos. A third category, the rock-cut tombs, probably began as simple caves, but in time came to acquire architectural façades which, like the house tombs, imitate wooden architecture. Fourth, there are the so-called sarcophagus tombs, like those of Merehi and Payava. With their seemingly gothic-arched gables, they are perhaps translations into stone of thatch-roofed, wooden buildings.

To judge from its funerary monuments, from the number of inscriptions and from the coins minted there, Xanthos was by far the most important of all the Lycian cities. Writing around 450–430 BC, the Greek historian Herodotos recalls the fall of Lycia to the Persians *c.* 545–540 BC and treats the capture of Xanthos as if that were the same as Lycia itself.[14] The Xanthians, he says, 'retreated to their Acropolis, whereupon they collected their women, children, slaves and other property and shut them up in the citadel, set fire to it and burnt it to the ground. Then, having sworn to do or die, they marched out to meet the enemy and were killed to a man.'

The episode may owe more to fiction than history, for stories of such collective suicide are a common feature in the national legends of Classical antiquity.[15] None the less, it says something of the heroic temper that was associated with the Lycian race. The city did not remain long abandoned. Apart from the return of eighty families who survived by being away from Xanthos at the time of the fire, the city was probably resettled by a mixed Lycian and Persian immigrant population. To judge from their names the local governing dynasty appears to have been Lycian, while the whole of Lycia remained ultimately under the control of Persia.[16] The Persians never appointed a satrap in the province itself; instead Lycia was ruled from the Lydian capital at Sardis, where the Persian satrap governing western Anatolia had his palace.[17] The Lion tomb is thought to be one of the earliest surviving funerary monuments at Xanthos and was perhaps erected *c.* 530–525 BC for one of the first Xanthian dynasts to rule after the Persian conquest.[18]

In 480–479 BC Lycians were conscripted into the Persian fleet gathered for King Xerxes' ill-fated invasion of mainland Greece. Herodotos describes their battle dress: 'They wore cuirasses and greaves, carrying bows of cornel-wood and unfeathered arrows and javelins; goat-skins hung from their shoulders, and they wore on their heads caps set about with feathers; daggers they had too, and scimitars.'[19] The leader of the Lycian contingent of forty to fifty ships was Kybernis, whose name in Greek means 'helmsman'. The so-called Harpy tomb was perhaps built for him *c.* 485–480 BC.[20] Following the Persian defeat, the Athenian general Kimon led a counter-offensive across the Aegean sea to attack Persian colonies in Lycia and Karia. A fire on the acropolis at Xanthos *c.* 475–470 BC may have been caused by Kimon's campaign.[21] Kuprlli seems to have been the successor of Kybernis.[22] He minted coins at Xanthos *c.* 480–440 BC and will have presided over the rebuilding of the acropolis. So-called Buildings F, G and H were erected around 470–460 BC, after the fire.[23]

Kuprlli was probably succeeded by his grandson Kheriga. He pursued a pro-Persian policy and, as a reluctant member of the Athenian empire, brought his city into conflict with Athens. The Inscribed Pillar, which stands partially reconstructed near the acropolis at Xanthos, was perhaps his tomb. Unfortunately, the vital place in the Greek text is damaged, and some prefer to restore it with the name of Kheriga's brother, Kherēi.[24] The tomb was first recorded by Charles Fellows, who had casts made of the inscriptions. It was topped by a burial chamber decorated with carvings of the owner's military exploits. The text, which is not fully translated, is in three parts, two parts in different forms of the Lycian language, the third a twelve-line epigram in Greek:[25]

> Since the time when the ocean separated Europe from Asia, no Lycian has ever yet raised such a stele to the Twelve Gods in the holy temenos of the agora, this immortal monument to his victories in war (?). It was [Kheriga/Kherēi?], the son of Harpagos, having excelled in all respects the youth of his day in his prowess at wrestling, who conquered many acropolises with (the support of) Athene, sacker of cities, and distributed part of his kingdom amongst his kin. In recognition of this, the immortal (gods) made him just recompense. He killed seven Arkadian hoplites in a single day, he who of all mankind set up the most numerous trophies to Zeus and garlanded by his illustrious exploits the family of Karika.[26]

Athletic and military prowess are recurring themes of the tomb carvings and, as we have seen, the inscription boasts of the deceased having killed seven Arcadian mercenaries in one day, presumably hirelings of the Athenians. Also found in the Pillar text is the name Melesandros. He is perhaps to be identified with the Athenian general who, as Thucydides tells us, was despatched in 430/429 to collect tribute in Karia and Lycia, but who was defeated and lost part of his army.[27] More probably, however, the Melesandros of the inscription was another, later Athenian general of 414/413, who is mentioned in a financial document.[28]

The date and especially the ownership of the monument are much disputed.[29] According to differing reconstructions of names in the inscription it is either the tomb of Kheriga, who is thought to have reigned c. 440–410 BC, or it is the tomb of his probable successor Kherēi, thought to have reigned c. 410–390 BC. To judge from the chronology of coinage, Kheriga's brother Kherēi was his direct successor.[30] Kherēi was succeeded by his nephew, Kheriga's son, Erbinna. The Inscribed Pillar tomb mentions a tomb of Erbinna, and this is arguably a reference to the construction of the Nereid Monument, thought to be Erbinna's tomb.[31] This mention of Erbinna in the text may suggest that the Inscribed Pillar tomb was not put up until Erbinna himself came to power c. 390 BC. According to one theory, Erbinna erected the monument, after he had overcome his uncle Kherēi, as a celebration of the life of his father Kheriga. Commemorating father and son, the Inscribed Pillar tomb and the Nereid Monument must have been the most remarkable buildings of their time in the city of Xanthos. The Inscribed Pillar is the only monument of its kind to bear an inscription lauding its honorand, and this has been seen as a part of Erbinna's propaganda to reinstate the honour of his father and legitimize his own control of Xanthos.[32]

The statue bases found in the sanctuary of Leto between 1962 and 1976, inscribed in Lycian and Greek, throw some light on Erbinna's career.[33] One mentions a bronze statue set up to Artemis by Erbinna and refers to his conquest of Xanthos and, to the west, Telmessos and Pinara. The other base refers to Erbinna's building of a temple of Leto and bears an elegy composed, as the Greek text tells us, by Symmachos of Pellana. It records the deeds of Erbinna (Arbinas) and refers to the erection of a statue dedicated to Leto. The translation of this reconstructed text should be read against the background of the podium friezes of Erbinna's supposed tomb, the Nereid Monument. The text is far from complete, and the following reconstruction may be taken as one scholar's view.

> [Arbin]as, son of Gerg[is] (= Kheriga), [dedicated me, having accomplished deeds worthy of the] valour [of his forefathers].

[Within the tomb chamber lies] (his) cor[pse]. But the stele [that one] s[ees] here commemorates how he est[ablished his rule over the Lycians] by his resourcefulness, his s[upreme] might and po[wer]. In his youth he conquered in one month three cities – Xanthos, Pinara and Tel[messos] with its fine harbour – striking terror into many Lycians and becoming their mas[ter]. A monument to these (achievements) he set up on the advice of the god Apoll[o]. Having sought counsel at Pytho, he dedicated me to Leto – his own image, whose *outward appearance* (??) expres[ses the prowess?] of his achievements. Having slain many people, having brought honour to his father G[ergis], having conquered many cities, Arbinas made his own and his forefathers' name renowned [through the whole] land of Asia. He was conspicuous amongst all in all human wisdom, in bowmanship, in courage, in horsemanship. From beginning to end, Arbinas, [you have] acc[omplished] great deeds, [you have presented] pleasing gifts to the immortal gods.

Symmachos of Pellana, son of Eumedes, seer w[ithout reproach], skilfully produced (this) elegy as a gift for Arbinas.[34]

A second Greek text on the same block of stone also tells us that Erbinna was only twenty years old at the time. Interestingly, for comparison with figures in the Nereid podium friezes, he likens himself to Greek mythological heroes in battle, including Achilles, Hector and Herakles.[35] Elsewhere on the Nereid Monument, in one of two pediments, Erbinna is enthroned Zeus-like in a blatant borrowing from the image of the Olympian on the Parthenon frieze (see fig. 180). In the other pediment, the dynast was shown riding into battle like a Greek hero. If he has pretensions to compare himself with the heroes of Greece to the west, Erbinna also looked to the east for his self-image (see fig. 186). For all his Hellenic aspirations, the standard of the hexameters written for him has been described as 'pitiful', and he is best seen as a self-propagandist borrowing elements of Greek and Persian imagery to impress his fellow Lycians.[36] That is certainly how he appears in the lesser podium frieze of the Nereid Monument, seated under a parasol, wearing Persian dress, his feet raised off the ground. Again, on the cella frieze (see fig. 190), he is shown reclining in the manner of an oriental banqueter, holding aloft a Persian drinking horn.[37]

Erbinna was of Lycian royal descent, but the statue-base from the sanctuary of Leto suggests that he had to fight his way to the succession, besieging his own capital of Xanthos. His military struggles are reflected in the embattled cities represented in the lesser podium frieze of the Nereid Monument.[38] Whereas his royal predecessors at Xanthos had chosen the traditional pillar form of tomb, he glamourized his life and eventual death by building the Nereid Monument as a temple-like tomb. In this he probably emulated the hero shrine of legendary Sarpedon, which must have stood on the Acropolis as memorial of the archetypal Lycian hero and is perhaps to be identified with Building G.[39] Indeed, the battle waged on the greater podium frieze of the Nereid Monument has an atmosphere of legend suggesting that Erbinna was inclined to see himself as latter-day Homeric hero. The grandeur and siting of Erbinna's tomb, dominating the approach to the city by the principal, seaward road, was intended as a sign of Xanthian power at a time when the city's pre-eminence was being challenged by the leaders of other, previously subservient Lycian cities, including Perikles of Limyra.[40]

Following Erbinna's death *c.* 370 BC, Autophradates, satrap at Sardis, appointed Arttum̃para to govern western Lycia and Mithrapata to govern the eastern cities of the province.[41] Erbinna's influence it seems, had been restricted to western Lycia, while other dynasts ruled central and eastern regions of the country. Their rising power is reflected in the construction of hero shrines, comparable in grandeur with that of Erbinna. A large monument was discovered at Trysa by August Schönborn in 1841 and was taken to Vienna in 1883 by Otto Benndorf (fig. 148).[42] Situated in central Lycia between Antiphellos (Kaş) and Myra, it occupied a lofty position on

148 Model of the Trysa hero shrine, *c.* 370 BC. Its many sculptures demonstrate the influence of Athenian temple sculpture and, in particular, that of the Parthenon. Kunsthistorisches Museum, Vienna.

the side of an acropolis. The entrance gateway and interior walls of the enclosure were heavily decorated with sculpture illustrating subjects drawn from Greek mythology, including Amazonomachy, Centauromachy, the Seven against Thebes, Bellerophon and the Chimaera, Odysseus and the Suitors, the Hunt for the Calydonian Boar, the Rape of the Daughters of Leukippos, the Deeds of Theseus, Perseus and Medusa.[43] This assemblage of Greek subjects, featuring much pictorial borrowing from Athenian monuments, is the most substantial and eloquent evidence to be found anywhere in Lycia of the ruling aristocracy's attachment to Greek culture. However, other themes represented at Trysa, such as battle and city-siege, hunting and banqueting, are more typically Lycian. The Trysa monument has been dated to a decade after the Nereid, to *c.* 370 BC.[44]

A more recent discovery is the hero shrine of Perikles at Limyra in eastern Lycia, built *c.* 370–360 BC (figs 149–50).[45] Appropriately for the name of this dynast, Perikles' tomb borrows heavily in its sculptural decoration from the monuments of Periklean Athens. Thus we find Caryatids, copied naively from those of the Erechtheum, and a frieze with clear echoes of that of the Parthenon. Perikles was the last of the dynasts to mint coins with legends in Lycian script. He asserted his dominance over his Lycian neighbours and *c.* 370 BC is thought to have revolted against Persian control of Lycia, driving out Arttum̃para, the satrap's governor designate.[46] He may subsequently have participated in the general uprising of the Great King of Persia's western dominions, which has become known as the Satraps' Revolt.[47] There is a suggestion that Mausolus of Karia re-ingratiated himself with the Great King at the end of his own participation in the Satraps' Revolt by putting down the rebellion in Lycia.[48] It is not probable, however, that Lycia was controlled absolutely by the Hekatomnid Karians until the reign of Mausolus' younger brother Pixodaros, whose power over Xanthos is made clear, as we saw above, by the Trilingual Stele of the sanctuary of Leto.

Following the suppression of Perikles' rebellion, Autophradates, satrap of Lydia, is thought to have appointed Payava to be his puppet at Xanthos. He did not mint coins in his own name and appears not to have been a king as such, but rather a governor. Payava is shown paying homage to the satrap in one of the carvings of the tomb erected for Payava, perhaps *c.* 360 BC.[49] The failure of the Xanthian dynasts to hold Lycia loyal to Persia was to forfeit their local independence. By 337 BC, Persia had let Pixodaros of Karia assume direct control of Lycia. Both Karia and Lycia remained Persian possessions until Alexander the Great swept through western Turkey in 334/333 BC. In the wake of his conquest Lycia became thoroughly hellenized and, to judge from funerary inscriptions, Lycian language was supplanted by Greek. Burial practice

149 Model of the hero shrine of Perikles of Limyra, *c.* 370–360 BC. Like the Trysa monument, the Limyra shrine borrows much from Athenian temple architecture and sculpture, including the Erechtheum Caryatid porch. Institut für Modelbau der Hochschule für angewandte Kunst, Vienna. Model by F. Hinizdo.

150 Silver coin of Perikles of Limyra. British Museum.

itself, however, was preserved and, although no more great hero shrines were to be built, many lesser tombs from late Hellenistic and Roman times speak of the durability of Lycian traditions.

THE TOMBS

The chronology of the surviving funerary monuments of Lycia can be divided into four phases, all represented by tombs from Xanthos in the British Museum. The first phase includes those tombs that fall between the Persian sack of Xanthos *c.* 545–540 BC and the burning of the citadel by Kimon *c.* 475–470 BC. Into this category fall the Lion tomb at Xanthos, constructed *c.* 530–525 BC, and the somewhat later so-called Harpy tomb, *c.* 485–480 BC, or tomb of Kybernis. The second is the period immediately after the second destruction of the acropolis at Xanthos when Kuprlli rebuilt the citadel. To this phase belong so-called buildings F, G and H on the Xanthian acropolis. The third phase, which includes the Inscribed Pillar tomb and perhaps the tomb of Merehi, occurs towards the end of the fifth century BC, when Athens was weakened by the Peloponnesian War, and Xanthos enjoyed a period of prosperity as the principal Lycian city. The fourth relates to the period after Erbinna's death around 370 BC, when the Persian governors Arttum̃para and Mithrapata were appointed to interfere directly in Lycian affairs. To this phase can be assigned Payava's tomb, the Landscape tomb at Pinara and many more funerary monuments besides.[50]

THE LION TOMB

The Lion tomb is one of the oldest Lycian monuments and probably dates soon after the Persian sack, around 530 BC. It is one of a number of so-called pillar tombs erected at Xanthos, probably all for ruling dynasts. When Charles Fellows first saw the monument, it stood partially buried in the cemetery of Xanthos to the east of the acropolis (fig. 151). In December 1843, during Fellows' last Lycian campaign, the pillar was laid down on its side and the sculptured parts detached.[51] In total the monument must have stood more than 4 metres high, comprising a base, the pillar, the sculptured chamber and a cap worked separately, which was not found. The top bed of the pillar is somewhat hollowed so as to extend the cavity of the chamber contained by the sculptured parts.[52]

151 The Lion tomb at Xanthos, the burial chamber still in place on its monolith pillar. Drawing George Scharf junior (1820–95). British Museum.

152 Lion carved on the principal side of the tomb at Xanthos, *c.* 530 BC. British Museum.

153 Warrior stabbing a rearing lion. West side of the tomb.

The burial chamber consisted of a single block of limestone, which had been hollowed out. Fellows found it in fragments, and these were rejoined.[53] On one side was carved a lion in high relief. The beast rests on its belly and looks out at the spectator, its tail curled around the haunch of the left, rear leg (fig. 152).

On one return was carved a warrior stabbing a rearing lion with a sword (fig. 153). This scene is strongly reminiscent of Achaemenid Persian art, where the same compositional formula is often found as a token of royal power. To the left of this scene, there was at least one, and probably two rectangular openings, separated by a central mullion.[54] These must have been closed with a stone panel and opened when offerings were to be placed in the chamber. The body itself will have been installed from above, before the opening was closed with a heavy stone lid.

The side opposite that carved with a lion is broken away. Built into a nearby wall, however, Fellows found a relief carved with a lioness guarding her young, which is thought to represent a fragment of the missing part. This lioness is rather leaner and more stylized than the lion.

KYBERNIS' (HARPY) TOMB

The Harpy tomb was so-called after the mistaken identification as Harpies of the winged female demons that punctuate the corners (fig. 154). They are in fact Sirens, the mythical bird-women who among other exploits lured sailors to shipwreck by confounding their senses with their mesmerizing song. The monument is thought to have been constructed as the tomb of Kybernis who, as we have already seen, struck coins at Xanthos around 520–480 BC. Before Fellows removed the sculptured burial chamber, now replaced by casts, Kybernis' tomb stood intact between the theatre and the south gate into the agora or marketplace of Xanthos. Although not the only funerary monument in the area, it appears in the Hellenistic period to have been the only late-archaic tomb to have survived. And when in the Roman period the surrounding area was much developed, it continued to stand isolated as a relic of a bygone age.[55]

Except for its sculptured chamber of marble, the tomb was constructed of local, grey-blue limestone. It stood in all some 9 metres high and consists of a great monolith weighing about 80 tons and measuring some 5.43 metres high, raised upon a virtually square plinth. The top bed of the monolith was hollowed out to a depth of about 1.65 metres, so as

154 Kybernis' tomb with the sculptured burial chamber in place on its massive pillar. Drawing George Scharf junior. British Museum.

155 Kybernis' tomb, west side. British Museum.

to enlarge the burial chamber above, which was enclosed by the marble reliefs now in the British Museum. The whole was topped by an overhanging cap, cut from a single block into three receding sections.[56]

The relief carvings are arranged as eight separate segments. Four of these create the corners, and four others fill the spaces in between.[57] The west side is exceptional by virtue of its additional insert panel, showing a cow suckling its calf, placed over the rectangular cutting through which the body was inserted (fig. 155). The scenes on each side are framed by a simple moulding, which is more elaborate along the bottom. This framing device represents the original thickness of the blocks before the sculpture was carved into them. Each side measures 1.02 metres high, around 2.5 metres long on the longer east and west sides and around 2.3 metres on the short south and north sides.

The west side is the best preserved and perhaps best conceived. Flanking the central scene are two seated women dressed in long tunics draped with mantles, their prominent breasts plainly visible through the fine folds. Their wrists are decorated with bracelets. They occupy elaborately worked thrones. On the left-hand throne the armrest, terminating in a ram's head, is supported by a seated Sphinx; on the right-hand throne the top of the backrest terminates in a swan's head. One figure holds a libation bowl in her left hand, while the other holds a pomegranate in her left hand and a flower between index finger and thumb of the right. Each rests her feet on a footstool, while the hem of the dress she wears trails back from it. This richness of ornament and variety of surface texture is found again in the procession of three female figures in the central panel. Like the seated figures, they are clad in long tunics, draped with over-mantles, and wear diadems in their hair and pointed shoes on their feet. While the hair of the seated figures is worn up, theirs is down, falling over the shoulders and breasts in long tresses. They hold objects including an egg, pomegranate and flowers.

The east side is the most weathered (fig. 156). The central panel shows a bearded male figure facing right, much in the manner of the seated females of the west side. The arm of his throne is supported by a miniature, fish-tailed Triton. The seated figure's left hand rests on a staff, which in turn rests on his left shoulder, while his right hand brings a flower to his nose. A boy approaches with a cockerel in one hand and some object in the other. From the left, approach two walking figures, whose sex is now hard to determine. Each one holds a flower to the nose, while the lead figure carries a pomegranate. On the extreme right is shown another approaching figure, a youth with a dog looking up at him. He holds a stick in one hand and a now lost object was held in the other. This was attached in metal, as were the bands that adorned the hair of all but the boy.[58] The compositional formula for this scene brings to mind the iconography of royal audience, as found in Assyrian and Persian palace art. From the throne room of the Apadana at Persepolis comes a relief

156 Kybernis' tomb, east side. British Museum.

157 Kybernis' tomb shows influence from Persian art as seen in an audience with the Persian king on a relief from the treasury building of the Achaemenid palace at Persepolis. Iran-e-Bastan Museum, Tehran.

showing Darius, or possibly his son Xerxes, seated with a retinue behind and a cringing suppliant before him (fig. 157).

The north and south sides are similarly composed (fig. 158). In the central panel of the north a powerfully built warrior stands before an older, bearded figure seated on a stool (fig. 159). The warrior wears a cuirass over a short tunic. He supports a shield with his left hand while with his right he receives, or alternatively hands over, a crested helmet. The seated figure is draped in tunic and cloak and supports a staff on his shoulder. The animal beneath the stool resembles a pig but has paws and is perhaps an unusual dog.

Sirens are carved into the angle blocks of both the north and south sides. They are best known as the fantastic bird-women who with their hypnotic song lured sailors to shipwreck. Here, however, they are seen carrying both in their hands and claws diminutive female human figures. Each of these reaches up with one hand to touch the chin of the Siren in an apparent act of supplication. In the extreme right of the picture, a grieving female figure squats and holds her head in her hands. She wears a voluminous tunic, crinkled like that of other female figures on the monument, and a diadem in her hair.

The angle-blocks of the south frieze bear almost identical scenes, while a heavily built figure appears in the centre, seated on a throne. The sex is hard to determine but is probably male. He wears the usual chiton form of tunic, draped with a mantle, and on his feet are shoes with turned up, pointed toes. A staff rests against his left shoulder. He holds a

158 OPPOSITE TOP Kybernis' tomb, north side. British Museum.

159 OPPOSITE BOTTOM Kybernis' tomb, south side. British Museum.

pomegranate in his left hand and another fruit in the right. The French excavations located a fragment preserving the upper part of the head of this figure, a cast of which is now in the British Museum.[59] Another epicene figure approaches and is usually seen as male. The left hand bears by the wings the offering of a dove, while the right is extended in worship. The face is entirely broken away.

The apparent majesty of the seated figures has inclined some to the view that they must be gods, probably those of the Underworld whom the standing figures are propitiating. The alternative view is that the seated figures are the heroized dead, the incumbent of the tomb and his dynasty, to whom family members are bringing offerings.[60] Lycian funerary practice probably required that the tomb chamber was periodically opened and that fresh offerings were inserted. The living and the dead, therefore, are – if we follow the second theory – glamorized by their timeless representation in stone as givers and receivers of gifts.

The courtly, ornate and late archaic style of the reliefs carved, it would seem, by Ionian workmen suggests a date around 500–480 BC. If this is indeed the tomb of Kybernis, son of Kossikas, who commanded the Lycian contingent of the Persian fleet at the Battle of Salamis,[61] it is possible to conjecture that the Lycian king died of wounds sustained at the battle, in which Greece defeated the Persians and their allies, and that his remains were brought home to Lycia.

There is no indication that, as with the Inscribed Pillar tomb, the cap stone was mounted with a sculpture of the dynast. In 1953, however, the French excavators located a fragment of a stylized lion carved in marble. This and perhaps another may have guarded the base of the monument.[62]

SHRINES AND TEMPLES ON THE ACROPOLIS OF XANTHOS: BUILDINGS F, G AND H

The acropolis at Xanthos falls sharply on its western and southern sides into the valley of the river far below. In its earliest phases the extent of the town was probably restricted to its highest point, and only gradually did civic buildings, such as the theatre, get planted around its lower slopes. In the extreme north-west corner of the acropolis, French excavations between 1951 and 1959 identified four phases in the history of the site.[63] The earliest remains were fragments of pottery with geometric decoration, dated to c. 725–700 BC. The Persian sack of Xanthos (c. 545–540 BC) destroyed this earliest phase of the city. Occupation on the citadel, however, seems to have resumed immediately in its second phase, since many Athenian black-figured sherds and some fragments of archaic East-

Greek pottery were found there. In its south-east corner the excavators identified a royal residence and, in the vicinity, a temple (C) with three parallel compartments.[64] In front of the central compartment was a votive pit (favissa). Around 520 BC, to judge from the finds of Athenian and East-Greek Fikellura pottery, a second temple (D) was constructed.[65] These buildings are thought to have been destroyed by fire, and the spread of broken pottery dating down to *c.* 475–70 BC suggests that this was caused by the Athenian general Kimon's campaign against Persia's subject allies, following the defeat of the Persian invasion of Greece in 480/479 BC. Entering its third phase, the acropolis was quickly renewed with buildings of stone, including so-called buildings F, G and H, perhaps replacing earlier wooden ones, and retaining many of the construction features of these wooden predecessors. The fourth and final phase covers the Hellenistic and Roman periods. It was introduced by the conquest of Alexander in 334 BC and of Ptolemy in 309 BC. The town expanded beyond archaic and Classical limits and the old acropolis became a fortification. It did not withstand the sack of Brutus in 42 BC and, if it was rebuilt in Roman times, very little of what was done then survives. Philon of Alexandria says that the Xanthians defied capture by Brutus' troops and repeated the mass-suicide of their sixth-century ancestors.[66]

In the south-west corner of the acropolis French excavations uncovered a level terrace comprising a rectangle measuring 15.5 metres east to west and 10.25 metres north to south. Here were found the foundations and some architectural members of buildings F, G and H, dismantled in late antiquity to make rough Byzantine walls.[67] The area had already been explored over a hundred years earlier by Fellows' expedition, and a number of sculptures sent by him to the British Museum are thought to come from these buildings.[68] Although similar to Lycian tombs in general appearance and technique of construction, these buildings have been interpreted as serving a cult, rather than funerary purpose. They may have been hero shrines, connected to the celebration of local Lycian heroes, such as Homer's Sarpedon (see fig. 145).[69] All seem to have been richly sculptured in a Graeco-Persian style.[70]

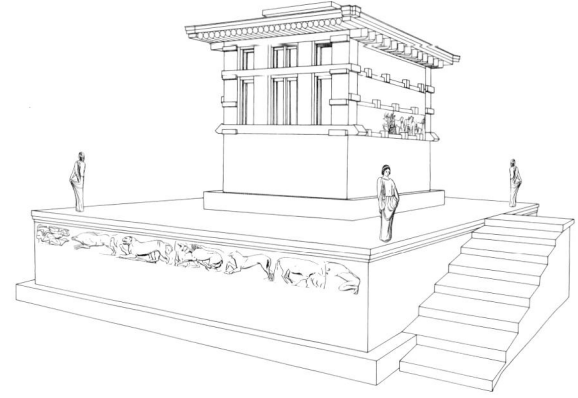

160 Shrine, known as Building G, on the acropolis of Xanthos.

Building G can be reconstructed as a tall, flat-roofed, rectangular construction with projecting beams, thought to imitate lost Lycian domestic architecture in timber (fig. 160). A line of mouldings cut to resemble the ends of wooden poles ran immediately beneath the flat roof slabs, and the short ends of the building were divided with a series of blind recesses, probably

161 Frieze block carved in relief with a Satyr wielding a tree branch. British Museum.

162 Lion devouring a deer. British Museum.

163 Panther. British Museum.

inspired by the window openings of timber buildings. The form of Building G is a typical tomb type, but the French excavators favoured its purpose as a hero shrine or a temple built around 460 BC after the destruction of *c.* 470 BC. Its estimated dimensions are 6.4 by 4.26 metres and it stood around 5 metres high.

An animal frieze is thought to have run around the top of a podium supporting the building (figs 161–3), and was itself crowned by a moulding made up of a double egg and dart above a single line of bead and reel.[71] The top bed of a surviving portion of this moulding preserves a cutting which may have been set with a freestanding sculpture. The torsos of three female figures, draped in a tunic (peplos), were found by Fellows, and figures to which they belong are thought to have been placed around the floor of the podium (fig. 164).[72] A fragment of a female head in the British Museum perhaps belongs to one of the group, and in 1951 French excavations discovered a further such fragment, perhaps even part of the same head. This fragment is now in Antalya Museum.[73]

The building itself is thought to have been decorated with both external and internal friezes. To the external frieze are assigned a series of blocks of equal height (77 centimetres), all with the same moulding running along the top face. They were placed on one of the long sides and show a procession of horsemen, figures riding in horse-drawn chariots and others walking in procession (fig. 165).[74] Two further blocks of frieze showing a procession measure just 71 centimetres high and are thought to belong to an interior frieze.[75]

164 Girl in a peplos, perhaps one of four who stood at each corner of the podium of Building G. British Museum.

165 A groom walks beside a horse in a procession that probably ran around the walls of Building G. British Museum.

Building H was located on the extreme western limit of the acropolis, bounded by cliffs on three sides descending into the valley below (fig. 167).[76] The foundations, comprising a series of irregular-shaped blocks jointed together and fixed with butterfly clamps, were already drawn by George Scharf during Fellows' expedition.[77] The French excavations relocated this footing and established its measurements as 5.17 by 3.34 metres. It carried a rectangular building measuring north to south 2.84 and east to west 2.34 metres. The height, including the podium, is reconstructed at 6 metres.

A series of blocks once built into a Byzantine wall to the south are thought to have belonged to this structure. As with Building G, the façades rose in a series of tiers, with mock-wooden beam ends and styles framing false doors and windows. The tentative reconstruction shows, in the short sides, a false door at 'ground-floor' level, above which are two further tiers of false windows, the uppermost crowned by a gable in the form of a sarcophagus lid. Here are assigned two triangular reliefs in the British Museum.[78] They feature an 'attic' window flanked by sphinxes, with two lions facing one another above (fig. 166). No blocks, it seems, survive of the long sides of the monument, nor of its pitched roof covering. In spite of apparent affinity with tomb architecture, the French excavators once more prefer to invest Building H with a cult rather than a funerary purpose. Largely on the basis of building technique, they date it to around 460 BC, the same as Building G.

Lycian Tombs 173

166 Two parts of a gable attributed to Building H carved with sphinxes and lions. British Museum.

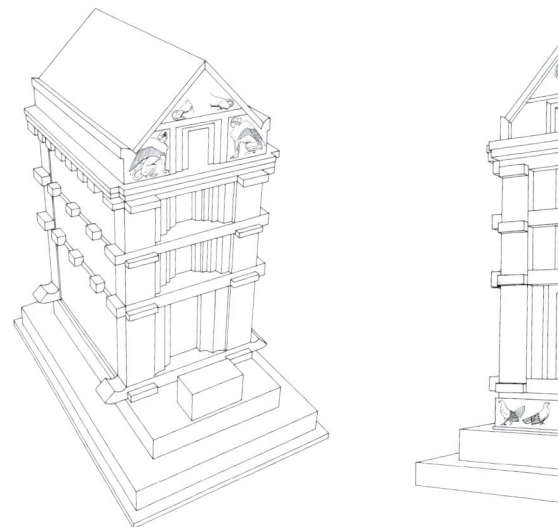

167 Building H (left) on the acropolis of Xanthos.

168 Building F (right) from the acropolis of Xanthos.

169 Gable end attributed to Building F drawn by George Scharf junior. In the centre a Siren perches on an Ionic column while, on either side, a male figure sits, one bearded, the other clean-shaven. Indications of colour include blue on the background, which can still be seen, and yellow and red on the figures and on the column. British Museum.

170 A frieze of cockerels and hens is tentatively attributed to Building F. British Museum.

Building F lay to the east of G and H (fig. 168). Of all three monuments, it is the least well preserved and its foundation is represented only by a rectangular cutting measuring 3.6 by 2.9 metres.[79] Assigned to Building F is a gable relief in the British Museum, found by Fellows built into a Byzantine wall on the south side of the acropolis, and two blocks of masonry of similar workmanship.[80] The relief shows two male figures seated and facing each other, the one bearded and the other not (fig. 169). Between them is an Ionic column on which perches a Siren with very large wings.[81] The building is thought to have been of similar kind to H and, with its stepped podium, stood not more than 6 metres high. To it is assigned the splendid frieze of fighting cocks, several blocks of which are in the British Museum.[82] The frieze is thought to have run around the base of the monument. The cockerel frieze (fig. 170) has been dated to the end of the sixth century BC, principally on the basis of comparisons with cockerels painted on contemporary Athenian vases and especially the class of so-called 'Little Master Cups'.[83] Since, however, the acropolis was destroyed around 475–470 BC and the frieze is unlikely to have survived the conflagration, it is perhaps more probable that it belongs early in the period of reconstruction, around 460 BC.

THE TOMB OF THE INSCRIBED PILLAR

The standing remains of this monument are located on the other side of the Roman agora from Kybernis' tomb (fig. 171). Like the latter, it must have seemed to the inhabitants of Hellenistic and Roman Xanthos a wonderful bygone of a heroic age. From the base to the top of the crowning sculpture it stood over 10 metres high. Built entire of local limestone, it comprised a podium, on which was raised a 4-metre-high inscribed monolith, now broken into two fragments. Above this was the funerary chamber, richly ornamented with sculpture. This was capped like Kybernis' tomb with a block of stone cut into three receding levels. On it stood a pedestal supporting a sculpture, which is thought to have represented the dynast of the tomb sitting on a throne, flanked by projecting lions.[84]

The sculptured chamber was made up of a series of hollowed blocks, comprising middle and corner pieces. Fellows retrieved three fragments from the site, which are now in the British Museum,[85] while the French excavated others, now in Istanbul. Partial reconstruction of the chamber was eventually possible, using original fragments and casts of pieces discovered at Xanthos. The reconstruction was achieved, however, only after a remarkable intervention by Professor J. Marcadé, who, reviewing the excavators' published report, realized that a fragment in London joined two others found at Xanthos.[86] Thus, it became apparent that the Inscribed Pillar tomb was embellished at the corners by protomes or bosses in the form of the foreparts of a bull. Parallels for these exist in the

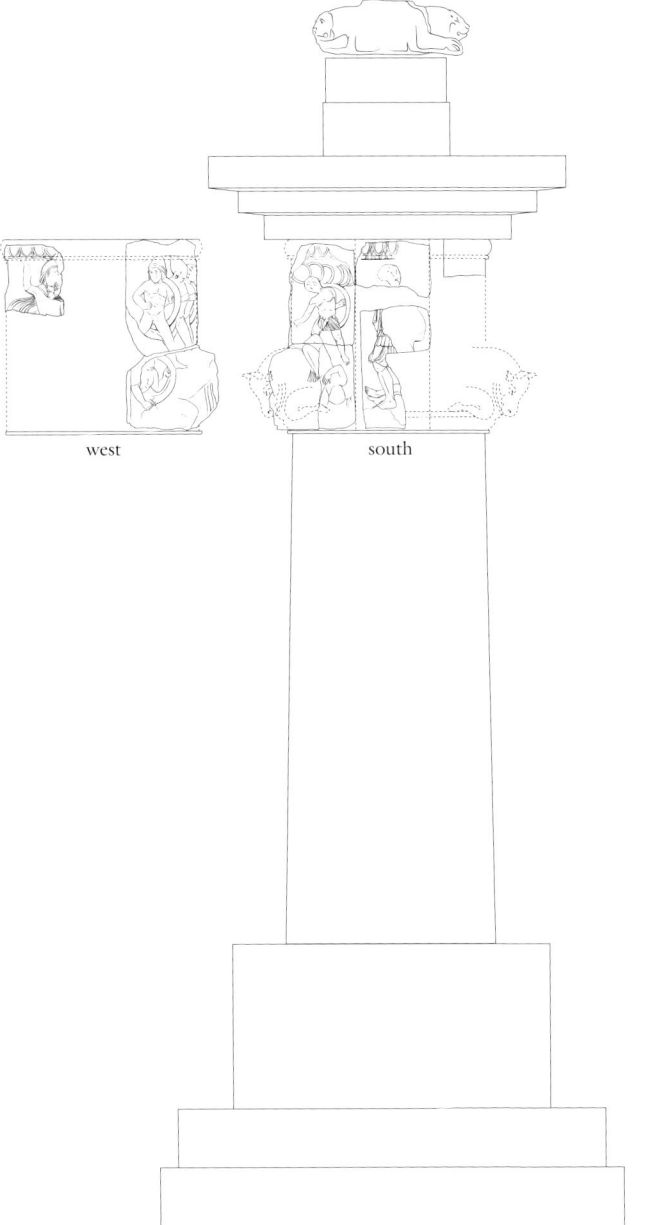

171 South elevation of the Inscribed Pillar tomb at Xanthos with its distinctive projections (protomes) in the shape of bulls. The inset shows part of the west face.

monumental architecture of Achaemenid Persia, and we are reminded here of the great empire that lay to the east of Lycia. We are reminded too of Greece to the west, both in the Greek form of the inscription[87] and in the motif of the dying figure falling over the flank of the bull. Here a parallel can be drawn with battle scenes on the outside of the shield of the Athena Parthenos in Athens (see fig. 68). Over this victim, on the south side of the Inscribed Pillar monument, triumphs the dynast, brandishing sword and shield, while above him is hung a series of shields, intended as emblems of his victories. In the central panel to the right, and on a larger scale, another warrior walks over his fallen victim. To the left, round the corner on the west side, a troop of warriors advance, naked but for the conical (pilos) helmet favoured in Lycia and the round shields they carry. Below, and strangely, a bearded warrior appears to be rearing up beside the bull. This remarkable ensemble was crowned by a capping stone, on which was placed a block carved with two projecting lion heads.[88] These remind us of the lion head protomes that protrude from the curving roofs of such monuments as the tombs of Payava and Merehi. Each rests its muzzle on the paws. One head is shown with just the neck, while the other includes part of the shoulder. Both turn slightly to one side and seem to have projected a little beyond the edge of the pedestal support. It is difficult now to envisage quite how these beasts were incorporated into what must have been a composite sculpture. It is thought that they formed protective elements in the throne of a lost seated figure of the dynast.[89]

Before the building of the Nereid Monument, the tomb of the Inscribed Pillar was perhaps the grandest sight in Xanthos. Its inscribed stele, richly ornamented sepulchral chamber and crowning sculpture proclaimed the kingly power of the dynast. The sculpture will have been all the more striking when, as surely they were, the various figures were picked out in contrasting colours.[90]

THE TOMB OF MEREHI

To the east and north of the acropolis of Xanthos lies a hill, enclosed by the walls of the Hellenistic and Roman city and on the slopes of which were constructed several tombs. These include, on its northern slope, the sarcophagus tomb of Merehi who, although not a dynast, must have been a significant person to merit such a splendid monument.[91] It was found in ruins by Fellows, who extracted the sculptured cover and brought it to London (fig. 172). Unlike Payava's tomb of the same type, Merehi's was just one storey high. On a shallow plinth sat the hollowed-out block that provided the funerary chamber, while above it rested the cover. The

Lycian Tombs 177

172 Merehi's tomb in ruins at Xanthos, drawn by George Scharf junior. British Museum.

173 Merehi's tomb reconstructed in the British Museum *c.* 1875.

chamber was carved with external panels and projecting beams simulating in limestone the wooden architecture of Lycian houses. The cover was carved all over with figured sculpture, including the flat sides of the ridge. Both curving sides of the cover are carved with a four-horsed chariot, the one accompanied by a panther, the other by a Chimaera. A driver in Persian dress, including sleeved tunic and bonnet, holds the reins, while his passenger is dressed in the clothes and armour of a Greek foot soldier.

The pointed arches of the ends were divided into four compartments by a central mullion and cross beam (fig. 173). In the apex of one end were carved two sphinxes facing each other, while below a male and female figure also facing each other sit on draped stools. The upper compartments of the other end are again carved with sphinxes, while the lower compartments are broken in. The arch was crowned by the flat end of the roof ridge, carved with acanthus.

The roof ridge itself displayed contrasting scenes of war and peace. On one side, a scene of battle before the walls of a city (fig. 174). A figure

174 and 175 The sculptured sarcophagus lid of Merehi's tomb. Drawing George Scharf junior. British Museum.

in Persian dress sits and commands the siege. This is perhaps Merehi himself. Behind him is represented a sequence of hand-to-hand combats around wounded victims. On the other side is a series of peaceful episodes, perhaps from the life of Merehi (fig. 175).[92] On the right, he is to be identified as the bearded figure seated on a stool draped in the Lycian manner and accompanied by a dog. He is approached by another bearded figure, wearing a Greek cloak (himation), leaning on a staff. On the left, he is perhaps again the bearded figure reclining on a couch, holding up a drinking horn in his right hand. From the left he is approached by a page, while the seated figure of a woman, perhaps his wife, looks on accompanied by the diminutive figure of a girl, possibly his daughter. Between these two stand three pairs of bearded men and clean-shaven youths. The first youth, from the left, is being crowned by his companion, while the others appear to be greeting each other. These scenes of what appear to be civic life seem to parallel similar compositions on the cella frieze of the Nereid Monument. The upper surface of the ridge has a number of cuttings, evidently for finials that now are lost. These perhaps took the form of figurative sculptures.

The burial chamber, left behind by Fellows, bears a Lycian inscription, which has been variously read. A recent interpretation translates it: This residence was built by 'Merehi, son of Kudala . . . under the authority of Kheriga'.[93] This apparent mention of the Xanthian dynast Kheriga, whom the Greeks called Gergis, would date the tomb to his reign c. 440–410 BC, making this one of the earliest known Lycian sarcophagus tombs, contemporary with the Lion Sarcophagus erected to the southeast of Merehi's.[94] Certainly, a date for Merehi's tomb in the last quarter of the fifth century would fit well with the style of the sculpture of the roof ridge. The chariots, however, are close to those of Payava's sarcophagus tomb, which is dated c. 370–350 BC. If Merehi's tomb is contemporary with Payava's, then the 'Kheriga' of the inscription cannot mean the dynast of the Inscribed Pillar tomb.[95]

THE TOMB OF PAYAVA

On the gentler southern slopes of the same hill on which to the north stands Merehi's tomb, is one of the most beautiful assemblages of tombs in all Lycia. Commanding fine views towards the sea, carved into and around an outcrop of rock, was a cluster of rock-cut tombs, thought to have been made c. 400–350 BC, with architectural façades simulating the wooden houses of Lycia. The rock itself is crowned by a towering, undecorated pillar tomb, and not far away were built two freestanding sarcophagus tombs. One small and undecorated is still there; the other monumental and richly sculptured was transported by Charles Fellows to the British Museum (fig. 176).[96]

The monument is identified by its inscriptions as the tomb of Payava, who is thought to have been governor of Xanthos. It stood 7.85 metres high, made up of a series of rising tiers.[97] The first tier remains at the site and comprises a stepped base, which supports a plinth of four massive slabs, capped by a flat lid. The steps are themselves hollowed so as to form a chamber with the space enclosed by the orthostates above. The lid of this chamber also served as the footing of the next tier, comprising a monolith with carved sides. These carvings were expertly sawn off by

176 Payava's tomb, drawn by George Scharf junior, standing in the necropolis of Xanthos. British Museum.

Fellows' men and are now in the British Museum,[98] while the remainder of the monolith, of which they were once a part, remains in place on the plinth. Above this was the third tier, an even greater monolith, partially hollowed out at the top to form an upper chamber capped by the fourth tier, which was the roof-like sarcophagus cover, similar to that of Merehi's tomb.

The second and fourth tiers were richly carved. One long side of the second tier shows a battle. Payava is to be identified as a victorious horseman riding in from the left at the head of a troop of cavalry (fig. 177, left). They are opposed by a force of infantry advancing from a rocky place on the extreme right. The loss of the face of Payava's helmeted head is to be regretted, but he makes an imposing figure all the same with his flying cloak, spear arm raised, body armour and leather (?) apron protecting his legs. The 'beam' above his head is inscribed: 'Payava manakhine made this tomb'.[99] The meaning of the second word, which occurs only on this Lycian monument, is obscure; it is perhaps a term denoting Payava's regional origin.

The other long, west side of the monument features a much-ruined figure in Persian dress seated on a draped stool (fig. 177, right). He wears a cloak around the shoulders over a tunic and leggings. From his belt hangs a sheathed dagger. The weathered head is bearded and covered by a Persian headdress (tiara). Behind this figure stood two servants in sleeved and belted tunics, their arms folded across their breasts. The better preserved (not shown here) was carved on a corner fragment found at the site by the French excavators of the 1950s.[100] The seated dignitary is approached by four male figures. The leader is almost destroyed, but was perhaps bearded like the figure to the right, and wore a similar sleeveless tunic. The thick, wig-like hair is distinctive and can be seen elsewhere on the monument. The two seemingly younger figures to the right wear the himation. The subject of this scene is probably to be identified as a Lycian delegation, led by Payava before the Persian satrap. An inscription on the beam above is imperfectly understood but is thought to include the words 'Autophradates, Persian satrap'. We can make out *Ksadrapa*, the Lycian word for satrap, and before it, *wat . . . ata*, which from another Lycian inscription has been identified as *wat[aprd]ata* or 'Autophradates'.[101]

177 Two elevations of Payava's tomb (east and west) with the sculptures. Drawing George Scharf junior. British Museum.

178 Two elevations of Payava's tomb (south and north) with the sculptures. Drawing George Scharf junior. British Museum.

Round the corner, on the south side of the same tier (fig. 178, left), there are two impressive figures with a long inscription to the right. Each is in military dress, a muscled cuirass with pendant leather straps (pteryges) over a tunic, a cloak and greaves. Their right hands are raised. The figure on the right appears to be crowning his companion on the left. Each has the bushy wig-like hair and beard of the figure in the Lycian delegation on the south side. Indeed, we might see here the same two figures shown this time in armour. The inscription is imperfectly understood, but begins 'Payava, son of Ed [. . .] . . .'[102]

On the opposite short side of this same tier, were carved three figures (fig. 178, right). Two are in the British Museum, while a third (not shown here) is carved on the return of the corner fragment found by the French and now in the Antalya Museum, which also preserves the second of the two Persian servants of the satrap. The central figure is draped in a Greek himation and coiffed like others we have seen. He raises his arm to crown a naked athlete, while a second youthful figure, preserved in the unattached corner fragment, stands on the right in a short tunic. The two youths may perhaps be equated with the younger men of the Lycian delegation in the satrap scene.

In the next tier up, the pointed arches above these reliefs on the short sides of the monument were each divided by beams into four compartments. The upper sections were filled with facing sphinxes, while below and again facing each other were carved figures seated on stools. On the south end of the tomb a youthful male figure is seen on the right, his right hand supported by a staff; to the left sits a young mother who holds out her veil with her left hand, while a child stretches a hand out to her. On the north end a similar mother and boy are only partly preserved, while the panel which once contained her pair is now missing.

At the same level, the two curving sides of the cover were each carved in the manner of the tomb of Merehi (and other tombs of this period) with a four-horse chariot, each driven by a youthful charioteer wearing a conical helmet, flying cloak and body armour with hanging straps or pteryges. His passenger is mounting or dismounting the carriage in the manner of the athletic foot soldier (apobates) of the Parthenon frieze. He is bearded and shown in full armour with round shield, crested helmet, cuirass and greaves, worn with a cloak and short tunic. The carving of Payava's chariots is deeper and the expression more lively than those of Merehi. In the latter case, the back legs of all the horses touch the ground line, or nearly so, while the fore-hooves are arranged on two levels. On Payava's tomb, the horses fly through the air. There is no ground line, and the position of the hooves is reversed: here it is the front hooves that follow virtually the same line, while the rear hooves arranged on two levels seem to dance. The balletic quality of these scenes is augmented by the turning of the head of the first and third horses.

The chariots are rendered the more extraordinary by lions, which in nightmarish fashion burst out with gaping jaws, hanging tongues, bulging eyes, hackles raised and claws exposed. These projections began as uncarved bosses employed in the lifting of the cover. Whereas in the case of Merehi's tomb they were knocked out and their place carved over, here they have been incorporated into the design to serve as apotropaic guardians of the deceased.

Again, as in Merehi's tomb, the sides of the roof ridge are carved. On one side a hunt, on the other a battle. Three mounted huntsmen, each with wind-blown cloak and spear-arm raised, pursue a different quarry, consecutively a deer, boar and a bear. A dog-handler brings up the rear. In the battle scene two mounted warriors ride down foot soldiers. One of the two is a miniature version of the figure who dominates the picture of one of the long sides. Most striking is the same apron or leg guard worn in both instances. To the right of this figure an inscription already seen is repeated, 'Payava manakhine made this tomb'.

The tomb of Payava with its inscription mentioning the historical person of the Persian satrap Autophradates, who assumed the satrapy of Sardis in 392/391 BC, has been seen to offer a rare clue to the chronology of the Lycian tombs.[103] Payava appears in the sarcophagus relief as a subject of Autophradates, and their relationship may have intensified during the Satraps' Revolt around the year 362 BC, when Autophradates himself joined in a general uprising against the authority of the Great King of Persia. A date of *c*. 360 BC for the construction of Payava's tomb has been suggested on these historical grounds, but has been disputed on the basis of the style of the sculpture, which has been placed well into the second half of the fourth century. The historical event, after all, provides only a *terminus post quem* for the monument and need not be exactly contemporary with it.[104]

CONCLUSION

We may conclude this chapter by remarking upon a peculiar aspect of Lycian tomb art, which appears not to have been noticed hitherto. For those who like to see iconographic programmes in the subject matter of ancient architectural sculpture, the Lycian tombs are pleasingly predictable in a way that is not always the case in Greek temple sculpture. From archaic times on, there is a self-conscious tendency to apply contrasting but complementary themes to opposite sides of a monument. Thus on one side of the Lion tomb is found a predatory lion devouring a bull, while on the opposite side a lioness mothers her cubs. The contrasted themes appear to be those of death and renewal, where the lion appears as killer and the lioness as life-giver. On the two other sides, we find a cavalryman and foot soldiers opposite a royal hunt and the despatch of a lion. Here, as so often in the Lycian tombs, male prowess in the arts of war is complemented with hunting as one of the arts of peace. In the one scene, moreover, man appears as the tamer of horses, while in the other he kills the untameable lion.

Not all the monuments of ancient Xanthos can be read so simply as the Lion tomb, but even Kybernis' tomb, where the carvings have proved notoriously difficult to interpret, can be seen to have been planned, at least so far as formal composition goes, as a set of opposites. So, on the west side two seated women frame a procession of girls, while on the east side standing youths flank a seated male. Again, on the north side Sirens flank a figure standing on the left, who faces another figure seated on the right, while on the south side Sirens frame a similar pair, this time the standing figure on the right and the seated person on the left. The gifts exchanged in the scene shown on the north side are weapons of war, while on the other side they are fruit and a bird.

The same apparent liking for parallel scenes is found in the fourth-century monuments. The scenes carved on Payava's tomb appear especially earnest to set out in binary opposites the identity of a Lycian leader. On one long side of the monument we see Payava in audience with the Persian satrap, while on the other he is at the head of a cavalry charge. Again, on one short side he is shown in civic dress crowning a victorious athlete, while on the other he is dressed as a soldier crowning a general. Above, on one side of the roof ridge, he rides in war, while on the other side he rides in a hunt. These contrasts of static and dynamic imagery, of peace and war, of statesmanship and warriorship seem mechanically calculated, and their message is the more urgent, no doubt, because of the especial vanity of Payava to prove himself to be more than merely a puppet of the Persian governor. His last resting place was not the acropolis among the heroized kings of Xanthos but a remote, if beautiful, corner of the vast necropolis. Payava's political position was very different from that of Erbinna, who was the last of the great kings of Xanthos. The Nereid Monument too is a very different building from Payava's tomb but, as we shall see, it shared a common purpose and method in presenting a record of the life of the owner, albeit in a uniquely grandiose manner.

Chapter Eight

The Nereid Monument

THE NEREID MONUMENT

Of all the sculptured tombs of Lycia, that known as the Nereid Monument is not only the grandest to survive but was probably also the grandest ever built (fig. 179). At the time of its discovery, it was associated with the Persian conquest of Xanthos (*c*. 545–540 BC) and seen as the tomb of Harpagos, commander of the Persian army.[1] Although this dating to the archaic period was quickly abandoned on the basis of the late style of the sculpture, nevertheless it is only relatively recently that Lycian history has been pieced together, and the Nereid Monument given an agreed place in its narrative. The consensus is that it was constructed *c*. 390–380 BC as the tomb of Erbinna, the last of the great rulers of Xanthos, who reigned *c*. 390–370 BC.[2] This date is consistent with what we know of Erbinna's life, as set out in the previous chapter, and with a stylistic analysis of the sculpture.[3]

Erbinna's tomb is a temple-like structure raised on a high podium, and standing in all about 15 metres high to command a lofty position overlooking the road leading to the principal gate into the city. It was perhaps deliberately intended from a distance to evoke the small Ionic temple of Athena Nike that stood on the Athenian Acropolis, which was raised on a high bastion giving an impression not unlike the podium of the Nereid Monument (see fig. 101).[4] Such podia are indicative of Persian royal tombs, including that of Cyrus the Great at Pasargadae, but one could also say that, as a sculptural chamber raised on a podium, the Nereid Monument was conceived in the Lycian tradition of pillar and house tombs.[5] P. Demargne's excavations within the podium in the 1950s found that earlier masonry had been reused in the structure and also uncovered sherds of Athenian black-figured pottery of the sixth century BC, no doubt left over from a previous use of this prominent site.[6]

The Monument appears to have stood until Byzantine times, when so much was destroyed at Xanthos by its Christian communities quarrying stone from their pagan legacy of fine buildings and robbing metal from the clamps holding the masonry together. In the early 1840s Charles Fellows and his team of sailors found the Monument in ruins, and the sculptures strewn around the foot of the podium. Unfortunately, detailed

179 Nereid Monument partially reconstructed in the British Museum.

The Nereid Monument 187

records of their find-places were not kept, and the problem of determining what went where on the building is made the more difficult for this omission. Fellows' written reports, however, and those of other witnesses, including the surgeon of the expedition ship, HMS *Medea*, do provide some clues.[7] There is also a numbered plan drawn by Rhode Hawkins, a son of Edward Hawkins, Keeper of Antiquities at the British Museum (1826–61), who joined Fellows' expedition in 1843–44 and acted as draughtsman, along with George Scharf junior (1820–95).[8] Hawkins' and especially Scharf's drawings are an important part of the archive of Fellows' archaeological activities.

Although the precise place of many sculptures in the architectural scheme remains uncertain, their broad arrangement is clear. The podium was decorated with two friezes, one above the other. The upper, lesser frieze was crowned by a decorative cornice, above which rose four columns on the short sides and six on the long. These are in the Ionic order, and their capitals closely resemble those of the Erechtheum in Athens (see fig. 107).[9] Between the columns, at least on three sides, there stood figures of girls in wind-blown drapery. These are the eponymous Nereids of the Monument, daughters of the sea-god Nereus. The columns supported an architrave carved in the Ionian manner. On the short façades the entablature was crowned by a pediment, with carvings in relief. The corners and apex of the pediment triangle were punctuated with sculptured ornaments (acroteria), taking the form of human figures carved in the round. Finally, a fourth frieze ran around the top of the cella wall, under the ceiling of the colonnade and above the door into the burial chamber, which contained four funerary couches.[10]

THE PODIUM FRIEZES

The likely correct positions of the surviving podium frieze blocks can be determined by a combination of evidence. This includes their find-places, detailed study of cuttings for clamps and dowels in the top and bottom beds, and the composition and style of the sculpture itself.[11] The task of reconstruction is not an easy one since, unlike that on the north and south sides of the Ionic frieze of the Parthenon, the figural composition does not run over the vertical joint between one block and another. Rather, as with the interior frieze of the temple of Apollo at Bassai and the Amazon frieze of the Mausoleum, each block has a self-contained scene that may or may not relate pictorially to that which was placed next to it. The latest arrangement proposed by Childs and Demargne differs somewhat from the British Museum's reconstruction of part of the Monument in the Museum gallery. This was completed in 1969 and relied partly upon

Demargne's architectural conclusions and partly upon the evidence of the sculptured blocks themselves; for example, on the principle that long blocks were deployed on long sides of the Monument and short ones on the short sides. Neither the British Museum's reconstructed arrangement nor the revised scheme of Childs and Demargne is secure.[12]

In their arrangement Childs and Demargne take into account a perceived stylistic division between the productions of two apparently different workshops, which they assign to separate sides of the building. So, for example, in the case of the angle blocks of the greater frieze, which have two faces and where there is a choice as to whether the blocks are arranged left or right on the Monument, Childs and Demargne place

180 East front of the Nereid Monument. The locations of some of the sculpture differ from the reconstruction of the same façade in the British Museum (fig. 179). In the pediment, carved in relief, Erbinna is enthroned with his wife facing him. Together they resemble Zeus and Hera on the east frieze of the Parthenon (see fig. 93). Drawing A. Lemaire.

1 central acroterion
2 corner acroterion
3 pediment
4 architrave frieze
5 cella frieze
6 Nereids
7 lesser podium frieze
8 greater podium frieze

181 North side of the Nereid Monument. Drawing A. Lemaire.

them according to how a given face relates in style to other blocks on the same façade.[13] First proposed by W.A. Schuchhardt,[14] the two workshops may be divided as Master I and Master II. The first is the better sculptor. He has a developed sense of pictorial illusion, modelling his volumes to render flesh that appears soft and yielding and near transparent drapery that falls, clings and flies naturalistically, responding faithfully to the energy of the body that moves it (for example, fig. 183). By contrast, Master II's figures often appear as if formed by the pastry-cutter (for example, fig. 185). They are flat and barely modelled. They lack the power of invention and the expressive quality visible in Master I's work. Master II likes to overlap one figure on another. He fills his frame often with the hard and smooth surfaces of armour, hiding the more challenging soft parts of human flesh and drapery from view.[15] Master I was perhaps the principal craftsman. We may even speculate that he was the master, while the other was an apprentice. The long north side of the Monument was the most important, being approached by a terrace, while the short, west side faced the gateway into the city. The opposite, south and east sides overlooked sloping ground falling to the road below. The work of Master I was, therefore, concentrated on the north (fig. 181) and west sides.[16]

THE GREATER PODIUM FRIEZE

The larger of two friezes that decorated the podium comprised twenty-two blocks, the angle members being cut in an L shape. Only eleven out of eighteen straight blocks survive and three of the four angles. There are

182 A heroic rider with streaming cloak and wearing a hat made from a feline pelt tramples a fallen victim. Greater podium frieze. British Museum.

183 A young warrior falls onto his knees, the flat smooth face of a shield contrasting exquisitely with the fine detail of his transparent tunic and the body beneath. Greater podium frieze. British Museum.

besides a number of fragments, including some excavated by the French. The majority of preserved blocks are by Master I.[17]

The frieze shows scenes of heroic combat involving male warriors, usually dressed in Greek costume and armour.[18] These scenes are contained as individual compositions within the frame of the block. Many are pictorially related to other known Greek architectural friezes and illustrate the extent to which such friezes were composed formulaically. Thus we may compare one of Master I's finest productions showing a youthful warrior, sinking beneath the onslaught, with the death of Kaineus in the Centauromachy frieze of the temple of Apollo at Bassai (see figs 134 and 135).[19]

Two distinct groups of combatants can be discerned according to the preference of each of the two workshops.[20] Many, for example, of the warriors carved by Master I wear a long chiton form of tunic, without cuirass. Master II, by contrast, prefers the hoplite type of foot soldier, with body armour and round shield (fig. 183). Unusually, for battle friezes of this type in Greek art, the participants are all male and not pitched against Amazons, such as we find in the podium frieze of the Mausoleum at Halikarnassos and other monuments, including the Parthenon west metopes and Bassai frieze. Nor are these male warriors shown as distinct, opposed races, such as we find on the south frieze of the temple of Athena Nike in Athens, where Greeks fight figures in oriental, probably Persian costume. When Persian figures do appear in

184 OVERLEAF TOP LEFT Two foot soldiers clash shields while, on the left, an archer aims an arrow. Greater podium frieze. British Museum.

185 OVERLEAF TOP RIGHT The stiff carving of the rider suggests a different hand from the one that produced the subtle forms of figs 182–3. Greater podium frieze. British Museum.

186 OPPOSITE TOP
Erbinna sits enthroned in the Persian manner, his head shaded by a parasol and his feet lifted from the ground by a footstool. A body guard of youthful warriors stands behind him. Facing him a pair of old, bearded men in civilian dress may be seen as elders of a captured city come to negotiate terms. Lesser podium frieze. British Museum.

187 OPPOSITE CENTRE
A scaling ladder is thrown up against the wall of a besieged city. Two warriors pull on ropes to secure it, while others make the perilous climb to the top of the defences. Lesser podium frieze. British Museum.

188 OPPOSITE BOTTOM
Warriors sally forth to defend a walled city from an attacking force, their hands raised to hurl stones as missiles. Within the city helmeted heads and hands holding missiles appear over rounded merlons. A solitary woman tears her hair with one hand and raises the other hand with fingers spread in obvious distress. Lesser podium frieze. British Museum.

the north and west greater podium frieze, they are few and seemingly incidental to the main action.[21] They are, however, distinctive in their long-sleeved tunics and caps.[22] Also distinctive are the archers.[23] Some figures sport long hair,[24] which is perhaps an indication of heroic status, or possibly intended as a sign of Lycian ethnic origin: Aristotle remarks that, at the time of Mausolus of Karia, Lycians wore their hair long.[25] Especially distinctive is the warrior who wears a lion-skin helmet[26] and who seems to prefigure the later type of Alexander the Great on horseback (fig. 182).

Long hair, Persian dress, archers and a lion-helmet, these are tantalizing clues to the intended meaning of the frieze. Unlike the friezes of the hero shrine at Trysa, however, the Nereid frieze calls no specific story to mind. Although we may perhaps here see the exploits of the hero Herakles or of Theseus, the greater podium frieze of the Nereid Monument nevertheless seems deliberately generalized, so as to suggest a heroic underpinning to the parallel real-life exploits of the dynast, explicitly recorded in the lesser frieze that rested physically upon it.

THE LESSER PODIUM FRIEZE

The lesser frieze originally comprised twenty-two blocks of which, as with the larger frieze, four were angle blocks carved in an L shape. All four of these survive, along with fifteen out of the eighteen straight blocks.[27] There are besides a number of fragments found by the French excavations. The lesser frieze rested on the top bed of the greater, with the short returns (headers) of the angle blocks of the lesser frieze sitting for structural reasons on the long returns (stretchers) of the greater frieze.[28]

On all four sides the lesser frieze features the siege of a city. We find scenes of battle between rival armies of foot soldiers in front of the walls of

The Nereid Monument

a city while elsewhere the besieging army attacks defenders within the walls. Not only are the walls shown with their characteristic Lycian merlons but there are also buildings and even a sculptured monument within the walls.

The west appears to be the principal side, to which a man in Persian dress is assigned, seated, and with his head shaded by a parasol and his feet raised from the ground (fig. 186).[29] This seated figure has variously been identified as the Lydian satrap and even as the Great King of Persia. The likeliest solution, however, is that this is Erbinna, the dynast who most probably commissioned the Monument and who is the presumed incumbent of its burial chamber.[30] A bodyguard of beautiful youths is lined up behind him, while from the front he is approached by two elderly emissaries. These are perhaps an embassy sent out from the city to negotiate a surrender. Elsewhere a warrior draped in a chiton with helmet and cuirass pulls a victim by the hair, while another seems to crown the victor. This last motif is also to be found on Payava's sarcophagus and on that of Merehi. On the lesser podium frieze of the Nereid Monument, it is perhaps a representation of the dynast, this time in Greek costume.

Each instance of city-siege has its own peculiar set of events. Thus we find prisoners being led away, warriors shaded from the sun by servants holding parasols, a ladder erected for scaling a city wall (fig. 187), an attacking force entering a city by means of a levée. Warriors are of various types, including heavily armed hoplites wearing the cuirass, others clad in a chiton without the cuirass, and archers. Then there is the occasional figure in Persian garb.

The city-sieges of the lesser podium frieze appear to illustrate the catalogue of Erbinna's exploits recorded in the statue base inscriptions found in the Letoon, mentioned in the previous chapter. These pictorial episodes of battle and siege seem real and documentary. They are altogether different from the battles of the greater podium frieze, deliberately borrowed from generic scenes traditional in Greek architectural friezes to create the right quasi-mythological tone. If the greater podium frieze looks back to 'old Greece' then the lesser frieze carries reminders of an even older civilization, that of Assyria. Erbinna's conceit seems to take its lead from the palace relief carvings that record the historical actions of the Assyrian kings. Such motifs as the siege of a city with scaling ladders, battlements and distressed women, the despatch of prisoners, the seated ruler with a bodyguard at his back are all familiar from Assyrian royal palace reliefs.[31] The Assyrian palaces were in ruins when the Nereid Monument was built and are unlikely to have been a direct source of inspiration, but their themes may have circulated in portable objects that were either produced in Assyria, or were influenced by Assyrian art. Whatever the source, in the lesser podium frieze we see Erbinna as successful general and potentate on the oriental model. Conspicuously absent, however, are scenes of atrocity that are a feature of the art of the Assyrians. No corpses on spikes or soldiers juggling with the heads of their victims appear on the Lycian reliefs. The people Erbinna subdued were, after all, fellow Lycians and, although he spilt their blood as he fought to claim his birthright, none of it flows on the tomb designed to glorify him.

ARCHITRAVE FRIEZE

The architrave sitting on the columns was carved pictorially in the Ionian manner. Thirteen blocks survive, including two angles, and their precise order is not certain.[32] As with the podium friezes, a variety of evidence has been employed for the suggested arrangement by Childs and Demargne.[33] First there are the places where the blocks were found in relation to the four sides of the building. Second, since the blocks are not only decorative but also load-bearing elements within the structure, there is the evidence of their length, orientation of angle blocks and the relationship of top and bottom beds to the adjoining architecture. This includes capitals of the supporting columns.[34]

It is hard to make out any preconceived plan in the slight scenes of combat (fig. 189), hunting and of figures bearing offerings which do not seem to cohere into any harmonious pattern, but appear to fall almost at random. At least one may say that the boar hunt of the east side was placed immediately under the pediment, as if to emphasize the prowess of the dynast shown seated above (fig. 180).[35] The subject of a hunt looks both to Greek and to Persian culture. We may see here either a Lycian royal hunt echoing that in the paradise gardens of the Great King of Persia or a hunt in a Greek mythological context such as that of Meleager for the Calydonian Boar. As if to emphasize this ambiguity, most of the huntsmen wear Greek dress, while one wears that of a Persian.[36]

189 Pairs of warriors in combat were carved in a simple, naive manner on the architrave frieze. British Museum.

190 A bearded and elaborately coiffed figure, probably Erbinna himself, reclines on a dining couch holding a bowl in his left hand and a Persian-style drinking horn in his right. A courtier leans forward and speaks into the ear of the dynast, while a favourite dog lies beneath the couch. To the left, youths in loose tunics rush around, earnest to serve their master. Cella frieze. British Museum.

CELLA FRIEZE

A fourth exterior frieze ran around the top of the cella wall and above the doorway into the burial chamber. Partially screened by the columns, it was the least visible of all the sculpture on the Monument. In all, eleven blocks survive, including the four angles.[37] We see scenes of banqueting and of sacrifice but, as in the architrave frieze, so here it is difficult to detect a design.[38] At a banquet, eight couches are occupied each by two male banqueters, while two more couches are filled by one occupant each. One of these two[39] is the dynast, while the other[40] is perhaps his son and heir, or some other significant person of the court. The dynast (fig. 190), head turned to face the viewer, is shown bigger than the other banqueters. He wears a diadem and is bearded and coiffed in the manner of the kings of Assyria and Persia. He holds a Persian drinking horn decorated with a griffin in the right hand, and a cup in the left. Another such vessel, this time featuring a winged horse, is carried by a servant, and other simpler drinking horns appear elsewhere.[41] Other vessels carried by the numerous servants seem to be Greek in shape. The servants are dressed in long or short tunics.

The scenes of sacrifice are most likely connected with the banquet and perhaps indicate cult status of the dynast in the afterlife, his soul being replenished with meat and drink. In addition to the themes of banqueting, there are scenes of standing male figures, who appear to be conversing casually in a manner similar to the heroes or magistrates carved on either side of the gods on the east frieze of the Parthenon.[42]

NEREIDS

The Monument takes its modern name from its most distinctive sculpture, the series of girls thought to represent sea-nymph daughters of Nereus, god of the sea. They are shown in wind-blown draperies placed between the columns. We find in them strong echoes of the style of the

Parthenon pedimental figures in the rich sculptural treatment of female form and of moving cloth. The shape and texture of this material, inspired by the elements of air or water, is especially evocative of the figure of Iris from the Parthenon's west pediment (fig. 191). Eleven figures survive from the Nereid Monument, of which six are substantially preserved, while two are preserved above the waist and three are no more than large fragments.[43] None has its head. There are just enough Nereids to fill the intercolumniations of the north, west and east sides of the Monument, and there may therefore never have been figures between the columns of the less conspicuous south side. They fall naturally into two roughly equal groups, depending on whether they turn to the left or to the right.[44] Owing to poor preservation of the pedestals and of the cuttings in the stylobate to receive them, no figure can be assigned its certain place on the Monument. Only reported find-places can serve as a clue to their placement. For example, three Nereids were discovered near the north-west angle, on the northern terrace, and are therefore likely to be from the north side.[45]

The identification as sea-nymphs seems assured by the marine animals – dolphin, fish, crab, seabird – to be found under the feet of seven of them.[46] In Greek vase-painting Nereids traditionally appear in scenes depicting the bearing of new arms made by Hephaistos for the hero Achilles, or as sisters of the sea-nymph Thetis during her tussle with her suitor Peleus. From the eventual union of Peleus and Thetis was Achilles born. The Nereids of Xanthos are not shown in either of these roles; instead, their purpose appears to be that of supernatural companions for the soul of the deceased in his passage over the waves into the afterlife.[47] This function is attested in literature. For example, in Euripides' tragedy *Andromache*, Thetis promises her husband Peleus the gift of divinity upon death. She will come to search for him with her Nereid sisters and, finding him, will escort him to eternal life in the home of her father, the sea god Nereus.[48]

The identification of the freestanding figures as daughters of Nereus is generally accepted, but a powerful argument has been made for

191 Striking sculptures of young women, probably sea-nymphs or Nereids, were placed on the podium between the columns. The drapery of this exceptionally animated figure moulds itself to the body as if, wet and clinging, or is sent flying by the rush of a sea breeze. This personification of air and water calls to mind Iris, goddess of the rainbow, from the Parthenon west pediment (fig. 83). British Museum.

recognizing them as a Lycian variant of Greek water nymphs, who may have less to do with the sea than with local sources of fresh water such as those at the nearby sanctuary of Leto. Erbinna is closely associated with the cult through the inscriptions found there that mention him. The Lycian text of the trilingual inscription discussed in Chapter Seven makes especial reference to the *Eliyãna*, and these are equated in the Greek version with the nymphs.[49]

ACROTERIA

The angles and apex of a Greek pediment were often crowned by a floral or zoomorphic figure (acroterion). Two fragmentary sculptural groups are thought to have been the central acroteria on the west and east sides of the Nereid Monument.[50] One group was found in a cistern to the east of the Monument and perhaps belongs to that side. It represents a naked youth carrying a girl (fig. 180).[51] The heads are missing and only the torso of the young man survives, along with the right leg of the draped girl. The youth holds her knee with his right hand and her inner thigh with his left.

The other central acroterion[52] also shows a youth carrying a young woman. Here the head of the youth is preserved (fig. 192), and attached to it is a hand, presumed to be that of a girl, tugging at the hair and dragging the head to one side. The hair is close cropped and bound with a ribbon. The remainder of the girl is altogether lost. A further three female figures can readily be identified as corner acroteria.[53] They comprise girls draped to the feet and moving rapidly to one side.

One interpretation of the acroteria as an ensemble sees the rape of the daughters of Leukippos by the twins Castor and Pollux.[54] This was a popular subject at the time, as seen among the sculpture for the monument at Trysa.[55] Another is that here was the Nereid Thetis, mother of Achilles, being carried off by her husband-to-be, Peleus.[56] Yet a further argument has been made for an exploit of Herakles.[57]

192 Sculptures (acroteria) were placed at the corners and apex of the roof gable. Here a young man was combined with another, probably female figure, represented in what survives only by a hand clutching the back of the youth's hair. The pair together perhaps represented Peleus capturing Thetis. British Museum.

PEDIMENTS

The sculpture that filled the pediments of the Nereid Monument was not carved in the round, as in the case of so many Greek temples, but as relief panels.[58] The east pediment shows the dynast enthroned in the company of his wife and children (fig. 180).[59] The appearance of the royal pair is in keeping with other Lycian tombs, where a dynast and his wife regularly appear. Interestingly, here the royal couple seem to have been inspired by the divine pair of Zeus and Hera on the east frieze of the Parthenon.[60] There, as on the Nereid Monument, the female deity lifts her veil in the bridal gesture of newly married girls (apokalypsis). Two accompanying figures of the Nereid Monument shown on a smaller scale perhaps represent the royal children. Even a family pet, a dog, is curled up under the dynast's throne. On either side is gathered the royal retinue.

This static and peaceful scene was complemented in the west pediment by a dynamic scene of battle (fig. 193).[61] The dynast was probably shown on horseback in the missing part intimidating a fallen enemy. Here again we see the influence of Athens, where for example Dexileos – who died in the year 394/393 – was shown on his tombstone, now in the Keremeikos Museum, Athens, riding down a victim. The subject was an unusual choice for a pediment sculpture, but the dynamic contrast it provides with the static composition of the east pediment sets up a counterpoint, which is typical of Greek pediment sculpture, as for example in the contrasting pedimental compositions of the temple of Zeus at Olympia.

193 The pedimental figures were not carved all the way round, as for example in the Parthenon, but as sections of relief sculpture. Here the composition is clumsily adapted to the raking gable with figures awkwardly reducing in size and then kneeling to fill the corner. Erbinna was probably shown on horseback in the missing right section. Only part of a leg and hoof survives here. British Museum.

OTHER SCULPTURE

Two freestanding statues (figs 194–5), one male and the other female, are difficult to place with any certainty.[62] It is perhaps plausible to argue from the style and composition of the female's drapery that she could not have been a Nereid, unless the pair together were intended to represent Peleus and Thetis. Alternatively, they could be portrait statues of the dynast and his wife. They need not have been placed among the freestanding Nereids, and could have stood on the terrace before the north front. Demargne would like to place them with the Nereids between columns and, while others have seen them as parents of the Nereids or as the dynast and his wife, he prefers to identify them as Peleus and Thetis.[63]

A lion and lioness were found near the Monument (fig. 196).[64] Their purpose was most probably to serve as guardian figures. In style they appear somewhat archaizing by comparison with the high Classical modelling of the architectural sculptures. This, combined with their large, round and deeply set eyes, was probably a deliberate device to impress the spectator. The attitude is definitely aggressive, heads down and haunches raised, as if on the point of attack. The bristling manes are arranged in a series of locks in parallel rows.

Such guardian figures stand in a long Anatolian and Middle-Eastern tradition, looking back perhaps to the age of the Hittite, Assyrian and Persian palaces, when gates and doorways

194 and 195 Parts of two miscellaneous figures, one male the other female, may perhaps represent the dynast and his wife, or perhaps legendary Peleus and Thetis. British Museum.

were protected by flanking fierce or fantastic beasts. These two lions probably formed part of a pride deployed around the north terrace or at its approach.

A SCULPTURAL PROGRAMME

There is in the Nereid Monument, as in Payava's tomb and in the earlier Lion tomb, a calculated accumulation of elements that add up to a holistic vision for a dynast's self-image. Erbinna appears at least five times: once in each of the two pediments; once as the Persian-style ruler of conquered cities; again as a reclining banqueter; and perhaps as a figure in Persian dress crowning a warrior on the lesser podium frieze.[65] The pediments present, on the one hand, Erbinna in action leading a military charge while, on the other hand, he sits enthroned in repose. The architrave and cella friezes portray hunting and feasting, while the podium friezes show real and heroic battle.

196 A lioness crouches ready to spring. This was one of possibly four guardian figures placed perhaps on the terrace on the northern approach to the tomb. British Museum.

In the cultural mix of Erbinna's self-image – Lycian, Greek and Persian – it is taste for Greek things and ideas that ultimately prevails. Like Perikles of Limyra and later Mausolus of Karia, Erbinna projects himself as a deified Greek-style hero in the hereafter.[66] The presence of the Nereids, risen from the sea to escort his soul, seems to invite comparison between the death of the dynast and that of Peleus. It is most probably this same hero who is shown grappling with his bride in one of the central acroteria, and perhaps Peleus and Thetis are to be seen again in the freestanding male and female figures that possibly stood among the Nereids.

CONCLUSION

The Lycian tombs represent a rich and fascinating fusion of styles in architecture and sculpture. We find native Lycian traditions of woodworking preserved in a variety of architectural types rendered in stone. We also find adaptation of Greek temple architecture, as in the Nereid Monument. These buildings are decorated in sculpture that is pure Greek, as in Kybernis' tomb, or in a mixed Graeco-Persian style, as in so-called Building G. Its frieze of chariots and horsemen is described by John Boardman as 'almost a cross between Persepolis and the Parthenon'.[67] The lesser podium frieze of the Nereid Monument looks back, albeit indirectly, to the city-siege reliefs of Assyria, while its temple form, raised on a high Lycian podium and with figures standing between the columns, looks forward to the Mausoleum of Halikarnassos. This great monument seems to have been directly inspired by the Nereid Monument. Perhaps more than any other Lycian building, the Nereid Monument epitomizes the confluence of mainland Greek, especially Athenian, Lycian and Middle-Eastern artistic traditions, while the column bases and sculptured architrave are Ionian.

There is a slightly painful self-consciousness about this deliberate borrowing. It is perhaps eloquent of the insecurity of the Lycian dynasts, caught as they were between Persia to the east and Greece to the west. The Trysa monument, Boardman again remarks, 'gives very much the impression of Greek myth bought by the metre'.[68] The appropriation of Greek style and iconography is not always successful. The Caryatids of Perikles' funerary monument at Limyra, free copies of those on the Erechtheum in Athens, are nothing short of barbaric. None the less, combined with recent advances in the knowledge to be found in their coins and stone inscriptions, Lycian architecture and its sculpture represents a chapter in the history of the ancient peoples of western Anatolia that ought to be better known than it is. The story, moreover, takes on even greater significance when we consider the exceptional nature of such building activity for its time. The great architectural projects of the sixth century BC in the eastern Aegean dried up in the fifth century following the suppression of the Ionian revolt. It was not until the 360s of the next century that the Ionian renaissance would see a resurgence of east Greek architecture. It was precisely during this hiatus of a hundred years or so that the Lycian rulers, who had remained loyal to the Persians, erected their remarkable tombs. Kuprlli's recreation of the Xanthian acropolis monuments in stone may be seen as a deliberate act of national defiance in the face of Athenian imperial aggression. The last of the great Lycian tombs – the Nereid, Trysa and Limyra monuments – were completed at a time when, following the demise of Athens, a new political stability in Ionia and Karia saw renewed monumental building there. The Lycian tombs, however, could not compete in grandeur with the great funerary monument of Mausolus and his sister Artemisia that will be visited in the next chapter.

Chapter Nine

The Mausoleum at Halikarnassos

THE HEKATOMNID DYNASTY

Karia is a coastal region of south-west Turkey that lies between Ionia to the north and Lycia to the south and east. The most famous of Karian royals to live before Mausolus was Artemisia, daughter of Lygdamis of Halikarnassos. She was a warrior queen who served under Xerxes, king of Persia, during his invasion of mainland Greece in 480 BC. Herodotos records how Artemisia was a squadron leader, commanding the ships of Halikarnassos and the nearby islands of Kos, Nisyros and Kalymnos. During the battle of Salamis, she rammed a friendly vessel blocking her escape from an Athenian ship that was pursuing her. Xerxes watching from his perch above the straits of Salamis was heard to say, 'my men have become women and my women men'.[1] There is no proof of a dynastic link between this Artemisia, daughter of Lygdamis, and Artemisia, daughter of Hekatomnos and sister of Mausolus, but an alabaster vessel in the British Museum may indicate that the two were related (fig. 197). It was found with fragments of several others by Charles Newton on the lower landing of the steps leading down to the tomb chamber of the Mausoleum. It dates from the time of the earlier Artemisia and must have been placed in the tomb at the order of the later Artemisia. In Old Persian, Elamite, Babylonian cuneiform and in Egyptian Hieroglyphs can be read 'Xerxes, Great King'. It seems very probable that this heirloom or its contents had been a gift of Xerxes, which afterwards passed down through the Karian royal family before it was interred with the body of Mausolus.[2]

197 A Hekatomnid family heirloom found on the site of the Mausoleum. Calcite jar inscribed 'Xerxes Great King' in Old Persian, Elamite, Babylonian and Egyptian, c. 486–465 BC. British Museum.

Following the failure of the invasion of mainland Greece in 480/479 BC, Persian influence declined in the Aegean and for much of the

Dates of the Karian satrapy in the fourth century BC	
Hekatomnos	c. 392–377
Mausolus with his sister/wife Artemisia	377–353
Artemisia (alone)	353–351
Idrieus with his wife Ada I	351–344
Ada I (alone)	344–341
Pixodaros (alone); married to Aphneis	341–336
Pixodaros with his son-in-law, the Persian Orontobates	336–336
Orontobates, possibly with his wife Ada II	336–334
Ada I (alone, reinstated by Alexander)	334–?

fifth century BC Athens dominated the sea and its Asian shore (see table opposite). Squeezed between Athenian (and later Spartan) aggression from the west and the satrapal power of the Persian empire to the east, Karia and its native rulers remained politically unremarkable until 392/391 BC when Hekatomnos, father of Mausolus, was appointed to his own satrapy. Hitherto, the western reaches of the Persian empire had been governed by the satrap of Sardis, the capital city of the province of Lydia. The Persian purpose in creating this separate satrapy of Karia was to establish loyal resistance to Sparta's ambition, following its success against Athens in the Peloponnesian War and, more recently, its defeat of a Persian army outside the walls of Sardis itself.[3] In 391 BC the Great King of Persia ordered Hekatomnos to move against the rising power of Euagoras I, rebellious king of Salamis on Cyprus.[4] Hekatomnos allied himself with Autophradates, the satrap of Lydia, and by this alliance participated in the defence of Persian interests in the west and thereby confirmed his new authority. In 387/386 a treaty with Athens, known as the King's Peace, brought to an end Athens' long pretence to protectorship over the nominal freedom of the Greek city states of East Greece.[5] The eastern Aegean was Persian once more.

In the new political stability that Persian rule brought, the Ionian Greeks to the north and Karians to the south enjoyed a cultural renaissance. Presiding over it was Mausolus who succeeded his father Hekatomnos in 377/376 BC.[6] The Hekatomnids, Mausolus and his four siblings, were jealously to guard their father's dynasty. Keeping power within the family, they practised brother–sister marriage, foreshadowing that of the later Ptolemies of Egypt. Mausolus married his sister Artemisia and ruled for twenty-four years until his death, probably as Diodorus says, in 353 BC.[7] Mourning the loss of her brother–husband, Artemisia ruled alone for a further two years until her death in 351 BC.

The remainder of the history of the dynasty can be summarised as follows. Mausolus and Artemisia were succeeded by their younger brother Idreus, who ruled with his sister Ada I.[8] Idreus died in 344/343 BC, and Ada ruled alone until 341 BC. In that year she was ousted from power by her younger brother Pixodaros and retired to the Karian town of Alinda.[9] Pixodaros, whom we have already met in Chapter Seven extending his power over Lycia, had married Aphneis, a Cappadocian.[10] He tried to strengthen his political position with an alliance between Karia and the rising power of Macedonia by offering a daughter, Ada II, in marriage to Philip Arrhidaeus, son of Philip II of Macedon.[11] When he heard of the plan, Philip's ambitious son Alexander (the Great) attempted to outmanoeuvre his brother by himself offering to marry the Karian princess, at which point his father broke off all negotiations. Ada was married instead to a Persian, Orontobates. After Pixodaros' death in 336 BC, Orontobates probably ruled alone or as satrap with Ada II.[12]

In the spring of 334 BC the young Alexander enters the saga once more. In that year he crossed from Europe into Asia and defeated a Persian army at the Battle of the River Granikos. On his march south he went from one Greek city to another offering freedom from Persian rule. On the way to Halikarnassos, he was approached by Ada I who, seeing a political opportunity to regain power, asked permission to adopt him. He accepted, and Karia and Macedonia were united by family ties at last. Alexander laid siege to Halikarnassos, expelled Orontobates and the Persian garrison and reinstated Ada I as queen.[13] She thus became the last of the Hekatomnid satraps and, one might say, the first of the so-called Diadochoi or followers of Alexander. At Halikarnassos she was succeeded by Philoxenos, one of Alexander's officers.[14]

Before Mausolus came to power, Karia had comprised a scattered community of villages with a capital at Mylasa. Mausolus sought to strengthen his rule over his people by encouraging them to adopt the Greek polis or city model of civic life. On the peninsula of Myndos, he pursued a policy of synoicism, gathering villages together and moving the capital from inland Mylasa, 50 kilometres to coastal Halikarnassos (fig. 198).[15] From here Mausolus and his successors extended their power over

198 Bodrum from the crusader castle. The Mausoleum was situated in the grove of trees, below and to the right of the ancient stone theatre.

the whole of Karia and beyond. Kaunos, for example, was just within Karian territory, on the eastern frontier close to the neighbouring land of Lycia. The Kaunians set up statues of Hekatomnos and of Mausolus, and the walls of the city were probably fortified at this time.[16] Also in Karia, south of Halikarnassos, was the city of Knidos. The Knidians synoicized, perhaps at the instigation of Mausolus, and founded a new city at the tip of their long, thin peninsula.[17] Further afield, Miletos in Ionia employed Satyros to erect statues of Idreus and Ada I in the panhellenic sanctuary at Delphi.[18] Near to Miletos, in the 330s BC the Ionian city of Priene was refounded on the slopes of Mount Mycale.[19] A portrait statue of one of the female members of the dynasty, probably Ada I – Alexander's adoptive mother – was dedicated in the temple of Athena Polias.[20] Among the off-shore islands that felt the influence of Karia were nearby Kos, Rhodes, Samos to the north and Crete to the south.[21]

In the reign of Pixodaros, Lycia seems to have been a Karian possession. In Chapter Seven mention was made of a trilingual inscription with texts in Lycian and Greek and a résumé in Aramaic, a court language of Persia.[22] It records a decree passed in 337 BC setting up a cult of Basileus Kaunios, imported from Kaunos on the Lycian–Karian border. The same text announces the establishment of a garrison commander at Xanthos and the appointment of two governors of Lycia. Hekatomnid dominance over Lycia probably began under Mausolus, encouraged by Persia, which governed its dominions through loyal satraps. During Mausolus' lifetime the principal governor in the western provinces was Autophradates at Sardis. When in 362 BC Autophradates joined a general rebellion against the Great King of Persia, the Satraps' Revolt, Mausolus is said also to have joined in.[23] The revolt collapsed, but Mausolus retained his satrapy, perhaps because he had proved himself loyal in suppressing another revolt by the Lycian dynast Perikles of Limyra.[24] Mausolus' return to the satrapy in 361/360 BC reflects his ultimate dependence upon the political stability given by the Persian empire. To the west, however, he encouraged squabbling among rival Greek states and sought to thwart Athenian aggression in the Aegean.[25] When Athens' allies revolted against it during the so-called Social War (357–355 BC) he gave them help. The refounding of the capital at Halikarnassos around 377–362 BC may itself have been precipitated by the need for greater military defence against Athenian military aggression.[26]

HALIKARNASSOS AND THE SETTING OF THE MAUSOLEUM

To appreciate the physical setting of the Mausoleum, the modern tourist town of Bodrum is best approached from the sea with a copy of Vitruvius

199 The crusader castle of St Peter, Bodrum.

in hand. The impression gained is of a vast natural theatre, the rising auditorium provided by the hills surrounding the harbour. On the western horn of the harbour of Halikarnassos was the fountain of the nymph Salmakis, located in 1995 in an area not publicly accessible.²⁷ On the eastern of the two harbour promontories, the Zephyrion, Mausolus built his palace, where now stands the crusader castle of St Peter (fig. 199).²⁸ Some wall foundations, part of a stone staircase and other features of this palace incorporated into the fabric of the castle have recently been uncovered by archaeologists, but nowhere are to be seen the fine apartments, which Vitruvius tells us were decoratively veneered in Proconnesian marble.²⁹ The crusader castle itself was built between 1494 and 1522, much of it reusing blocks of stone taken from the Mausoleum.

As at Knidos, Priene and other towns, Halikarnassos was laid out with an orthogonal (grid) plan according to the design principles associated with the fifth-century BC town-planner Hippodamos of Miletos.³⁰ The city (fig. 200) boasted a fine, broad high street stretching from the relatively well-preserved Myndos gate in the west (fig. 201) to the now totally destroyed Mylasa gate in the east. Vitruvius tells us that the Mausoleum was situated on this street running 'through the middle of the rising curve'.³¹ The modern Turgut Reis Caddesi today occupies the much-reduced line of this street. The Mausoleum was indeed situated close to

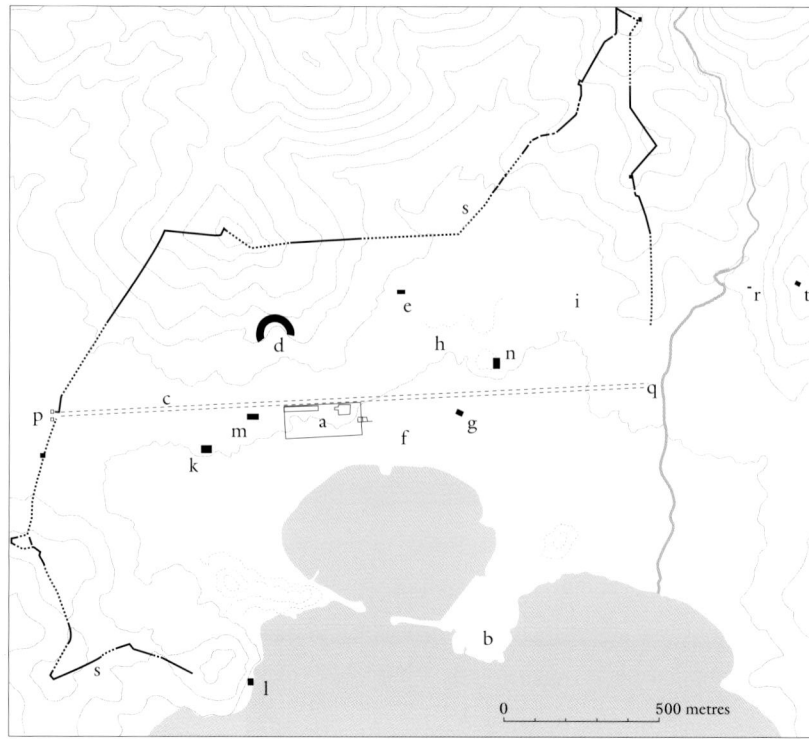

200 Plan of Halikarnassos.

a   the Mausoleum
b   presumed palace of Mausolus
c   main street of ancient Halikarnassos
d   the theatre
e   sanctuary of Ares
f   presumed location of the agora
g   sanctuary of Demeter
h   presumed location of gymnasion
    (= 'doric stoa')
i   the stadion
k   late Roman villa
l   Roman villa and Salmakis Fountain
m   Hellenistic house
n   approximate location of
    Türkkyusu temple
p   Myndos Gate
q   presumed location of Mylasa Gate
r   approximate location of 'Tomb of the
    Karian Princess'
s   city wall
t   fortification tower

the centre of the city, to the north and west of the agora, or ancient marketplace, and just below the high street. It was set in its own precinct, measuring some 242 metres long and 105 metres wide, enclosed by a temenos wall and entered through a monumental gateway (propylon).[32] It was necessary to retain the sloping ground of the natural site with terrace walls. These were made of drafted limestone blocks, above which sat further courses of white marble topped by a marble coping.[33] The Mausoleum enclosure was most likely planted with trees and flowering shrubs to provide shady walks.

The Mausoleum terrace was planned as part of the overall design of the new city. To the north-east of it, another platform was terraced to contain the sacred enclosure and temple of the war god Ares. To the north-west and with a good view of the Mausoleum was the stone-built theatre, terraced into the steeply rising hillside. Its precise date is uncertain, but it was probably built in time for Theopompos, historian and political exile from the island of Chios, to deliver his winning funeral speech as part of the 'games' organized by Artemisia in Mausolus' honour.[34] Also performed here, no doubt, were the plays staged in a dramatic competition won by Theodektes of Phaselis in Pamphylia.[35] Artemisia's grief for her brother became legendary in antiquity, and she was said to have daily drunk a pinch of his ashes mixed in a cup of wine.[36]

MAUSOLUS AND THE MAUSOLEUM

Some five hundred years after the building of Mausolus' great funerary monument, the second-century AD author Lucian wrote an anecdotal collection entitled *Dialogues of the Dead*. Among them is an imagined meeting between the fourth-century BC Cynic philosopher Diogenes, of barrel-occupying fame, and Mausolus. Lucian had travelled in the eastern Aegean and had himself seen the Mausoleum, as he had the statue of Aphrodite by Praxiteles at nearby Knidos, and about which he also wrote a memorable anecdote.[37] The following conversation takes place in the Underworld between the ghosts of the vain and materialistic Mausolus and the self-denying Diogenes, who before migrating to Athens had been a native of Sinope on the Black Sea coast.

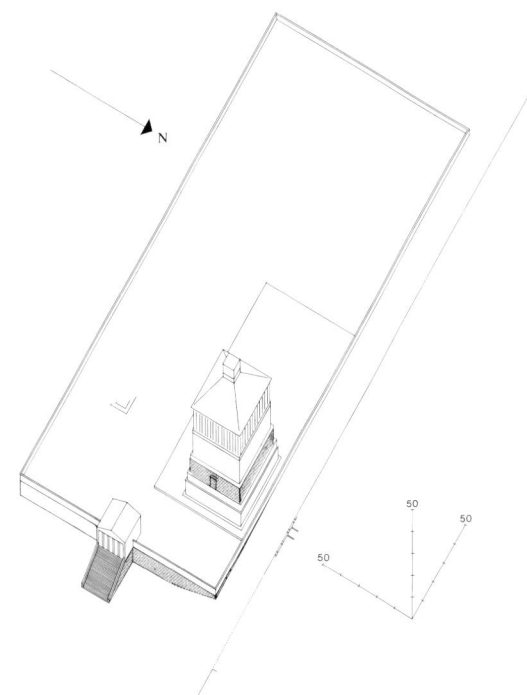

201 Aerial reconstruction of the Mausoleum and its precinct. Drawing K. Jeppesen.

> DIOGENES: Why, Carian, are you so proud, and expect to be honoured above all of us?
>
> MAUSOLUS: Firstly, Sinopean, because of my royal position. I was king of all Caria, ruler also of part of Lydia, subdued some islands, too, and advanced as far as Miletus, subjugating most of Ionia. Moreover, I was handsome and tall and mighty in war. But, most important of all, I have lying over me in Halicarnassus a vast memorial, outdoing that of any other of the dead not only in size but also in its finished beauty, with horses and men reproduced most perfectly in the fairest marble, so that it would be difficult to find even a temple like it. Don't you think I've a right to be proud of these things?

DIOGENES: Of your royal position, you say, and your beauty, and the weight of your tomb?

MAUSOLUS: Good heavens, yes.

DIOGENES: But my handsome Mausolus, the strength and the beauty you mention aren't still with you here. If we chose a judge of beauty, I can't see why your skull should be thought better than mine. Both of them are bald and bare, both of us show our teeth in the same way, and have lost our eyes, and have snub noses now. Perhaps your tomb and all that costly marble may give the people of Halicarnassus something to show off, and they can boast to strangers of the magnificent building they have, but I can't see what good it is to you my good fellow, unless you're claiming that, with all that marble pressing down on you, you have a heavier burden to bear than any of us.

MAUSOLUS: Will all that, then, be of no good to me? Will Mausolus and Diogenes be on an equal footing?

DIOGENES: No, indeed, your excellency; we shan't be on an equal footing. Mausolus will groan when he remembers the things on earth above, which he thought brought him happiness, while Diogenes will be able to laugh at him. Mausolus will talk of the tomb erected to him at Halicarnassus by his wife and sister, Artemisia, whereas Diogenes has no idea whether he even has a tomb for his body, for he didn't care about that, but he has left for the best of those who come after the report that he has lived the life of a man, most servile of Carians, that towers above your memorial, and is built on surer foundations.[38]

The Cynics were an extreme philosophical sect with a moral resolve to lead a dog's life, devoid of material comforts (kuon is the Greek word for dog). By juxtaposing one of antiquity's great showmen with the arch Cynic, Lucian nicely brings out Mausolus' essential character. That he was beautiful, as Lucian portrays him, we need have no doubt. Perhaps his very face is to be found in the colossal figure which was discovered in many fragments during Charles Newton's excavations (fig. 202).[39] At the very least we are given a record of the family likeness which, if not a portrait of Mausolus himself, is likely to be one of his ancestors: lion-maned, strong and even-featured, full-mouthed and with large, deep-set and hooded eyes. If not this man, then one like him was heroized, perhaps even deified in the grandest tomb the Greek world had ever seen. Grand indeed it seemed to Roman writers, including Pliny[40] and Vitruvius.[41] The description of the building to be found in Pliny's *Natural History* is especially important for an understanding of its possible appearance. Pliny was working from earlier, Greek texts copied and recopied by hand. Pliny's text itself comes down to us in many Latin manuscripts, which do not all agree.[42] It is easy therefore to see how errors could creep in and, although some of his 'facts' can be reconciled with the archaeological evidence, not all that he says can be confirmed.

> The sculptor Scopas had as his rivals and contemporaries Bryaxis, Timotheus and Leochares, whom we must discuss together, because they jointly carved the sculptures of the Mausoleum. This is the tomb built by his wife Artemisia for Mausolus, king of Caria, who died in the second year of the 107th Olympiad. These artists in particular were responsible for making the building one of the seven wonders of the world. It is 63 feet long on the north and south sides, shorter on the façades, its total circumference is 440 feet, it rises to a height of 25 cubits, and is surrounded by 36 columns. They called the circumference a 'colonnade'. The sculptures on the east side were carved by Scopas, those on the north by Bryaxis, those on the south by Timotheus, and those on the west by Leochares; and before they finished the queen died. But they did not stop the work until it was completed, considering it to be a monument to their own glory and artistic skill; and to this day their hands compete with one another. A fifth artist took part. For above the colonnade is a pyramid, equal in height to the lower part, contracting by 24 steps to the topmost point; on the summit is a marble four-horse chariot, made by Pythis. When this is included it brings the whole building to a height of 140 feet.[43]

202 Head of a colossal portrait statue found on the north side of the Mausoleum, perhaps Mausolus himself. British Museum.

RECONSTRUCTION

Before Charles Newton's excavations of the Mausoleum site in 1857–8, there was no archaeological evidence to restrain the many and fantastic attempts at its reconstruction.[44] Even following the excavations, suggested solutions to the problem of reconstruction can seem fanciful (fig. 203).[45] Newton's own architect Richard Pullan, for example, wrongly assigned a carved frieze to the external entablature above the columns.

203 Fanciful reconstruction of the Mausoleum by C.R. Cockerell, exhibited at the Royal Academy of Arts in 1858. British Museum.

One of the problems intrinsic to the task is not knowing the ancient foot length used on the Mausoleum. The Greeks had no standard system of measurement, such as we use today, and their foot and indeed other units of measurement could vary from time to time and place to place.[46] Moreover, where Pliny writing in the first century AD gives measurements in feet, he is not thinking of a measurement known to Romans of his day (usually 29.57 centimetres), but is quoting Greek sources that go back to the Mausoleum architects' own treatise on their building. We can only guess at what foot measurement they had in mind.[47]

Given such difficulties, the level of disagreement among those who have attempted to resolve them, the fragmentary nature of the material evidence and the high degree of specialist knowledge needed to interpret it, there is no agreed way of reconstructing the Mausoleum in detail. There are, however, some elements in Pliny's account and some firm facts of archaeology that can be agreed upon (fig. 205). We can say for certain that the building was raised in three parts, the lowest of which was a podium base. The footprint of this was not square but, as the excavated foundation cutting into the bedrock itself demonstrates, a rectangle with two long and two short sides.[48] On top of the podium stood an Ionic colonnade of thirty-six columns, and above this again was a pyramid roof, crowned with a colossal chariot and four horses in marble. We can say for certain that a continuous frieze carved in low relief with a battle between Greeks and Amazons was located around the top of the podium (fig. 204). Also certain is the fact that the 'lids' of the coffers of the ceiling in the colonnade were carved in low relief showing battle scenes.[49] That the corners of the roof were decorated with sculptured ornaments (acroteria) is sure, but the assignment of surviving fragments of sculpture to these positions remains tentative. Other details of the architecture are known, such as the floral carving of the marble roof guttering (sima) with its lion-head spouts, and the design of the Ionic column capitals and ornamental column bases standing on low, square plinths.

204 Reconstruction of one corner of the Mausoleum incorporating the Amazon frieze in a combination of podium cornice, stylobate and column base. After K. Jeppesen.

A broad outline of the building emerges, but we soon find controversy when we attempt to go beyond these 'facts'. Disputed, for example, are the relative heights of the podium, colonnade and roof. Pliny is not very helpful in giving the height of the building as 25 cubits or 37.5 feet, when he later tells us that it rose to a total height of 140 feet. Equally problematic is his assertion that it measured 63 feet long, which is difficult to reconcile with a given circumference of 440 feet. One way out is to argue that the lesser measurements refer to parts only of the elevation and length of the building, but scholars cannot agree on whether this is the case, or what parts these would be. Apart from its height, there is also the disputed shape of the podium. As we have seen, it supported thirty-six columns. The width of the spacing of these columns, if it can be agreed upon, will determine the lengths of the colonnades on the four sides of the building and hence the dimensions of the top of the podium on which the columns

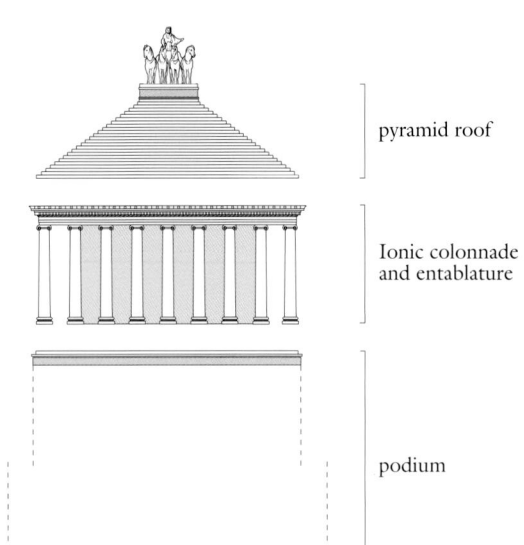

205 Sketch of the Mausoleum illustrating the basic known elements.

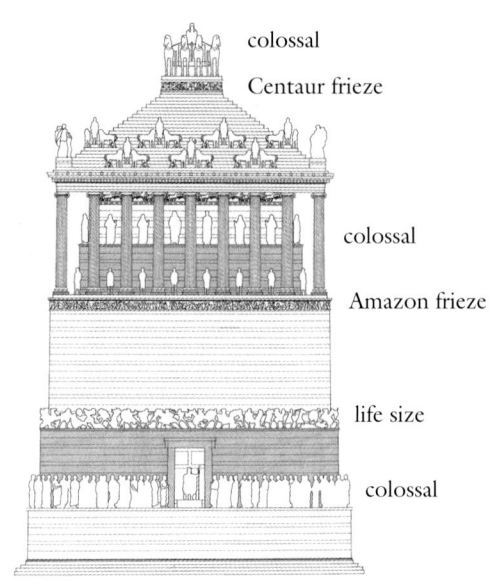

206 The Mausoleum according to K. Jeppesen.

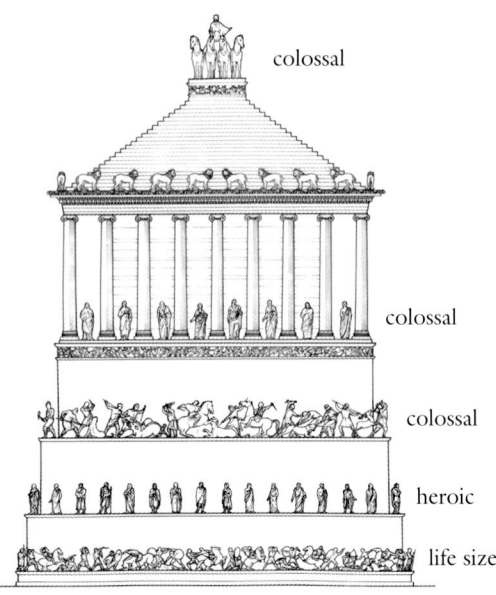

207 The Mausoleum according to G. Waywell.

208 The Mausoleum according to W. Hoepfner.

stood. The dimensions of the top of the podium determine how its sides were built. If the top and base measurements of the podium are roughly the same, then the sides could have risen vertically from the base. If, however, in relation to its base there was a reduction of the dimensions of the podium at the top, then the sides must have tapered inwards. Alternatively, they could have risen vertically, but in steps (figs 206–8). In his reconstruction, for example, W. Hoepfner prefers a wider spacing of columns (3.15 metres) and has straight sides to the podium, while Kristian Jeppesen, who from 1966 to 1977 led the Danish excavations at the site of the Mausoleum, has insisted upon a 3-metre spacing of eleven columns along the long sides and nine on the short.[50] Such an arrangement would give a top to the podium measuring 32 by 26 metres, which is less than the base. Accordingly, Jeppesen restores steps in the side walls of the podium, a solution which is also favoured by Geoffrey Waywell in his study of the Mausoleum sculpture but, whereas Jeppesen has two steps only, Waywell has three.

THE SCULPTURE

The question of whether there were steps or not in the podium sides is crucial to the problem of how the freestanding sculpture was displayed on the building, for in addition to no fewer than three friezes carved in low relief, numerous sculptures and fragments of sculpture carved in the round have been found. These represent three different scales, the colossal, so-called heroic and life size.

As with the Nereid Monument, so here some figures are thought to have been located between the columns and these include the colossal portrait figures, popularly known as Mausolus and Artemisia (fig. 209). There are, however, too many fragments of sculpture for them all to have been accommodated thus, and hence the argument for introducing steps into the podium, on which sculpture could have been displayed. Geoffrey Waywell has made the fullest study of these sculptures and he argues for three steps in the podium, one for each of the three scales.[51] The colossal includes human standing figures (about 2.7–3 metres high), hunt scenes and scenes of sacrifice. The heroic scale comprised

209 Colossal portrait statues perhaps to be identified as Mausolus and Artemisia. British Museum.

210 Left, colossal head from a royal portrait statue. The unusual coiffure of tight curls encircling the head is a feature of the Hekatomnid dynasty and is found again in a smaller portrait head, right, thought to represent Mausolus' younger sister Ada I, found at the site of the temple of Priene. British Museum.

211 Colossal rider wearing trousers under a tunic and probably representing a Persian. Traces of blue paint and gilding, not visible here, are the remains of a painted saddle cloth. British Museum.

212 'Heroic' bearded male head carved on a scale between colossal and life-size. British Museum.

213 Life-size head of a Persian. British Museum.

standing figures (about 2.4 metres high) in either Graeco-Karian or Persian dress. The life-size figures (about 1.8 metres high) comprise repeating groups of battle between Greeks and Persians. Added to these are the fragments of the colossal chariot group, which Pliny says crowned the roof and a series of lions, which Waywell arranges in two files around the base of the roof.

Major differences between Waywell's and Jeppesen's reconstructions are to be found in the deployment of the sculptured remains.[52] According to Jeppesen, a blue limestone plinth ran around the wall of the cella on which colossal portrait statues of the dynastic family and their ancestors were displayed (fig. 214). Here he assigns the work of the famous sculptors named by Pliny. Jeppesen suggests that the colonnade could be reached by a staircase rising inside the monument.[53] He believes that one statue was placed behind each pair of columns, six on each short and eight on each long side, numbering twenty-eight in all. These he believes were the colossal male figures, such as the so-called Mausolus. Paired with the male statues were females, represented in the surviving fragments by a head which is slightly larger in scale than that of the so-called Artemisia.[54] The smaller female statues of the 'Artemisia' type he believes are too small to have stood here, and these he assigns to the spaces between the columns, as he does a presumed series of bodyguard figures in Persian dress.[55]

Jeppesen accommodates the remainder of the colossal and life-size sculpture on just two plinths around the podium. He insists on only two plinths in the podium because, once he has restored more than one foot moulding (krepidoma) to the base, his calculation of the available space will not allow more.[56] The life-sized sculptures are assigned to the first, upper plinth. It is suggested that they were set in shallow recesses cut into the cornice of an entire band of blue limestone masonry running around the podium face.[57] This use of blue limestone, as a contrast with the white marble used elsewhere in the monument, is a striking feature of Jeppesen's reconstruction. (It includes the sculpture podium of the cella and square plinths beneath the

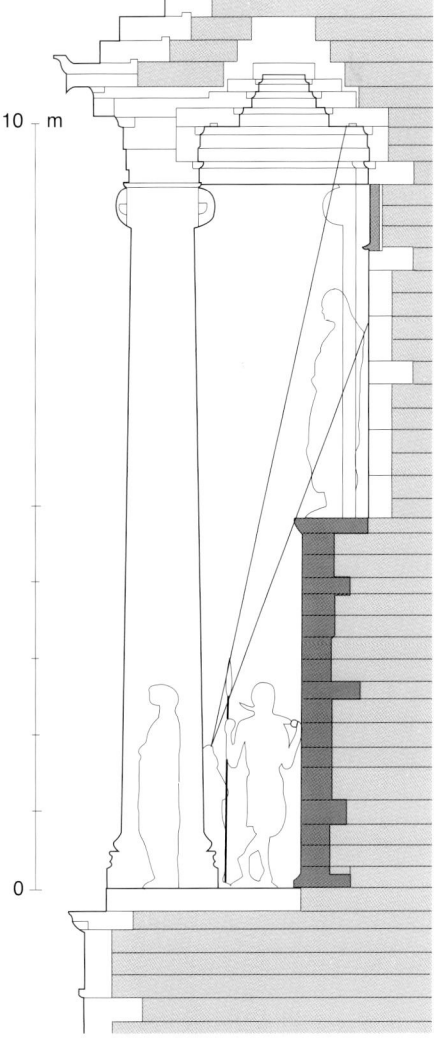

214 Proposed shelf of blue limestone for displaying colossal sculpture along the cella wall of the Mausoleum. After K. Jeppesen.

215 Colossal seated figure, perhaps of Mausolus himself. When first excavated, the drapery was coated in purple paint, which discoloured upon exposure to the air into a dull brown. British Museum.

circular column-bases). Jeppesen's second, lower plinth is assigned an estimated more than 120 colossal figures. These include a seated statue, which has been seen as a representation of Mausolus, with one arm raised and resting on a spear or sceptre (fig. 215). When found, Newton records that the drapery was coated in purple paint, which discoloured to a rusty brown on exposure to the air. Jeppesen sets the figure in a niche in the form of a false door, let into the podium as a recess, and he reconstructs the remainder of sculpture set on the same plinth as a procession leading sacrificial victims in honour of the deified Mausolus.[58]

The contention that there were just two sculpture plinths on the podium leaves no place for figures of the larger than life, so-called 'heroic' scale, which Jeppesen assigns to the steps of the roof along with the lions.[59] Also at roof level, Jeppesen attempts to identify the acroterial statues that stood at the corners of the entablature. It is suggested that at least two of the four bases were filled with representations of the goddess Leto and her son Apollo, slaying Niobe and her children. A fine head of Apollo (fig. 216) and an assumed head of Leto are assigned to a putative acroterial group.[60]

One aspect of the decoration of the Mausoleum on which all scholars agree is the location of the Amazon frieze around the upper edge of the podium (fig. 217). Jeppesen has shown beyond doubt that this frieze was mounted here and crowned by an egg and dart moulding, of which fragments survive.[61] Like most architectural friezes, the Amazon frieze of the Mausoleum was carved on the building, as is made clear by the figures that were carved across the joints between two blocks. Measuring around 90 centimetres high, the frieze blocks vary between some 1.5 and 2 metres long and are presumed to have run in a continuous band around the full perimeter of the building. The composition is looser than that of the Parthenon and Bassai friezes, but can still be quite complex with occasional overlapping of figures. A figure of the hero Herakles, recognizable by his club and lion's skin, makes this Amazonomachy specific to the story of his quest for the belt of the Amazon queen, Hippolyte. It was said that the battle-axe also taken from her by Herakles could be seen in the temple of Zeus in the Hekatomnid sanctuary at Labraynda.

The Amazon frieze was just one of three ornamental friezes.[62] Little survives of the so-called Centaur frieze – one block only and some fragments of others – and it may not originally have been extensive (fig. 218). It may be assigned to the sides of the plinth supporting the colossal chariot group, crowning the monument.[63] Then there is the Chariot frieze. This is very fragmentary, but sixteen individual chariots, each with a driver (fig. 219) and drawn by four horses galloping one behind another, have been identified. These may be assigned to the top of the cella wall, possibly on the short front sides only. The thickness of the blocks

216 Over life-size head thought to represent the god Apollo. British Museum.

varied between 9.6 and 15.5 centimetres. Made of particularly fine marble, they were carved separately as individual plaques and inserted into the wall.[64]

KRISCHEN'S AND HOEPFNER'S MAUSOLEUM

For those seeking a ready-made solution to its detailed reconstruction, the Mausoleum brings little comfort, and controversy continues to surround it. Recently, W. Hoepfner has raised several major objections to Jeppesen's scheme.[65] He insists that the inter-axial span of the columns must be commensurate with the architectural elements above, and form a regular and symmetrical pattern with, for example, the lion-head spouts. Hoepfner's own reconstruction resembles in many ways that of Fritz Krischen, who was at pains to find a system of proportions that could be reconciled with the measurements given by Pliny. He insisted, therefore, as does Hoepfner, on an inter-axial span of 3.15 metres. For Krischen this had represented nine so-called Ionic feet of 35 centimetres.[66] Hoepfner prefers a foot of 30.08 centimetres. A span of 315 centimetres therefore represents 10.5 feet. This is the equivalent of three blocks of the stone guttering (sima) that ran around the base of the pyramid roof. Such a span would allow a regular and co-ordinated sequence of column and lion-head spout, as indeed is the case with Pytheos' other great work, the temple of Athena Polias at Priene, which we shall explore in the next chapter.[67]

In Krischen's and Hoepfner's reconstructions the wider spacing of the columns, resting on a stepped stylobate, means that the need to insert steps into the podium is eliminated. Unlike Waywell and Jeppesen, therefore, they have no place to accommodate the greater part of the freestanding sculpture. Hoepfner resorts to the suggestion that this was displayed

The Mausoleum at Halikarnassos 221

217 Two blocks of the frieze that ran around the top of the podium, showing a battle between Greeks and Amazons. British Museum.

218 Block of a frieze that shows a battle of humans against Centaurs. A rump only of the mythical beast appears exiting from the right of the picture. The centaur frieze may have decorated the base of the chariot group crowning the roof. British Museum.

219 Charioteer in a long flowing tunic from a frieze that may have run around the top of the cella wall. British Museum.

along walkways near ground level on the Mausoleum terrace, but there is no evidence for this. Hoepfner does accept, at least for the long sides, Jeppesen's suggestion of a raised plinth running along the cella wall in order to accommodate some colossal freestanding figures. Others he places between the columns, but set back behind the line of them.[68]

Hoepfner shares Krischen's desire to reconcile his reconstruction with the measurements given by Pliny. For him, however, as for Krischen, the hardest of Pliny's measurements to resolve is the impossible length of the building given as 63 feet. Krischen got around the problem by amending the text. This altering of a literary source to make the text fit the theory, instead of the other way round, always weakens any argument. Hoepfner's solution is to accept the received version and to take this as the length of the cella. In so doing he reduces the size of the cella and accordingly enlarges the surounding space for the columns (pteron). This increased space he fills with a second series of columns and in the porches at either end he has a third row of three columns in each to create a forest effect similar to that of the great temple of Artemis at Ephesos.[69]

Hoepfner's is a fully rational and regular Mausoleum. Pliny, for example, says that the upper part of the building, that is to say the roof, is equal to that below, which can only mean the colonnade. Hoepfner, therefore, devises a scheme which divides the elevation into three equal parts. The first is the podium from its foot (krepidoma) to the first step of the top of the podium; the second part comprises the distance between the top of the podium and the top of the guttering (sima); the third comprises the top of the sima to the top of the heads of the figures that Hoepfner assumes stood in the chariot. Each division measures 46⅔ of his foot of 30.08 centimetres, equal to 140 feet.[70]

Krischen and Hoepfner place the Centaur frieze under the Amazon frieze. As they are the same thickness, this seems possible, but Jeppesen had already discounted the idea in 1975, on account of the unique foot moulding of the Centaur frieze, which he thought incompatible with the smooth ashlar masonry immediately below.[71] Like Jeppesen, Krischen had placed the chariot frieze as a crown to the cella wall, but Hoepfner objects on grounds that this would run counter to what he perceives to be the grammar of Greek architecture. It is not, he says, possible to place the frieze at the same height as the columns.[72] Hoepfner locates the chariot frieze around the walls of the burial chamber, which according to him was barrel-vaulted in its ceiling.[73] The surviving fragments, however, of the chariot frieze indicate too many blocks of too great a length to be accommodated around the walls of the chamber.

It is usually assumed that the burial chamber placed off-centre in the podium was the only room in the entire building. Krischen, however, argued the case for a room in the cella, arranged around a massive central pillar supporting the pyramid of the roof. Hoepfner too believes that the cella could be entered through a porch from the colonnade and that there was a cult space with a high false-vaulted or corbelled ceiling reaching up into the apex of the pyramid roof.[74] Without horizontal beams connecting the upper parts of the walls, however, the outward thrust of the pyramid and the weight of the quadriga pressing down on them may have caused Hoepfner's cella building to have fallen down.[75]

Hoepfner concludes that the Mausoleum was an Ionic, regular grid-building with signs of arithmetical planning. Pliny says the circumference of the Mausoleum was 440 feet, and as we have seen the cutting for the foundations of the monument suggest a width for the building of 100 feet and a length of 120 feet. Pliny gives the height of the monument as 140 feet. These measurements may suggest a relationship of 5, 6, 7, where one is equal to twenty. The Mausoleum is seen to have such features in common with other buildings erected in the Hekatomnid era, including the temple of Athena at Priene and the temple of Zeus at Labraynda. In this last, for example, the diameter of the underside of the lowest column drum is in a 3 : 8 relation to the inter-axial span of the intercolumniation; at Priene it was 4 : 7; on the Mausoleum it was 5 : 9. This greater width in the Mausoleum can be accounted for by the intention of placing sculpture between the columns.[76]

Hoepfner's is on paper at least a compelling argument and is likely to be taken up by those seeking a tidy Mausoleum, but it has been rejected by Jeppesen on the basis of the concrete evidence, which he himself has discovered, and his authority is difficult to challenge. If we were to sum up the three proposals for reconstruction, we might say that Waywell's is primarily concerned with the sculpture, while Hoepfner's is motivated more by an interest in architecture and a desire to apply a literal reading of Pliny. Jeppesen's is the one that makes the most conscientious attempt at considering all the evidence together and at finding a fully integrated solution. At the end, therefore, we are left with three competing options for reconstructing the Mausoleum of Halikarnassos, each with individual merit and none of them fully consistent with the testimony of Pliny.

THE SCULPTORS

Pliny mentions the names of four famous Greek sculptors who were, he says, each responsible for a different side of the building: Timotheos on the south, Bryaxis on the north, Skopas on the east and Leochares on the west.[77] In addition he says that the chariot group (fig. 220) that crowned the pyramid of the roof was by Pytheos who, together with Satyros, wrote

220 Forepart of a colossal horse, one of four harnessed to a chariot crowning the roof of the Mausoleum. British Museum.

a lost treatise about the Mausoleum.[78] This same Pytheos went on to design the temple of Athena at Priene and is also thought to have designed buildings at Labraynda in Karia, perhaps working both for Mausolus and, after his death, for Idreus.[79] Satyros is a more shadowy figure but is thought to be the same as a Satyros, son of Isotimos of Paros, who around 345/354 BC signed a statue base at Delphi designed to support bronze portrait statues of Idreus and his sister–consort Ada.[80] Jeppesen considers Pytheos and Satyros as having an equal responsibility for architecture and sculpture alike. Satyros is thought to have been the senior partner, while the junior Pytheos was to succeed him.[81] Vitruvius is another source for the names of the sculptors and he largely confirms the account of Pliny, except that he includes Praxiteles in place of Timotheos. We also learn from Vitruvius that Pytheos was opposed to the use of the Doric order and that he created the temple of Athena at Priene, about which he wrote another treatise.[82]

Timotheos is known for his work *c.* 375–370 BC as a sculptor on the temple of Asclepius at Epidauros in the eastern Peloponnese, where he is mentioned in the inscribed temple accounts as a maker of 'typoi', which here perhaps means reliefs.[83] Timotheos is not the only sculptor to have worked on the Epidaurian temple decoration, and in the assignment of different tasks to different craftsmen the accounts for building and decorating the temple may be seen to provide a model for the making of the Mausoleum.[84]

The Bryaxis who worked on the Mausoleum is to be distinguished from the sculptor of the same name who was active in the early third century BC and who was commissioned by the Ptolemys to create the cult statue of the god Serapis for the Alexandrian Serapeion and who sculpted a portrait of Seleukos I, the Macedonian successor to much of Alexander's empire.[85] A number of works are mentioned in the ancient authors as being by a Bryaxis, but without specific reference as to which sculptor of that name is intended. Our man was probably the Athenian who signed a base for a monument commemorating a victory in the festival at Athens known as the anthippasia.[86] He probably also made a statue of Dionysos at Knidos, which city took advantage of the presence of the Mausoleum sculptors at nearby Halikarnassos to commission works from them.[87] Given the tendency for Greeks to name their sons after the grandfather, the later Bryaxis may very well have been related to the earlier.

Skopas of Paros is perhaps best known for his work at Tegea in the Arcadia region of the Peloponnese.[88] There some very fine pediment sculpture from the temple of Athena Alea is attributed to his workshop. The old temple of Athena was destroyed by fire in 395 BC and was rebuilt some time after that date. Precisely when is not known, but it was perhaps around 345 BC, following Skopas' service to Mausolus.[89] A curious connection between the Hekatomnids and Tegea itself may be found in a relief in the British Museum discovered at Tegea and showing Zeus of Labraynda, the principal deity of the Karians, flanked by Idreus and Ada (fig. 221).[90] Could it be that when Skopas moved his workshop west from Halikarnassos to Arcadia he was commissioned by his former patrons to

221 Marble relief from Tegea in western mainland Greece showing Zeus of Labraynda flanked by Idreus and Ada I, joint rulers of Karia 351–344 BC. British Museum.

set up this token of their religious piety? Again, like Bryaxis, Skopas also provided sculpture, a Dionysos and an Athena, for the new Knidian sanctuaries.⁹¹

Pliny tells us that the Athenian Leochares flourished in the 102nd Olympiad, around 372/371–369/368 BC.⁹² These dates are too early not only for his participation in the decoration of the Mausoleum but also for his other known achievements. Alexander's father, Philip II, is said to have engaged him after the Battle of Chaironeia (338 BC) to work on family portraits in Philip's family shrine, the Philippeion at Olympia.⁹³ There is an unavoidable comparison to be made between the Mausoleum as commemoration of the Hekatomnids and the Philippeion as commemoration of the Macedonian dynasty of Philip and Alexander. As with all the other named sculptors of the Mausoleum, Leochares is also connected with Knidos, this time as the sculptor most likely to have carved the Demeter now in the British Museum.⁹⁴ Other work in Karia may have included the cult statue in the temple of Ares at Halikarnassos, which is also attributed to Timotheos.⁹⁵

Of all the named sculptors, the most famous is Praxiteles, best known for his naturalistic representation of fleshy gods, especially Aphrodite.⁹⁶ Like the others his activity in the region of Halikarnassos is corroborated by association with other projects, namely the two statues of Aphrodite, one on Kos and the other at Knidos. The date of these works is not known but could have been early in his career *c.* 360 BC, when the Mausoleum was being built and close to the date of the re-founding of Kos in 366/365 BC.⁹⁷ Although doubted by some, because he is omitted by Pliny, Praxiteles' involvement in the Mausoleum project must be considered a possibility.

There has been much speculation as to which of the surviving sculptures of the Mausoleum should be attributed to which of these sculptors. Given that Pliny says each one of four sculptors was allocated a different side of the building, the original position of the sculpture on the Mausoleum becomes critical. Charles Newton's excavation records find-places of the sculptures he retrieved, and these should tell us from which side of the building each fell. Unfortunately, however, already by the time Newton arrived on the scene, few of the sculptures he found were in the place they occupied when they fell or were pulled from the building. Only the undisturbed cache of fragments found outside the wall that bounded the Mausoleum precinct on its north side can with certainty be said to have fallen from the north side of the Mausoleum.[98] They include the most important of all the sculptures to survive, the colossal portrait statue of a Hekatomnid dynast – perhaps Mausolus himself – and of a female relative. These should be by Bryaxis. Doubt remains, however, because Waywell has questioned whether Pliny's assignment of sides to sculptors applies to all levels of the Mausoleum. In his analysis of the various compositions, Waywell noted that the subject matter of the sculptures tends to change from level to level, rather than from side to side.[99] The portrait statues are thought to have been arranged within the colonnade around all four sides of the building and thus one sculptor is likely to have taken responsibility for all of these.

As we have seen, the Amazon frieze crowned the top of the podium, and its subject matter turned at least one, and probably all four corners. It was once a focus of interest in the possibility that individual styles could be detected in the sculpture. Charles Newton was the first to speculate that a run of four frieze blocks found on the east side of the Mausoleum site must be given to Skopas.[100] The reliability, however, of the find-site has been challenged along with the whole notion that the frieze had anything to do with the involvement of the named sculptors.[101] It is more likely that their role was restricted to the freestanding sculpture only and that the frieze was treated as an architectural ornament in the master-plan. That is not to say that it is devoid of artistic personality.

SUCCESSORS OF THE MAUSOLEUM

Through the succeeding Hellenistic period and into Roman imperial times, Mausolus' sepulchre had a powerful and sustained influence over monumental tomb-building across the Mediterranean world.[102] None of those it inspired was ever so grand, but there were to be many lesser versions of its three-part design, with a high podium supporting a colonnade, topped by a pyramidal roof. Naturally, Karia itself had its share of such monuments. The best preserved of them is that known to Turks as Gümüşkesen,[103] still standing on the outskirts of the modern town of Milas, which occupies the site of the old Karian capital of Mylasa. Others are known only through the efforts of archaeologists. These include the Lion tomb at Knidos and the Scylla Monument from Bargylia, elements of which are in the British Museum and are therefore selected for detailed description here.

222 Colossal marble lion from a tomb in the necropolis of Knidos, about two and a half times life size, c. 325–300 BC. British Museum.

223 Charles Newton, right, with Corporal Jenkins and the lion of Knidos, after its rediscovery by R. Pullan in 1858.

THE LION TOMB AT KNIDOS

Half a day's sail south of Halikarnassos, at the end of a long thin promontory, stand the ruins of the Classical city of Knidos. The archaic city lies to the east in the region of the modern tourist resort of Datcha, but around 360 BC, perhaps as part of Mausolus' programme of urbanization in his kingdom of Karia, the Knidians re-founded their city and continued to develop it into a flourishing centre of Hellenistic culture and commerce.[104] One sign of the wealth of the Knidians is the extent of their necropolis, which stretches for several kilometres along the ancient road leading from the eastern gate of the city. The southern limit of this cemetery is the coastline, which in one place forms a headland jutting out into the sea, with a 60-metre drop to the water from its highest point. On this commanding position was built a fine monumental tomb, surmounted by a colossal reclining lion (fig. 222).[105] This magnificent beast weighs around 7 tons and was carved from a single block of marble brought from Mount Pentelikon near Athens. Its hidden belly was hollowed to reduce the weight, while the eyes were also hollowed to carry inlays in contrasting metal or different coloured stone. Pliny writes of a lion that topped the tomb of a certain king Hermias on Cyprus, whose flashing coloured eyes frightened away the fish in the sea.[106] The lion of Knidos will have served as a landmark to passing sea traffic, but those looking up from a boat will certainly not have appreciated the subtlety of its carving. For all the distance of the intended viewpoint, however, and the battering the lion has taken from the weather and its fall, the sculpture nevertheless rewards close inspection. The surface of the pelt and mane is multi-faceted and made mobile through a play of light over its sensitive modelling. The lower jaw is missing, but still the asymmetrical face wears a noble and somewhat pathetic expression, suggested principally by the outward slant of the eyes.

The lion was found in May 1858 by Richard Pullan, who was serving as architect to Charles Newton's excavations at Knidos (fig. 223).[107] Pullan is better known as the excavator of the temple of Athena Polias at Priene. The unsung hero of the lion's modern discovery, however, is Robert Murdoch Smith, a Lieutenant of the Royal Engineers attached to Newton's expedition. He masterminded the removal of the sculpture, its descent to the water and its eventual transport to England aboard ship.[108] It had fallen on its face from a monument that before its destruction had risen some 18 metres or so above the ground. The limestone core still stands (fig. 224), but its superstructure lies scattered around it, and its marble facings had been carried off before Newton's time. Newton's men turned over every stone that had fallen from the monument for Pullan to incorporate in his published reconstruction.[109] Pullan, therefore, had better knowledge of the evidence for reconstruction than anyone has since his time. His elevation is likely to be broadly right, but some of the details have been challenged.

Beyond dispute is the plan, which is some 12 metres square (figs 225–6). Pullan shows this set in its own enclosure, marked by a wall with an entrance on the landward side. The tomb chamber in the base formed a circle with chambers for individual burials radiating out from it.

224 Remains of the masonry core of the lion tomb at Knidos.

230   Greek Architecture and Its Sculpture

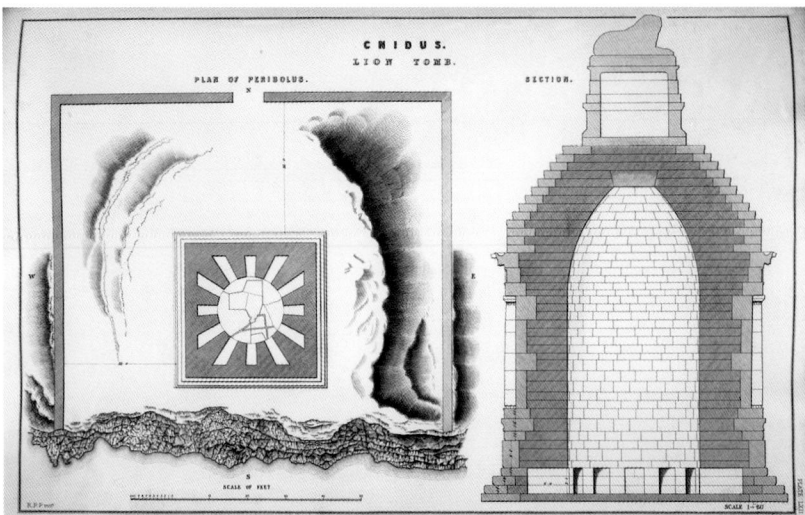

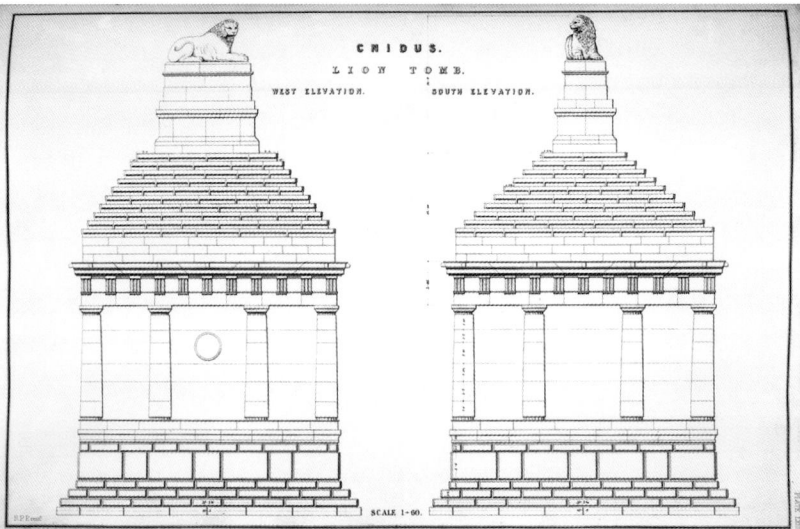

225 and 226 Reconstructed plan, section and elevations of the lion tomb by R. Pullan.

These can be seen today, but the partition walls are largely broken away. The burial chamber is cased in a low podium resting on a three-stepped foot moulding (krepidoma). Above this podium rose an engaged colonnade of four Doric half-columns on each of the four sides. Pullan spaces the inner pair more widely than the outer. The central intercolumniation of one side at least was set with a carved shield. One of these, and there may only ever have been one, is among the ruins at the site. The colonnade was crowned by a metope and triglyph frieze carrying the cornice. Pullan's roof comprises a low attic of three courses of masonry supporting a ten-stepped pyramid, and he shows the lion mounted on a double base rising above it. F. Krischen is probably right to challenge the existence of

227 The lion tomb promontory at Knidos viewing the location of the monument 60 metres above the water.

the attic and also the double base of the lion (fig. 227). He removes the attic and lowers the base to a single storey, adds two more steps to the pyramid and also lengthens the columns to three times the height of the entablature.[110]

The date of the lion tomb is disputed: Newton identified it as a mausoleum for casualties in a famous naval victory won by the Athenian admiral Konon over Sparta, which was fought off Knidos in 394 BC.[111] There is no inscription, however, and the shield seems to be a formal device that does not convey any military message other than a general symbol of strength. It was, for example, a feature of the principal pediment of the second-century AD Corinthian temple that once stood at Knidos itself.[112] The deity of this temple is unknown, but Ares does not come to mind. Krischen argued a second-century BC date for the Lion tomb, comparing its Doric engaged architecture with that of the council house (Bouleuterion) at Miletos (175–164 BC).[113] More obvious parallels are, however, to be found in the architecture of other monuments crowned by lion sculptures. Those at Chaironeia and Amphipolis in mainland Greece are usually dated to the late fourth or early third century BC.[114]

The lion itself is probably the best indication of date and for the closest comparisons we need only look across the water to Halikarnassos and the lions of the Mausoleum (fig. 228). In the shape of the face, in its surface treatment and modelling and in the carving of the mane there are similarities that are not to be found in other surviving lions and certainly not in other colossal ones. On this evidence, a date in the later fourth century seems justified for the Lion tomb at Knidos.

THE SCYLLA MONUMENT FROM BARGYLIA

The site of ancient Bargylia lies to the north of Halikarnassos on the coastal road that now links modern Bodrum with ancient Iasos.[115] The place is not much remarked upon by ancient historians, but Polybius records that in 201/200 BC Philip V of Macedon, at war with Pergamon and Rhodes, wintered his ships in the harbour.[116] On a headland beside the harbour there stood a tomb monument, the remains of which were first remarked upon in 1865 by Alfred Biliotti. He was British Consul on Rhodes and together with Auguste Salzmann was conducting excavations where Charles Newton had left off on the site of the Mausoleum at Bodrum. Biliotti gathered fragments of sculpture and a few pieces of architecture from his visit to Bargylia and brought them to the British Museum. Others were collected in 1872 from the voyage of the Duke of St Albans aboard his yacht *Xantha*.[117]

228 Marble lion from the Mausoleum at Halikarnassos, *c.* 360–350 BC. British Museum.

Biliotti recorded in his diaries that much of the monument had survived above ground until some seventeen years before, when the area was ravaged by a woodland fire.[118] Subsequently the ancient worked stone was quarried by the crews of Turkish warships collecting building materials for harbour works at Istanbul. These included the blocks of the foundations, removal of which had exposed the ancient foundation-cutting measuring 7.5 by 6.5 metres and 1.2 metres deep. Biliotti remarks that the superstructure was of marble, that the order was Doric and that the columns were engaged (fig. 229). The roof, he says, was pyramidal and crowned by a sculptured group. Following Biliotti's visit, the location of the monument was forgotten until it was rediscovered in 1991 by Geoffrey Waywell, who went on to publish a full account of it. From Biliotti's remarks, an examination of the physical remains and comparisons with other tomb monuments, such as the Lion tomb at Knidos and the third-century BC mausoleum at Belevi south of Ephesos, Waywell arrived at a tentative but plausible reconstruction of the architecture.[119]

The restored monument stands just under 12 metres high. At its foot is placed a three-stepped moulding (krepidoma), on which rested the ashlar walls of the podium enclosing one or more sepulchral chambers. A framed door is restored to one of the long sides of the tomb and one side of this frame is set with the inscribed block found by Biliotti that is thought to record the name of the apparently wealthy, but otherwise unknown man for whom the tomb was built, Melas, son of Hermaiskos.[120] Above the podium we find a colonnade of engaged half columns, four on each side. On the long sides the extra length may be taken up by spacing the central intercolumniation wider than it is on the short sides. The columns carried an architrave and Doric frieze of metopes and triglyphs. Above this rose the pyramid roof of eleven steps of equal height and a taller extra one acting as a base for the Scylla.[121]

Scylla first enters the record of the ancient human imagination in Homer's Odyssey, where she is described by the witch Circe as a monster with twelve feet and twelve necks, each terminating in a vile head, which in turn displayed an unappealing triple row of thick and close-set teeth.[122] From the vantage point of her cave high in a cliff she overlooked one side of a narrow ocean strait, while the whirlpool Charybdis guarded the other. Together they menaced every ship that attempted to pass between them, Scylla plucking helpless sailors from the decks to devour them alive. Down the centuries of Classical antiquity Homer's ogress transformed herself into a beautiful *femme fatale* with a sexy, naked upper body, rising from a pack of sea-hounds, with one or more fish tails stretching out behind.[123] So she appeared at Bargylia with a skirt of seaweed to mask the awkward transition between her human and animal parts. These comprised the foreparts of three dogs, one at the front, one at each side and two fish tails at the back. One of her hounds preserves its head, which turns back to observe its mistress with an insincerely pathetic expression, no doubt intended to beg from her some dismembered part of a hapless victim.

Scylla herself was carved about one and a half times life size from a higher-quality marble than that chosen for the rest of the sculpture (fig. 230). The body twists backwards to the left with the right arm raised, while the left hung closer to the body. The right hand probably dangled a sailor teasingly over an expectant hound, while the left probably clutched a steering oar, such as we find in other representations of the same subject. Her possession of this vital tool of navigation betokened the futility of the

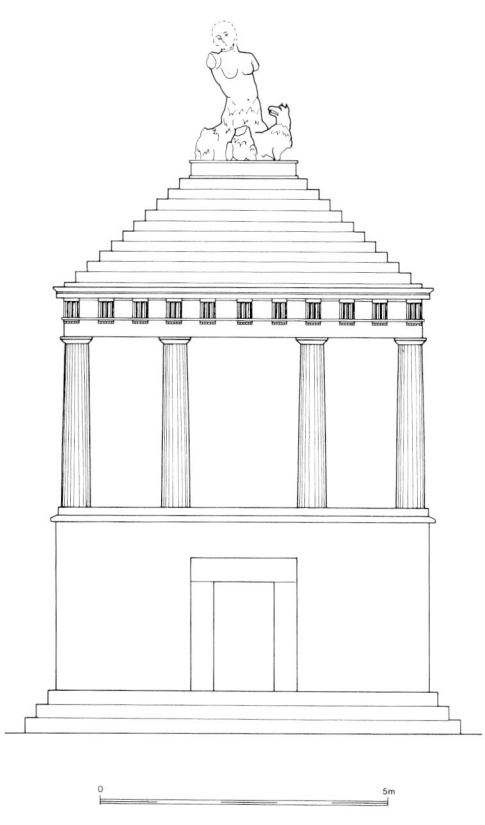

229 The Bargylia monument reconstructed by G. Waywell.

230 Remains of the Scylla group from Bargylia. British Museum.

voyage she and Charybdis had interrupted. This formula is repeated in numerous representations in all forms of Hellenistic and Roman art from the third century BC onwards. Our monument stands in the mainstream of this tradition, and probably dates to around 200–150 BC.[124]

Sharing some elements of the type, but in many respects a grandiose aberration from it, is the now famous colossal group discovered in a cave in 1957 at Sperlonga on the Adriatic coast in Italy.[125] This complex sculpture of the Roman early-Imperial period replicated part of the ship itself, while the enlarged scale permitted Odysseus' sailors to be shown as terrified individuals. The Bargylia monument has no such focus on the terror of the human victims but concentrates instead upon the awfulness of the perpetrator, the humanized Scylla and her accomplices. As the stuff of nightmares, the Scylla group of the Bargylia monument was probably chosen not primarily for her maritime connection or for the sake of any literary pretensions that Melas may have had. Rather, Scylla was almost certainly a frightening guardian of the tomb and a warning against those who might violate its contents and as such she was part of a family of real and fanciful apotropaic creatures like the Sirens of Kyberniskos' tomb at Xanthos and, indeed, the lions that prowled the perimeter of the roof of the Mausoleum at Halikarnassos.

CONCLUSION

The Lion tomb at Knidos and the Scylla monument of Bargylia are direct descendants of the Mausoleum at Halikarnassos. Elements in common include the podium base and burial chamber, the colonnaded superstructure and the pyramid roof. The tombs of Knidos and Bargylia are far smaller and greatly simplified with their engaged columns and sculptural decoration reduced to a single, apotropaic image crowning the roof. They were none the less impressive designs that demonstrated the wealth of those who commissioned them and the taste and skill of those who built them. Their seaside setting amplified their beauty and contributed to the successful marriage of monument and landscape.

In tracing back the origin of these tombs to the great mother of all monumental tombs, that of Mausolus, we should not forget the debt that the Mausoleum in turn owed to the tomb of Erbinna of Xanthos. It was remarked in Chapter Eight how elements of the Nereid Monument, notably the high podium base and the figures between the columns, anticipate the Mausoleum of Halikarnassos. Both monuments, moreover, employed a plethora of sculpture at all levels of the elevation to project the identity of the tomb occupant as a figure worthy of present fame and future legend. Both monuments shared subjects to do with the kingly exploits of war, hunting and sacrifice, and both were concerned with dynasty. Erbinna seems to have been content to root his heroic ancestry in the mythical warriors of ancient Greece. Mausolus and Artemisia were more conscious of recent and immediate family and, whereas Erbinna had the daughters of the sea god Nereus in pride of place between the columns of his tomb, Mausolus had portrait statues of himself and his relatives. The anonymous architect of the Nereid Monument had looked, as we have seen, to the Athenian Acropolis for inspiration, while Pytheos and Satyros in designing the order of the Mausoleum no doubt had in mind the great temple of Artemis at Ephesos but also, or so it would appear, the pyramids of Egypt. Whereas the Nereid Monument has a pedimented, temple-like roof, the Mausoleum set a new trend in Greek tomb architecture in carrying a roof that referenced the dynastic civilization of old Egypt.

The vanities of Erbinna, the Lycian warrior-king, and Mausolus, the Karian satrap-statesman, were well served by their respective monuments. In the next and final chapter we shall visit another of Pytheos' works that was a prominent feature in the renaissance of the Ionian enlightenment. Whereas the Mausoleum was designed to advertise the achievements of a royal patron, and its tomb architecture became a vehicle for the message of its decorative sculpture, the temple of Athena Polias at Priene was a civic commission and, as its relative lack of sculpture shows, the architect was thereby freed of the obligation to introduce the documentary detail of personality cult. In short, if the Mausoleum is about sculpture, the Priene temple is a celebration of architecture.

Chapter Ten

The Temple of Athena Polias at Priene

PRIENE

Perched on a natural shelf below the towering cliffs of Mount Mycale and overlooking the flood plain of the River Maeander, Priene is one of the most dramatically situated of all the sites of western Turkey (figs 231–2).[1] The Prieneans had not always lived here. The original city was on the coast at the mouth of the river. The coastline, however, had a tendency to march rapidly westwards as alluvial silt was brought down in the river's winter spate. Nowhere is there a more dramatic demonstration of this phenomenon than the envelopment of the former island of Lade at nearby Miletos. Around the island in 494 BC a naval battle had been fought and lost by the allied Ionian cities who had rebelled against the Persians. Today it is no more than a rocky knoll.

The new city of Priene was founded around 350–330 BC. Some historians would take the earlier date and attribute the impulse to the influence of the Hekatomnids of Halikarnassos, while others would see Alexander as re-founder, thus eliminating the Karians.[2] It was laid out in a series of elegant terraces, with streets crossing at right angles according to the rational principles of town planning associated with Hippodamos of Miletos.[3] New Priene was on the coast, but such was the rapidity of the alluviation of the Maeander valley that already by Roman times the sea had receded some 6 kilometres distant. Today, therefore, not only is the old town submerged and still unlocated in the deep deposit of river silt, but the later city is also robbed of its access to the sea. The isolation of Priene meant that it escaped heavy rebuilding in Roman times, and it is the best preserved of the Hellenistic towns of western Anatolia.

231 Reconstructed columns of the temple of Athena Polias with the fertile flood plain of the River Maeander below.

Priene is in the ethnic region of Ionia. Although always small, it had its own political dimension in being the controlling member of the religious assembly of the Ionian cities, the Panionion. The sanctuary itself was in Prienean

232 The walled city of Priene perched on a shelf of towering Mt Mycale, the temple of Athena highlighted. Drawing A. Zippelius, 1908.

territory. Knidos in Karia had a comparable role in managing the meeting place of the union of Dorian cities at the Triopian sanctuary of Apollo.

REDISCOVERY

Unlike Knidos, Priene did not have a significant Byzantine phase and it lay in ruins for centuries before its modern archaeological discovery. It was visited in the seventeenth century by the travellers Jacob Spon and George Wheler,[4] and the principal monument they remarked upon was the temple of Athena Polias, goddess of the city. It was not surveyed systematically, however, until the next century when in 1764–5 Richard Chandler headed an expedition to Asia Minor under the auspices of the Society of Dilettanti.[5] With Chandler were William Pars (fig. 233), painter and draughtsman, and the architect Nicholas Revett. Their detailed investigations of the temple were printed as part of a folio volume entitled *Ionian Antiquities* (1769). In 1811–12 a second Dilettanti expedition comprised William Gell, topographer and draughtsman, Francis Bedford and Joseph Michael Gandy.[6] The temple was surveyed and drawn a second time, and Bedford's reconstruction drawings of the temple and of the unfinished propylon (gateway) at the eastern end of the sanctuary were published in 1821. Bedford improved upon Revett's earlier rendering of the Ionic order of the temple, and the publication of his drawings may have

233 The ruins of the Priene temple in 1765 drawn by William Pars. British Museum.

provided Robert Smirke with a model for the capitals of the columns for the British Museum, designed in 1823.[7]

A third expedition sponsored by the Dilettanti was that of the architect Richard Pullan in 1868–9.[8] He had served a decade earlier in the excavations of Charles Newton and worked both at Bodrum and at Knidos. Pullan's investigation at Priene was more extensive than any previous one. Employing a grid-reference system, he carefully plotted not only the architectural remains but also the find-places of sculpture and the many inscribed bases that had once supported sculpture dedicated in the sanctuary. Pullan's record of his excavations, his drawings, notebooks, letters and photographs were never fully published, but a summary was presented in Part IV of *Antiquities of Ionia* with engravings based on Pullan's drawings.[9] Sadly, after his departure, the temple was much plundered for its stone, and today we see far less than he did. Fortunately, however, he brought back to the British Museum a number of sculptures, architectural fragments and inscriptions.[10] Pullan was the last of the British explorers to carry out extensive work in the Athena temple at Priene. Since his time, architectural excavation and survey have been carried out in large parts of the town chiefly by German archaeologists and notably by Th. Wiegand and H. Schrader in 1895–9.[11] As a consequence of these efforts, sculpture and architectural members have been added to the collections of the Berlin and Istanbul museums. So rich was the archive gathered by Pullan, however, that in the late twentieth century the American archaeologist Joseph Coleman Carter drew on it extensively in his re-examination of the sculptured remains of the temple of Athena Polias. His book was published in 1983.

234 Cut-away view of the Priene temple. Drawing H. Schleif, 1931.

THE TEMPLE

According to Vitruvius, the architect of the temple of Athena (fig. 234) was Pytheos.[12] This Pytheos is the same, Vitruvius tells us, as the man who wrote a book about the Mausoleum at nearby Halikarnassos.[13] As we saw in the previous chapter, another Roman writer, Pliny, also mentioned Pytheos in connection with the Mausoleum. From these literary references, and from numerous points of comparison between the architectural orders of the two buildings, it seems clear that Pytheos was responsible for both buildings. Many of the workmen who had laboured on the construction of the tomb are likely to have been employed on the temple.[14]

The building of the temple is connected with an even more famous historical person, Alexander the Great. His name was prominently carved

235 Inscription recording the dedication of the Priene temple by Alexander the Great in 334 BC: 'King Alexander dedicated the temple to Athena Polias'. British Museum.

on the end of one of the flank walls of the temple (fig. 235),[15] and the inscribed block, together with others carved with records of Prienean civic decrees, was found by Pullan and brought back to England. Alexander is named as the dedicator of the temple to Athena Polias, and the inscription raises the question of how Alexander came to be associated with it. The traditional explanation assigns the date of the dedication to the immediate aftermath of the Battle of the River Granikos in 334 BC, which forced the Persian king to withdraw his armies from western Anatolia. Alexander proceeded south through the cities of the Aegean seaboard, declaring their freedom from Persian rule. As we saw in Chapter Three, at Ephesos he offered to pay for the rebuilding of the temple of Artemis,[16] which offer was famously refused. When Alexander reached Priene further down the coast, he found the inhabitants there more inclined to flatter him by accepting his generosity. There is also some evidence to suggest that there was a shrine to the deified Alexander in the town.[17]

A temple to Athena was a fitting memorial to the role of Alexander as liberator of the Ionian Greeks. Athena Polias was the principal goddess of the Athenian Acropolis. Some 150 years earlier, Athens had covered itself in glory by defeating the Persian invasion of mainland Greece at the Battle of Marathon. Alexander's Granikos was a new Marathon in the age-old struggle of Greece for freedom from eastern domination. Moreover, there was a special relationship between Priene and Athens. Like other Ionians, the Prieneans saw Athens as a mother-city tracing the foundation of their city back to Kodros, one of the legendary kings of Athens. This tradition would be reinforced at Priene by a replica of the Athena Parthenos of Pheidias to serve as a cult statue in the temple of Athena Polias.[18]

There seem to have been at least two principal construction phases, to judge from the variation in form and style of the mouldings. Some variation in moulding shape and size is to be expected in any great temple, built over decades by more than one hand. On the basis of variation in the proportions of its various parts, a capital from the Athena temple can be assigned to one or another side of the building. Thus, a capital in the British Museum is thought to come from the rear porch.[19] It can also, not least on the basis of its close comparison with the very similar capitals of the Mausoleum at Halikarnassos, be said to belong to the first phase of the work. Other capitals, however, and diverse elements of the superstructure, including most of the carved coffer frames, are treated so differently as to make it clear that the work was carried on over many years before the temple was finally completed at ceiling and roof level. A late phase of operations, which is estimated to have involved some two-thirds of the superstructure, is traditionally dated to the mid second century BC and the patronage of King Orophernes of Cappadocia, who reigned *c.* 158–156 BC

The Temple of Athena Polias at Priene   241

(fig. 236).²⁰ He is known to have financed other works in the city including a fine colonnaded hall (stoa). In the Roman period the temple would find another benefactor in the person of the emperor Augustus, and it was not finally completed until his reign. In return, the deified Roman had his name carved into the east architrave and he became joint dedicatee with Athena. In all these benefactions, a pattern emerges of rich patrons seeking to legitimize their power by attaching their names to the cultural achievements of a small but venerable city.

One more name that should be mentioned is Megabyzos of Ephesos.²¹ An inscription that was carved into a stele set up in front of the building records honours to him for 'completing the temple', including the erection of a bronze statue.²² The letter forms have recently been dated to *c*. 290 BC, after the death of Alexander. Strabo says that all the priests of Artemis at Ephesos were eunuchs called Megabyzos. There is no reason, therefore, to identify this Megabyzos with the priest of Artemis at Ephesos of that name, who was featured by Apelles along with Alexander in pictures painted inside the new temple of Artemis.²³ The Megabyzoi are likely to have acted as independent agents for seeing that the funds given to Priene by Alexander were properly used.²⁴ The Megabyzos of the inscription is unlikely actually to have completed the temple, but probably played a prominent role in advancing its progress.

236 Two sides of a coin of Orophernes of Cappadocia, *c*. 158–156 BC. It was found by A. Clarke in 1870 under the remains of the cult-statue base. The inscription reads: 'Of King Orophernes Nikephoros [victorious]'. British Museum.

THE ARCHITECTURE

Pytheos seems self-consciously to have designed the temple of Athena Polias at Priene as the embodiment of a canon of proportions.²⁵ For example, the length of the colonnade measured from axis to axis of the corner columns is exactly twice the width of the colonnade. The interaxial measurement between the columns is equal on all sides, and the width of each square column plinth is exactly half of the column spacing, measuring from central axis to central axis. These regular proportions allow for the axes of the walls of the cella building to be aligned on the axes of the columns, so that the whole building was planned on a grid, which is reflected in the pattern of the joints of the paving stones.²⁶ An explanation of such features must have been included in Pytheos' lost book on the temple and, as we saw in Chapter Two, was to inspire Pytheos' admirer Hermogenes to imitate the same principles in his own work.

The order of the architecture is thoroughly Ionian and seemingly intended as a homage to that of the temple of Artemis at Ephesos. The column bases had square plinths like those of the Artemision and are among many features that the Priene temple shares with Pytheos'

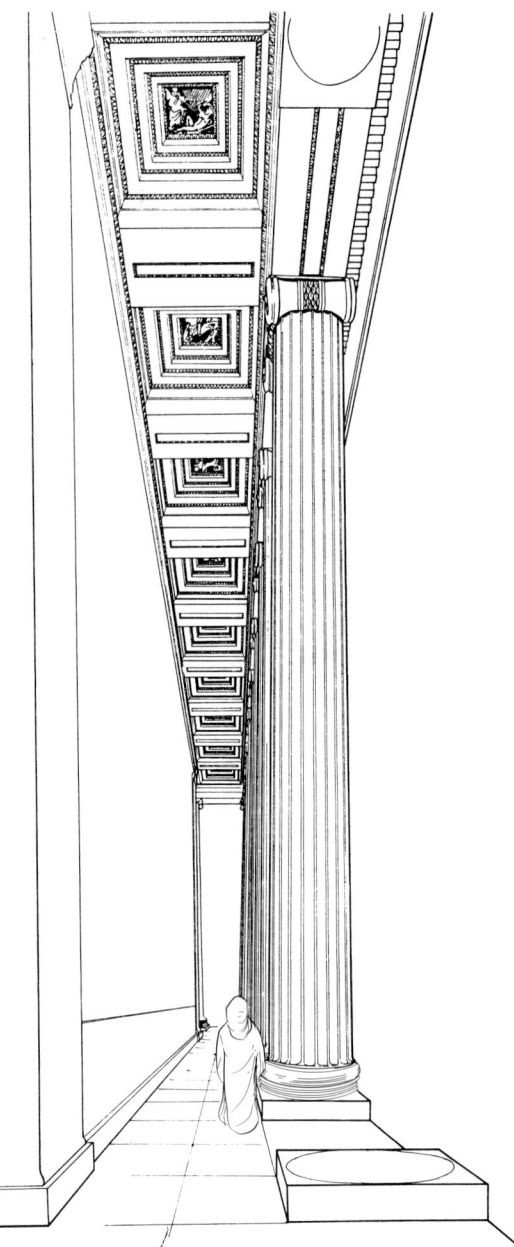

237 View along one of the Priene temple colonnades showing the carved coffers, one in each intercolumniation. Drawing S. Bird.

Mausoleum at Halikarnassos. The bases themselves were in the Asiatic style of western Anatolia and not in the Attic style, which would later become dominant in the Ionic order. The columns rise to a height of around 11.5 metres and were crowned by capitals which, as we have already remarked, closely resemble those of the Mausoleum. The architrave supported no frieze, again in conformity with the Asiatic tradition. The regularity of the plan allowed for equal regularity at ceiling level, where one sculptured coffer was fitted above each column space (fig. 237).

THE CEILING COFFERS

The temple boasted in all twenty-six individual coffers.[27] The coffers themselves comprised a number of mouldings framing a series of square openings, decreasing by steps until the aperture was finally closed by a relief carving in the coffer 'lid', which was roughly 65 centimetres square. The idea for coffer lids carved pictorially at Priene will have come with Pytheos from the Mausoleum, where they were first introduced. The relief in the Mausoleum coffers is more shallow and figures do not, as at Priene, stand or sit on a pictorial ground line. There are, however, close similarities between the two, including the choice of carved mouldings for the framing.[28] On the Mausoleum carved coffers are just one of many sculptured elements in the architect's design. There the piling up of carved imagery reflects the ambitions of Hekatomnid patrons, and the building may have seemed overloaded with decoration. By contrast, the coffers at Priene were the sole figured ornament, and even they were tucked discreetly away into the ceiling of the peristyle. Pytheos, it seems, wanted to emphasize the refinement of his architecture uncluttered by elaborate sculptural decoration.

A specific problem concerns the date of the

carving. To judge from surviving fragments, the style is remarkably homogeneous. Moreover, stylistic and anatomical affinities between figures in the coffers and those in the Amazon frieze of the Mausoleum may suggest that the coffers were carved not long after the transfer of Pytheos' workshop from Halikarnassos to Priene upon completion of the Mausoleum. The coffer sculptures would thus date *c.* 350–325 BC.[29] With, however, so much at ceiling-coffer level apparently unfinished before the second phase of construction, it seems improbable that the ready-carved coffers were fitted immediately upon manufacture. If we accept the later date for completion of the temple, that would mean that they must have been stored for up to two hundred years. Alternatively, therefore, it has been argued that the coffer sculptures were not themselves carved until the second century and, on both stylistic and iconographic grounds, parallels have been drawn with the gigantomachy of the Pergamon altar reliefs dated *c.* 170 BC (fig. 238). This, the greatest surviving Hellenistic work of art, has been seen as the inspiration for the Priene sculptures.[30] The comparison with the Pergamon altar once seemed especially apposite to scholars who mistakenly believed the relief sculptures of the Priene temple belonged to a continuous frieze.[31] Even though we now know that not to be the case, nevertheless a second-century date for the carving of the Priene coffer lids seems probable.[32]

238 Battle of gods and giants from the great altar of Zeus at Pergamon. Berlin Pergamon Museum.

The principal subject of the Priene coffers is, as we have seen, a battle between gods and giants.[33] This theme had featured large in the decoration of the Parthenon in Athens, where it is employed in the metopes of the east and principal façade. It was engraved or painted on the inside of the shield of the statue that stood within the Parthenon. It was also woven pictorially into the robe that was dedicated on the Athenian Acropolis to Athena Polias at the Panathenaic festival. In the case of the Parthenon the gigantomachy has readily been interpreted as an allegory of Athenian victory over the Persians. There was no better way for Prieneans to demonstrate affinity with Athens and, if he was involved, to flatter their Persian-slaying hero Alexander, than to choose the same subject for their new temple.

So far as it is possible to say from fragments, there were usually two protagonists in the Priene reliefs, sometimes combined with an animal. By no means all figures can be identified for certain. Cybele, the oriental mother goddess, was certainly there (fig. 239),[34] as was the sun god Helios;[35] near certain identifications include Zeus, ruler over the divine realm,

239 Fragment of one of the carved coffers showing Cybele riding a lion and holding her tympanum. British Museum.

240 Reconstruction of the fragment in fig. 239 with an associated piece representing a young giant partially sunk into the ground. Drawing S. Bird.

241 Striding goddess restored as Athena spearing a winged and serpent-tailed giant. Drawing S. Bird.

his daughter Athena as goddess of the temple (fig. 241) and Dionysos, god of wine. The anonymous giants usually go naked except for a cloak and, while most are in human form, at least one, who is the probable opponent of Athena, is snake-legged.[36] At least two coffers feature Amazons, probably fighting in support of giants, rather than to be seen as a separate theme.[37] Forms are exaggerated so as to be visible from below. The relief is extremely high, with some figures barely attached to the parent block. Added paint, of which some traces survive, will also have helped with legibility of the images. Not only were figures picked out in colour, but the framing mouldings were also coloured in a manner consistent with that of the Mausoleum coffers. The carved ovolo (egg moulding) was, for example, reserved as the white of the marble against a painted blue background, and the bead and reel was similarly reserved against red.

242 Reconstruction of the colossal cult statue of Athena Polias. Drawing S. Bird.

THE STATUE OF ATHENA

The cult statue was a freestanding, reduced but still colossal replica of the Athena Parthenos by Pheidias (fig. 242).[38] By the late first century AD, the statue was being shown on the coins of Priene as emblematic of the city.[39] When found, the statue survived only as a mass of fragments scattered across the floor of the temple. These have been joined to comprise ten principal fragments of various parts of head and limb. It is clear from cuttings in some of these that the statue was not all of marble, but was acrolithic, that is to say only the extremities were of stone. These were supported on a wooden armature, concealed by a casing of, probably, gilded metal plates representing drapery, which were perhaps combined with real garments. Gilded bronze wings found in the temple by Pullan must have belonged to the statuette of Nike (Victory) which stood in the palm of Athena's outstretched hand.[40]

The base of the statue also survives and comprises a conglomerate, hollow core, which was then faced with marble. It used to be thought that both statue and base belonged to a

243 The Priene temple altar reconstructed. Drawing S. Bird.

later phase of construction. They have been connected in date with a number of silver coins of Orophernes of Cappadocia that were found in and around the base. One of these coins is in the British Museum.[41] The likeliest date for the hoard is *c.* 158–156 BC, the years of Orophernes' brief reign. The base appears, however, to be earlier – at least to judge by its moulded decoration, which is similar in form to that of the fourth-century capitals from phase one of the construction. The sculpture itself may also be fourth-century, and therefore made in a local tradition. Leochares, for example, one of the sculptors of the Mausoleum at Halikarnassos, made an acrolithic statue of Ares for the Hekatomnid temple at Halikarnassos.[42]

THE ALTAR

Like most Greek temples, that of Athena Polias at Priene had a monumental altar placed in front of the principal entrance (fig. 243).[43] Almost immediately after Pullan's departure from Priene, the site was pillaged for building stone and what remained of the altar was destroyed, except for the core and part of the foundation.[44] The plan seems to have echoed that of the temple with six by eleven columns, except that in the case of the altar the columns were engaged. Between them were carved single figures representing Apollo and the Muses. Together, columns and figures were part of a screen enclosing three sides of the pen-like area in which animals were sacrificed.[45] Photographs taken by Pullan's expedition show three figures surviving in the vicinity of the altar, an Apollo now lost and two Muses, one now in Berlin, the other in the tea garden of the Istanbul Archaeological Museum, where it was identified by Carter from a sketch by Pullan.[46] The design of the altar, which has been dated to the last quarter of the third century BC, is foreshadowed in that of the sarcophagus of the so-called 'mourning women' from the royal cemetery at Sidon (modern Lebanon). This sarcophagus, on the evidence of the date of the figure type, has been dated to the second half of the fourth century BC.[47]

THE SANCTUARY DEDICATIONS

During its cult life, the temple was a favourite place for the dedication of freestanding votive sculpture. Pullan collected around a hundred fragments, including nine heads, from within the temple and its precinct. The north and west walls of the porch were lined with inscribed bases that had once carried honorific sculpture or inscribed stelae, while other bases were set up along the wall of the sanctuary (fig. 244).[48] Among the sculpture found in the temple itself is the headless 'charioteer' (fig. 245), a less-than-life-size male standing figure draped in the long, high-belted tunic associated with charioteers, such as the more famous bronze in the museum at Delphi.[49] This is perhaps part of a victory monument commemorating

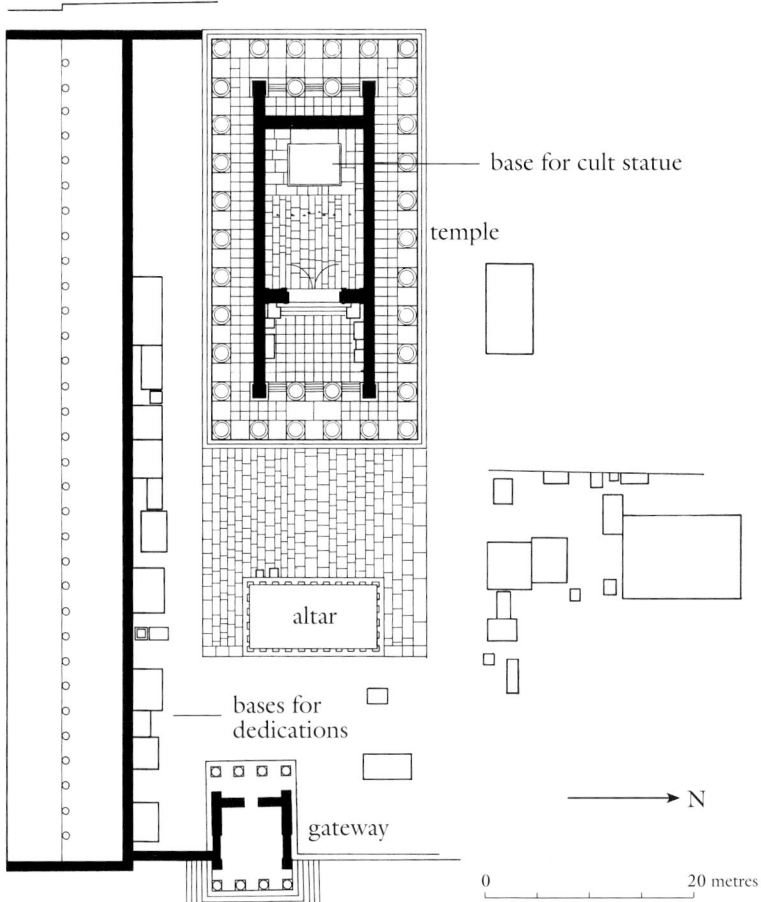

244 Plan of the sanctuary of Athena Polias.

245 Marble statue of a youth draped in a long tunic, belted in the manner of a charioteer. British Museum.

success at one of the local or panhellenic games. Other sculpture found in the temple includes the head of a colossal portrait statue with the distinctive coiffure associated with the Hekatomnid royal family of Halikarnassos (see fig. 210, right).[50] This find might seem to support an argument for the participation of the Hekatomnids in the foundation of Priene, against the view that this had more to do with Alexander.[51] With its painted hair net (sakkos) and frontal crown of so-called snail curls, this head has been identified as Ada I.[52]

We have already seen evidence of other patronage of Priene in the Roman period in the re-dedication of the temple of Athena to Augustus and the goddess. In addition, numerous inscribed Roman bases have been found in the sanctuary, along with several battered torsos wearing the Roman cuirass. Among fragmentary portrait heads, one has been identified with Julius Caesar[53] and another as the emperor Claudius.[54]

CONCLUSION

The temple of Athena Polias at Priene was an exquisite study in the rational principles of Ionic architecture. Unburdened by the Mausoleum's plethora of figurative sculpture, and on a scale less overwhelming than that of the colossal temple of Artemis at Ephesos, Pytheos' design may be seen as the distilled essence of an East-Greek rational tectonic tradition. The temple was begun, probably under the Hekatomnids who presided over a revival of Ionian enlightenment architecture, following a century and more of decline in Ionia and their native Karia. The temple's rediscovery in the eighteenth century of the modern era was to influence another architectural renaissance, that of the neoclassical Greek revival. The Ionic temple-like British Museum now houses much of what survives of the architecture and sculpture of Priene, along with the remains of many other great buildings that together tell the story of this book.

Today most of Priene lies in romantic ruin, and yet enough survives to make it possible for the modern visitor to understand what it was like to inhabit a model Hellenistic city, designed not only for practical living but also for aesthetic pleasure. It is possible still to walk the ancient streets and to visit various sacred and civic buildings, and an extensive domestic quarter besides. Above the city looms the great grey rock of Mount Mycale, while below lies the lush green flood plain and its winding river ever pushing against the retreating sea. 'The cities of Ionia', wrote Herodotos, 'were built in places more favoured by skies and seasons than any country known to us'.[55] Today, as in ancient times, summer and winter, morning and evening, the changing light that Herodotos saw, moving its shadows over theatre and fountain-houses, temple and marketplace, stoa and stadium, acropolis and necropolis, transforms the shapes and colours of stones crafted to crown nature with human artifice.

Priene was by no means exceptional and, sailing the Aegean and Mediterranean coasts of antiquity, the voyager could go from one beautiful city to another, each seeming perfectly to complement what nature had supplied by way of land and sea, mountain and river valley. Apart from this variety of their natural setting, Greek cities gained a pleasing homogeneity from the disciplined application of rational town-planning and the restricted use of building materials. In contrast with modern city-sprawl, the constant threat of military attack inhibited urban development beyond the limits of fortified walls. Within this contained uniformity, however, every city sought to distinguish itself with one or more exceptional feature. Thus Pergamon had its altar to Zeus, Ephesos its Artemision, Miletos its Apollo temple at Didyma, and Halikarnassos the Mausoleum. Knidos had the so-called hanging stoa, constructed by Sostratos, who also built the famous lighthouse at Alexandria. To Roman commentators these were *mirabilia opera*, works made to inspire wonder in the beholder, and such was their reputation in antiquity that even now, broken into scattered fragments or destroyed altogether, their fame lives on, and still we feel drawn to them with melancholy longing for what we have lost.

Notes

Chapter One
1. Here, pages 137–8.
2. Vitruvius, *About Architecture*, 4.1.9; Wesenberg 1994; Wesenberg 1999.
3. Coulton 1993; and Barletta 2001, 125–33 for a wooden Doric tradition.
4. Dinsmoor 1950, 51; Coulton 1977, 35–6; Winter 1993, 12–20, 109–15; Gruben 2001, 33–8; Gebhard 2001; Barletta 2001, 54–83.
5. Coulton 1977, 32–3; Østby 2001.
6. Coulton 1977, 39.
7. Cf. Kienast 2001; Bammer 2001b.
8. Boardman 1980, 111–41.
9. *Ibid.*, 131–2; BM Vases, 1888.6-1.392.
10. BM Sculpture B391–433; Dinsmoor 1950, 125–6. Lethaby, 1929a; Barletta 2001, 87–90 and 184, note 11. See also 108 and 189, note 46.
11. Herodotos, *Histories*, 2.178.
12. Boardman 1980, 135.
13. Dinsmoor 1950, 59; Betancourt 1977, 18–23.
14. Dinsmoor 1950, 61; Betancourt 1977, 61 and passim.
15. Lethaby 1929b, 1020.
16. Betancourt 1977, 122–33; Boardman 2000, 41–2.
17. Dinsmoor 1950, 132–3; Barletta 2001, 84–124, who makes a case for the Cycladic origin of the order.
18. Dinsmoor 1950, 136–7; Barletta 1983.
19. Dinsmoor 1950, 87–8.
20. Curtis 2000, 34–59.
21. Boardman 2000, 129–30.
22. Diodorus Siculus 17.69.
23. Vitruvius, *About Architecture*, 7, Preface 15; Dinsmoor 1950, 91.
24. Cook 1961; Cook 1962, 122–3.
25. Hellström 1994, 37–40.
26. *Ibid.*, 40–42.
27. Tomlinson 1963, 139.
28. Hornblower 1994, 49 and 79; Pedersen 1994; Pedersen 2001/2002.

Chapter Two
1. *Inschriften von Priene* 207. For Hermogenes, Dinsmoor 1950, 273–5; Coulton 1977, 70–71; Hoepfner and Schwandner 1990; Gruben 2001, 422 ff.
2. For Pytheos and the Priene temple, see here, Chapter Ten.
3. Gruben 2001, 422.
4. Vitruvius, *About Architecture*, 4.3.1–2; Tomlinson 1963.
5. Hoepfner 1990, 8–20; Uz 1990; Gruben 2001, 426–9. The Artemis temple was seemingly not dedicated until *c.* 130 BC, after Hermogenes' death.
6. Vitruvius, *About Architecture*, 7, Preface 5.
7. Mordaunt Crook 1972, 120.
8. Vitruvius, *About Architecture*, 4.1.4–7.
9. *Ibid.*, 3.1.1–5.
10. Euclid 6.3; 6.30; 3.1.1–5.
11. Coulton 1977, 65; Kidson 1998; Robbins 1998.
12. Dinsmoor 1950, 161, note 1; Coulton 1975; Coulton 1977, 65–6.
13. Haselberger 2005, 115 and note 21 for bibliography.
14. Vitruvius, *About Architecture*, 4.3.3.
15. Dinsmoor 1950, 54, note 4.
16. *Ibid.*, 152; Gruben 2001, 56–7.
17. See here, Chapter Four.
18. Vitruvius, *About Architecture*, 2.6.1.
19. Bundgaard 1957, 44–5 and 93–7; 139–42.
20. Pliny, *Natural History*, 36.21.96–7.
21. Coulton 1974; Coulton 1977, 48 and 144.
22. Bundgaard 1957, 94–7; Coulton 1977, 57; Haselberger 2005.
23. Coulton 1977, 1 ff.
24. Bundgaard 1957, 184.
25. Rubens 1986, 98–105.
26. Vitruvius, *About Architecture*, 1.1.4.
27. Haselberger 1983 and 1999b; Coulton 1998. This specifically relates to the design of entasis (tension) in the columns.
28. Vitruvius, *About Architecture*, 1.1.2.
29. *Ibid.*, 1.1.4 ff.
30. *Ibid.*, 1.1.12.
31. Coulton 1977, 23–4.
32. Pliny, *Natural History*, 7.56.198.
33. Buschor 1930, old temple; Reuther 1957, Polykrates temple. Betancourt 1977, 123–4; Dinsmoor 1950, 124–5 and Pedersen 1983 and 1994, 27 ff, influence: Gruben 2001, 355–65.
34. Vitruvius, *About Architecture*, 7, Preface 12.
35. See here, Chapter Three.
36. Dinsmoor 1950, 145.
37. See here, pages 119–20 and 125–6.
38. Scranton 1960; Burford 1969, 54 ff.
39. Plutarch, *Life of Perikles*, 12.1–7; Meiggs 1963, 41.
40. Stern 1985.
41. For an excellent recent discussion and bibliography of this difficult topic, Ridgway 1999, Chapter Four; also Manzelli 1994; Brinkmann 2003a and 2003b; Pfaff 2003, 185–9.
42. Jeppesen 1992 and 1997.
43. Walker and Matthews 1997.
44. Jenkins and Middleton 1988.
45. Gunn 2000.
46. Von Graeve and Preusser 1981.
47. Carter 1983, 67.
48. Lethaby 1908, 183.
49. Waywell 1978, 66; Jenkins, Gratziu and Middleton 1997.
50. Pryce 1928, 49.
51. Wood 1877, 245; Pryce 1928, 43, Cat. B50; Jenkins, Gratziu and Middleton 1997, 38.
52. Jenkins, Gratziu and Middleton 1997, 39.
53. Hellmann et al. 1982; Jenkins and Middleton 1988, 183–7; Jenkins 1992, 48–54.
54. Jenkins, Gratziu and Middleton 1997, 36.
55. BM Sculpture 1047; Waywell 1978, 108–110, cat. 33, pl. 17. Jenkins, Gratziu and Middleton 1997, 36.
56. BM Sculpture 435; Penrose 1888, 58; Lethaby 1908, 153; Jenkins and Middleton 1988, 191–2. For this Ionic cornice of the central building of the Propylaea, see Dinsmoor 2004, 207, especially note 224.
57. BM Sculpture 357 and 358.
58. BM Sculpture 436; Lethaby 1908, 156–7; Büsing 1990.
59. Pryce 1928, 127.
60. Jenkins 2001.
61. Jenkins and Middleton 1988, 186.
62. Harrison 1988, 339–41.
63. Frantz 1954; Jenkins 2001, 27–8.
64. Harrison 1988, 339–40.
65. Kouzeli, Dogani and Belogiannis 1990; cf. Ebersole 1899, 431–2.

66. Jenkins and Middleton 1988, 188.
67. Ridgway 1999, Chapter Five.
68. See here, page 158.
69. Cook 2005, 35.
70. Hersey 1988; Onians 1988; Barletta 2001, 137–43.
71. Bammer 1985, 74–8.
72. Ridgway 1999, Chapter Two.
73. Corbett 1970; Coldstream 1985; Barringer 2005; Hurwit 2005a.

Chapter Three
1. Strabo, *Geography*, 14.1.22.
2. Plutarch, *Life of Alexander*, 3.5–6.
3. Strabo, *Geography*, 14.1.22; Rügler 1988, 18–19.
4. Lanowski 1965; Trell 1988, 78.
5. Foss 1979, 3, note 3 for sources.
6. Knibbe 1998.
7. Herodotos, *Histories*, 1; Huxley 1966, 75–117.
8. Nicolas of Damascus, *Fragments of Greek Historians*, 90, fr. 65; Herodotos, *Histories*, 1.92.
9. Muss 1994, 25–7.
10. Boardman 2000, 53–6.
11. Hussey 1972, 66.
12. Shipley 1987, 69–99.
13. Walter 1976; Shipley 1987, 73.
14. See here, Chapter Two, note 33; see also Shipley 1987, 78–9.
15. Shipley 1987, 86.
16. Asios quoted by Athenaeus, *Table Talk*, 12.525 f.
17. Gruben 1963, 106–112.
18. Hussey 1972, 11–31; Kirk, Raven and Schofield 1983; Gorman 2001, 72–85.
19. Hussey 1972, 31–59.
20. Herodotos, *Histories*, 6.19.
21. Wood 1877.
22. BM Inscriptions 481; Wood 1877, 73, 111 ff.
23. MacLean Rogers 1991, 80–115.
24. Pausanias, *Description of Greece*, 7.2.9.
25. Wood 1877, 155.
26. Hogarth 1908.
27. Strabo, *Geography*, 14.1.23; Rügler 1988, 14; Muss, Bammer and Büyükkolancı 2001.
28. Morris 2001.
29. Hogarth 1908, 1–8; Rügler 1988, 16–23 and 185–93.
30. Vitruvius, *About Architecture*, 7, Preface 12.
31. Athenaeus, *Table Talk*, 12.525c.
32. Rügler 1988, 19.
33. Pliny, *Natural History*, 36.21; Wesenberg 1983a, 32–68.
34. Vitruvius, *About Architecture*, 3.2.7–8.
35. Philo of Byzantium, *Seven Wonders of the World*, 6.
36. Rügler 1988, 44.
37. See here, page 31.
38. BM Sculpture B86–B268; Muss 1994.
39. Lethaby 1917, 1 ff; Muss 1994, 12 ff; Barletta 2001, 118 with note 88.
40. Muss 1994, 17–18.
41. Bammer 1972, fig. 5.
42. Rügler 1988, 37, fig. 2 and note 158.
43. Muss 1994, 20–21.
44. Bammer 1964–1965, 134–5.
45. Muss 1994, 5–6 and 21.
46. Lethaby 1929a.
47. Muss 1994, 6.
48. Herodotos, *Histories*, 1.92.
49. Muss 1994, 110.
50. *Ibid.*, 43 ff.
51. Hanfmann 1975, 12–13.
52. Root 1985; cf. Castriota 1992, 185–7.
53. Murray 1889, 1–4.
54. Hanfmann 1975, 9.
55. Muss 1994, 57 ff.
56. *Ibid.*, 69 ff.
57. Hogarth 1908, 7.
58. Rügler 1988, 6–7.
59. Strabo, *Geography*, 14.1.22.
60. Bammer 1972, 6–13; Rügler 1988, 40–44.
61. Rügler 1988, 45.
62. Fergusson 1882–1883, 162 ff.
63. Rügler 1988, 13.
64. Lethaby 1908, 18.
65. Rügler 1988, 30–33, fig. 1a; Wesenberg 2001.
66. Trell 1945; Rügler 1988, 27–8.
67. Rügler 1988, 27, note 123, 7 and 9; Bammer 1964–1965, 135, fig. 75.
68. Rügler 1988, 27, note 123.
69. Lethaby 1913, 87 ff; 1914, 76 ff; 1916, 25 ff.
70. BM Sculpture 1200; Rügler 1988, 48–9, cat. page 133, pls 1–2.
71. BM Sculpture 1204; Rügler 1988, 49–50, cat. page 137, pl. 3.
72. BM Sculpture 1206; Rügler 1988, 54–6, cat. pages 151–5, pls 13–15.
73. Robert 1879.
74. Cf. Rügler 1988, 69–73.
75. BM Sculpture 1213; Rügler 1988, 56–8, cat. pages 159–62, pl. 18.
76. BM Sculpture 1202 and 1203; Rügler 1988, 58–9, cat. pages 148–51, pl. 11.
77. Rügler 1988, 65–8, following Wiegartz 1968.

Chapter Four
1. Thucydides, *History of the Peloponnesian War*, 2.65.9.
2. Mark 1993, 99–102 and 132–3; Green 1996, 239–41.
3. Meiggs 1963, 38–40; Badian 1987; Hornblower 2002, 45.
4. Plutarch, *Life of Kimon*, 13.8; Camp 2001, 63–72.
5. Plutarch, *Life of Perikles*. Two recent biographies are Kagan 1991 and Podlecki 1998.
6. Cohen 1991.
7. Zanker 1995, 27–9.
8. Plutarch, *Life of Perikles*, 5.1. Loeb translation.
9. *Ibid.*, 7.4.
10. Thucydides, *History of the Peloponnesian War*, 2.39.1.
11. Dinsmoor 1950, 159–209; Randall 1953; Stanier 1953; Boersma 1970, 42–104; Mark 1993, 132–4; Hurwit 1999, 157–9; Camp 2001, 72–117; Hurwit 2004.
12. Dinsmoor 1950, 181–2; cf. Boersma 1970, 76–8. The remains of a Periklean temple in the Athenian agora used to be included in this list. It has long been recognized that this building did not start life in the marketplace of Athens and it is thought to have been moved there by the Romans. It was once thought to have been a presumed temple of Ares at Acharnai, but there was no temple there, only a sanctuary. It is now established that the temple in the agora was moved from a former sanctuary of Athena Pallenis near modern Stavro: Goette 2001, 81; Korres 1992–1998, 83–104.
13. Meiggs 1963, 40–45.
14. Plutarch, *Life of Perikles*, 31.4.
15. Delivorrias 1994, 135, with bibliography.
16. Plurarch, *Life of Perikles*, 12.2. Translation Meiggs 1963, 41.
17. Penrose 1888, 9–57; Orlandos 1977–1978; Korres 1983–1994; Korres 1995; Beard 2002.
18. Korres 1995.
19. Dinsmoor 1950, 161; Korres 1994, 80.
20. Penrose 1888.
21. Wesenberg 1983a; Korres 1994a; good English summary in Barletta 2005, 74–86.
22. Dinsmoor 1950, 164; Korres 1994b, 79.
23. Penrose 1888, 22 ff; Dinsmoor 1950, 165–9; Coulton 1977, 108–111; Korres 1994b, 66–7; Hurwit 1999, 167; Haselberger 2005.
24. Penrose 1888, 24; Korres 1994b, 66.
25. Plutarch, *Life of Perikles*, 13.4; Vitruvius, *About Architecture*, 7, Preface 12.
26. McCredie 1979; Wesenberg 1982; Barletta 2005, 88–95.
27. Coulton 1977, 113–15; Mallwitz 1972, 211–34.
28. Dinsmoor 1950, 160 and 176.
29. For good surveys of the whole, see Boardman and Finn 1985; Delivorrias 1994; Hurwit 1999, 168–88.
30. Leipen 1971; Nick 2002.
31. Lapatin 2001, 63–79.
32. Ridgway 1989; Creighton 1991.
33. Harrison 1996.
34. Brommer 1967; Berger 1986; Mantis 1997, with bibliography at note 4; Schwab 2005.
35. Cf. Wilson Jones 2002; cf. Barletta 2001, 128–37.
36. For other explanations see Yeroulanou 1998, 420–21 with bibliography.

37. Brommer 1963; Berger 1974; Palagia 1993.
38. Korres 1994b, 61–4.
39. Burford 1963, 31–2.
40. Simon 1986.
41. Palagia 1993, 27 for another view.
42. Again, Palagia 1993 offers another view arguing for a static central composition.
43. Binder 1984.
44. Brommer 1977; Jenkins 1994; Berger and Gisler-Huwiler 1996; Neils 2001; Mizuta 2001; Delivorrias 2004.
45. Coulton 2000, 70–72, argues against my view.
46. Childs 1985, 210 with note 14, argues against my view.
47. Bird, Jenkins and Levi 1998, 18–19; Jenkins 2005, 155, fig. 13.11.
48. Plutarch, *Life of Perikles*, 13.6.
49. See, for example, Connelly 1996.
50. Jenkins 2005.
51. Castriota 1992.

Chapter Five
1. Plutarch, *Life of Perikles*, 14.1 and 2; Meiggs 1963, 44; Hurwit 1999, 158; Camp 2001, 72–117.
2. Neils 2001, 25–6.
3. Hurwit 2004, 94.
4. Stuart and Revett 1762–1816, 1, chapter 2, pls 1–8; Dinsmoor 1950, 185.
5. Picon 1978; Childs 1985; Mark 1993, 82–6; McNeil 2005; and see bibliography collected by Palagia 2005, 190, note 7.
6. Miles 1980.
7. Plommer 1950; Hodge and Tomlinson 1969; Boersma 1970; Delivorrias 1974; Miles 1989; Mark 1993, 77.
8. Bundgaard 1957; Tanoulas 1994a; Tanoulas 1994b; Tanoulas 1997; Hurwit 1999, 192–7; Dinsmoor 2004.
9. The Doric capital, BM Sculpture 433, second column from the south end of the east portico, came to the British Museum with the Elgin collection along with part of a drum from one of the Ionic columns, BM Sculpture 434, and a wall-crowning member, BM Sculpture 435, from the interior Ionic order.
10. Pausanias, *Description of Greece*, 1.32.6.
11. Shoe 1949.
12. Mark 1993; Ziro 1994; Hurwit 1999, 209–213.
13. Stuart and Revett 1762–1816, 2, chapter 5, pls 2, 12 and 13.
14. BM Sculpture 421–424. They were accompanied by two architectural members thought to come from the temple: an Ionic angle capital, BM Sculpture 2735, and an anta-capital, BM Sculpture 436.
15. Ross, Schaubert, Hansen 1839.
16. Balanos 1956.
17. Ongoing at the time of writing; Ziro 1994.
18. Boersma 1970, 11–27.
19. *IG* I² 24 = *IG* I³ 35; for the disputed dating of the decree and the temple see Wesenberg 1981; Childs 1985, 240 and 250 with note 195; Mark 1993, 104–107; Korres in Bouras et al. 2000, 29.
20. Wesenberg 1981, 53.
21. Brouskari 1999.
22. Fuchs 1959, 12 ff, pl. 2.
23. Dinsmoor 1950, 340.
24. Despinis 1974.
25. Boulter 1969; cf. Schulz 2001.
26. For bibliography see Boardman 1985, 245; Stewart 1985; Palagia 2005.
27. Palagia 2005, 188–9.
28. Harrison 1997, 109–126.
29. Stevens et al. 1927; Wycherley 1978, 143–54; Hurwit 1999, 200–209.
30. Pausanias, *Description of Greece*, 1.26.7.
31. *Ibid.*, 1.26.6.
32. Stevens et al. 1927, 479.
33. *Ibid.*, 287.
34. Pausanias, *Description of Greece*, 1.26.5; Plutarch, *Life of Lycurgus*, 843e.
35. Jeppesen 1987; cf. Mansfield 1985, 245–52.
36. Stevens et al. 1927, 455; Shear 1963, 408–24; Mark 1993, 130–33; Hurwit 1999, 205–206.
37. Mark 1993, 140–41.
38. Stevens et al. 1927, 454.
39. BM Inscriptions 35; *IG* I² 372 ff.
40. Stevens et al. 1927, 277–321.
41. *Ibid.*, 322–70.
42. *Ibid.*, 370–416.
43. *Ibid.*, 416–22.
44. *Ibid.*, 411–13; see also Wesenberg 1985, 57–8.
45. BM Sculpture 408; Stevens et al. 1927, 18, 54 and 207.
46. Vitruvius, *About Architecture*, 4.8.4.
47. BM Sculpture 413; Stevens et al. 1927, 54.
48. BM Sculpture 414: once thought to come from the south side of the building, it was probably all part of Elgin's removals from the north-east corner of the temple and probably met BM Sculpture 413 at right angles.
49. BM Sculpture 409 shares the same number as three blocks from the south wall but not to be confused with them – see note 73 below.
50. Stevens et al. 1927, 151–61; Wycherley 1978, 149–52 (follows I. Travlos); Hurwit 1999, 203–204.
51. Pausanias, *Description of Greece*, 1.26-7.
52. *IG* I² 372, lines 9, 58, 62 and 83.
53. Stevens et al. 1927, 161–70.
54. *Ibid.*, 104–109.
55. *Ibid.*, 89–90.
56. BM Sculpture 416.
57. Stevens et al. 1927, 58–9.
58. *Ibid.*, 54–76.
59. *Ibid.*, 75, note 2.
60. BM Sculpture 420. Another piece of cornice from the Erechtheum is in the British Museum, which is said to belong to the west front and, although the block itself is considered as part of the original building, its top bed is thought to have been reworked when it was reincorporated in the Roman reconstruction. Stevens et al. 1927, 75; BM Sculpture 415.
61. For the Roma and Augustus temple see Binder 1969. For cross-connections on the Acropolis see Hurwit 2005.
62. Stevens et al. 1927, 110–11.
63. *Ibid.*, 110–19.
64. BM Inscriptions 35, lines 83–92.
65. Hurwit 1999, 207 and fig. 178.
66. Stevens et al. 1927, 232–8; Scholl 1995.
67. BM Sculpture 407.
68. Papanikolaou 1994.
69. Stevens et al. 1927, 239–76; Boulter 1970.
70. Karousou 1954–1955, 79–94; Kosmopoulou 2002, 126–30.
71. Stevens et al. 1927, 389, lines 2–9.
72. BM Sculpture 409, not to be confused with the corner piece sharing the same number but from the east wall – see notes 49 and 73.
73. Stevens et al. 1927, 52, and fig. 180 on 303. Sharing the same number are two pieces of wall-crown (epicranitis) which, together with a third piece once attributed to the wall of the east porch and a piece formerly in the von Hallerstein collection and now in Munich, probably all come from the long south wall of the temple.
74. See here, page 34.
75. Pedersen 1989.

Chapter Six
1. Pausanias, *Description of Greece*, 8.41.9; Cooper, *Bassitas* 1, 1996, 369–379; Gruben 2001, 128–35; Barletta 2005, 90–91.
2. Thucydides, *History of the Peloponnesian War*, 2.54.5.
3. Cooper, *Bassitas* 1, 1996, 75–9.
4. *Ibid.*, 58–9.
5. *Ibid.*, 80.
6. *Ibid.*, 60–80.
7. Kourouniotes 1910, 1–25; Cooper, *Bassitas* 1, 1996, 68–73 and 81.
8. Yalouris 1973; Kelly 1995; Cooper, *Bassitas* 1, 1996, 80–86.
9. Kelly 1995, 271–5, figs 18–20; Cooper, *Bassitas* 1, 1996, 61 and 90–92.
10. Cooper, *Bassitas* 1, 1996, 6 and 73–4.

11. *Ibid.*, 6–7 and 74–5.
12. *Ibid.*, 97.
13. *Ibid.*, 42.
14. *Ibid.*, 13, note 9.
15. *Ibid.*, 12–31. The proprietors were the architects Charles Cockerell and John Foster, the wealthy landowner Thomas Leigh of Lyme Park, the aristocratic but by no means wealthy Haller von Hallerstein, the painter and watercolourist Jacob Linckh and their agent George Gropius.
16. Cockerell 1860.
17. Cooper, *Bassitas* 1, 1996, 3. The original and a second copy are in Strasbourg.
18. *Ibid.*, 31–5.
19. Papers in the Greek and Roman Department library. See note 68, below.
20. Kourouniotes 1904 and 1910.
21. Cooper, *Bassitas* 1, 1996, 3.
22. *Ibid.*, 7 and 138–40.
23. *Ibid.*, 122–3.
24. *Ibid.*, 4; Epitropé Epikouriou 1995. A commission set up in 1975 to conserve it and ensure its future safety, the 'Epitropé Epikouriou', soon lapsed and was not reconvened until March 1995, when an international meeting gathered under its aegis to report on the condition of the temple and consider its future.
25. Cooper, *Bassitas* 1, 1996, 8 and 98.
26. Rhys Carpenter quoted by Cooper, *Bassitas* 1, 1996, 98.
27. Cooper, *Bassitas* 1, 1996, 249.
28. *Ibid.*, 9 and 148.
29. *Ibid.*, 280.
30. *Ibid.*, 268–76; BM Sculpture 505; Cooper, *Bassitas* 3, 1996, pl. 55a–c.
31. Cooper, *Bassitas* 1, 1996, 258–66, 276–7; BM Sculpture 509.1; Cooper, *Bassitas* 3, 1996, pl. 59a and b.
32. Cooper, *Bassitas* 1, 1996, 266–8; BM Sculpture 509.2; Cooper, *Bassitas* 3, 1996, pl. 54b, which is wrongly captioned.
33. Cooper, *Bassitas* 1, 1996, 277–9.
34. *Ibid.*, 283–92 and 301–304.
35. *Ibid.*, 293–5 and 305–324.
36. Pedersen 1989.
37. Vitruvius, *About Architecture*, 4.1. 8–10.
38. Cooper, *Bassitas* 1, 1996, 301–304.
39. *Ibid.*, 296–300; BM Sculpture 508; Cooper, *Bassitas* 3, 1996, inv. 37, IM 10.
40. Büsing 1970, 31–3 and 44.
41. Madigan, *Bassitas* 2, 1992. Previous studies include Sauer 1895, Hahland 1959, Hofkes-Brukker 1963 and Yalouris 1967.
42. Madigan, *Bassitas* 2, 1992, 10–11, figs 1, and 18, fig. 2; see also 30–31, figs 3–4.
43. Evidence for the assignment of some fragments to the south or the north side of the building is given in the Danish traveller P.O. Brønsted's statement that in 1812 two major fragments, which he describes as a 'silen' and a 'dancer' were found on the south side: Brønsted 1861; Madigan, *Bassitas* 2, 1992, 3–5. His descriptions suggest these are the flaccid torso of a mature male (BM Sculpture 519; Madigan, *Bassitas*, 2, 1992, cat. 43, pl. 14) and another piece showing a female with wind-blown drapery, who may be dancing but is also being grabbed by the throat: BM Sculpture 517; Madigan, *Bassitas* 2, 1992, cat. 35, pl. 12. Two other prominent fragments are not mentioned as coming from the south side and so, Madigan asserts, they must come from the north. These are a kithara-player (BM Sculpture 510; Madigan, *Bassitas* 2, 1992, cat. 58, pl. 20) and a female dancer with castanets: BM Sculpture 512; Madigan, *Bassitas* 2, 1992, cat. 45, pl. 15. In Madigan's own words, 'the assignment of the kitharoidos and the dancer with the krotala to the north metopes and Brønsted's "silen" and "dancer" to the south provides the starting point for reconstructing the two sets of metopes': Madigan, *Bassitas* 2, 1992, 4. The argument *ex silentio* is not very strong, and besides there is a contradictory account from Cockerell: Cockerell Letters, BM Greek and Roman Department Library. He was not actually at Bassai at the time and must have had the information from another source, but says that all the major fragments are from the south side of the temple.
44. Higgs forthcoming a, whose work will incorporate many unpublished joins made by Dyfri Williams.
45. Palagia 2002.
46. Madigan, *Bassitas* 2, 1992, 13–15.
47. BM Vases E224; Burn 1987, pl. 1a.
48. Pausanias, *Description of Greece*, 3.16.1.
49. Picon 1981, 323–8; Madigan, *Bassitas* 2, 1992, 16–22.
50. Cockerell 1860, 52.
51. BM Vases E543.
52. *LIMC* 7.1, *Orpheus*, 4 (M.-X. Garezou).
53. Larson 2001, 73–4.
54. *Ibid.*, 96–8.
55. Madigan, *Bassitas* 2, 1992, 35–7.
56. BM Sculpture 520–542; Yalouris 1967; Hofkes-Brukker and Mallwitz 1975; Madigan, *Bassitas* 2, 1992, Amazonomachy 70–78, Centauromachy 78–83.
57. Madigan, *Bassitas* 2, 1992, 91–4.
58. BM Sculpture 541; Madigan, *Bassitas* 2, 1992, 73–8.
59. BM Sculpture 530.
60. BM Sculpture 536.
61. Madigan, *Bassitas* 2, 1992, 70–78.
62. BM Vases B210.
63. Madigan, *Bassitas* 2, 1992, 78–9.
64. *Ibid.*, 48–52; Jenkins and Williams 1993.
65. There are, for example, in the bottom bed of the frieze two sets of cuttings, apparently for metal dowels, while in the top bed of the architrave there are two sets of cuttings, but there is no agreement as to which dowel fixing went with which cutting.
66. Felten 1984; Hofkes-Brukker and Mallwitz 1975.
67. E.g. 520 (right end); 542 (right end).
68. Madigan, *Bassitas* 2, 1992, 57–63. The last time that the problem of the arrangement was considered in detail was in 1990–1991, when a refurbishment of the British Museum's gallery afforded an opportunity to dismantle the installation and examine all sides of the frieze. A conference was held at the British Museum in May 1991. The arrangement then (as now) was that of P. and G.U.S. Corbett, whose work on the problem had begun in the 1950s and whose conclusions would challenge the results of an earlier study by the American scholar W.B. Dinsmoor: Dinsmoor 1956. The Corbett arrangement had in its turn been contested by F. Cooper, whose work at the site itself had thoroughly re-examined the architectural evidence for the setting of the frieze: Cooper 1978. The blocks were rearranged in the order proposed by Cooper, placing the Centauromachy on the long east side and the Amazonomachy on the west, instead of the other way round, as they are in Corbett's arrangement. The short run of four blocks along the north side was also disturbed. Only the short corner block 520, which had been securely placed by Dinsmoor, a fact also recognized by the Corbetts, was left *in situ*. The other three were replaced. The result was a near-total reworking of the Corbett arrangement but, when actually assembled, Cooper's order was found not to fit. For example, blocks 535 and 540 proposed as the south-east corner, do not actually make a corner: a rebate is cut into the left-hand margin of 540 that will not accommodate the swelling volume of the sculptured figure towards the right of 535. Again, in assigning a different run of three blocks to the right of 520 on the north side, Cooper ignored vital evidence in the trimming of sculpture towards the right side of 520 and the left of 527 that proves they went

together. These and other mistakes in the proposed rearrangement of the frieze meant that there was no alternative but to reinstate the Corbett order in the gallery. This may not be correct in every placement, but it has many arguments in its favour.
69. Jenkins and Williams 1993, 67 contra Madigan and Cooper, *Bassitas* 2, 1992, 52–3.
70. Pausanias, *Description of Greece*, 8.30.3; Cooper, *Bassitas* 1, 1996, 70.
71. BM Sculpture GR 1815.10-20.42-52; Madigan 1993; Madigan, *Bassitas* 2, 1992, 121, 66–7.
72. Morrow 1985, 96–7.
73. Cockerell 1860, 59, pl. 16; Madigan 1993.

Chapter Seven
1. Bean 1989a; Bryce 1986, 14 ff.
2. Bryce 1986, 21 ff; Keen 1998, 1–2, 25–6.
3. Herodotos, *Histories*, 1.173.
4. Homer, *Iliad*, 2.876–7.
5. Robinson 1995a.
6. Bryce 1986, 54–5.
7. *Ibid.*, 42 ff.; Keen 1998, 7 ff.
8. Mørkholm and Neumann 1978.
9. Mørkholm and Zahle 1972 and 1976.
10. *FdX* 6, 31 ff; Blomquist 1982.
11. Bryce 1986, 91–3.
12. *Ibid.*, 48.
13. Jenkins 1992, 140–53; Slatter 1994.
14. Herodotos, *Histories*, 1.176.
15. Ellinger 1993, 269–91.
16. Bryce 1986, 168.
17. Herodotos, *Histories*, 3.90; Keen 1998, 91–3.
18. See here, the Lion tomb.
19. Herodotos, *Histories*, 7.92, Loeb translation.
20. Herodotos, *Histories*, 98; *FdX* 1, 44–5; Keen 1992, 56–7; Keen 1998, 89; see here, Kybernis' tomb.
21. *FdX* 2, 81; Keen 1998, 105.
22. Keen 1998, 112–16.
23. *FdX* 2, 49–75; see here, buildings F, G and H.
24. See here, the Inscribed Pillar tomb.
25. *FdX* 8, 254; Bryce 1986, 84 and 97–8; Robinson 1999, 367–8.
26. Translation Bryce 1986, 97–8.
27. Thucydides, *History of the Peloponnesian War*, 2.69.
28. Thompson 1967, 105–106; *FdX* 5, 113; Bryce 1986, 107.
29. Bousquet 1975; Childs 1979; Bryce 1986, 97 note 126; Keen 1992, 59, and 1998, 129–30.
30. Mørkholm and Zahle 1976; Keen 1998, 129–30.
31. See here, Chapter Eight.
32. Robinson 1999, 366–7.
33. Bousquet 1975; Robert 1978, 3 ff; Bryce 1986, 94–5; *FdX* 9, 149 ff; Keen 1998, 141.
34. The transcription and reconstruction are by Bousquet 1975. The translation is by Bryce 1986, 96; cf. *FdX* 9, 160–61.
35. *FdX* 9, 160; *FdX* 8, 404; Robinson 1999, 371.
36. Hornblower 1982, 120.
37. See here, Chapter Eight.
38. Robinson 1999, 371.
39. See here, Building G.
40. Bryce 1980; Keen 1998, 148–70.
41. Keen 1998, 167.
42. Benndorf and Niemann 1889; Eichler 1950; Oberleitner 1994.
43. Childs 1978, 10 ff; Bruns-Özgan 1987, 56 ff.
44. Childs 1976, 281–316.
45. Borchhardt 1967; 1970a and b; 1976; Bruns-Özgan 1987, 81 ff.
46. Childs 1981, 73–6; Bryce 1986, 111; Keen 1998, 167.
47. Hornblower 1982, 170 ff.
48. *Ibid.*, 181 ff.
49. *FdX* 5, 85–6; cf. Bruns-Özgan 1987, 141–6.
50. Childs 1981, 62–72.
51. *FdX* 1, 29.
52. *Ibid.*, 30.
53. BM Sculpture B286; Akurgal 1941, 3 ff; *FdX* 1, 29–35, pls II–III.
54. *FdX* 1, 31.
55. *Ibid.*, 38–9.
56. *Ibid.*, 39–41; *FdX* 5, 112–13.
57. BM Sculpture B287; Tritsch 1942, 42; *FdX* 1, 42.
58. Pryce in BM Sculpture B287.
59. *FdX* 1, 45–6.
60. Pryce in BM Sculpture B287; Froning 2002/2003, 147–8; Froning 2004, 315–17.
61. *FdX* 1, 44; Keen 1992, 59.
62. *Ibid.*, 47.
63. *FdX* 2, 7–84.
64. *Ibid.*, 28–32.
65. *Ibid.*, 39–42.
66. Philon of Alexandria, *Every Good Man Is Free*, 118–20.
67. *FdX* 2, 49–75.
68. *Ibid.*, 50 ff.
69. Keen 1992, 55.
70. Bruns-Özgan 1987, 20–33; Castriota 1992, 221–5; Boardman 1995, 189–90, figs 213–16.
71. BM Sculpture 961 (moulding); BM Sculpture B292–298 (animal and satyr frieze).
72. BM Sculpture B316–318.
73. Robertson 1938–1939, 39, pl. 18; *FdX* 51, note 10.
74. BM Sculpture B311, 312, 313 and 314; *FdX* 2, 52–4.
75. BM Sculpture B309 and B310; *FdX* 2, 57–8.
76. *FdX* 2, 63 ff.
77. *Ibid.*, 63, pl. 56.
78. BM Sculpture B290 and 291.
79. *FdX* 2, 71 ff.
80. BM Sculpture B289.
81. Bruns-Özgan 1996/1997, 48.
82. BM Sculpture B299–306; Coupel and Metzger 1976.
83. Pryce in BM Sculpture B299.
84. *FdX* 1, 79–105; Bruns-Özgan 1987, 53–6.
85. BM Sculpture 679 – two joining pieces; BM Sculpture 953.
86. Demargne and Klincksieck 1960, 41–7; *FdX* 5, 113–16.
87. See here, pages 155–6.
88. BM Sculpture 288.
89. *FdX* 1, 100–102.
90. Keen 1992, 59.
91. BM Sculpture 951; *FdX* 5, 88–96.
92. Bruns-Özgan 1987, 50–51, fig. 4.
93. *FdX* 5, 134; cf. *FdX* 9, 172–3.
94. *FdX* 5, 46–60; *c.* 430–400 BC.
95. *Ibid.*, 96.
96. *FdX* 1, 113–26.
97. *FdX* 5, 61–87.
98. BM Sculpture 950.
99. *FdX* 5, 137.
100. *Ibid.*, 78.
101. *Ibid.*, 86 and 139; Bruns-Özgan 1987, 142.
102. *FdX* 5, 137–8.
103. *Ibid.*, 85–6.
104. Bruns-Özgan 1987, 141–6.

Chapter Eight
1. *FdX* 8, 3–4.
2. *Ibid.*, 404.
3. Childs 1973; Bruns-Özgan 1987, 35–51; Childs, *FdX* 8, 377 ff; for a full bibliography, Barringer 1995, 233–4, no. 385.
4. *FdX* 3, 157; Robinson 1999, 370.
5. Boardman 2000, 53–7.
6. *FdX* 8,15.
7. *Ibid.*, 21–2.
8. Jenkins 1992, 144–5.
9. *FdX* 3, 75 and 157.
10. *FdX* 8, 253.
11. *Ibid.*, 44 and 139.
12. *FdX* 3, 57–9.
13. *FdX* 8, 139 and 153.
14. Schuchhardt 1927; Bruns-Özgan 1987, 35–6 and 51–2.
15. *FdX* 8, 319ff.
16. *Ibid.*, 153–4, 157 and 374.
17. *Ibid.*, 45 ff.
18. Bruns-Özgan 1987, 209–210.
19. BM Sculpture 858; *FdX* 8, 51–2, pl. 16. Bassai Kaineus, BM Sculpture 530.
20. *FdX* 8, 257–8.
21. BM Sculpture 850 c, 853 and 857; *FdX* 8, 70–71, pl. 33.1; 64–5, pl. 29.1; 69–70, pl. 32.1.
22. *FdX* 8, 259.
23. BM Sculpture 859 and 855; *FdX* 8, 55–6, pl. 20.1; 57–8, 22.1.
24. BM Sculpture 860 L, 862, 850 L; *FdX* 8, 46–7, pl. 9.1; 50–51, pl. 17.1; 59–61, pl. 24.2.
25. Aristotle, *Economics*, 2.1348; *FdX* 8, 260.
26. BM Sculpture 850 L; *FdX* 8, 59–61, pl. 25.1 and 2.

27. *FdX* 8, 44.
28. *Ibid.*, 140.
29. BM Sculpture 879; *FdX* 8, 97–9, pl. 57.2.
30. *FdX* 8, 265 ff.
31. Childs 1978, 48 ff; *FdX* 8, 268; Robinson 1999, 372.
32. BM Sculpture 885–897; *FdX* 8, 185 ff.
33. *FdX* 8, 234 ff.
34. *Ibid.*, 240 ff. As in the actual reconstruction in the British Museum, it is still thought that blocks 889, 887 and 888, showing a hunt, certainly comprised the east side. Two of them are the surviving angle blocks, with their distinctive oblique joints. The meeting of block 890 with 889 at the south-east corner is also confirmed, and this gives the clue to the placement of three further blocks on the south side showing scenes of combat, namely 891, 894 and 892, while a fourth is missing, along with the south-west angle block. The length of these blocks together correspond with that of the stylobate, or floor formed by the top of the podium. The actual sequence of these blocks on the south side is not entirely certain, but from east to west Demargne places 890 first, followed by 891, 894 and 892. The loss of the south-west and north-west angle blocks makes the reconstruction of the west and especially the north sides all the more difficult.
35. *FdX* 8, 280 ff.
36. Bruns-Özgan 1987, 193–5.
37. BM Sculpture 898–908; *FdX* 8, 185.
38. *FdX* 8, 284 ff.
39. BM Sculpture 903; *FdX* 8, 207–208, pl. 133.
40. BM Sculpture 902; *FdX* 8, 208–209, pl. 134.3.
41. Ebbinghaus 2000.
42. BM Sculpture 906; *FdX* 8, 213–14, pl. 137; Bruns-Özgan 1996/1997, 49–50, and 53, fig. 3.
43. BM Sculpture 909–912, 914 and 918 (statues); BM Sculpture 913, 915–916 and 920–921 (fragments).
44. *FdX* 8, 167 ff.
45. BM Sculpture 909, 910 and 915; *FdX* 8, 168.
46. Birch 1844, 202; *FdX* 8, 270; Barringer 1995, 63–4; Six 1892–1893, suggested Aurai (sea-breezes).
47. *FdX* 8, 271 ff; Barringer 1995, 17–58.
48. Euripides, *Andromache*, 1254–68; *FdX* 8, 273, 302; Barringer 1995, 65.
49. Robinson 1995b.
50. *FdX* 8, 223, 297 ff.
51. BM Sculpture 926; *FdX* 8, 223–4, pl. 147.
52. BM Sculpture 927; *FdX* 8, 225–6, pl. 149.
53. BM Sculpture 919, 922 and 923; *FdX* 8, 227 ff, pls 150–52.
54. Furtwängler 1882, column 347. *FdX* 8, 301; Barringer 1995, 62.
55. Benndorf and Niemann 1889, 163–8.
56. Demargne 1987, 190–205; *FdX* 8, 302–303; Barringer 1995, 62 and 65.
57. Harrison 1992.
58. *FdX* 8, 291 ff.
59. BM Sculpture 924; *FdX* 8, 216–20, pls 140–44.
60. *FdX* 8, 293.
61. BM Sculpture 925; *FdX* 8, 220–23, pls 145–6.
62. BM Sculpture 940–942; *FdX* 8, 183–6, pls 112–13.
63. Demargne 1987; *FdX* 8, 277–9; Barringer 1995, 65.
64. BM Sculpture 929–930; *FdX* 8, 231–3, pls 156–8.
65. BM Sculpture 868a.
66. Demargne 1976.
67. Boardman 1995, 189–90.
68. *Ibid.*, 192.

Chapter Nine
1. Herodotos, *Histories*, 8.99.2; *MAH* 5, 171–3.
2. *MAH* 1, 41–4.
3. Hornblower 1982, 38.
4. Diodorus Siculus, *Library of History*, 14.98.3; Hornblower 1982, 35–7; Watkin 1988, 23.
5. Hornblower 1982, 78; Pedersen 2001/2002, 122–3; also known as the Peace of Antalcidas: see Green 1970, 48, notes 23–5.
6. Diodorus Siculus, *Library of History*, 16.36.2.
7. Pliny, *Natural History*, 36.30.47, puts Mausolus' death two years later in 351 BC, but seems to confuse this with the death of Artemisia – Hornblower 1982, 39–41.
8. Hornblower 1982, 41–5.
9. Diodorus Siculus, *Library of Knowledge*, 16.74.2; Hornblower 1982, 45–6.
10. Strabo, *Geography*, 14.2.17.
11. Plutarch, *Life of Alexander*, 10; Green 1970, 99–101; Hornblower 1982, 220–21.
12. Strabo, *Geography*, 14.2.17; Hornblower 1982, 49–50.
13. Arrian, *Anabasis*, 1.23.8; Hornblower 1982, 51.
14. Hornblower 1982, 51.
15. *Ibid.*, 78 ff.
16. *Ibid.*, 114–15.
17. Bean and Cook 1952; Hornblower 1982, 115 ff; Bruns-Özgan, 2002.
18. Tod 1948, 180–81, Inscr. 161B, signed by Satyros, son of Isotimos of Paros; Hornblower 1982, 111 and 241.
19. Hornblower 1982, 110 and 323; see here, page 236.
20. BM Sculpture 1151; Carter 1983, 271–6, cat. 85, pl. 39.
21. Hornblower 1982, 123 ff, 331.
22. *Ibid.*, 46–7.
23. *Ibid.*, 170 ff.
24. Treuber 1987, 102 ff; but doubted by Hornblower 1982, 181–2.
25. Hornblower 1982, 209.
26. *Ibid.*, 188.
27. Vitruvius, *About Architecture*, 2.8.10–15; Hornblower 1982, 301–5; *MAH* 2, 73–101; Isager 1998; Pedersen 2004.
28. *MAH* 2.
29. Vitruvius, *About Architecture*, 2.8.10; Pedersen 2001/2002, 103.
30. Hoepfner and Schwandner 1986, 187–91; *MAH* 3.1, 95–7.
31. Vitruvius, *About Architecture*, 2.8.11.
32. *MAH* 3.1, 95–6.
33. *Ibid.*, 10–39.
34. Hornblower 1982, 259, 334; *MAH* 2, 102–108.
35. Hornblower 1982, 333–5; *MAH* 2, 104–105.
36. Aulius Gellius 10.18.3; Hornblower 1982, 258.
37. Lucian, *Amores*, 11–17.
38. Lucian, *The Dialogues of the Dead*, 430–31 (Loeb Classical Library, Lucian 7).
39. BM Sculpture 1000; Waywell 1978, 97–103, cat. 26; Hornblower 1982, 272–3; *MAH* 5, 173–9.
40. Pliny, *Natural History*, 36.4.30–31.
41. Vitruvius, *About Architecture*, 2.8.11–12 and Preface to Book 7, Chapters 12 and 13.
42. Waywell 1978, 54–5; Hornblower 1982, 225; Wesenberg 1983b, 68–87; *MAH* 2, 13–51; Waywell 1988, 103; Jeppesen 1998, 164 ff; *MAH* 5, 29–42.
43. Translation Waywell 1998.
44. Newton 1862, 72–212.
45. Lethaby 1908, 49–53; Van Breen 1942, 44–117; Bury 1998, 49, fig. 12.
46. Dilke 1987, 26; cf. Cooper 1996, *Bassitas* 1, 131–2 with bibliography.
47. That guess tends to depend on one of two approaches: the first may be characterized as the 'tell it like it is'; the second as the 'tell it like it ought to be'. The leading exponent of the first has been Kristian Jeppesen. He found that 30 centimetres, or more precisely 29.90 centimetres, often recurs among the architectural members and has argued that this may have been the Mausoleum foot: Jeppesen and Zahle 1975, 78; Jeppesen 1998, 163, 187 ff. He is also open, however, to the alternative suggestion that the key measurement used in the actual construction may not have been a foot, but a lesser unit of daktyls, where one daktyl is the equivalent of 2 centimetres. The recurring 30-centimetre unit,

therefore, was the equivalent of 15 daktyls in a system where 16 daktyls make a foot, and a foot is the equivalent of 32 and not 30 centimetres. The daktyl-based unit is preferred by Poul Pedersen in conclusions that he draws from an analysis of the Mausoleum terrace and its entrance gateway: *MAH* 3.1, 93–4. More recently, Jeppesen has concluded with Pedersen that the foot unit was indeed 32 centimetres: *MAH* 3, 1.43–54. W. Hoepfner has put forward an alternative foot of 30.08 centimetres, which he equates with the planning unit: Hoepfner 1996, 98. This fits with his reconstruction which is arrived at by a different method from the more empirical attempt of Jeppesen. Hoepfner's starting point is the text of Pliny, which he combines with a theoretical system of proportions to arrive at a pleasing but, Jeppesen claims, largely hypothetical Mausoleum. Hoepfner's method has much in common with an earlier attempt by Fritz Krischen. Jeppesen has been critical of both, describing Hoepfner's work as a 'house of cards'. Hoepfner's Mausoleum is discussed further below.

48. Newton measured 127 by 108 feet for the foundation cutting, using a modern foot measurement of 30.48 centimetres. This translates as c. 38.71 by 32.92 metres. K. Jeppesen measured the cutting in different places as 38.15–38.4 by 32.5–32.75 metres: Jeppesen and Zahle 1975, 75, note 31. Both Newton's and Jeppesen's measurements are roughly consistent with the 120 by 100 feet suggested by Pliny's circumference of 440 feet, whatever the precise foot measurement was that he had in mind.

49. For the coffers see Carter 1983, 59–63; Tancke 1989, 18–22, pls 10–19; *MAH* 5, 77–94; Cook 2005, 71–3, cat. 230–53, pls 27–9.

50. As traditionally argued, for example, by Lethaby 1908, 43. Now, however, Jeppesen argues that it was so only on the short sides, while on the long sides it was 2.88 metres: Jeppesen 1992, 88–90; 1998, 161–2.2, 187; *MAH* 5, 77–87. These modifications represent a significant and it must be said awkward refinement of Jeppesen's own original confirmation that the inter-axial measurement was 3 metres. In other respects the Mausoleum appears to be a regular building planned along the lines of a grid, in which for example a single carved ceiling coffer and its framing were roughly square and occupied one space between the columns. It might have been expected that these intercolumniations remained the same, but in Jeppesen's latest reconstruction this is not the case.

51. A summary reconstruction was published in Waywell 1978, 54 ff. Afterwards, Waywell worked with the graphic artist Susan Bird to produce an image of one of the short sides of the Mausoleum in greater detail: Waywell 1988, 119, fig. 61. Waywell has since modified his argument to suggest that the slightly smaller colossal female figures were located between the columns, while the male figures were placed on the upper of the podium plinths: Waywell 1989, 29.

52. Jeppesen 1992. See also Jeppesen 1997, 1998, and *MAH* 5, 15–18. Another major difference between Waywell and Jeppesen is in their respective readings of Pliny's text. Waywell accepts the figure of 25 cubits (37.5 feet) as that intended by Pliny and applies it to the height of the colonnade. Jeppesen, however, rejects this figure and argues instead that it should have read 75 cubits (112.5 feet). This he sees as the height of the podium and the colonnade together. The height of the roof must, therefore, be 27.5 feet (140 minus 112.5), a figure Jeppesen finds compatible with the archaeological remains (*MAH* 5, 38) He reconstructs the 140-foot-high monument as: podium and colonnade measured to the lowest pyramid step, 112.5 feet; 24 pyramid steps, 22.5 feet; height of the quadriga pedestal only, 5 feet (*MAH* 5, 207).

53. Jeppesen 1998, 161.1, 162.5; 185, fig. 15; 164–82.

54. BM Sculpture 1053; Waywell 1978, 108, cat. 32, pl. 17; Jeppesen 1998, 169, erstens; *MAH* 5, 178–82.

55. BM Sculpture 1001; Waywell 1978, 103, cat. 27, pl. 13 (Artemisia). BM Sculpture 1048; Waywell 1978, 113–14, cat. 42, pl. 19 (Persian). Jeppesen 1998, 162.5, 169 zweitens and 170 drittens, fig. 3; *MAH* 5, 147. For a sceptical view of differences of scale in the female heads, see Higgs 1997, 31–2.

56. Jeppesen 1997, 45; 1998, 192.2; *MAH* 5, 200–201.

57. Jeppesen 1998, 161.1, 185, fig. 15; *MAH* 5, 155–63.

58. BM Sculpture 1047; Waywell 1978, 108–110, cat. 33, pl. 17; *MAH* 5, 194–9.

59. BM Sculpture 1049; Waywell 1978, 115, cat. 44, pl. 19 (heroic scale standing male); Jeppesen 1998, 170–71; *MAH* 5, 118–24.

60. BM Sculpture 1051; Waywell 1978, 106–107, cat. 30, pl. 16 (Leto). BM Sculpture 1058; Waywell 1978, 118–19, cat. 48, pl. 22; *MAH* 5, 109–117.

61. Jeppesen and Zahle 1975, 76, fig. 5; Jeppesen 1998, 177, fig. 8; *MAH* 5, 183–7. See also Ashmole 1972, 165–6; Cook 2005, 31, 42–64, cat. 1–181, pls 2–23.

62. For the friezes see Jeppesen 1998, 162.3–4; Ashmole 1972, 159 ff. All these sculptures are the subject of a special study by Brian Cook and he is in agreement with Jeppesen as to their location on the building: Cook 2005.

63. Jeppesen 1998, 175; *MAH* 5, 70; Cook 2005, 31–2, 65–70, cat. 182–229, pls 24–6.

64. Jeppesen 1998, 175; *MAH* 5, 154; Cook 2005, 32–3, 100–115, cats 636–869, pls 46–63.

65. Hoepfner 1996, 97–8; Hoepfner 2002.

66. Krischen 1956, 96 ff.

67. Hoepfner 1996, 98.

68. *Ibid.*, 106–107.

69. *Ibid.*, 98–100.

70. *Ibid.*, fig. 7.

71. Jeppesen and Zahle 1975, 76.

72. Hoepfner 1996, 107.

73. *Ibid.*, 107–110.

74. *Ibid.*, 110–111.

75. *MAH* 5, 55.

76. Hoepfner 1996, 111–13.

77. Pliny, *Natural History*, 36.30–31; Waywell 1978, 79–84; Hornblower 1982, 226–7; Stewart 1990, 281–6; Wesenberg 1993; Waywell 1997, 60–64; Cook 2005, 17–22.

78. Waywell 1978, 83–4; Hornblower 1982, 227–8.

79. Hornblower 1982, 228; Hellström 1994, 51–2.

80. Tod, note 18 above.

81. Jeppesen 1992, 99–101.

82. Vitruvius, *About Architecture*, 7, Preface 12.4.31; Hornblower 1982, 227–8.

83. *IG* IV^2, 1.102; Burford 1969, 57; Stewart 1990, 273–4; Waywell 1997, 61–2.

84. Waywell 1997, 61–4; Posch 1991.

85. Stewart 1990, 282.

86. Athens National Museum 1733; Camp 1998, 30, fig. 43.

87. Pliny, *Natural History*, 36.20–21.

88. Stewart 1977; Stewart 1990, 182–5 and 284–6; Palagia 2000.

89. Stewart 1990, 182.

90. BM Sculpture 1914.7–14.1; Tod 1948, 161 A; Hornblower 1982, 241; Waywell 1993.

91. Pliny, *Natural History*, 36.20–21.

92. *Ibid.*, 35.49–52; Hornblower 1982, 243; Stewart 1990, 282–4.

93. Pausanias, *Description of Greece*, 5.20.9.

94. Ashmole 1951; Bruns-Özgan 2005.

95. Vitruvius, *About Architecture*, 2.8.11.

96. *Ibid.*, 7, Preface 13; Corso 2004, with bibliography.
97. Corso 1997, 91–6.
98. Newton 1862, 102 ff.
99. Waywell 1997, 61.
100. Cook 1989, 36–7.
101. *Ibid.*; Cook 2005, 14–22.
102. Fedak 1990.
103. *Ibid.*, 171, fig. 254.
104. Note 17, above.
105. BM Sculpture 1350; Newton 1862, 485–511; Waywell 1998.
106. Pliny, *Natural History*, 37.66.
107. Jenkins 1992, 187–8.
108. Dickson 1901, 119–33.
109. Newton 1862, pls 62–3.
110. Krischen 1944.
111. Newton 1862, 493.
112. Mert 2002.
113. Krischen 1944; Büsing 1970, 21, 83, figs 1a and 29.
114. Waywell 1998, 239–40.
115. Bean 1989b, 62–6, Waywell 1996, 76–7.
116. Polybius 16.24.
117. Waywell 1996, 76 and 80.
118. *MAH* 3.1, Appendix 1, 130–34, 140–41; Waywell 1996, 77–81.
119. Waywell 1996, 80–83, figs 10 and 11.
120. BM Inscriptions 1039.
121. BM Sculpture 1542.
122. Homer, *Odyssey*, 12.73–126 and 222–59.
123. Waywell 1996, 86–91.
124. *Ibid.*, 91.
125. *Ibid.*, 91–5 with bibliography.

Chapter Ten
1. Wiegand and Schrader 1904; Hoepfner and Schwandner 1986, 141–86; Rumscheid and Koenigs 1998; Dontas 2000.
2. Hornblower 1982, 323; Carter 1990, 130 and 134.
3. Hoepfner and Schwandner 1986, note 1.
4. Carter 1983, 1.
5. *Ibid.*, 1–5.
6. Stoneman 1987, 130–36.
7. Mordaunt Crook 1972, 120.
8. Carter 1983, 5–24.
9. *Antiquities of Ionia*, 4, 28–30. See also volume 5, 25–31.
10. Carter 1983, 24–5.
11. Koenigs 1983.
12. Vitruvius, *About Architecture*, 1.1.12.
13. *Ibid.*, 7, Preface 12.
14. See here, Chapter Nine.
15. BM Inscriptions 399; *Inschriften von Priene* 156; Hornblower 1982, 323; Carter 1983, 26.
16. Strabo, *Geography*, 14.1.22.
17. Rumscheid and Koenigs 1998, 93–8.
18. See here, pages 245–6.
19. BM Sculpture 1125 and 1126; Koenigs 1983, 150.
20. Schede 1934; Koenigs 1983, 149–74; Carter 1983, 235–7.
21. Carter 1983, 36–8.
22. *Inschriften von Priene*, 3.
23. Strabo, *Geography*, 14.1.65.
24. Carter 1990, 133–4.
25. Dinsmoor 1950, 222.
26. Coulton 1977, 70–71.
27. BM Sculpture 1165–1176; Carter 1983, 38 ff; Tancke 1989, 30–38.
28. Carter 1983, 59–63 and 99–101.
29. *Ibid.*, 99–101; Cook 2005, 26–8.
30. Carter 1990, 129–30.
31. Recognized as coffer reliefs by Praschniker 1936.
32. Higgs forthcoming b.
33. Carter 1983, 88–9.
34. BM Sculpture 1170; Carter 1983, 121–3, cat. 14, pl. 11.
35. BM Sculpture 1168; Carter 1983, 132–5, cat. 23, pl. 14a.
36. BM Sculpture 1172; Carter 1983, 144–6, cat. 31, pls 17a and 18b (Athena). BM Sculpture 1173; Carter 1983, 146–9, cat. 32, pls 17c and 18c (giant).
37. Istanbul Archaeological Museum 1042; Carter 1983, 152, cat. 35, pl. 19c.
38. BM Sculpture 1150, 1–4; Carter 1983, 210–49; cat. 72–81, pls 33–7.
39. Carter 1983, 218–20.
40. BM Bronzes 1728; Carter 1983, 220–23, 82–3, pl. 37a–d.
41. Thompson, Mørkholm and Kraay 1973, 176, no. 1323.
42. Koenigs 1983, 160; Carter 1990, 135.
43. Carter 1983, 181–209, cat. 68–71, pls 5b, 29, 30, 32a; Webb 1996, 99–100.
44. Carter 1983, 8.
45. *Ibid.*, 191, fig. 17.
46. *Ibid.*, 192–6.
47. Fleischer 1983.
48. Carter 1983, 250–336.
49. BM Sculpture 1154; Carter 1983, 268–71, cat. 84, pl. 38.
50. BM Sculpture 1151; Carter 1983, 271–6, cat. 85, pl. 39.
51. Carter 1990, 134.
52. See here, page 205.
53. BM Sculpture 1152; Carter 1983, 283–5, cat. 90, pl. 42.
54. BM Sculpture 1155; Carter 1983, 286–9, cat. 91, pl. 43.
55. Herodotos, *Histories*, 1.142.

Bibliography

Akurgal 1941, E. Akurgal, *Griechische Reliefs des VI. Jahrhunderts aus Lykien.* Berlin.

Antiquities of Athens, see Stuart and Revett.

Antiquities of Ionia, 5 parts, 1821–1915. Dilettanti Society. London. See also *Ionian Antiquities* 1769.

Ashmole 1951, B. Ashmole, 'Demeter of Cnidus', *Journal of Hellenic Studies* 71, 13–28.

Ashmole 1972, B. Ashmole, *Architect and Sculptor in Classical Greece.* London.

Badian 1987, E. Badian, 'The Peace of Callias', *Journal of Hellenic Studies* 107, 1–39.

Balanos 1956, N. Balanos, 'The new reconstruction of the temple of Athena Nike (1935–1939)', *Archaiologike Ephemeris* 1937, part 3 (1956), 776–807.

Bammer 1964–1965, A. Bammer, 'Zum jüngeren Artemision von Ephesos', *Jahreshefte des Österreichischen Archäologischen Instituts in Wien*, 47, 126–45.

Bammer 1972, A. Bammer, *Die Architektur des jüngeren Artemision von Ephesos.* Vienna.

Bammer 1985, A. Bammer, *Architektur und Gesellschaft in der Antike*, 2nd edition. Vienna.

Bammer 2001a, see Muss.

Bammer 2001b, A. Bammer, 'Der Ephesische Peripteros und die Ägyptische Architektur', in Bietak (ed.), 71–82.

Barletta 1983, B. Barletta, *Ionic Influence in Archaic Sicily: The Monumental Art.* Göteborg.

Barletta 2001, B. Barletta, *The Origins of the Greek Architectural Orders.* Cambridge.

Barletta 2005, B. Barletta, 'The architecture and architects of the Classical Parthenon', in Neils (ed.), 67–99.

Barringer 1995, J. Barringer, *Divine Escorts: Nereids in Archaic and Classical Greek Art.* Michigan.

Barringer 2005, J. Barringer, 'The temple of Zeus at Olympia, heroes and athletes', *Hesperia* 74, 211–41.

Barringer and Hurwit 2005, J. Barringer and J. Hurwit (eds), *Periklean Athens and Its Legacy: Problems and Perspectives.* Austin, Texas.

Başgelen and Lugal 1989, N. Başgelen and M. Lugal (eds), *Festschrift für Jale Inan.* Istanbul.

Bean 1989a, G. Bean, *Lycian Turkey.* London.

Bean 1989b, G. Bean, *Turkey Beyond the Maeander.* London.

Bean and Cook 1952, G. Bean and J. Cook, 'The Cnidia', *The Annual of the British School at Athens* 47, 171–212.

Beard 2002, M. Beard, *The Parthenon.* London.

Belogiannis, see Kouzeli.

Benndorf and Niemann 1889, O. Benndorf and G. Niemann, *Das Heroon von Gjölbaschi-Trysa.* Vienna.

Berger 1974, E. Berger, *Die Geburt der Athena im Ostgiebel des Parthenon.* Mainz.

Berger 1986, E. Berger, *Der Parthenon in Basel: Dokumentation zu den Metopen.* Mainz.

Berger and Gisler-Huwiler 1996, E. Berger and M. Gisler-Huwiler, *Der Parthenon in Basel: Dokumentation zum Fries.* Mainz.

Betancourt 1977, P. Betancourt, *The Aeolic Style in Architecture.* Princeton.

Bietak 2001, M. Bietak (ed.), *Archaische griechische Tempel und Altägypten.* Vienna.

Binder 1969, W. Binder, *Der Roma-Augustus Monopteros auf der Akropolis in Athen und sein typologischer Ort.* Stuttgart.

Binder 1984, J. Binder, 'The west pediment of the Parthenon: Poseidon', in *Studies Presented to Stirling Dow.* Greek, Roman and Byzantine Studies Monographs 10. Durham, North Carolina, 15–22.

Birch 1844, S. Birch, 'Observations on the Xanthian marbles recently deposited in the British Museum', *Archaeologia* 30, 176–204.

Bird, Jenkins and Levi 1998, S. Bird, I. Jenkins and F. Levi, *Second Sight of the Parthenon Frieze.* London.

Biscontin and Volpin 1990, G. Biscontin and S. Volpin (eds), *Superfici dell' architettura: le finiture.* Acts of a conference, Bressanone 26–9 June.

Blomquist 1982, J. Blomquist, 'Translation Greek in the Trilingual Inscription of Xanthus', *Opuscula Atheniensia* 14, 11–20.

BM Bronzes, see Walters.

BM Inscriptions, see Hicks et al.

BM Sculpture, see Pryce or Smith.

BM Vases, see Smith or Walters.

Boardman 1980, J. Boardman, *The Greeks Overseas.* London.

Boardman 1985, J. Boardman, *Greek Sculpture: The Classical Period.* London.

Boardman 1995, J. Boardman, *Greek Sculpture: The Late Classical Period.* London.

Boardman 2000, J. Boardman, *Persia and the West: An Archaeological Investigation of the Genesis of Achaemenid Art.* London.

Boardman and Finn 1985, J. Boardman and D. Finn, *The Parthenon and Its Sculptures.* London.

Boersma 1970, J. Boersma, *Athenian Building Policy from 561/0 to 405/4 BC.* (*Scripta Archaeologica Groningana* 4). Groningen.

Borbein 1973, A. Borbein, 'Die griechische Statue des 4. Jahrhunderts v. Chr.', *Jahrbuch des Deutschen Archäologischen Instituts* 88, 108–113.

Borchhardt 1967, J. Borchhardt, 'Limyra, Sitz des lykischen Dynasten Perikles', *Mitteilungen des Deutschen Archäologischen Instituts, Abteilung Istanbul* 17, 151–67.

Borchhardt 1970a, J. Borchhardt, 'Das Heroon von Limyra – Grabmal des lykischen Königs Perikles', *Archäologischer Anzeiger* 85, 353–90.

Borchhardt 1970b, J. Borchhardt, 'Archaeology in Asia Minor', *American Journal of Archaeology* 74, 169–70.

Borchhardt 1976, J. Borchhardt, *Die Bauskulptur des Heroons von Limyra.* Berlin.

Boulter 1969, P. Boulter, 'The acroteria of the Nike temple', *Hesperia* 38, 133–40.

Boulter 1970, P. Boulter, 'The frieze of the Erechtheion', *Antike Plastik* 10, 7–28.

Bouras et al. 2000, C. Bouras, M. Sakellariou, K. Straïkos and E. Touloupa, *Athens from the Classical Epoch until the Present Day*. Athens.

Bousquet 1975, J. Bousquet, 'Arbinas, fils de Gergis, dynaste de Xanthos', *Comptes Rendus de l'Académie d'Inscriptions*, 138–48.

van Breen 1942, J. van Breen, *Het Reconstructieplan voor het Mausoleum te Halikarnassos*. Amsterdam.

Brinkmann 2003a, V. Brinkmann, *Bunte Götter – die Farbigkeit antiker Skulptur*. Exhibition catalogue. Munich.

Brinkmann 2003b, V. Brinkmann, *Die Polychromie der archaischen und frühklassischen Skulptur*. Munich.

Brommer 1963, F. Brommer, *Die Skulpturen der Parthenon-Giebel*. Mainz.

Brommer 1967, F. Brommer, *Die Metopen des Parthenon*. Mainz.

Brommer 1977, F. Brommer, *Der Parthenonfries: Katalog und Untersuchung*. Mainz.

Brønsted 1861, P. O. Brønsted, 'Udgravningen af Templet ved Phigalia', *Nordisk Universitets Tidskrift* 7.1, edited by M. Hamerich, 64–86.

Brouskari 1999, M. Brouskari, 'The parapet of the Temple of Athena Nike', *Archaiologike Ephemeris* 137 (1998).

Bruns-Özgan 1987, C. Bruns-Özgan, *Lykische Grabreliefs des 5. und 4. Jahrhunderts v. Chr.*, Istanbuler Mitteilungen, Beiheft 3, Tübingen.

Bruns-Özgan 1996/1997, C. Bruns-Özgan, 'Philosophische Gespräche in Lykien', *Lykia* 3 (Antalya), 46–57.

Bruns-Özgan 2002, C. Bruns-Özgan, *Knidos: Ein Führer durch die Ruinen*. Konya. English translation 2004.

Bruns-Özgan 2005, C. Bruns-Özgan, 'Attische Bildhauer in Knidos', in V.M. Strocka (ed.), *Meisterwerke: Internationales Symposion anlässlich des 150. Geburtstages von Adolf Furtwängler, Freiburg 2003*. Munich, 179–91.

Bryce 1980, T. Bryce, 'The other Perikles', *Historia* 29, 377–81.

Bryce 1986, T. Bryce, *The Lycians in Literary and Epigraphic Sources*. Copenhagen.

Büsing 1970, H. Büsing, *Die griechische Halbsäule*. Wiesbaden.

Büsing 1990, H. Büsing, 'Zur Bemalung des Nike-Tempels', *Archäologischer Anzeiger*, 71–6.

Büyükkolancı, see Muss.

Buitron-Oliver 1997, D. Buitron-Oliver (ed.), *The Interpretation of Architectural Sculpture in Greece and Rome*. Studies in the History of Art 49. Washington DC.

Bundgaard 1957, J.A. Bundgaard, *Mnesicles: A Greek Architect at Work*. Copenhagen.

Burford 1963, A. Burford, 'The builders of the Parthenon', in Hooker (ed.), 23–34.

Burford 1969, A. Burford, *The Greek Temple Builders at Epidauros*. Liverpool.

Burn 1987, L. Burn, *The Meidias Painter*. Oxford.

Bury 1998, J. Bury, 'Chapter III of the Hypnerotomachia Poliphili and the Tomb of Mausolus', *Word and Image* 14, 40–60.

Buschor 1930, E. Buschor, 'Heraion von Samos: frühe Bauten', *Mitteilungen des Deutschen Archäologischen Instituts, Athenische Abteilung* 55, 1–90.

Camp 1998, J. Camp, *Horses and Horsemanship in the Athenian Agora*. Athens.

Camp 2001, J. Camp, *The Archaeology of Athens*. New Haven and London.

Carter 1979, J. Carter, 'The date of the sculptured coffer lids from the temple of Athene Polias at Priene', in Kopcke and Moore (eds), 139–51.

Carter 1983, J. Carter, *The Sculpture of the Sanctuary of Athena Polias at Priene*. London.

Carter 1990, J. Carter, 'Pytheos', *Akten des XIII. Internationalen Kongresses für klassische Archäologie Berlin 1988*. Mainz, 129–36.

Caskey, see Stevens.

Castriota 1992, D. Castriota, *Myth, Ethos and Actuality – Official Art in Fifth-Century BC Athens*. Madison.

Childs 1973, W. Childs, 'Prolegomena to a Lycian chronology: the Nereid Monument from Xanthos', *Opuscula Romana* 9, 105–116.

Childs 1976, W. Childs, 'Prolegomena to a Lycian chronology, II: the Heroon from Trysa', *Revue Archéologique*, 281–316.

Childs 1978, W. Childs, *The City-Reliefs of Lycia*. Princeton.

Childs 1979, W. Childs, 'The authorship of the Inscribed Pillar of Xanthos', *Anatolian Studies* 29, 97–102.

Childs 1981, W. Childs, 'Lycian relations with Persians and Greeks in the fifth and fourth centuries re-examined', *Anatolian Studies* 31, 55–80.

Childs 1985, W. Childs, 'In defence of an earlier date for the frieze of the temple on the Ilissos', *Mitteilungen des Deutschen Archäologischen Instituts, Athenische Abteilung* 100, 207–51.

Clayton and Price 1988, P. Clayton and M. Price, *The Seven Wonders of the Ancient World*. London and New York.

Cockerell 1860, C. Cockerell, *The Temples of Jupiter Panhellenius at Aegina and of Apollo Epicurius at Bassae near Phigaleia in Arcadia*. London.

Cohen 1991, B. Cohen, 'Perikles' portrait and the Riace Bronzes: new evidence for schinocephaly', *Hesperia* 60, 462–502.

Coldstream 1985, N. Coldstream, 'Greek temples: why and where', in Easterling and Muir (eds), 67–97.

Connelly 1996, J. Connelly, 'Parthenon and Parthenoi: a mythological interpretation of the Parthenon Frieze', *American Journal of Archaeology* 100, 53–80.

Connolly and Dodge 1998, P. Connolly and H. Dodge, *The Ancient City*. Oxford.

Cook 1984, B. Cook, *The Elgin Marbles*. Revised edition 1997, London.

Cook 1989, B. Cook, 'The sculptors of the Mausoleum friezes', in Linders and Hellström (eds), 31–41.

Cook 1993, B. Cook, 'The Parthenon, east pediment A–C', *Annual of the British School at Athens* 88, 183–5.

Cook 2005, B. Cook, *Relief Sculptures of the Mausoleum at Halicarnassus*. Oxford.

Cook 1961, J. Cook, 'The problem of Classical Ionia', *Proceedings of the Cambridge Philological Society* 187, 9–18.

Cook 1962, J. Cook, *The Greeks in Ionia and the East*. London.

Cooper 1978, F. Cooper, *The Temple of Apollo at Bassai*. PhD Dissertation, University of Pennsylvania 1970.

Cooper 1996, F. Cooper (with N. Kelly), *The Temple of Apollo Bassitas* 1 and 3, *The Architecture*. Princeton. See also Madigan (with F. Cooper) *Bassitas* 2.

Corbett 1970, P. Corbett, 'Greek temples and Greek worshippers: the literary and archaeological evidence', *Bulletin of the Institute of Classical Studies* 17, 149–58.

Corso 1997, A. Corso, 'The Cnidian Aphrodite', in Jenkins and Waywell (eds), 91–8.

Corso 2004, A. Corso, *The Art of Praxiteles. The Development of Praxiteles' Workshop and its Tradition until the Sculptor's Acme (364–1 BC)*. Rome.

Coulson, see Palagia.

Coulton 1974, J. Coulton, 'Lifting in early Greek architecture', *Journal of Hellenic Studies* 94, 1–19.

Coulton 1975, J. Coulton, 'Towards understanding Greek temple architecture design', *Annual of the British School at Athens* 70, 59–99.

Coulton 1977, J. Coulton, *Greek Architects at Work: Problems of Structure and Design*. London.

Coulton 1993, J. Coulton, 'The Toumba building: description and analysis of the architecture', in Popham et al., 33–70 with plate 28.

Coulton 1998, J. Coulton, 'Greece, ancient. Architectural theory and design: Drawings, models and specifications', *Dictionary of Art* 13, 409–410.

Coulton 2000, J. Coulton, 'Fitting friezes: architecture and sculpture', in Tsetskhladze et al. (eds), 70–79.

Coupel and Metzger 1976, P. Coupel and H. Metzger, 'La frise des coqs et poules de l'acropole de Xanthos: essai de restitution et d'interprétation', *Revue Archéologique*, 247–64.

Creighton 1991, W. Creighton, *The Parthenon in Nashville*. Nashville.

Curtis 2000, J. Curtis, *Ancient Persia*. London.

Delivorrias 1974, A. Delivorrias, *Attische Giebelskulpturen und Akrotere des fünften Jahrhunderts*. Tübingen.

Delivorrias 1994, A. Delivorrias, 'The sculptures of the Parthenon', in Tournikiotis (ed.), 100–135.

Delivorrias 2004, A. Delivorrias, *The Parthenon Frieze*. Athens.

Deltour-Levie 1980, C. Deltour-Levie, *Les piliers funéraires de Lycie*. Louvain-la-Neuve.

Demargne 1976, P. Demargne, 'L'iconographie dynastique au monument des Néréides de Xanthos', *Recueil Plassart: Etudes sur l'antiquité grecque offertes à A. Plassart*. Paris, 81–95.

Demargne 1987, P. Demargne, 'Thétis et Pélée: un mythe grec au monument des Néréides de Xanthos', *Comptes rendus de l'Académie d'Inscriptions*, 190–205.

Demargne and Klincksieck 1960, P. Demargne and C. Klincksieck, 'Le Pilier Inscrit de Xanthos, Note complémentaire aux Fouilles de Xanthos 1', *Revue des Études Anciennes* 62, 41–7.

Despinis 1974, G. Despinis, 'The sculpture of the pediments of the Temple of Athenian Nike', *Archaiologikon Deltion* 29, 1–24.

Dickson 1901, W. Dickson, *The Life of Major-General Sir Robert Murdoch Smith*. Edinburgh and London.

Dilke 1987, O. Dilke, *Mathematics and Measurement*. London.

Dinsmoor 1950, W. Dinsmoor, *The Architecture of Ancient Greece*. 3rd edition. London.

Dinsmoor 1956, W. Dinsmoor, 'The sculptured frieze from Bassae (a revised sequence)', *American Journal of Archaeology* 60, 401–52.

Dinsmoor 2004, A. Dinsmoor (ed.), *The Propylaia to the Athenian Akropolis*, volume 2, *The Classical Building*. Princeton.

Dogani, see Kouzeli.

Dontas 2000, N. Dontas et al., *Priene*. Athens.

Easterling and Muir 1985, P. Easterling and J. Muir (eds), *Greek Religion and Society*. Cambridge.

Ebbinghaus 2000, S. Ebbinghaus, 'A banquet at Xanthos: seven rhyta on the northern cella frieze of the Nereid Monument', in Tsetskhladze et al. (eds), 99–109.

Ebersole 1899, W. Ebersole, 'Metopes of the west end of the Parthenon', *American Journal of Archaeology* 3, 409–432.

Eichler 1950, F. Eichler, *Die Reliefs des Heroon von Gjölbaschi in Trysa*. Vienna

Ekonomakis 1994, R. Ekonomakis (ed.), *Acropolis Restorations: The CCAM Interventions*. London.

Ellinger 1993, P. Ellinger, 'La légende nationale phocidienne', *Bulletin de Correspondence Hellénique*, Supplement 27.

Epitropé Epikouriou 1995, *1st Meeting on the Conservation of the Temple of Apollo Epikourios*, Athens 1995, published Praktika 1996.

FdX = Fouilles de Xanthos.

FdX 1. *Les Piliers Funéraires* by P. Demargne, drawn and reconstructed by P. Coupel and P. Prunet. Paris 1958.

FdX 2. *L'acropole Lycienne* by H. Metzger, architectural reconstructions by P. Coupel. Paris 1963.

FdX 3. *Le monument des Néréides, architecture* by P. Coupel and P. Demargne. Paris 1969.

FdX 4. *Les céramiques archaïques et classiques de l'acropole Lycienne* by H. Metzger, with D. von Bothmer and J.N. Coldstream. Paris 1972.

FdX 5. *Tombes-maisons, tombes rupestres et sarcophages* by P. Demargne, reconstructed by P. Coupel and P. Prunet, Lycian epitaphs by E. Laroche. Paris 1974.

FdX 6. *La stèle trilingue du Létôon* by H. Metzger, A. Dupont-Sommer, E. Laroche, M. Mayrhofer and P. Demargne. Paris 1979.

FdX 7. *Inscriptions d'Époque impériale du Létôon* by A. Balland. Paris 1981.

FdX 8, 1 and 2. *Le monument des Néréides, le décor sculpté* by W. Childs and P. Demargne, reconstructions and architectural studies by P. Coupel and A. Lemaire, with S. Flatko, D. Bylund and N. Laos. Paris 1989.

FdX 9, 1 and 2. *La région nord du Létôon* by H. Metzger, A. Bougarel and G. Siebert, the sculptures by A. Devesne and J. Marcadé, the Graeco-Lycian inscriptions by J. Bousquet with C. Le Roy and appendix by A. Lemaire. Paris 1992.

Fedak 1990, J. Fedak, *Monumental Tombs of the Hellenistic Period*. Toronto.

Felten 1984, F. Felten, *Griechische tektonische Friese in archaischer und klassischer Zeit*. Waldsassen-Bayern.

Fergusson 1882–1883, J. Fergusson, 'The Temple of Diana at Ephesus, with especial reference to Mr Wood's discoveries of its remains', *Transactions of the Royal Institute of British Architects*, 3, 147 ff.

Fleischer 1983, R. Fleischer, *Der Klagefrauensarkophag aus Sidon, Istanbuler Forschungen* 34. Tübingen.

Foss 1979, C. Foss, *Ephesus after Antiquity: A Late Antique, Byzantine and Turkish City*. Cambridge.

Fowler, see Stevens.

Frantz 1954, A. Frantz, 'The Hephaisteion revisited', *Archaeology* 7, 244–8.

Froning 2002/2003, H. Froning, 'Das sogenannte Harpyienmonument von Xanthos etc.', *Archäologie* (Nuremberg) 19, 137–58.

Froning 2004, H. Froning, 'Das sogenannte Harpyienmonument etc.', in Korkut (ed.), 315–20.

Fuchs 1959, W. Fuchs, *Die Vorbilder der neuattischen Reliefs*. Berlin.

Furtwängler 1882, A. Furtwängler, 'von Delos', *Archäologische Zeitung* 40, 322–68.

Gebhard 2001, E. Gebhard, 'The archaic temple at Isthmia: techniques of construction', in Bietak (ed.), 41–61.

Gisler-Huwiler, see Berger.

Goette 2001, H. Goette, *Athens, Attica and the Megarid: An Archaeological Guide*. London and New York.

Gorman 2001, V. Gorman, *Miletos, the Ornament of Ionia: A History of the City to 400 BCE*. Minneapolis.

von Graeve and Preusser 1981, V. von Graeve and F. Preusser, 'Zur Technik griechischer Malerei auf Marmor', *Jahrbuch des Deutschen Archäologischen Instituts* 96, 120–56.

Gratziu, see Jenkins.

Green 1970, P. Green, *Alexander of Macedon 356–323 BC*. London.

Green 1996, P. Green, *The Greco-Persian Wars*. Berkeley.

Gruben 1963, G. Gruben, 'Das archaische Didymaion', *Jahrbuch des Deutschen Archäologischen Instituts* 78, 78–182

Gruben 2001, G. Gruben, *Griechische Tempel und Heiligtümer*, 5th edition. Munich.

Gunn 2000, J. Gunn (ed.), *The Years without Summer*, BAR International Series. Oxford.

Hahland 1959, W. Hahland, 'Einige Bermerkungen zur Deutung und Anordnung der Metopenreliefs von Bassae', *Jahreshefte des Österreichischen Archäologischen Instituts in Wien* 44, 37–53.

Hanfmann 1975, G. Hanfmann, *From Croesus to Constantine: The Cities of Western Asia Minor and their Arts in Greek and Roman Times.* Minneapolis.

Hansen, see Ross.

Harrison 1988, E. Harrison, 'Theseum east frieze colour traces and attachment cuttings', *Hesperia* 57, 339–49.

Harrison 1992, E. Harrison, 'New light on a Nereid Monument Acroterion', *Kotinos, Festschrift für Erika Simon*, Mainz, 204–210.

Harrison 1996, E. Harrison, 'Pheidias', in Palagia and Pollitt (eds), 16–65.

Harrison 1997, E. Harrison, 'The glories of the Athenians: observations on the program of the frieze of the temple of Athena Nike', in Buitron-Oliver (ed.), 108–125.

Haselberger 1983, L. Haselberger, 'The construction plans of the temple of Apollo at Didyma', *Scientific American* 253/256 (December), 126–32.

Haselberger 1998, L. Haselberger, 'Greece, ancient. Architectural theory and design: Measurement', *Dictionary of Art* 13, 410–12.

Haselberger 1999a, L. Haselberger (ed.), *Appearance and Essence: Refinements of Classical Architecture: Curvature.* Philadelphia.

Haselberger 1999b, L. Haselberger, 'Curvature: the evidence of Didyma', in Haselberger 1999a (ed.), 173–84.

Haselberger 2005, L. Haselberger, 'Bending the truth: curvature and other refinements of the Parthenon', in Neils (ed.), 101–157.

Hellmann et al. 1982, M.-C. Hellmann et al., *Paris. Rome. Athènes: Le Voyage en Grèce des architectes français aux XIX et XX siècles.* Exhibition catalogue. Paris.

Hellström 1989, see Linders.

Hellström 1994, P. Hellström, 'Architecture: characteristic building-types and particularities of style and technique. Possible implications for Hellenistic architecture', in Isager (ed.), 36–57.

Hersey 1988, G. Hersey, *The Lost Meaning of Classical Architecture: Speculation on Ornament from Vitruvius to Venturi.* Cambridge, Massachusetts.

Hicks et al. 1874–1916 (abbreviated as BM Inscriptions), E. Hicks et al. (eds), *The Collection of Ancient Greek Inscriptions in the British Museum.* Oxford.

Higgs 1997, P. Higgs, 'A newly found fragment of free-standing sculpture from the Mausoleum at Halicarnassus', in Jenkins and Waywell (eds), 30–34.

Higgs forthcoming (a), P. Higgs, 'The Bassai metopes'.

Higgs forthconming (b), P. Higgs, 'Back to the second century BC: new thoughts on the date of the sculptured coffers from the temple of Athene Polias at Priene', in van den Hoff and Schulz forthcoming.

Hodge and Tomlinson 1969, A. Hodge and R. Tomlinson, 'Some notes on the temple of Nemesis at Rhamnous', *American Journal of Archaeology* 73, 185–92.

Hoepfner 1990, W. Hoepfner, 'Bauten und Bedeutung des Hermogenes', in Hoepfner and Schwandner (eds), 1–34.

Hoepfner 1996, W. Hoepfner, 'Zum Maussolleion von Halikarnassos', *Archäologischer Anzeiger*, 95–114.

Hoepfner 2002, W. Hoepfner, 'Das Mausoleum von Halikarnassos: Perfektion und Hybris', in *Die griechische Klassik: Idee oder Wirklichkeit.* Exhibition catalogue, Berlin, 417–23.

Hoepfner and Schwandner 1986, W. Hoepfner and E.-L. Schwandner, *Haus und Stadt im klassischen Griechenland.* Munich.

Hoepfner and Schwandner 1990, W. Hoepfner and E.-L. Schwandner (eds) *Hermogenes und die hochhellenistische Architektur.* Mainz.

von den Hoff (forthcoming), R. von den Hoff and P. Schulz (eds), *Structure, Image, Ornament: Architectural Sculpture of the Greek World*, Proceedings of the Conference Held in Athens 27–9 November 2004.

Hofkes-Brukker 1963, C. Hofkes-Brukker, 'Die Metopen des Bassaetempels. Versuch zur Deutung', *Bulletin Antieke Beschaving* 38, 52–83.

Hofkes-Brukker and Mallwitz 1975, C. Hofkes-Brukker and A. Mallwitz, *Der Bassai-Fries.* Munich.

Hogarth 1908, D.G. Hogarth, *Excavations at Ephesus: The Archaic Artemision.* London.

Hooker 1963, G. Hooker (ed.), *Parthenos and Parthenon, Greece and Rome Supplement to Volume 10.* Oxford.

Hornblower 1982, S. Hornblower, *Mausolus.* Oxford.

Hornblower 1994, S. Hornblower, 'Persia', *The Cambridge Ancient History*, 2nd edition, Cambridge, 45–96.

Hornblower 2002, S. Hornblower, *The Greek World 479–323 BC.* London and New York.

Hurwit 1999, J. Hurwit, *The Athenian Acropolis.* Cambridge.

Hurwit 2004, J. Hurwit, *The Acropolis in the Age of Pericles.* Cambridge.

Hurwit 2005a, J. Hurwit, 'Space and theme: the setting of the Parthenon', in Neils (ed.), 9–34.

Hurwit 2005b, see Barringer.

Hussey 1972, E. Hussey, *The Presocratics.* London.

Huwiler 1996, see Berger.

Huxley 1966, G. Huxley, *The Early Ionians.* London.

IG = *Inscriptiones Graecae.* Many volumes from 1873.

Inschriften von Priene, F. Hiller von Gaertringen, *Inschriften von Priene.* Berlin 1906.

Ionian Antiquities 1769. Dilettanti Society. London. See also *Antiquities of Ionia*, 1821–1915.

Isager 1994, J. Isager (ed.), *Hekatomnid Caria and the Ionian Renaissance.* Acts of the International Symposium at the Department of Greek and Roman Studies, Odense University, 28–9 November, 1991. Odense.

Isager 1998, S. Isager, 'The pride of Halikarnassos', *Zeitschrift für Papyrologie und Epigraphik* 123, 1–23.

Isager and Pedersen 2004, S. Isager and P. Pedersen (eds), *The Salmakis Inscription and Hellenistic Halikarnassos.* Halicarnassian Studies 4. Odense.

Jenkins 1992, I. Jenkins, *Archaeologists and Aesthetes in the Sculpture Galleries of the British Museum 1800–1839.* London.

Jenkins 1994, I. Jenkins, *The Parthenon Frieze.* London.

Jenkins 1998, see Bird.

Jenkins 2001, I. Jenkins, 'Cleaning and controversy: the Parthenon sculptures 1811–1939'. British Museum Occasional Paper 146. London.

Jenkins 2005, I. Jenkins, 'The Parthenon frieze and Perikles' cavalry of a thousand', in Barringer and Hurwit (eds), 147–61.

Jenkins and Middleton 1988, I. Jenkins and A. Middleton, 'Paint on the Parthenon sculptures', *Annual of the British School at Athens* 83, 183–207.

Jenkins and Waywell 1997, I. Jenkins and G. Waywell (eds), *Sculptors and Sculpture of Caria and the Dodecanese.* Proceedings of the 1994 conference at the British Museum and King's College, London.

Jenkins and Williams 1993, I. Jenkins and D. Williams, 'The arrangement of the sculptured frieze from the temple of Apollo Epikourios at Bassae', in Palagia and Coulson (eds), 57–77.

Jenkins, Gratziu and Middleton 1997, I. Jenkins, C. Gratziu and A. Middleton, 'The polychromy of the Mausoleum', in Jenkins and Waywell (eds), 35–40.

Jeppesen 1987, K. Jeppesen, *The Theory of the Alternative Erechtheion*. Aahrus.

Jeppesen 1992, K. Jeppesen, 'Tot operum opus: Ergebnisse der dänischen Forschungen zum Maussolleion von Halikarnassos seit 1966', *Jahrbuch des Deutschen Archäologischen Instituts* 107, 59–102.

Jeppesen 1997, K. Jeppesen, 'The Mausoleum at Halikarnassus, sculptural decoration and architectural background', in Jenkins and Waywell (eds), 42–8.

Jeppesen 1998, K. Jeppesen, 'Das Maussolleion von Halikarnass: Forschungsbericht 1997', *Proceedings of the Danish Institute at Athens* 2, 161–231.

Jeppesen and Zahle 1975, K. Jeppesen and J. Zahle, 'Investigations on the site of the Mausoleum 1970/1973', *American Journal of Archaeology* 79, 67–79.

Kagan 1991, D. Kagan, *Pericles of Athens and the Birth of Democracy*. New York.

Karousou 1954–1955, S. Papaspyridi-Karousou, 'Alkamenes und das Hephaisteion', *Mitteilungen des Deutschen Archäologischen Instituts, Athenische Abteilung* 69–70, 66–94.

Katsonopoulou, see Schilardi.

Keen 1992, A. Keen, 'The dynastic tombs of Xanthos – who was buried where?', *Anatolian Studies* 42, 53–63.

Keen 1998, A. Keen, *Dynastic Lycia: A Political History of the Lycians and Their Relations with Foreign Powers c. 545–362 BC*. Leiden.

Kelly 1995, N. Kelly, 'The Apollo temple at Bassai: correspondences to the classical temple', *Hesperia* 64, 227–77.

Kelly 1996, see Cooper.

Kidson 1998, P. Kidson, 'Architectural proportion, 1, 2: Before 1450', in *Dictionary of Art* 2, 343 ff.

Kienast 2001, H. Kienast, 'Samische Monumentalarchitektur – Ägyptischer Einfluss?', in Bietak (ed.), 35–9.

Kirk, Raven and Schofield 1983, G. Kirk, J. Raven and M. Schofield, *The Presocratic Philosophers*, 2nd edition. Cambridge.

Klincksieck, see Demargne.

Knibbe 1998, D. Knibbe, *Ephesus: Geschichte einer bedeutenden antiken Stadt und Portrait einer modernen Grossgrabung*. Vienna.

Koenigs 1983, W. Koenigs, 'Der Athenatempel von Priene, Bericht über die 1977–82 durchgeführten Untersuchungen', *Istanbuler Mitteilungen* 33, 134–76.

Koenigs 1998, see Rumscheid.

Kopcke and Moore 1979, G. Kopcke and M. Moore (eds), *Studies in Classical Art and Archaeology: A Tribute to Peter Heinrich von Blanckenhagen*. Locust Valley, New York.

Korkut 2004, T. Korkut (ed.), *Festschrift für Fahri Işık zum 60. Geburtstag*. Istanbul.

Korres 1983–1994, M. Korres et al., *Study for the Restoration of the Parthenon*, 5 volumes. Athens.

Korres 1992–1998, M. Korres, 'From Stavros to the ancient agora', *Horos* 10–12, 83–104.

Korres 1994a, M. Korres, 'Der Plan des Parthenon', *Mitteilungen des Deutschen Archäologischen Instituts, Athenische Abteilung* 109, 53–120.

Korres 1994b, M. Korres, 'The architecture of the Parthenon', in Tournikiotis (ed.), 56–97.

Korres 1995, M. Korres, *From Pentelicon to the Parthenon*. Athens.

Korres 2000, M. Korres, 'Classical Athenian architecture', in Bouras et al. (eds), 2–45.

Kosmopoulou 2002, A. Kosmopoulou, *The Iconography of Sculptured Statue Bases in the Archaic and Classical Periods*. University of Wisconsin.

Kourouniotes 1904, K. Kourouniotes, 'Excavation at Kotilion', *Archaiologike Ephemeris* 1903 [1904], columns 151–88.

Kourouniotes 1910, K. Kourouniotes, 'The ancient Sanctuary of Apollo at Bassai', *Archaiologike Ephemeris*, columns 271–332.

Kouzeli et al. 1990, K. Kouzeli, Y. Dogani and N. Belogiannis, 'Study of the remaining colour on the architectural surfaces of the Parthenon', in Biscontin and Volpin (eds), 241–3.

Kraay 1973, see Thompson.

Krischen 1938, F. Krischen, *Die Griechische Stadt*. Berlin.

Krischen 1944, F. Krischen, 'Löwenmonument und Maussolleion', *Mitteilungen des Deutschen Archäologischen Instituts. Römische Abteilung* 59, 173–81.

Krischen 1956, F. Krischen, *Weltwunder der Baukunst in Babylonien und Jonien*, Tübingen.

Lanowski 1965, J. Lanowski, 'Weltwunder', *Paulys Realencyclopädie der klassischen Altertumswissenschaft*, Supplement 10, 1020 ff.

Lapatin 2001, K. Lapatin, *Chryselephantine Statuary in the Ancient Mediterranean World*. Oxford.

Larson 2001, J. Larson, *Greek Nymphs: Myth, Cult and Lore*. Oxford.

Lazzarini 2002, L. Lazzarini (ed.), *Interdisciplinary Studies on Ancient Stone, Asmosia* 6. Padua.

Leipen 1971, N. Leipen, *Athena Parthenos: A Reconstruction*. Toronto.

Lethaby 1908, W.R. Lethaby, *Greek Buildings Represented by Fragments in the British Museum*. London

Lethaby 1913, W.R. Lethaby, 'The sculptures of the later temple of Artemis at Ephesus', *Journal of Hellenic Studies* 33, 87–96.

Lethaby 1914, W.R. Lethaby, 'Further notes on the sculpture of the later temple of Artemis at Ephesus', *Journal of Hellenic Studies* 34, 76–88.

Lethaby 1916, W.R. Lethaby, 'Another note on the sculpture of the later temple of Artemis at Ephesus', *Journal of Hellenic Studies* 36, 25–35.

Lethaby 1917, W.R. Lethaby, 'The earlier temple of Artemis at Ephesus', *Journal of Hellenic Studies* 37, 1 ff.

Lethaby 1929a, W. Lethaby, 'More Greek studies 10, The Ionic order, Naucratis I and II', *The Builder*, 6 December, 967–8.

Lethaby 1929b, W. Lethaby, 'More Greek studies 10, The Ionic order continued', *The Builder*, 13 December, 1019–20.

Levi 1998, see Bird.

LIMC = Lexicon Iconographicum Mythologiae Classicae. Zurich and Munich.

Linders and Hellström 1989, T. Linders and P. Hellström (eds), *Architecture and Society in Hekatomnid Caria*, Proceedings of the Uppsala Symposium 1987, *Boreas* 17. Uppsala.

Lugal, see Başgelen.

McCredie 1979, J. McCredie, 'The architects of the Parthenon', in Kopcke and Moore (eds), 69–73.

MacLean Rogers 1991, G. MacLean Rogers, *The Sacred Identity of Ephesos: Foundation Myths of a Roman City*. London and New York.

McNeill 2005, R. McNeill, 'Notes on the subject of the Ilissos temple frieze', in Barringer and Hurwitt (eds), 103–110.

Madigan 1992, B. Madigan (with F. Cooper), *The Temple of Apollo Bassitas 2: The Sculpture*. Princeton.

Madigan 1993, B. Madigan, 'A statue in the temple of Apollo at Bassai', in Palagia and Coulson (eds), 111–18.

MAH = The Maussolleion at Halikarnassos

MAH 1. *The Maussolleion at Halikarnassos* 1, *The Sacrificial Deposit* by K. Jeppesen, F. Højlund and K. Aaris-Sørensen. Copenhagen 1981.

MAH 2. *The Maussolleion at Halikarnassos* 2, *The Written Sources and their Archaeological Background* by K. Jeppesen and A. Luttrell. Moesgaard 1986.

MAH 3.1. *The Maussolleion at Halikarnassos* 3.1–2, *The Maussolleion Terrace and Accessory Structures* by P. Pedersen. Moesgaard 1991.

MAH 5. *The Maussolleion at Halikarnassos 5. The Superstructure, a Comparative Analysis of the Architectural, Sculptural and Literary Evidence* by K. Jeppesen. Moesgaard 2002.

Mallwitz 1962, A. Mallwitz, 'Cella und adyton des Apollotempels in Bassai', *Mitteilungen des Deutschen Archäologischen Instituts, Athenische Abteilung* 77, 140–47.

Mallwitz 1972, A. Mallwitz, *Olympia und seine Bauten*. Munich.

Mansfield 1985, J. Mansfield, 'The Robe of Athena and the Panathenaic Peplos', PhD Dissertation, University of California, Berkeley. UMI. Ann Arbor.

Mantis 1997, A. Mantis, 'Parthenon central south metopes: new evidence', in Buitron-Oliver (ed.), 67–81 gives bibliography for other articles on the same subject.

Manzelli 1994, V. Manzelli, *La policromia nella statuaria greca arcaica*. Rome.

Mark 1993, I. Mark, *The Sanctuary of Athena Nike in Athens: Architectural Stages and Archaeology*. Hesperia Supplement 26. Princeton.

Matthews, see Walker.

Meiggs 1963, R. Meiggs, 'Political implications of the Parthenon', in Hooker (ed.), 36–45.

Mert 2002, I. Mert, 'Der korinthische Tempel in Knidos', *Archäologischer Anzeiger* 9–22.

Metzger, see Coupel.

Middleton, see Jenkins.

Miles 1980, M. Miles, 'The date of the temple on the Ilissos river', *Hesperia* 49, 309–25.

Miles 1989, M. Miles, 'A reconstruction of the temple of Nemesis at Rhamnous', *Hesperia* 58, 131–249.

Mizuta 2001, A. Mizuta, *Iconographic and Stylistic Observations on the Parthenon Frieze*. Tokyo.

Moore, see Kopcke.

Mordaunt Crook 1972, J. Mordaunt Crook, *The British Museum*. London.

Mørkholm 1973, see Thompson.

Mørkholm and Neumann 1978, O. Mørkholm and G. Neumann, *Die lykischen Münzlegenden: Nachrichten der Akademie der Wissenschaften in Göttingen*. Number 1. Göttingen.

Mørkholm and Zahle 1972, O. Mørkholm and J. Zahle, 'The coinage of Kuprlli', *Acta Archaeologica* 43, 57–113.

Mørkholm and Zahle 1976, O. Mørkholm and J. Zahle, 'The coinages of the Lycian dynasts, Kheriga, Kherêi and Erbbina', *Acta Archaeologica* 47, 47–90.

Morris 2001, S. Morris, 'The prehistoric background of Artemis Ephesia: a solution to the enigma of her breasts', in Muss (ed.), 135–51.

Morrow 1985, K. Morrow, *Greek Footwear and the Dating of Sculpture*. Madison.

Muir, see Easterling.

Murray 1889, A. Murray, 'Remains of the archaic temple of Artemis at Ephesus', *Journal of Hellenic Studies* 10, 1–10.

Muss 1994, U. Muss, *Die Bauplastik des archaischen Artemisions von Ephesos*. Vienna.

Muss 2001, U. Muss (ed.), *Der Kosmos der Artemis von Ephesos*, Vienna.

Muss, Bammer and Büyükkolancı 2001, U. Muss, A. Bammer and M. Büyükkolancı, *Der Altar des Artemisions von Ephesos, Forschungen in Ephesos* 12/2, 2 volumes. Vienna.

Neils 2001, J. Neils, *The Parthenon Frieze*. Cambridge.

Neils 2005, J. Neils (ed.), *The Parthenon from Antiquity to the Present*. Cambridge.

Neumann, see Mørkholm.

Newton 1862, C. Newton, *A History of Discoveries at Halicarnassus, Cnidus and Branchidae*. London.

Nick 2002, G. Nick, *Die Athena Parthenos: Studien zum griechischen Kultbild und seiner Rezeption*. Mainz.

Niemann, see Benndorf.

Oberleitner 1994, W. Oberleitner, *Das Heroon von Trysa*. Mainz.

Onians 1988, J. Onians, *Bearers of Meaning: The Classical Orders in Antiquity, the Middle Ages and the Renaissance*. Princeton.

Orlandos 1977–1978, A. Orlandos, *The Architecture of the Parthenon*. 3 volumes, Athens.

Østby 2001, E. Østby, 'Der Ursprung der Griechischen Tempelarchitektur', in Bietak (ed.), 17–33.

Palagia 1993, O. Palagia, *The Pediments of the Parthenon*. Leiden.

Palagia 2000, O. Palagia, 'Scopas of Paros and the Pothos', in Schilardi and Katsonopoulou (eds), 219–25.

Palagia 2002, O. Palagia, 'A new metope from Bassai', in Lazzarini (ed.), 375–82.

Palagia 2005, O. Palagia, 'Interpretations of two Athenian friezes: the temple on the Ilissos and the temple of Athena Nike', in Barringer and Hurwit (eds), 177–92.

Palagia and Coulson 1993, O. Palagia and W. Coulson (eds), *Sculpture from Arcadia and Laconia: Proceedings of an International Conference Held at the American School of Classical Studies at Athens, April 10–14, 1992*, Oxbow Monograph 30. Oxford.

Palagia and Coulson 1998, O. Palagia and W. Coulson (eds), *Regional Schools in Hellenistic Sculpture*, Conference Proceedings. Oxbow Monograph 90. Oxford.

Palagia and Pollitt 1996, O. Palagia and J. Pollitt (eds), *Personal Styles in Greek Architecture*. Cambridge.

Papanikolaou 1994, A. Papanikolaou, 'The restoration of the Erechtheum', in Ekonomakis (ed.), 137–49.

Paton, see Stevens.

Pedersen 1983, P. Pedersen, 'Zwei ornamentierte Säulenhälse aus Halikarnassos', *Jahrbuch des Deutschen Archäologischen Instituts* 98, 87–121.

Pedersen 1989, P. Pedersen, *The Parthenon and the Origin of the Corinthian Capital*. Odense.

Pedersen 1994, P. Pedersen, 'The Ionian Renaissance and some aspects of its origins within the field of architecture and planning', in Isager (ed.), 11–35.

Pedersen 2001/2002, P. Pedersen, 'Reflections on the Ionian Renaissance in Greek architecture and its historical background', *Hephaistos* 19/20, 97–130.

Pedersen 2004, see Isager.

Penrose 1888, F. Penrose, *The Principles of Athenian Architecture*, 2nd edition. London

Pfaff 2003, C. Pfaff, *The Argive Heraion Volume 1: The Architecture of the Classical Temple of Hera*. Athens.

Picon 1978, C. Picon, 'The Ilissos Temple reconsidered', *American Journal of Archaeology* 82, 47–81.

Picon 1981, C. Picon, 'The Orpheus metope from Bassai', *Annual of the British School at Athens* 76, 323–8.

Plommer 1950, W. Plommer, 'Three Attic temples', *Annual of the British School at Athens* 45, 66–112.

Podlecki 1998, A. Podlecki, *Perikles and His Circle*. London and New York.

Pollitt, see Palagia.

Popham et al. 1993, M. Popham, P. Calligas and L. Sackett (eds), *Lefkandi II: The Protogeometric Building at Toumba, Part 2 The Excavation, Architecture and Finds*. Oxford.

Posch 1991, W. Posch, 'The typoi of Timotheos', *Archäologischer Anzeiger*, 69–73.

Prag, see Tsetskhladze et al. 2000.

Praschniker 1936, C. Praschniker, 'Die Gigantomachie-Reliefs von Priene',

Jahreshefte des Österreichischen Archäologischen Instituts in Wien 30, 45–9.

Praschniker 1952, C. Praschniker, 'Das Basisrelief der Parthenos' *Jahreshefte des Österreichischen Archäologischen Instituts in Wien* 39, 1–12.

Preusser, see von Graeve.

Pryce 1928 (abbreviated as BM Sculpture), F. Pryce, *Catalogue of Sculpture in the Department of Greek and Roman Antiquities of the British Museum*, Volume I, Part I, *Prehellenic and Early Greek*, London.

Randall 1953, R. Randall, 'The Erechtheum workmen', *American Journal of Archaeology* 57, 199–210.

Raven, see Kirk.

Reuther 1957, O. Reuther, *Der Heratempel von Samos: Der Bau seit der Zeit des Polykrates*. Berlin.

Revett, see Stuart.

Ridgway 1989, B. Ridgway, 'Parthenon and Parthenos', in Başgelen and Lugal (eds), 295–305.

Ridgway 1999, B. Ridgway, *Prayers in Stone*. Berkeley and Los Angeles.

Robbins 1998, D. Robbins, 'Golden section', *Dictionary of Art* 12, 871.

Robert 1879, C. Robert, *Thanatos. 39. Programm zum Winckelmannsfeste der Archäologischen Gesellschaft zu Berlin*.

Robert 1978, L. Robert, 'Les Conquêtes du dynaste Lycien Arbinas', *Journal des Savants*, 3–48.

Robertson 1938–1939, M. Robertson, 'A fragment of marble sculpture from Xanthos', *British Museum Quarterly* 13, 39–41.

Robinson 1995a, T. Robinson, *Lycia and the Highlands from Archaic to Hellenistic: A Transhumant Relationship?* Unpublished MA thesis, University of Oxford.

Robinson 1995b, T. Robinson, 'The Nereid Monument at Xanthos or the Eliyãna monument at Arnña', *Oxford Journal of Archaeology* 14, 355–8.

Robinson 1999, T. Robinson, 'Erbinna, the Nereid Monument and Xanthos', in Tsetskhladze (ed.), 362–77.

Root 1985, M. Root, 'The Parthenon frieze and the Apadana reliefs at Persepolis', *American Journal of Archaeology* 89, 103–120.

Ross, Schaubert, Hansen 1839, L. Ross, E. Schaubert and C. Hansen, *Die Akropolis von Athen nach den neuesten Ausgrabungen*, 1, *Der Tempel der Nike Apteros*. Berlin.

Rubens 1986, G. Rubens, *William Richard Lethaby*. London.

Rügler 1988, A. Rügler, *Die Columnae Caelatae des jüngeren Artemisions von Ephesos*. Tübingen.

Rumscheid and Koenigs 1998, F. Rumscheid and W. Koenigs, *Priene – a Guide to the Pompeii of Asia Minor*. Istanbul.

Sauer 1895, B. Sauer, 'Die Metopen des Apollontempels von Phigalia', *Sitzungsberichte der Sächsischen Akademie der Wissenschaften zu Leipzig* 47, 207–55.

Schaubert, see Ross.

Schede 1934, M. Schede, 'Heiligtümer in Priene', *Jahrbuch des Deutschen Archäologischen Instituts* 49, 97–108.

Schilardi and Katsonopoulou 2000, D. Schilardi and D. Katsonopoulou (eds), *Paria Lithos*. Athens.

Schofield, see Kirk.

Scholl 1995, A. Scholl, 'Choephoroi: zur Deutung der Korenhalle des Erechtheion', *Jahrbuch des Deutschen Archcologischen Instituts* 110, 179–212.

Schrader, see Wiegand.

Schuchhardt 1927, W. Schuchhardt, 'Die Friese des Nereiden-Monumentes von Xanthos', *Mitteilungen des Deutschen Archäologischen Instituts, Athenische Abteilung* 51, 94–161.

Schulz 2001, P. Schulz, 'The Akroteria of the Temple of Athena Nike', *Hesperia* 70, 1–47.

Schulz (forthcoming), see von den Hoff.

Schwab 2005, K. Schwab, 'Celebration of victory: the metopes of the Parthenon', in Neils (ed.), 159–97.

Schwandner, see Hoepfner.

Scranton 1960, R. Scranton, 'Greek architectural inscriptions as documents', *Harvard Library Bulletin* 14, 159–82.

Shabazi 1975, A. Shabazi, *The Irano-Lycian Monuments*. Tehran.

Shear 1963, I. Shear, 'Kallikrates', *Hesperia* 32, 375–424.

Shipley 1987, G. Shipley, *A History of Samos 800–188 BC*. Oxford.

Shoe 1949, L. Shoe, 'Dark stone in Greek architecture', *Hesperia* Supplement 8, 341–52.

Simon 1986, E. Simon, 'El nacimento de Atenea en el frontón oriental del Partenón', in *Coloquio sobre et puteal de la Moncloa*. Madrid, 65–85.

Six 1892–1893, J. Six, 'Aurae: the Xanthian Heroon and an Attic Astragalos', *Journal of Hellenic Studies* 13, 131–6.

Slatter 1994, E. Slatter, *Travels of Discovery in Turkey*. London.

Smith 1892–1904 (abbreviated as BM Sculpture), A. Smith, *A Catalogue of Sculpture in the Department of Greek and Roman Antiquities, British Museum*, 3 volumes. London.

Smith 1896 (abbreviated as BM Vases), C. Smith, *Catalogue of the Greek and Etruscan Vases in the British Museum. Volume 3, Vases of the Finest Period*. London.

Snodgrass, see Tsetskhladze et al.

Speltz 1914, A. Speltz, *The Coloured Ornament of all Historical Styles – Antiquity*. Leipzig.

Stanier 1953, R. Stanier, 'The cost of the Parthenon', *Journal of Hellenic Studies* 73, 68–76.

Stern 1985, E. Stern, 'Die Kapitelle der Nordhalle des Erechtheion', *Mitteilungen des Deutschen Archäologischen Instituts, Athenische Abteilung* 100, 405–426.

Stevens et al. 1927, G.P. Stevens with L.D. Caskey, H.N. Fowler and J.M. Paton, *The Erechtheum*. Cambridge, Massachusetts.

Stewart 1977, A. Stewart, *Skopas of Paros*. Park Ridge.

Stewart 1985, A. Stewart, 'History, myth and allegory in the program of the temple of Athena Nike, Athens', *National Gallery of Washington. Studies in the History of Art* 16, 53–74. Washington DC.

Stewart 1990, A. Stewart, *Greek Sculpture – An Exploration*, 2 volumes. New Haven and London.

Stoneman 1987, R. Stoneman, *Land of Lost Gods: The Search for Classical Greece*. London.

Stuart and Revett 1762–1816, J. Stuart and N. Revett, *The Antiquities of Athens*, 4 volumes. London

Tancke 1989, K. Tancke, *Figuralkassetten griechischer und römischer Steindecken*. Europäische Hochschulschriften, Series 38, volume 20. Frankfurt.

Tanoulas 1994a, T. Tanoulas, 'The Propylaea and the western access of the Acropolis', in Ekonomakis (ed.), 53–67.

Tanoulas 1994b, T. Tanoulas, *Study for the Restoration of the Propylaea*, 2 volumes. Athens.

Tanoulas 1997, T. Tanoulas, *The Propylaea of the Athenian Acropolis in the Medieval Period*. Athens.

Thompson 1967, W. Thompson, 'Two Athenian strategoi', *Hesperia* 36, 105–106.

Thompson, Mørkholm and Kraay 1973, M. Thompson, O. Mørkholm and C. Kraay, *An Inventory of Greek Coin Hoards*. New York.

Tod 1948, M. Tod, *A Selection of Greek Historical Inscriptions*. 2 volumes 1946 and 1948. Oxford.

Tomlinson 1963, R. Tomlinson, 'The

Doric order: Hellenistic critics and criticism', *Journal of Hellenic Studies* 83, 133–45.

Tomlinson 1969, see Hodge.

Tournikiotis 1994, P. Tournikiotis (ed.) *The Parthenon and Its Impact in Modern Times*. Athens.

Trell 1945, B. Trell, 'The temple of Artemis at Ephesus', *American Numismatic Society: Numismatic Notes and Monographs* 107.10. New York.

Trell 1988, B. Trell, 'The temple of Artemis at Ephesos', in Clayton and Price (eds), 78–99.

Treuber 1987, O. Treuber, *Geschichte der Lykier*. Stuttgart.

Tritsch 1942, F. Tritsch, 'The Harpy tomb at Xanthus', *Journal of Hellenic Studies* 62, 39–50.

Tsetskhladze 1999, G.R. Tsetskhladze (ed.), *Ancient Greeks West and East*. Leiden, Boston and Cologne.

Tsetskhladze et al. 2000, G. Tsetskhladze, J. Prag and A. Snodgrass (eds), *Periplous, Papers on Classical Art and Archaeology Presented to Sir John Boardman*. London.

Uz 1990, M. Uz, 'The temple of Dionysos at Teos', in Hoepfner and Schwandner (eds), 51–61.

Volpin, see Biscontin.

Walker and Matthews 1997, S. Walker and K. Matthews, 'The marbles of the Mausoleum', in Jenkins and Waywell (eds), 49–59.

Walter 1976, H. Walter, *Das Heraion von Samos: Ursprung und Wandel eines griechischen Heiligtums*. Munich.

Walters 1893 (abbreviated as BM Vases), H. Walters, *Catalogue of the Greek and Etruscan Vases in the British Museum, Volume 2, Black Figured Vases*. London.

Walters 1899 (abbreviated as BM Bronzes), H. Walters, *Catalogue of the Bronzes, Greek, Roman and Etruscan in the British Museum*. London.

Watkin 1988, H. Watkin, *The Development of Cities in Cyprus from the Archaic to the Roman Period*. PhD thesis, Columbia University (UMI Microfilm).

Waywell 1978, G. Waywell, *The Freestanding Sculptures of the Mausoleum at Halicarnassus*. London

Waywell 1988, G. Waywell, 'The Mausoleum at Halicarnassus', in Clayton and Price (eds), 100–123.

Waywell 1989, G. Waywell, 'Further thoughts on the placing and interpretation of the freestanding sculptures from the Mausoleum', in Linders and Hellström (eds), 23–30.

Waywell 1993, G. Waywell, 'The Ada, Zeus and Idreus relief from Tegea', in Palagia and Coulson (eds), 79–86.

Waywell 1994, G. Waywell, 'Sculpture in the Ionian Renaissance. Types, themes, style, sculptors. Aspects of origins and influence', in Isager (ed.) 1994, 58–72.

Waywell 1996, G. Waywell, 'The Scylla Monument from Bargylia', *Antike Plastik* 25, Munich, 75–119.

Waywell 1997, G. Waywell, 'The sculptors of the Mausoleum at Halicarnassus', in Jenkins and Waywell (eds), 60–67.

Waywell 1998, G. Waywell, 'The Lion from the Lion Tomb at Cnidus', in Palagia and Coulson (eds), 235–41.

Webb 1996, P. Webb, *Hellenistic Architectural Sculpture, Figural Motifs in Western Anatolia and the Aegean Islands*. Madison.

Wesenberg 1981, B. Wesenberg, 'Zur Baugeschichte des Niketempels', *Jahrbuch des Deutschen Archäologischen Instituts* 96, 28–54.

Wesenberg 1982, B. Wesenberg, 'Wer erbaute den Parthenon?', *Mitteilungen des Deutschen Archäologischen Instituts, Athenische Abteilung* 97, 99–125.

Wesenberg 1983a, B. Wesenberg, 'Parthenongebälk und Südmetopenproblem', *Jahrbuch des Deutschen Archäologischen Instituts* 98, 57–86.

Wesenberg 1983b, B. Wesenberg, *Beiträge zur Rekonstruktion griechischer Architektur nach literarischen Quellen*, Mitteilungen des Deutschen Archäologischen Instituts, Athenische Abteilung, Beiheft 9. Berlin.

Wesenberg 1985, B. Wesenberg, 'Kunst und Lohn am Erechtheion', *Archäologischer Anzeiger* 55–65.

Wesenberg 1993, B. Wesenberg, 'Mausoleumsfries und Meisterforschung', in *Der Stilbegriff in den Altertumswissenschaften*. Rostock.

Wesenberg 1994, B. Wesenberg, 'Die Entstehung der griechischen Säulen und Gebälkformen in der literarischen Überlieferung der Antike', in Schwandner (ed.), *Säule und Gebälk*. Mainz, 1–15.

Wesenberg 1999, B. Wesenberg, 'Virginis Peculia', *Archäologischer Anzeiger*, 313–15.

Wesenberg 2001, B. Wesenberg, 'BM 1206 und die Rekonstruktion der columnae caelatae des jüngeren Artemision', in Muss (ed.), 297–313.

Wiegand and Schrader 1904, T. Wiegand and H. Schrader, *Priene: Ergebnisse der Ausgrabungen und Untersuchungen in den Jahren 1895–1898*. Berlin.

Wiegartz 1968, H. Wiegartz, 'Zu den Columnae Caelatae des jüngeren Artemisions von Ephesos', *Marburger Winckelman-Programm*, 41–73.

Williams 1993, see Jenkins.

Wilson Jones 2001, M. Wilson Jones, 'Doric measure and architectural design 2: a modular reading of the classical temple', *American Journal of Archaeology* 105, 675–713.

Wilson Jones 2002, M. Wilson Jones, 'Tripods, triglyphs and the origin of the Doric frieze', *American Journal of Archaeology* 106, 353–90.

Winter 1993, N. Winter, *Greek Architectural Terracottas from the Prehistoric to the End of the Archaic Period*. Oxford.

Wood 1877, J. Wood, *Discoveries at Ephesus*. London.

Woodford 1981, S. Woodford, *The Parthenon*. Cambridge.

Wycherley 1978, R. Wycherley, *The Stones of Athens*. Princeton.

Yalouris 1967, N. Yalouris, 'Meaning in the composition of the sculptures of the temple at Bassai', *Archaiologike Ephemeris*, 187–99.

Yalouris 1973, N. Yalouris, 'Excavations in the temple of Apollo Epikourios at Bassai', *Archaiologika analekta ex Athenon* 6, 39–55.

Yeroulanou 1998, M. Yeroulanou, 'Metopes and architecture: the Hephaisteion and the Parthenon', *Annual of the British School at Athens* 93, 401–425.

Zahle, see Mørkholm.

Zahle 1975, see Jeppesen.

Zanker 1995, P. Zanker, *The Mask of Socrates: The Image of the Intellectual in Antiquity*. Berkeley.

Ziro 1994, D. Ziro, *Study for the Restoration of the Temple of Athena Nike*, 2 volumes. Athens.

Index

A
Abu Simbel 19
Academy gymnasium 72
Achilles 145–6, 157, 197–8
Ada I 25, 204–6, 216, 224–6, 248
Ada II 204–5
Aegina, temple of Aphaia, 133
Aeolic capital 19
Ajax 147–8
Akragas, temple of Zeus, 54
Alcestis 66, 68
Alcibiades 114, 119
Alexander the Great 20–21, 25, 47, 51, 60–61, 152, 159, 169, 192, 204–5, 226, 236, 239–41
Alkamenes 126
Alyattes 48
Anaximander 50
Anaximenes 50
Androklos 52
Antipater of Sidon 47
Antiphanes of Kerameis 128
Antiphellos, *see* Kaş
Antoninus Pius 64
Apelles 241
Aphrodite 87, 90, 102, 104, 131
Aphrodite of Knidos 209, 226
Apollo 103–4, 141, 149, 151, 157, 216
Apollo Bassitas 131
Apollo Epikourios 130–31, 150
Arbinas, *see* Erbinna
Argolid 17
Aristagoras 51
Aristotle 192
Arkas 142
Arñna 151
Artaxerxes I, 21
Artaxerxes II, 25
Artemis 103–4, 131, 142–3, 151, 156
Artemisia, daughter of Hekatomnos, 203–4, 209–11, 215, 235
Artemisia, daughter of Lygdamis, 203, 217

Artemision, *see* Ephesos
Arttum̃para 158–9, 161
Asios 50
Assyria 19–20, 29, 194–6
Astyages 20, 49
Athena Alea, temple at Tegea, 138, 150, 225
Athena, birth of, 87, 90
Athena, in contest with Poseidon, 90–93, 124, 144–5
Athena Parthenos, 74, 78, 80–83, 109, 116, 240, 245
Athena Polias, 96, 105, 117–18, 121, 206, 220, 244
Athena Promachos 125
Athens 14, 21–3, 33, 70, 71–129
Atreus, treasury of, 17
Augustus 53, 61, 124, 241
Autophradates 158–9, 181, 184, 204, 206

B
Babylon 20
Bargylia, Scylla monument, 232–5
Bassai, temple of Apollo Epikourios, 29, 35, 46, 79, 130–50, 191
Bedford, Francis, 237
Belevi mausoleum 232
Bellerophon 116, 151, 159
Benndorf, Otto, 158
Biliotti, Alfred, 232
Bocher, Joachim, 133
Boutes 122
Brønsted, Peter Oluf, 133
Bryaxis 211, 223, 225–7
Buildings F, G and H at Xanthos 154, 161, 168–74

C
Calydonian boar 159
Carrey, Jacques, 90, 92, 98

Caryatids 33, 45, 117, 125–7, 159
Castor and Pollux 141, 198
Chaironeia, battle of, 226
Chandler, Richard, 237
Charybdis 233
Cheirokrates 55
Chersiphron 29, 55
Chimaera 151, 159, 177
Chryse, temple of Apollo Smintheus, 57
Claudius 25, 248
'Cleaning' of the Parthenon sculptures 43
Cockerell, Charles, 133–5, 150, 212
Colour, *see* polychromy
Coressian Gate, Ephesos, 52
Corinthian order 14, 137–8
Crete 206
Cybele 244
Cyclades 20
Cyrus the Great 20, 48–9, 186

D
Dair al-Bahri 17, fig. 4
Damianus 52
Daphne 143
Darius 21–2, 166
Deinokrates 55
Delian Confederacy, also League, 22–3, 71, 75
Delos 20, 46, 50–51, 142
Delphi 49, 57, 60, 126, 142, 206, 224
Demeter 68, 89, 102–3
Demeter of Knidos 226
Demetrios 55
Demokritos 55
Diodorus Siculus 21
Didyma, temple of Apollo, 21, 23, 30, 48, 54
Dilettanti Society 237–8
Diogenes the Cynic 209–10
Dione 87, 90
Dionysos 86, 88–9, 102–3, 245

Doric order 15–16, 24, 25–6, 28, 31, 45, 130
Douris of Samos 50
Dryads 142

E
Egypt 17–18, 29, 31, 50
Egyptian blue 36
Eleusis 108, 127
Elgin, Lord, 112, 126
Eliyãna 198
Ephesos, Artemision, 17, 20–24, 29, 31–2, 35, 44–6, 47–70, 74, 240
Epidauros, sanctuary of Asklepios, 33, 225
Erbinna 23, 152, 154, 156–8, 161, 186–202, 235
Erechtheum 30, 33–4, 41, 109, 115, 117–29, 131, 138, 143, 150, 159, 188
Erechtheus 102, 118, 127
Eretria 21
Eros 103
Euagoras I 204
Euboea 15
Euclid 27
Euripides 66, 197
Eurymedon, River, 72
Exekias 145

F
Faraday, Michael, 43
Fellows, Charles, 154–5, 161–3, 169, 179, 186
Foster, John, 133

G
Gandy, Joseph Michael, 237
Gell, William, 237
Gergis, see Kheriga
Glaukos 151
Golden Section 27
Granikos, River and battle of, 60, 203–5, 240

H
Hades 68, 103
Hadrian 64
Halikarnassos 153, 203–8, 210
Hallerstein, Haller von, 128, 133

Halys, River, 20
Hamadryads 142
Harpagos 49, 155, 186
Harpy tomb, see Kybernis
Hawkins, Rhode, 188
Hebe 86, 89
Hekataios 50
Hekatomnos 24, 203–6
Hektor 157
Helios 86, 88–9, 244
Henderson, A.E., 53
Hephaistos 82, 87–8, 103–4, 116, 197
Hephaistos, temple of (also Hephaesteum), 43, 74, 109–10, 122
Hera 102–4, 199
Herakleitos 50–51
Herakles 65–6, 144–5, 157, 192, 198, 219
Hermes 66–8, 102–3, 122
Hermias of Cyprus 229
Hermogenes 26, 28, 241
Herodotos 19, 48, 50, 57, 154–5
Herostratos 23, 46
Hestia 87
Hilaira 141
Hippodameia 83
Hippodamos of Miletos 207
Hippolyte 144–5, 219
Hittites 151–2
Hogarth, D.G., 53
Homer 103, 158
Hyperboreans 142

I
Idreus 24, 204, 224–6
Iktinos 29, 79, 108, 130
Ilissos, River, 93
Ilissos, temple, 109
Imbrasos, River, 31
Inscribed Pillar tomb 154–6, 174–6
Ionic order 17–20, 24–7, 31, 45, 130
Iris 93, 102–4

J
Julius Caesar 25, 248
Justinian 47

K
Kaineus 144–5, 191

Kallias, Peace of, 72
Kallikrates 79, 108, 113, 118
Kallimachos 14, 138
Kallisto 142
Kalymnos 203
Karpion 79
Kaş 158
Kaunos 153, 206
Keats, John, 102
Kekrops 93, 102, 122, 124
Kherẽi 152, 155–6
Kheriga 152, 155–6
Kimon 22–3, 72, 75, 155, 160, 169
King's Peace, the, 25, 204
Knidos 206–7, 209, 225–6
Knidos, Lion Tomb, 227–31
Kodros 240
Kolophon 49
Konon 231
Kos 203, 226
Kotilion, Mount, 130, 132
Kourouniotes, Nikolaos, 132
Kroisos 20, 48–9, 57, 60
Kuprlli 23, 152, 155, 161
Kybernis' (Harpy) tomb 38, 42, 152, 154–5, 160, 163–8, 185, 201

L
Labraynda, temple of Zeus, 24, 70, 219, 225–6
Laossos of Alopeke 121
Lapiths 83–5
Lefkandi 15–16, fig. 2
Leochares 211, 223, 225–6, 246
LeQuire, Alan, 81–2
Leto 151
Leto, sanctuary of at Xanthos, 156–7, 159, 194, 198
Leukippos, daughters of, 141–2, 159, 198
Libon 28
Limyra, see Perikles
Lion Tomb at Knidos, see Knidos
Lion tomb at Xanthos 154–5, 160–62
Lokri Epizephyri 20
Lucian 209–10
Lukka 151
Lycia 23–5, 72, 151–201
Lydia 20, 47–8
Lygdamis 203
Lykos 151

M

Madrid well-head 86–8, 91
Magnesia, temple of Artemis Leukophryene, 26
Magnesian Gate, Ephesos, 52
Marathon, battle of, 22, 74, 76, 117
Mausoleum at Halikarnassos 23–6, 32, 34, 38, 44–5, 69–70, 188, 201–27, 240, 242–3
Mausolus 159, 201, 202–7, 211, 215, 217–18, 235
Medea, HMS, 188
Media 20
Medusa 82, 159
Megabyzos 241
Megalopolis 149
Meidias Painter 141
Melas, son of Hermaiskos, 233
Meleager 195
Melesandros 156
Merehi's tomb 154, 161, 176–9, 194
Messene 130
Messenia 141
Metagenes, Athens, 108
Metagenes, Ephesos, 55
Metis 87
Miletos 21–2, 48–51, 70, 206, 209, 231
Miltiades 72
Mithrapata 158, 161
Mnesikles 29, 110–12, 118
Morris, William, 30
Munich 128, 133
Mycale, Mount, 206, 236–7
Mycenae 15–17
Mylasa 205
Mylasa, Gümüşkesen, 227
Mylasa gate 207–8
Myndos gate 207–8
Myndos peninsula 205
Myra 158

N

Nashville Parthenon 82
Naukratis, temple of Apollo, 18–19, 50, 57
Neandria 19
Nemesis, temple of, 74, 110
Nereid Monument 23, 29, 32, 44–5, 154, 156–8, 186–202, 235
Nereus 188
Newton, Charles, 38, 203, 210, 226–9
Nike temple, Athens, 29, 41, 112–17, 109, 119, 186
Nikias, Peace of, 119
Nisyros 203

O

Odysseus 159
Olympia, Philppeion, 206
Olympia, temple of Zeus, 28, 46, 76, 78–80, 82
Olympieion, Athens, 54
Olympos 103, 106–7
Orontobates 204–5
Orophernes of Cappadocia 240–41, 246
Orpheus 142
Ostrogoths 47
Oxus, River, 20

P

Paionios 55
Pan 142
Panathenaic festival 22, 44, 83, 95–8, 101, 105, 113
Pandion 151
Pandora 82, 116
Pandrosos 122, 125
Parmenio 61
Pars, William, 237–8
Parthenon 54, 71–108
Parthenon frieze 22, 34, 41, 45, 57, 64, 94–106, 117, 157, 159
Parthenon, pictorial programme, 44
Parthenon, system of proportions, 28
Parthia 124
Pasargadae 21, 186
Patina, *see* polychromy
Pausanias 52, 87, 118, 122, 130, 149
Payava's tomb 154, 159, 161, 179–85, 194
Pegasos 59
Peisistratos 21
Peleus 197–8, 200
Penrose, Francis, 40, 78
Pentelikon, Mount, 34
Penthesilea 145–6, 148
Pergamon altar 243
Perikles of Athens 33, 71–5, 100, 105, 109, 129
Perikles, building programme, 74, 108–10
Perikles of Limyra 23, 33, 158–60, 201, 206
Perithoos 83, 146, 148
Persephone 68, 86, 89, 103

Persepolis 21, 57, 165–6
Perseus 159
Persia 20–21, 25, 47–9, 60, 70–72, 107, 117–18, 124, 151–2, 154, 157, 159, 162, 176, 184, 195–6, 200
Pheidias 74–5, 79–80, 82–3, 109, 117, 125, 245
Phigaleia 130–31, 149
Philip Arrhidaeus 205
Philip II of Macedon 61, 226
Philo of Byzantium 55, 61
Philon of Alexandria 169
Philostratus 52
Phoenicia 19
Phoibe 141
Phyromachos of Kephisia 128
Pinara 156
Pinara, Landscape tomb, 161
Pitys 142
Pixodaros 153, 159, 204–6
Plataea, battle and Oath of, 22, 72
Pliny 35, 55, 61, 210–13, 217, 220, 222–3, 226
Plutarch 28, 33, 72–4, 108–9
Polykleitos 27, 68
Polykrates 31, 50, 54
Polychromy 34–44, 173
Polybius 232
Poseidon 90–91, 92–3, 103–4, 107, 122–4, 144
Pozzolana sand 29
Praxias 128
Praxiteles 53, 68, 209, 225–6
Priene 48, 69
Priene, temple of Athena Polias, 25, 38, 206–7, 220, 223–5, 236–49; *see also* Athena Polias
Proconnesian marble 207
Prokne and Itys by Alkamenes 126
Propylaea, of the Athenian Acropolis, 29, 36, 108–12, 114–15, 118, 125
Ptolemy 169
Pullan, Richard, 211, 229–30, 238, 240, 246–7
Pythagoras 27, 31
Pytheos 24–6, 31, 220, 223–5, 239, 241–3
Pythis (for Pytheos) 211

R

Revett, Nicholas, 109, 112, 237
Rhamnous, *see* Nemesis
Rhodes 206

Rhoikos 18–19, 50, 54
Roma and Augustus temple 124
Ruskin, John, 30

S
Sadyattes 48
Salamis, battle of, 22, 74, 168
Salmakis fountain and inscription 207
Salutarius, C. Vibius, 52
Salzmann, Auguste, 232
Samos, temple of Hera, 17–18, 21–2, 31, 49–50, 54
Sardis 20, 22, 25, 48–9, 54, 57, 59, 154, 206
Sarpedon 151, 158, 169
Satrap's Revolt 159, 184, 206
Satyros 26, 206, 223–5
Scharf, George junior, 161, 163, 172–3, 177, 181–2, 188
Schönborn, August, 158
Schrader, H., 238
Scylla, *see* Bargylia
Selene (and her horse) 91
Seleukos I, 225
Selinous, temple G, 54
Serapis 225
Seven against Thebes 159
Seven Wonders 47
Sirens 166
Skopas 55, 211, 223, 225–7

Sleep (Hypnos) and Death (Thanatos) 151
Smirke, Robert, 238
Smith, Robert Murdoch, 299
Sparta 71, 73, 109, 112, 117, 130–31, 150
Sperlonga 234
Sphinx 164
Spon, Jacob, 237
Stackelberg, Otto Magnus von, 133
Strabo 55, 241
Stuart, James, 109, 112
Sunium, temple of Poseidon, 74
Susa 21
Symmachos of Pellana 156
Syrinx 142

T
Tegea, *see* Athena Alea
Telmessos 156
Teos, temple of Apollo, 26
Thales 50
Thanatos 66, 68
Thebes 49
Theodektes of Phaselis 209
Theodoros 18, 31–2, 50, 55
Theopompos of Chios 209
Thermon in Aetolia 16
Theseus 66, 102, 146, 159, 192
Thetis 197–8, 200

Theugenes of Piraeus 121
Thucydides 73, 117, 130, 156
Thucydides, son of Milesias, 74–5
Timotheos 211, 223–5
Trajan 52
Trilingual Stele 152–3, 159
Trysa monument 158–9, 192, 198, 202

V
Vitruvius 15, 26–8, 30–32, 35, 55, 79, 83, 121, 137, 206–7, 210, 225, 239

W
Wheler, George, 237
Wiegand, Th., 238
Wood, John Turtle, 51–3

X
Xanthos 23, 29, 42, 45, 151–202, 206
Xenikles 108
Xerxes 21, 109, 166, 203

Z
Zephyrion 207
Zeus 86–8, 102–4, 122, 141, 157, 199
Zeus Hypsistos 122
Zeus of Labraynda, *see* Labraynda

Illustration Acknowledgements

Title page: British Museum.

Map: Kate Morton. British Museum.

1	Kate Morton. British Museum.
2	British School of Archaeology at Athens.
3	Kate Morton. British Museum.
4	Hisham F. Ibrahim / Photodisc Green / Getty Images.
5	British Museum.
6	Kate Morton. British Museum.
7	From Speltz 1914.
8	British Museum ANE 124939A.
9	Kate Morton. British Museum.
10	Robert Harding World Imagery.
11	Krischen 1938 and Kate Morton.
12	Kate Morton after Coulton 1977.
13	Kate Morton. British Museum.
14	British Museum.
15	British Museum GR 1860.2-1.106.
16	British Museum Scientific Research.
17–18	BM Sculpture 1018.
19	BM Sculpture B50. Photo author.
20	From Newton 1862.
21	British Museum GR 1857.12-20.197.
22	Photo author.
23–4	BM Sculpture 435.
25	From Penrose 1888.
26	BM Sculpture 358.
27	From Penrose 1888.
28	British Museum computer-generated photo.
29	British Museum Parthenon east pediment F.
30	© Photo RMN / © Hervé Lewandowski.
31	Kate Morton after Gruben 1963.
32	BPK / Antikensammlung, Staatliche Museen zu Berlin. Photo Ingrid Geske.
33	British Museum.
34	Kate Morton. British Museum.
35	From Wood 1877.
36	© Photo SCALA, Florence – courtesy of the Ministero Beni e Att. Culturali.
37	Kate Morton. British Museum.
38	BM Sculpture B121.
39	BM Sculpture B90.
40	BM Sculpture B89.
41	BM Sculpture B91.
42	Krischen 1938 and Kate Morton.
43	Kate Morton. British Museum.
44	BM Sculpture B161.
45	BM Sculpture B215.
46	From Rügler 1988 (who adapts Wesenberg 1983).
47	From Rügler 1988.
48	British Museum Greek and Roman Department archive.
49	Kate Morton adapting Krischen 1938.
50	BM Coins Claudius 229.
51–2	BM Sculpture 1200.
53	Kate Morton after Lethaby 1916.
54–5	BM Sculpture 1206.
56	Kate Morton. British Museum.
57	BM Sculpture 1234.
58	BM Sculpture 549.
59	Photo author.
60	BM Sculpture 302.
61	British Museum Greek and Roman Department archive.
62	Photo author.
63	Photo French and Company, New York.
64	Kate Morton after Woodford 1981.
65	Kate Morton after Coulton 1977.
66	Kate Morton after Coulton 1977.
67	Kate Morton. British Museum.
68	Photo Gary Layda by courtesy of Wesley Paine, Metro Board of Parks and Recreation.
69–77	British Museum.
78	Facsimile copies of original drawings in the Bibliothèque Nationale, Paris. British Museum Greek and Roman Department archive.
79–83	British Museum.
84–5	British Museum computer-generated photo.
86	British Museum.
87–8	British Museum.
89	British Museum.
90	British Museum.
91	Acropolis Museum, Athens.
92	British Museum.
93	British Museum.
94	Acropolis Museum, Athens.
95	akg images / P. Connolly 1998, 56–7.
96	Engraving Stuart and Revett 1762.
97	Kate Morton. British Museum.
98	Drawing akg images / P. Connolly 1998, 64.
99–101	Photos author.
102	Athens, Acropolis Museum.
103	BM Sculpture 424.
104	BM Sculpture 422.
105	Kate Morton. British Museum.
106	Photo author.
107	BM Sculpture 408 (column), 409 part (wall crown) and 413 (architrave). Drawing Stevens 1927, adapted by Kate Morton.
108	Kate Morton. British Museum.
109	akg images / P. Connolly 1998, 76.
110	Drawing Stevens 1927, adapted by Kate Morton.
111	BM Sculpture 416.
112	BM Sculpture 420.
113	Stevens 1927.
114	BM Sculpture 407.
115	By courtesy of the Trustees of Sir John Soane's Museum. Photo Margaret Harker.
116	BM Sculpture 409 (part).
117	British Museum Greek and Roman Department archive.

Illustration Acknowledgements

118 British Museum Department of Prints and Drawings.
119 Kate Morton. British Museum.
120 British Museum Department of Prints and Drawings.
121 Photo author.
122a Drawing N. Kelly 1995, adapted by Kate Morton.
122b BM Sculpture 505.
122c BM Sculpture 509.1.
123 Engraving Cockerell 1860.
124 From Mallwitz 1962.
125–6 From Madigan 1992.
127 BM Sculpture 517.1.
128 BM Vases E224.
129 BM Sculpture 519.
130 BM Sculpture 510.
131 BM Sculpture 512.
132 BM Sculpture 523.
133 BM Sculpture 541.
134 BM Sculpture 530.
135 BM Sculpture 536.
136 BM Vases B210.
137 BM Sculpture 537.
138 BM Sculpture 538.
139 BM Sculpture 526.
140 British Museum.
141 BM Sculpture 522.
142 BM Sculpture 524.
143 BM Sculpture 543.
144 BM Sculpture 544 and other joining fragments.
145 The Metropolitan Museum of Art, Purchase, Bequest of Joseph H. Durkee, Gift of Darius Ogden Mills and Gift of C. Ruxton Love, by exchange, 1972 (1972.11.10). Photo © 1999 The Metropolitan Museum of Art.
146 (Top to bottom) BM Coins 9; BM Coins 68; BM Coins 1927.7-3.1; BM Coins 101; BM Coins 1897.4-4.1.
147 Kate Morton. British Museum.
148 © 2006 Kunsthistorisches Museum mit MVK und ÖTM, Wissenschaftliche Anstalt öffentlichen Techts, Burgring 5 1010 Wien, Austria.
149 University of Vienna, Institute of Classical Archaeology, Archaeological Collection.
150 BM Coins 1927.8-5.1.
151 British Museum Greek and Roman Department archive.
152–3 BM Sculpture B286.
154 British Museum Greek and Roman Department archive.
155–6 BM Sculpture B287.
157 Persepolis, Iran, Giraudon/ Bridgeman Art Library.
158–9 BM Sculpture B287.
160 Kate Morton. British Museum.
161 BM Sculpture B292.
162 BM Sculpture B295.
163 BM Sculpture B294.
164 BM Sculpture B318.
165 BM Sculpture B312.
166 BM Sculpture B290.
167–8 Kate Morton. British Museum.
169 BM Sculpture B289. Drawing British Museum Greek and Roman Department archive.
170 BM Sculpture B305 and B306. Drawing from Pryce 1928.
171 Kate Morton. British Museum.
172–6 British Museum Greek and Roman Department archive.
177–8 Kate Morton incorporating drawings by Scharf in British Museum Greek and Roman Department archive.
179 British Museum.
180–81 Drawing Lemaire in *FdX* 8.
182 BM Sculpture 850.
183 BM Sculpture 858.
184 BM Sculpture 859.
185 BM Sculpture 855.
186 BM Sculpture 879.
187 BM Sculpture 872.
188 BM Sculpture 869.
189 BM Sculpture 894.
190 BM Sculpture 903.
191 BM Sculpture 909.
192 BM Sculpture 927.
193 BM Sculpture 925.
194 BM Sculpture 940.
195 BM Sculpture 942.
196 BM Sculpture 929.
197 British Museum ANE 132114.
198–9 Photos author.
200 Kate Morton after O.A. Hansen and O.R. Andersen.
201 Drawing K. Jeppesen in *MAH* 3.1.
202 BM Sculpture 1000.
203 British Museum Greek and Roman Department.
204 Kate Morton after Jeppesen 1997.
205 Kate Morton. British Museum.
206 Jeppesen 1992.
207 British Museum.
208 Hoepfner 1996.
209 BM Sculpture 1000 and 1001.
210 BM Sculpture 1051 (left) and 1151.
211 BM Sculpture 1045.
212 BM Sculpture 1054.
213 BM Sculpture 1057.
214 Kate Morton after Jeppesen 1997.
215 BM Sculpture 1047.
216 BM Sculpture 1058.
217 BM Sculpture 1014 and 1015.
218 BM Sculpture 1032.
219 BM Sculpture 1037.
220 BM Sculpture 1002.
221 BM Sculpture 1914.7-14.1.
222 BM Sculpture 1350.
223 Lithograph Newton 1862.
224 Photo author.
225–6 Lithographs Newton 1862.
227 Drawing Kate Morton and photo author.
228 BM Sculpture 1075.
229 From Waywell 1996.
230 BM Sculpture 1542.
231 Photo author.
232 German Archaeological Institute Istanbul archives.
233 British Museum Department of Prints and Drawings.
234 Antikensammlung Berlin, SMPK archives.
235 BM Inscriptions 399.
236 BM Coins 1870.4-7.1.
237 British Museum.
238 Berlin Pergamon Museum.
239 BM Sculpture 1170.
240 British Museum.
241 Drawing of BM Sculpture 1172 and 1173.
242–4 British Museum.
245 BM Sculpture 1154.